ADVENTURES IN UNIX™ NETWORK APPLICATIONS PROGRAMMING

Bill Rieken
.sh consulting
Santa Clara, California

Lyle Weiman
Hewlett-Packard Company
Palo Alto, California

John Wiley & Sons, Inc.
New York · Chichester · Brisbane · Toronto · Singapore

In recognition of the importance of preserving what has been written, it is a policy of John Wiley & Sons, Inc. to have books of enduring value published in the United States printed on acid-free paper, and we exert our best efforts to that end.

This book was produced using FrameMaker 2.0 on an Apple MAC-IIcx with MAC OS 6.0.7 and A/UX 2.0. Camera ready copy was printed on an Apple LaserWriter. Source code was tested on SunOS, HP-UX, AIX, A/UX, UTS, SVR4, SCO Open Desktop (SVR3), and Hitachi OSF/1.

CONTENTS

Preface

Purpose of this Book

The aim of this book is to "jump-start" the network programming ability of experienced UNIX C programmers who are new to networking in a UNIX environment. Indeed, many of the examples are derived from real-world projects where the authors have helped seasoned C programmers with networking technology. This book will help UNIX programmers build distributed applications.

Characteristics of this Book

This book is characterized by an emphasis on real-world applications and their development. For example, breakpoint debugging with sdb is shown when it was needed to solve a core dump problem. In another example, the SVR4 truss command (trace on SunOS) is shown when it was used to find out why a process would hang when it ran on a customer's system. The crash command is used to show STREAMS control blocks in the kernel, and the netstat command is used to find out why data never reached the target system. Instead of showing only the final working version of a program, system administration commands and programming tools are shown where they were needed to troubleshoot problems encountered in the development cycle. In other words, you might say that this book teaches "conversational UNIX" rather than its syntax and grammar. The authors do not regurgitate manual pages for the reader. Commands and functions are introduced in the context of where and how they are used; readers are advised to read the reference manual for all the details of other options.

Special Topics in this Book

There are some differences between this book and other books on UNIX network programming. One difference is that we introduce a few helpful system administration commands in Chapter 1, and omit presentations of non-networking interprocess communication (IPC) facilities such as shared memory, semaphores, messages, and pipes. Another example is the omission of any discussion of getmsg() and putmsg() system calls, as they are rarely used by application programmers, who normally use Transport Level Interface (TLI) library functions (which are implemented with getmsg() and putmsg() system calls on STREAMS devices). A complete STREAMS device driver is included, partly because it helps a programmer understand the Transport Level Interface implementation, and partly because a programmer may be required to write a STREAMS module as part of developing a new transport provider. A STREAMS pseudo-tty device is used to insert CR/LF pairs to a line printer on a dumb network terminal server. The `poll()` system call is used for timeouts on a TCP socket. A point-to-point connection over a broadcast network is set up when needed by an end user. A complete example using the Network Selection facility of SVR4 is shown to demonstrate transport-level independence by running the same executable over TCP/IP and OSI transports.

Reader Prerequisites

Readers should have experience using the Berkeley "r-commands" (`rlogin`, `rsh`, `rcp`) and ARPA commands (`telnet`, `ftp`), and be experienced C programmers, who are comfortable with commandline arguments (`argc`, `argv[]`), standard library functions (such as `printf`, `popen`, `perror`, `assert`), system calls (such as `fork`, `exec`, `pipe`), and archive libraries (such as `libc.a`, `libcurses.a`).

Organization of this Book

This book is organized as follows:

- Chapter 1 is an introduction to some of the fundamental concepts and basic terminology of computer networking. Some important concepts are the **client/server model, virtual circuit connection-mode service,** and **connectionless datagram service.** Network administration commands essential for application development are also presented in Chapter 1.

- Chapter 2 introduces the **socket abstraction** and the **basic socket system calls** for interprocess communication among processes running on the same computer using the **UNIX socket domain.**

- Chapter 3 introduces the **Internet socket domain,** along with **Internet addresses** and some **(3N) network library functions** which are used to manipulate Internet addresses. System files **/etc/hosts** and **/etc/services** and library functions **gethostbyname()** and **getservbyname()** are shown. A Non-BSD socket implementation which was encountered during a development project is also presented.

- Chapter 4 shows some advanced datagram (UDP) programming techniques, including **how to recover from lost messages** and how to **select()** on more than one port.

- Chapter 5 shows the client/server pair from Chapter 4 rewritten with connection-oriented (TCP) services. It discusses the differences in service paradigms such as **record-oriented UDP versus byte-stream TCP,** and how these matter in programming.

- Chapter 6 introduces **STREAMS programming**. This includes a conceptual overview, basic system calls and header files, and a network printer application that uses a STREAMS pseudo-tty device. A **STREAMS pseudo-device driver** is added to the kernel, and the driver is tested by an application program.

- Chapter 7 presents the **Transport-Level Interface (TLI)** library functions introduced by AT&T Bell Labs and adopted by X/Open which promotes **XTI (X/Open Transport Independent)** library functions. A socket-based application from Chapter 3 is converted to TLI, and the Network Selection facility of SVR4 is shown to run with TCP/IP and OSI transport providers.

- Chapter 8 discusses how to integrate services with the **Internet Daemon (`inetd`)** and the advantages of doing so, as well as how this affects programming.

- Chapter 9 introduces some **advanced topics** in socket programming: **broadcasting, setting and getting options on a socket, sending and receiving "urgent" data**, and how to program **even more reliability** into your application (above and beyond that supplied by TCP).

- Chapter 10 introduces **X.25 sockets**, and shows differences in programming these from other kinds of sockets.

Many of the chapters are independent from the others. For example, Chapters 6 and 7 on STREAMS and TLI programming are not prerequisite reading for Chapter 10 on X.25 sockets. A reasonable grouping of chapter reading could be:

- Chapter 1 on network concepts, fundamentals, and terminology.

- Chapters 2 and 3 on basic socket programming.

- Chapters 4 and 5 on advanced TCP/UDP socket programming.

- Chapters 6 and 7 on STREAMS and TLI programming.

- Chapter 8 and 9 on the Internet Daemon (inetd) and advanced socket programming.

- Chapter 10 on X.25 sockets.

There is a tremendous amount of technology covered in these chapters, and it is unreasonable to expect one person to be an expert in all the areas presented in this book. Lyle Weiman has more experience with X.25 and advanced features of socket programming, so he wrote those chapters. Bill Rieken has more experience with System V STREAMS and TLI programming, and he wrote the chapters on those topics.

Acknowledgments

The authors wish to thank the following people:

George Leach	GTE Data Services, Tampa, Florida
Robert LaPrade	IBM Scientific Center, Palo Alto, California
Joanne Eglash	Santa Cruz Operations, Santa Cruz, California
Jean Stables	*.sh consulting*, Santa Clara, California
Jim Webb	*.sh consulting*, Ocean Township, New Jersey
Mike Guth	AT&T Bell Laboratories, Middletown, New Jersey
Rich Mayer	AT&T Federal Systems, Greensboro, North Carolina
David Korn	AT&T Bell Laboratories, Murray Hill, New Jersey
Ron Sawyer	Technical Services Associates, Mechanicsburg, Pennsylvania
Robert Chu	Hughes LAN Systems, Mountain View, California

George Leach, Bob LaPrade, Jean Stables and Joanne Eglash reviewed early versions of the manuscript. Their comments and suggestions improved the quality of this book in many ways. Jim Webb, Rich Mayer, and Mike Guth provided valuable insights to new UNIX technology. Dave Korn made several suggestions which improved the quality of the STREAMS chapter. Ron Sawyer contributed the remote database example, and Robert Chu helped with the pseudo-tty example. Tracy Weiman converted troff files to FrameMaker; Jean Stables did the final typesetting. Students in UNIX Networking classes gave very good feedback on the lecture notes that formed the basis of this book.

About the Authors

Bill Rieken has over 20 years experience as a computer programmer and educator. He taught at the University of Wisconsin and Southern Illinois University, where he began using UNIX version 6 in 1976. Bill provided UNIX System Support and Training at AT&T Bell Laboratories in New Jersey for five years from 1983 through 1988. He provided AIX System Support at the IBM Palo Alto Scientific Center for two years from 1988 to 1990, and currently teaches TCP/IP networking, Xlib/Motif programming, and OSF/MACH and SVR4 kernel internals and system administration. His undergraduate work in Mathematics and Computer Science was done at U.C. Berkeley, and his graduate work in Computer Science was done at Stanford University. He also has an M.S. in Mathematics from the University of Nevada at Reno. Bill is an International ACM Lecturer and a founder of **.sh consulting** based in Santa Clara, California.

Lyle Weiman has 23 years experience in computer software, with 16 of those in networking. He received his bachelor's degree in Computer Science in 1972 from the University of California in San Diego and his Master's Degree in Computer Science from San Jose State University in 1978. He helped implement TCP/IP protocol and X.25 socket interfaces for **Hewlett-Packard** in Cupertino, California, and is currently working in SNMP-based network management for H-P in Palo Alto. He has also helped in SNA and OSI-related development projects.

Purpose of different Fonts

The intent of using different fonts in this book is to emphasize something important (*italic font*), something new and important (**bold font**), and to distinguish commands and source code (`courier font`) from ordinary text (Times Roman font).

Example of different Fonts

Here is an excerpt that gives an example of each font:

It uses a *standard* RPC header file (`rpc.h`) and an *application-specific* header file (`fun.h`) which assigns a **program number**, **version number**, and **procedure number** to your service. That is, it maps your function, `fun()`, into the program number `1992`.

Sample Source Code Listing

Here is a small program listing that gives an example of ordinary courier font for familiar C code (`stdio.h`) and bold font to introduce (**rpc.h**) or emphasize (**FUNPROG**) something new for networking:

```
/* fun.c - fortune cookie client                              */

#include <stdio.h>   /* standard I/O header (NULL, FILE,...) */
#include <rpc/rpc.h> /* standard RPC header (xdr.h, svc.h, ) */
#include "fun.h"      /* RPCGEN header (prog/vers/proc #'s)   */

main( argc, argv )   /* local  fun  command                  */
char *argv[];
{
    int  cookie;      /* returned from  remote  fund  daemon */
    if ( argc != 2 ) { printf("Usage: %0 hostname\n"); exit(86);}
    if ( callrpc( argv[1], FUNPROG, FUNVERS, FUNPROC,
                 xdr_void, 0, xdr_int, &cookie ) != 0 )
      { printf( "RPC Error\n" ); exit(99); }
    printf( "\nYour fortune cookie is:\t%d\n", cookie );
}
```

Sample Command Line Listing

```
$  rpcinfo -p
   program vers proto  port
      1992   1   udp   1238
      1992   2   udp   1238
```

1 *Introduction to Network Programming*

by Bill Rieken

1.1   Introduction

Figure 1.1 lists some of the topics that will be covered in this chapter. Many of these topics could be the subject of an entire book. Since this book focuses on network application programming, these topics will be covered only to the level necessary to understand and determine programming alternatives.

Operating System Interface

- Sockets   (BSD)
- STREAMS (SysV)

Protocol Software

- TCP   (Transmission Control Protocol)
- UDP   (User Datagram Protocol)
- IP   (Internet Protocol)
- OSI   (Open System Interconnection)
- X.25   (Packet-Switched Virtual Circuits)

Physical Hardware

- Ethernet bus cable
- Token ring coax
- Twisted pair telephone line
- Microwave (T1) channel satellite links

Packets

- Logical (such as, TCP segments)
- Physical (such as, Ethernet frames)

Addressing

- Source and destination
- 32-bit Internet addresses
- TCP/UDP "ports"
- 48-bit Ethernet addresses
- X.25 virtual circuits

Figure 1.1   Network Fundamentals

1.2   Operating System Interface

There are two popular application programming interfaces (APIs) for network applications in a UNIX environment: sockets and STREAMS. Sockets have been available since 1983, when the University of California at Berkeley began distributing 4.2BSD. They form the basis on which the Berkeley "r-commands" (**rlogin**, **rsh**, **rcp**, **rwho**) are coded. Sockets were the only UNIX interface to the TCP/IP protocols until STREAMS were provided in the implementation known as STREAMS, distributed with System V Release 3 in 1986. STREAMS were originally developed at Bell Labs in 1983 to simplify and streamline the UNIX terminal I/O (**tty**) interface. However, their emphasis on modularity make them ideal for implementing protocol layers: **Each protocol layer can be implemented in a module, and modules can be creatively stacked together in a Stream.** Figure 1.2 shows a comparison of Sockets and STREAMS.

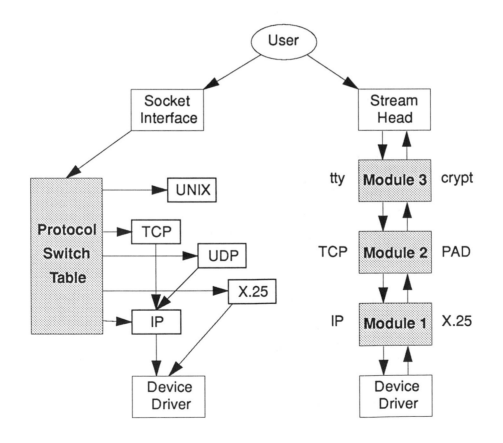

Figure 1.2   UNIX Sockets and STREAMS

Note that the TCP/IP protocols can be implemented using either API. System V Release 4 (SVR4), supports both socket and STREAMS interfaces to the TCP/IP protocols. The socket interface is provided by a socket compatibility library (lib**socket**.a) and a network services library (lib**nsl**.a) with functions that access a STREAMS-based TCP/IP implementation. OSF/1, on the other hand, glues a small STREAMS stack on top of the internal TCP/IP implementation distributed with BSD 4.4. Interoperability is maintained by the protocols. That is, one side of a network interaction may use the socket interface while the other end uses the STREAMS interface, and they both interoperate with each other via the TCP/IP protocols.

As shown in Figure 1.2, the BSD socket interface indexes a jump (switch) table to transfer control to one of the various protocols implemented in the kernel. The protocol switch table (**protosw**) is an array of C function pointers to the appropriate protocol handlers. Almost all systems have entries for TCP and UDP network protocols, which are described in the next section. Most systems also provide another protocol called the UNIX domain, which is used for interprocess communication (IPC) between processes running on the same computer (it does not use any networks).

Other protocols may be purchased and installed separately, such as the Xerox Network Services (**XNS**) protocol suite, **X.25**, **SNA**, and **DECNET**. Your choice of which one to use is driven mainly by which are available on all of the systems on which your network application is to run. **TCP** or **UDP** are very reasonable least common denominators, because they can be found on almost every UNIX system.

The STREAMS implementation provides a duplex connection between two endpoints. Data flows *downstream* from the user to a device, *upstream* from a device toward the user, in both directions concurrently. **Modules** are connected inside the kernel like command line pipelines to implement a **protocol stack,** as illustrated in Figure 1.2. Data is not actually copied between modules. Only pointers to the data are passed, and a module's **service procedure** (if any) operates on the data in the buffer. A clever idea of STREAMS is to use pointers to upstream and downstream modules. In this way, **modules can be dynamically pushed onto or popped from a protocol stack,** simply by changing the function pointers in the top (Stream Head) module. This offers more flexibility than a single pointer in the socket protocol switch table, as, for example, encryption/decryption or data compression/decompression modules can be pushed when needed and popped when not. A separate entry would be needed in the protocol switch table to access a protocol with encryption or data compression, or a flag would have to be sent as a parameter to enable these functions in the protocol code. STREAMS encourage modularity and reuse of network protocol software modules. For example, encryption or data compression modules could be pushed onto any protocol stack, because the intermodule interfaces are the same between any two modules.

1.3   Protocol Software

The main protocols discussed in this book are the ones "of most interest to programmers today." One could argue that proprietary protocols actually pump more data today than ever before, but anyone interested in using or interfacing with a proprietary protocol is advised to contact the vendor for more information about it.

1.3.1 Internet Protocol (IP)

The Internet Protocol (IP) interconnects independent and possibly different physical networks. For example, Figure 1.3 shows three interconnected networks, where Network 1 might be an Ethernet, Network 2 might be an X.25 network, and Network 3 could be a token-ring network. A packet from Host X to Host Y would be sent to Host 1, which is connected to both Networks 1 and 2. Host 1 forwards the packet to Host 2, which puts the packet on Network 3, where it will be delivered to Host Y.

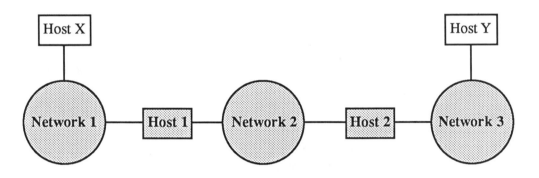

Figure 1.3   Internetwork Connections

Hosts 1 and 2 are called **routers** if the networks they connect use the same protocol; otherwise, they are called **gateways** between the two different protocols (such as token-ring on one side and Ethernet or X.25 on the other). **The important contribution of IP is that it hides the differences of the underlying physical networks and makes the entire Internet appear as a single network to the user.**

Packet size is often related to network reliability. For instance, packets can carry up to 4K bytes on a token-ring network, 1.5K on an Ethernet, and 128 bytes on X.25 networks. This is due in part to the cost of retransmitting packets when checksums are different at the receiving end. X.25 networks use telephone lines which are subject to interference from noise and thus are more likely to cause packet retransmissions; therefore these networks use smaller packet sizes. It is IP's job to break 4K token-ring packets into 128-byte X.25 packets and reassemble packets at the receiving end whenever packets are sent from a token-ring network to an X.25 network. This repackaging of data is called fragmetation and the smaller pieces of data are called **IP fragments**.

IP also provides a primitive form of flow control: An intermediate host is allowed to drop packets if it is out of memory buffers to hold them in transit. This means that end-to-end reliability must be provided by a higher level protocol (as in TCP) or by the applications running at either end (as in UDP).

1.3.2 Transmission Control Protocol (TCP)

TCP (**Transmission Control Protocol**) provides a virtual circuit **connection** with end-to-end reliability for sending messages. If the sender is going faster than the receiver, TCP provides **flow control** to throttle the sender. If the sender is overdriving any computer in between, that node can discard any packet that node is too busy to handle, because TCP has **lost-packet recovery** (the sending TCP will not receive an ACK for a missing packet, and after a timeout period will retransmit the lost packet). If packet size changes from one network to another, the Internet Protocol (IP) can handle it. If network routers decide to send part of your data via FrozenNose, Siberia, and another part by way of SunBaked, Saudi Arabia, TCP will reassemble the packets so that the **data gets to the receiver in the same order it was sent** (this is called **byte-stream** semantics, and it works just like reading or writing to a disk file). If any intermediate host has a memory parity problem and accidentally puts hiccups into the data, TCP's end-to-end checksumming will notice the error, and request a retransmission. The TCP layer is shown in Figure 1.4:

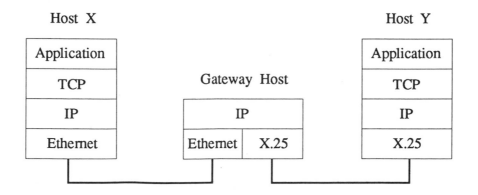

Figure 1.4 TCP/IP Protocol Layers

All of this reliability is very nice, but, like room service at the Ritz, it is not cheap. TCP has a **three-part** handshake for setting up a connection. There is an initial request for a connection, a reply from the far end, and finally an acknowledgment to the reply.

The third acknowledgment message adds slightly more overhead to establish a TCP connection than establishing an X.25 or ISO TP4 connection. The second and third packets in the connection setup sequence contain a "window size," which tells the other end how much data it can send without overflowing the receiver's buffers. Thus, both ends know how much "room" there is at the other end, and data can flow in both directions at the same time.

1.3.3 User Datagram Protocol (UDP)

Setting up a TCP connection may take a couple of seconds or more, depending on how long it takes to get this three-way handshake through the network. Not every application requires a continuous connection, and UDP (**User Datagram Protocol**) is one alternative for TCP. If, for example, you have **short messages** you want to send periodically, and if **it doesn't matter if some of them are lost**, UDP makes a very good choice. Rwho (remote "who") and ruptime (remote "uptime") are two services that take advantage of this. The rwhod daemon broadcasts "who data" over a local network once a minute for rwhod daemons running on other systems to grab and tuck away in /usr/spool/rwho/whod.* files. Users access these files via the rwho and ruptime commands to find out who is logged in to which systems and which systems are up. There is no great loss if you miss a few broadcasts now and then.

```
$ ruptime
UNIX0       down   4+00:13
earth       up       1:23,   1 user,    load 1.00, 1.02, 1.05
fire        up      22:06,   1 user,    load 1.00, 1.12, 1.06
unix0       up       0:21,   0 users,   load 0.00, 0.00, 0.00
wind        down   5+04:14
```

A system is declared "down" if an rwho broadcast packet is not received for five minutes. Notice that UNIX0 has been down for four days, and wind has been down for five days. These systems will continue to be reported as "down" until either a packet is received from them or the system administrator removes the whod.UNIX0 and whod.wind files from the /usr/spool/rwho directory (such as the system UNIX0 was renamed to unix0, but the UNIX0 "who data" file was not removed).

Another connectionless example is a database lookup request where a second request can be sent if a reply for the first request is not received within an application-specified timeout period. Transaction-oriented applications are good candidates for **UDP** rather than TCP.

TCP connections can be thought of as "virtual circuits" over a common physical link between two endpoints, and are similar to telephone calls. Once a connection is made, either or both sides can talk at the same time, messages are received in the same order in which they were sent, and messages are always sent to the connected endpoint.

A UDP datagram is similar to a letter in the mail, in that each envelope must be addressed, a mailbox may receive letters from more than one source, and there is no guarantee that the intended recipient will ever receive it. Also, everything in the envelope is received as a single unit, letters may be received in a different order than they were mailed, and duplicate letters may be sent if the sender does not receive a reply from the recipient within a reasonable amount of time. These comparisons are summarized in Figure 1.5.

The choice of whether to use datagrams or virtual circuits is usually decided by the kind of application you are programming. Rlogin and telnet would clearly use TCP virtual circuits, because the connection setup time is negligible compared to the service time, and it is very important that characters be received in the same order that they were sent. Ruptime (remote "uptime") and rwho use UDP datagrams, because a continuous connection is not required by these services.

The broadcast capability of Ethernets allow them to support datagrams easily, while the point-to-point characteristics of telephone lines lend themselves more naturally to support virtual circuits. However, virtual circuits can be implemented on Ethernets by internal TCP acknowledgments, timeouts, and retransmissions if necessary. Datagrams can be sent over point-to-point connections by establishing temporary connections for a short period to carry datagram messages. **TCP and UDP hide most aspects of the particular network hardware technology from the application.**

Connectionless Datagrams: *Like mailing a letter*

- individually addressed
- delivery not guaranteed
- sequence not guaranteed
- duplicate packets are possible
- atomic messages

Virtual Circuits: *Like making a phone call*

- connection setup
- delivery acknowledged by receiver
- sequence guaranteed
- duplicate packets are dropped
- character byte-streams

Figure 1.5 Datagrams and Virtual Circuits

1.3.4 Datagrams, Segments, Fragments, and Frames

When TCP packets are presented to IP to send, it first has to determine which network interface to use. In most computers, there is only one interface, but gateways are connected to more than one network. Once the interface is chosen, IP examines a data structure called the **ifnet** structure, which is kept for each interface, to determine the **maximum transmission unit (MTU)** size. This is the maximum size of a message that the particular interface can handle, and it varies by interface type. In the case of Ethernet, for example, the maximum is 1500 bytes. In the case of IEEE 802.3, it is 1492. The netstat command can be used to find the MTU.

```
$ netstat -i
```

Name	Mtu	Network	Address	Ipkts	Ierrs	Opkts	Oerrs	Coll
wdn0	1500	129.33	fire	8558	0	7682	0	0
lo0	2048	loopback	localhost	2112	0	2112	0	0

The wdn0 is an Ethernet interface device that can handle packets (frames) with a maximum of 1500 data bytes. The lo0 is an internal "pseudo-device" to send data between applications running on the same host, using TCP/IP protocols but without using any network hardware.

If the data unit presented to IP for transmission is larger than the MTU for the interface, then IP will break the message into several parts, called **fragments**. Each will be sent individually. IP has no way of determining if any of them reached the destination. The message is not complete until all of its fragments have arrived. If even one fragment should become lost, the whole message must be resent. Each fragment has a different message identifier in it, and **the user of UDP has no way of overriding that**. What this means is that you might be tempted to pack more data into larger messages to get better performance, but under some conditions throughput may decrease due to message retransmissions. An ideal solution would be to design your application program such that you can dynamically vary the message size, and begin to decrease the message size, say, after a retransmission counter reaches two or three.

IP fragmentation applies also to TCP, but TCP is a little smarter about it. This is because TCP endpoints negotiate a **Maximum Segment Size** (MSS), usually based on the MTUs between the two endpoints. If a user sends an amount of data that exceeds the MSS, TCP will perform an IP-like fragmentation (called **segmentation**, when TCP does it). The two TCPs negotiate the maximum segment size they will use on the basis of the MTUs of the interfaces used. If, for example, one endpoint shows an MTU of 1500 but the other shows 256, as can happen if the path through the network involves gateways and different physical links, then the smaller will be used. Also, TCP does not preserve message boundaries. This means it is free to send varying amounts of data, when it deems that the network is ready to carry it. If it "senses" a problem in network congestion, it can automatically scale back its segment size.

Each segment has a TCP header, and the sequence number of the first byte in the segment is stored in the header. In Figure 1.6, the segment sequence numbers are 1, 1501, and 3001. Given the sequence number in the byte-stream, TCP knows immediately where to place each segment. If can tell whether a segment has already been delivered to the user, and even whether a segment belongs to an "old" connection (thereby detecting when somebody is continuing to send even though this side has been rebooted, for example).

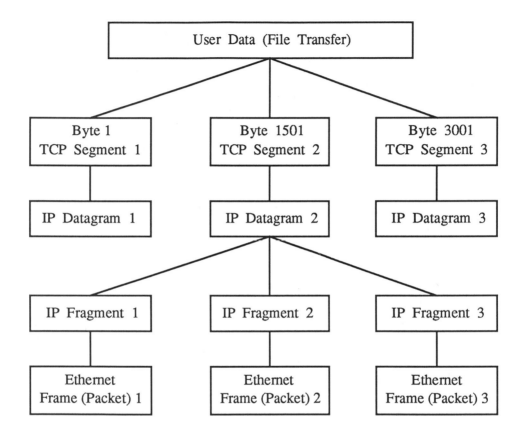

Figure 1.6   Data Transfer Units

When TCP receives a segment whose byte sequence number indicates that there is at least one missing segment, most implementations save the segment, in hopes the missing segment(s) will arrive shortly. If, for example, segment 1 in Figure 1.6 had not arrived, segments 2 and 3 would be kept in memory buffers until the sender retransmits segment 1. When segment 1 arrives, the receiver would then acknowledge all three segments by sending the sequence number 3001 back to the sender in a TCP header. If segment 1 were sent again, the receiving TCP would discard it, because the current sequence number has advanced well beyond that in segment 1.

This flow control and recovery mechanism is completely hidden from the user. That is, each byte appears in a byte-stream exactly as it would if the data were coming from a disk file instead of a network connection. Notice that the error handling is done by the endpoints, at the TCP (transport) level. TCP flow control is diagramed in Figure 1.7. Error handling and flow control could be done by the network equipment (ISO level 3), which we discuss in the next section.

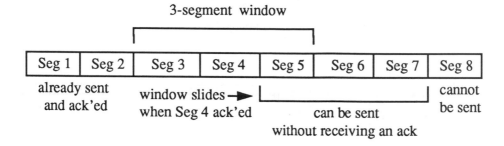

Figure 1.7 TCP Flow Control Windows

1.4   OSI Reference Model

The International Standards Organization (ISO) has published an **Open System Interconnection** (OSI) **Reference Model** for implementors to layer their networking functionality into seven levels. This model was developed by a committee of people who came from telephone company backgrounds, and its terminology is oriented toward point-to-point connections, rather than connectionless broadcast media such as Ethernet. It matches TCP/IP layering very closely, except that it adds a presentation and a session level between the application and transport levels. The model is not a protocol specification; it is a common reference for network people to use the same terminology and put their functions at the "correct" place in the protocol stack. It is different from TCP/IP in that it demands that each layer make service requests to the layer below it, and layers are not allowed to reach in and grab data or control from another layer. This means, for example, that the transport level (level 4) can only "talk" to the session level (level 5) above it and make service requests to the network level (level 3) below it. The dotted lines in Figure 1.8 indicate that messages are exchanged and understood by peer levels at both ends on (probably) remote systems, but the only physical data communication occurs at the physical level (level 1), shown with a solid line. Also, intermediate "packet switches" need not be general-purpose computers (as shown in Figure 1.4) but may be special-purpose network routers.

This reference model focuses the jargon and helps to keep designers from putting functionality in the wrong places in the hierarchy. Vendors have control over the vertical interfaces, but the horizontal "peer" may very likely be implemented by a different vendor.

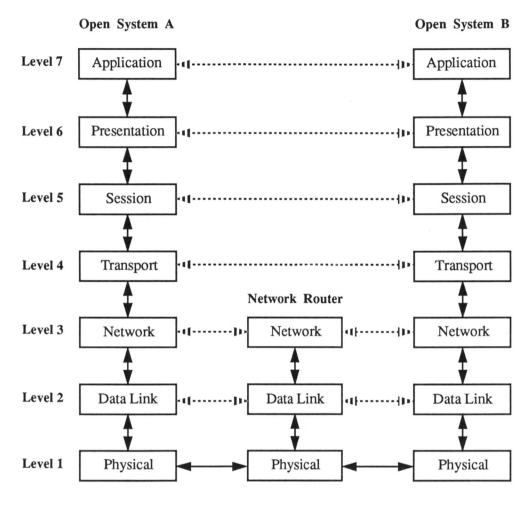

Figure 1.8   OSI Reference Model

One stack could use the socket interface and the other stack could use the Streams interface to communicate using the TCP/UDP/IP protocols. Each layer is on the "honor system" not to peek at the other layers' data. The messages at each layer are private, and a very basic requirement of the OSI model is that other layers do not "reach in and grab" information from a different layer. Each layer adds its own header information to the data, according to its protocol, and then sends the encapsulated message on to the next layer. A brief description of the functions of each level is given in Figure 1.9.

Level 7 -- **Application Layer**
   Provides services from all layers to a user

Level 6 -- **Presentation Layer**
   Provides data transformation/compression services
   Requests a session from the Session Layer

Level 5 -- **Session Layer**
   Establish and Terminate Connections
   Synchronize dialogues and Session recovery
   Provides normal and expedited data exchange

Level 4 -- **Transport Layer**
   Packetizes Session Layer messages
   Optimizes routing path
   End-to-end flow control, error detection and recovery
   Multiplexes single communication channel

Level 3 -- **Network Layer**
   Establishes, maintains, and terminates connections
   Provides cost information to Transport Layer
   Determines network routing and/or switching
   May provide sequencing of data

Level 2 -- **Data Link Layer**
   Provides one or more data link connections
   Provides error-free data delivery
   May provide flow control, sequencing
   Provides network id on multipoint connections

Level 1 -- **Physical Layer**
   Provides transmission of raw bit streams
   Provides activation, operation, and deactivation
      of physical connections

Figure 1.9   OSI Functional Layers

The data link layer is a device driver that packages data into physical packets (messages) for the physical device media to transmit. Network routing functions are done at level 3, and end-to-end reliability is provided by the transport level, 4. Virtual circuit connections are provided by TCP, and UDP provides a connectionless datagram transport service. Session-level functions are provided by Sun's Remote Procedure Calls (RPC) and Apollo's Network Computing System (NCS). Presentation-level functions are performed by Sun's XDR (External Data Representation) and Apollo's

NDR (Network Data Representation). RPC and NCS are popular transport-independent tools for developing distributed applications. The application level includes many of the standard Internet services, such as `telnet`, `ftp`, and `mail`. Figure 1.10 shows how TCP/IP fits in the OSI Reference Model.

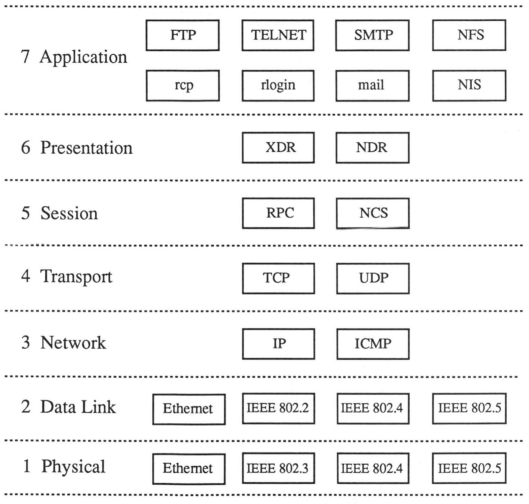

Figure 1.10   How TCP/IP Fits in the OSI Model

In the early days of computer networking, in the mid-1960s, data communication took place between computers and terminals over point-to-point connections. Typical applications were terminal login sessions, remote job entry, file transfers, and electronic mail. Generic Internet services are TELNET for terminal emulation over a network, FTP for file transfer protocol, and SMTP for simple mail transfer protocol. These services are available on UNIX and non-UNIX systems. Network commands `rlogin` (remote login), `rcp` (remote copy), and `mail` are available for use between UNIX systems only.

Figure 1.11 shows a typical wide area network topology. The equipment inside the "cloud" is usually provided by a telecommunications company, which is free to use any kind of technology the company feels is best, as long as a standard interface (such as X.25) is provided to the Data Terminating Equipment (computers and terminals) using the network. Data is packaged in packets, which are sent in a **"store and forward"** path through **point-to-point** connections between packet-switching equipment (PSE) in the network. Each PSE node provides network (ISO level 3) services and is not necessarily a general-purpose computer.

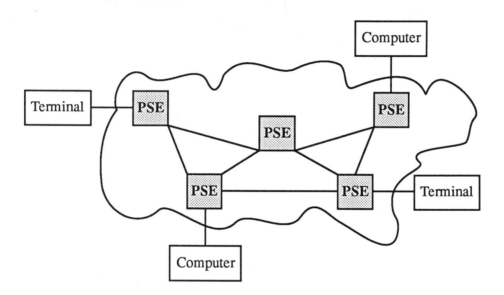

Point-to-Point Store-and-Forward Packet Switching Equipment (PSE)

Figure 1.11   Store-and-Forward Wide Area Network

1.5   Network Addressing

Each layer (Application/TCP/IP/Ethernet) may add its own header information to whatever was passed to it from the next higher level. The peer level at the other end will remove the header information before sending the rest of each packet upward to the next level. For example, the IP header contains a 32-bit **Internet address,** which is used to send the packet to the destination host. After the packet arrives, the IP code on the destination machine strips off the IP header before delivering the remaining bytes to the TCP layer. The TCP header contains a 16-bit **service port number**, which TCP uses to multiplex the packet to the service application process using that port number (for example, TELNET, FTP, and SMTP in Figure 1.12). UDP also uses a 16-bit number to multiplex packets. ICMP is a special Internet Control Message Protocol (for network control rather than user data transfer). ARP (Address Resolution Protocol) and RARP (Reverse ARP) are special protocols used to translate between IP addresses and physical network addresses.

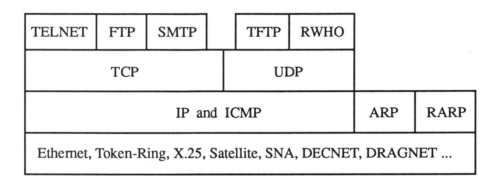

Figure 1.12 TCP/IP Layers

IP addresses are translated into physical network addresses by the data link (device driver) layer. When a packet travels over a wide area X.25 network, its header contains a 14-digit **X.121 International Data Number (IDN) address,** and reliable data transfer is guaranteed by an X.25 CRC (Cyclic Redundancy Check byte). The X.25 header and CRC byte are removed by the X.25 device driver when the packet arrives on a gateway to the local area networks at either end of the X.25 link. Ethernet headers, with a **48-bit Ethernet address** and CRC bytes, are used on Ethernet LAN; 48-bit token-ring or token-bus addresses and CRCs would be used on token-ring or token-bus LAN. Figure 1.13 shows a diagram of the protocol headers used by each layer.

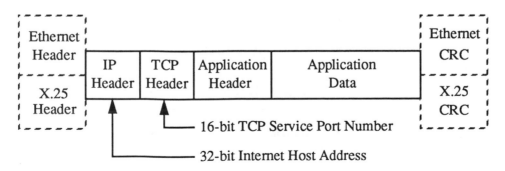

Figure 1.13 Protocol Headers

Figure 1.14 shows a typical Ethernet local area network (LAN) configuration. Each host computer on the LAN has at least one Ethernet controller, connected to an Ethernet by a drop cable with a transceiver (T in the figure) connection. The Ethernet bus is terminated at either end with a terminating resistor (E in the figure). Every packet on the cable is "seen" by every controller; however, the controller sends to IP only those packets addressed to it (that is, packets with its Ethernet address in the destination field) or those with a special broadcast address of all ones. The controller can be put in "promiscuous mode" to snoop on all packets travelling on the cable, but normally this is used only for diagnostic purposes. IP sends packets on up to TCP or UDP, depending on the transport protocol code in the IP header.

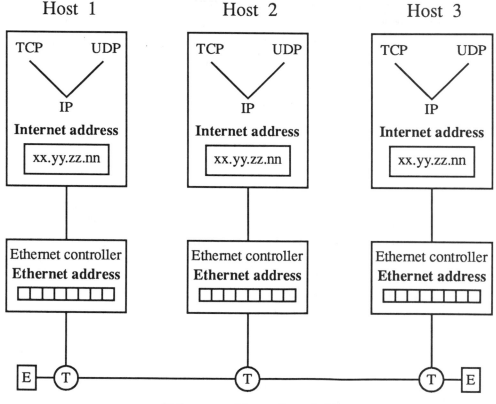

Ethernet **Broadcast** Bus

ARP(Internet) = Ethernet address
RARP(Ethernet) = Internet address

Figure 1.14   Internet-Ethernet Addresses

Internet addresses are assigned to network interface boards by the system command **/etc/ifconfig** (interface **config**uration). If a host has an Ungermann-Bass controller (un0) and a Pegasus controller (pg0), the following ifconfig commands assign Internet numbers to them:

```
/etc/ifconfig    un0    129.33.192.96
/etc/ifconfig    pg0    129.33.192.87
```

These command are usually executed at system startup time by an **/etc/rc** shell script (or a shell script invoked by /etc/rc). Consult your local system administration manual to see where this command is executed on your system. The ifconfig.c program executes an I/O control (**ioctl**) system call, with **SIOCSIFADDR** command, to set the interface's IP address. Ethernet addresses are "burned in" by manufacturers like serial numbers and are not easily changed. Internet addresses can be changed by specifying a different address on the ifconfig command line.

A special **address resolution protocol (ARP)** is used to find the Ethernet address of a destination system. The first time a remote system is accessed, an ARP request packet is broadcast on the LAN with the Internet address of the remote system, asking each host to respond with its Ethernet address if its Internet address matches the one in the ARP request. The Ethernet address in the ARP reply packet is then saved in a local ARP cache for subsequent communication with the other host. The **arp** command can be used to examine the ARP cache (arp -a) or learn the Ethernet or Internet address of any host on your LAN:

```
$ arp earth
earth (129.33.192.100) at 0:0:c0:47:ef:8
$ arp fire
fire (129.33.192.30) -- no entry
```

Internet addresses are shown in parentheses in "dotted decimal" format: one decimal digit per byte, separated by a decimal point. The dotted decimal form is easier for people to use; internally, the Internet address is stored as a 32-bit number. Ethernet addresses are six-byte (48-bit) "serial numbers" used to guarantee a unique address for each controller board. They are shown as a colon-separated sequence of six hexadecimal numbers and stored internally as a 48-bit number, one hexadecimal number per byte. The first three bytes are a vendor code assigned by the Xerox Corporation, and the next three bytes are assigned by the vendor.

Another special protocol, **reverse address resolution protocol (RARP)**, is used by diskless workstations. Without a disk, they know only the Ethernet address of their network interface controller, which they broadcast in a RARP request packet. The RARP server daemon (**rarpd**) running on a designated server host accepts the broadcasted request and looks up the Ethernet address in a system file called **/etc/ethers**. This file has the host name to use to search **/etc/hosts** to find the

Internet address. The server then puts the IP address in a RARP reply message, which is sent to the diskless workstation. Sample file entries are shown in Figure 1.15.

```
          /etc/ethers                              /etc/hosts

  00:12:45:00:11:23 snoopy            129.33.192.40 snoopy
  00:12:45:00:11:25 sneezy            129.33.192.50 sneezy
  00:12:45:00:11:27 grumpy            129.33.192.60 grumpy
  00:12:45:00:11:29 happy····┤-----┤··129.33.192.70 happy

  Ethernet address   Hostname         Internet address   Hostname

                          rarpd daemon

                          arp command
```

Figure 1.15 Sample `/etc/ethers` and `/etc/hosts` Files

Only the names and Ethernet addresses of diskless workstations (or X-terminals) need to be in the `/etc/ethers` file, and this file is needed only on the designated server (usually one per LAN) running the `rarpd` daemon.

The `ifconfig` command shows the Internet address(es) of your system:

```
$ ifconfig wdn0
```

```
wdn0:flags=23<UP,BROADCAST,NOTRAILERS>
        inet 129.33.192.30 netmask ffff0000 broadcast 129.33.255.255
```

This also shows the subnetmask in effect on your system and the broadcast address for the LAN. The name of an interface (`wdn0`) is required, and you can use the command **netstat -i** to learn the name(s) of the interface(s) in use on your host:

```
$ netstat -i
```

Name	Mtu	**Network**	Address	Ipkts	Ierrs	Opkts	Oerrs	Coll
wdn0	1500	**129.33**	fire	8558	0	7682	0	0
lo0	2048	loopback	localhost	2112	0	2112	0	0

Notice that `wdn0` is connected to the `129.33` network. This means that all packets addressed to hosts with Internet addresses that begin with `129.33` will be sent to the `wdn0` interface. This leaves two bytes (16 bits) to specify a host on that network. One byte would allow up to 255 hosts per network (all ones is a broadcast address), and the netmask could be set to **ffffff00** to use the third byte to specify an internal (local) network, with up to 255 hosts. For example, `129.33.`**192** could be an Ethernet in building A, `129.33.`**194** could be an Ethernet in building B, `129.33.`**196** could be a token ring, and `129.33.`**198** could be a token bus. Outside your organization, only the first two bytes (129.33) would be used to route packets to your network; inside your organization the third byte would be used to isolate traffic on Ethernets or route packets between different physical networks.

Another internal table is used to cache addresses for routing purposes. The `netstat` command can be used to examine this routing table:

```
$ netstat -r
```

Routing tables

Destination	Gateway	Flags	Refs	Use	Interface
localhost	**localhost**	UH	4	655	**lo0**
roid	localhost	UH	1	429	lo0
diamond	**aix03**	UH	1	12	**un0**
170.24	129.33.192.10	UG	0	0	pg0

This tells us which interface is used to reach the destination: The software loopback pseudo-device is used to reach `localhost` and `roid`, the Ungermann-Bass interface un0 is used to reach `diamond`, and the Pegasus interface pg0 is used to reach another network, 170.24, through the gateway at 129.33.192.10. The flag U means "up," H means "host," and G means "gateway." Host routes appear in the table in front of network gateways, which allows us to create direct paths to certain hosts before the gateway to the network is used.

A command called `ping` can be used to determine if a remote system is up:

```
$ ping moonbeam 64 1

PING 129.47.1.193: 64 data bytes
72 bytes from 129.47.1.193: icmp_seq=0, time=1 100th of sec
----129.47.1.193 PING Statistics----
1 packets transmitted, 1 packets received, 0% packet loss
round trip (100th of sec) min/avg/max=1/1/1
```

Here the `ping` sends an ICMP "Echo Request" packet to the remote system `moonbeam`, and reports its round-trip time if a reply packet is received; otherwise it reports 100% packet loss to let you know a reply was not received. The arguments are hostname, number of data bytes, and the number of packets to send. The default number of bytes is 64, and the default number of packets is an endless loop, so a control-C interrupt would be necessary to stop `ping` if the third argument were not given on the command line. It is instructive to examine the routing table with **netstat -r**, then **ping** a remote system and examine the routing table again to see how it changes.

The routing table is updated in one of three ways:

1. Static routing via the **/etc/route** command
2. Dynamic routing via the **/etc/routed** daemon
3. Rerouting via ICMP **"Redirect" packets** from IP routers

All TCP/IP implementations are required to support IP "Echo Requests," but IP "Redirects" are optional. Most IP routers send a special ICMP redirect packet to the source to let it know whenever a different path should be used. The `routed` daemon listens on UDP socket 520 for routing information packets. The internal routing table is broadcast every 30 seconds, using a variant of the Xerox Networking Services (XNS) Routing Information Protocol (RIP). Other routing protocols can be used, such as Exterior Gateway Protocol (EGP), Interior Gateway Routing Protocol (IGRP), or Hello, the original gateway protocol for NSFNET. Consult your local system administration manuals for more information about the different routing protocols.

Static routing is usually done at system startup time by **/etc/route** commands in an **/etc/rc** shell script, although it can be done from the command line by system administrators. The basic form of the command is as follows:

```
/etc/route {add|delete} [host|net] {dest|default} [gateway [metric]]
```

The `add` option uses an I/O control (`ioctl`) system call with an SIOCADDRT command to add an entry to the routing table; `delete` uses SIOCDELRT to delete an entry from the routing table. The `host` option with a hostname in the *dest* field can be used for "host routing," while the `net` option can be used to specify which *gateway* should be used to reach the *dest* network. The *metric* option specifies the number of hops (different networks) between this host and the *dest* host or network. The *metric* is used to find the "best" route to *dest*. The **default** option specifies the *gateway* to send all packets that are not on the local network after all other routes have been attempted.

Figure 1.16 shows a point-to-point connection added to a broadcast LAN.

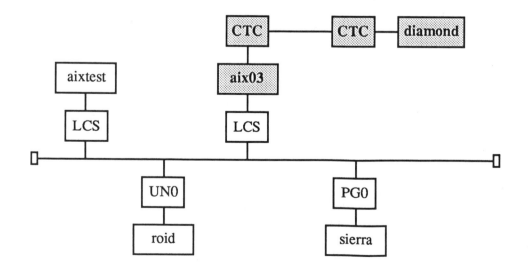

Figure 1.16   Point-to-point Gateway on an Ethernet

The systems `aixtest`, `aix03`, and `diamond` in Figure 1.16 are **virtual machines** running on a single mainframe computer. Mainframes connect to the LAN through a Lan Channel Station (LCS). The physical LCS is logically assigned to a virtual machine by the Control Program (CP) component of the VM operating system. Device interrupts are sent to the correct virtual machine by CP. Each virtual machine runs a different (prerelease) version of **AIX/370** (IBM's mainframe UNIX). Normally, only two versions of AIX/370 are needed at the same time: the current version and the previous version (in case applications break on the newest version). Therefore, only two LCS interfaces were allocated for our group's use. Unfortunately, one person needed to go back *two* releases to run his applications (there is one in every crowd :-).

The `diamond` system was kept intact on the VM mainframe, directly connected to the virtual machine `aix03` by a **channel-to-channel adapter** (CTC). Peripheral devices connect to IBM mainframes through a channel, and channel-to-channel adapters are used in mainframe environments for **computer-to-computer** data transfers. Thus, the CTC interfaces are **point-to-point** links between IBM mainframes, functionally equivalent to DEC's Computer Interconnect (CI) bus or a direct X.25 connection to another host. The command that must be executed for Ethernet hosts to reach the isolated `diamond` system is to route all packets through the `aix03` gateway:

```
/etc/route  add  host  diamond aix03 1
```

This command adds an entry to the host's routing table to direct all packets to `diamond` through the gateway `aix03`, and the destination host is one hop on the other side of the gateway. Hostnames `aix03` and `diamond` are used for clarity; their Internet addresses are obtained by a table lookup in the system file `/etc/hosts`.

How does `diamond` send packets to hosts on the Ethernet?

```
on diamond: /etc/ifconfig ctc0 diamond aix03 netmask 0xffffff00
            /etc/route  add  net    default aix03 1
```

The `ifconfig` command with *two* addresses specifies that the channel-to-channel adapter (`ctc0`) interface is a point-to-point connection from `diamond` to `aix03` (again, Internet addresses are found in `/etc/hosts`). The `route` command causes all outgoing packets to be sent to `aix03`, which has an entry in the routing table to the `ctc0` interface, thanks to the `ifconfig` command. The other end is initialized as follows:

```
on aix03:  /etc/ifconfig ctc0 aix03 diamond netmask 0xffffff00
           /etc/ifconfig lcs0 129.33.192.81 netmask 0xffffff00
```

The first `ifconfig` command enters a **point-to-point host route** table entry from `aix03` to `diamond`, and the second one enters a **broadcast network route** table entry for the Lan Channel Station (`lcs0`). This means that packets addressed to `diamond` will be sent to the channel-to-channel interface (`ctc0`), while other packets will be sent to the `lcs0` interface. This works because host entries are found before network entries in the routing table. Some systems may require the `ctc0` interface to have a different Internet address from that of the `lcs0` interface. If this is the case, you may need to add an entry `aix03-gw` to `/etc/hosts` with a different Internet address than that used by `aix03`. (That is, some implementations may allow you to use the same Internet address for the point-to-point interface and the broadcast interface, because host routing would send the "right packets" to the point-to-point interface, and network routing would send the "right packets" to the broadcast interface device. The only confusion would arise if the **same address** were assigned to **two different interfaces** on the same **broadcast** network.)

Workstations connect to the Ethernet with Ungermann-Bass (`un0`) interface boards, and personal computers use Pegasus (`pg0`) boards. Because a host may have more than one of the same type of interface board, each interface is numbered, (such as `pg0` or `pg1`). The commands used to initialize the Internet addresses are as follows:

```
on aixtest:
      /etc/ifconfig  lcs0  129.33.192.106  netmask  0xffffff00
on roid:
      /etc/ifconfig  un0   129.33.192.96   netmask  0xffffff00
on sierra:
      /etc/ifconfig  pg0   129.33.192.87   netmask  0xffffff00
```

Each interface must have a unique Internet address, or else those claiming the same address are "kicked out" of the Internet. To guarantee uniqueness, a designated person within an organization usually assigns Internet addresses. This person will assign a new Internet address for your workstation. What happens if, later on, your network needs to be connected to another? This could easily happen if your organization is bought or merges with another. There will almost certainly be address conflicts if **universally unique network numbers** were not initially used. That's why it's worth the effort to contact the Network Information Center (NIC) at SRI to get a unique Internet network number. The contact address is

```
              DDN Network Information Center
              SRI International
              333 Ravenswood Avenue
              Menlo Park, CA  94025
              USA
```

or you can request an electronic form (INTERNET-NUMBER-TEMPLATE.TXT) by email from **hostmaster@sri-nic.arpa** and submit it electronically. Numbers are usually assigned within two weeks.

Internet addresses are not hard-coded into programs. Fortunately, there is a library utility function **gethostbyname()** *to obtain the IP addresses of a host from the* **/etc/hosts** file. To change addresses, simply edit a new `/etc/hosts` file and then make sure all the hosts on the network use the new file. Examples of these network utility functions will be introduced in Chapter 3.

Figure 1.17 shows a sample **/etc/hosts** file. The Internet address is followed by the "official" host name, followed by your favorite aliases. The gethostbyname() function looks at all the names and aliases and, if it finds the name you requested, it returns the Internet address.

```
128.6.1.2          bubble       bubble.eecs.mit.edu
129.33.192.96      roid         roid.pasc.ibm.com
129.33.192.202     quixote      quixote.pasc.ibm.com
129.33.192.129     diamond      diamond.pasc.ibm.com
9.1.58.1           ibmpa        ibmpa.awd.ibm.com
136.4.1.22         hplabs       hplabs.palab.hp.com
148.1.9.1          wilbur       wilbur.nas.nasa.gov
192.12.102.3       ames         ames.arc.nasa.gov
```

Figure 1.17 A Sample /etc/hosts File

The /etc/hosts file makes it possible for people to reach systems by name rather than Internet address. For example, you can use

rlogin hplabs

instead of

rlogin 136.4.1.22

because the **rlogin.c** program uses the library function gethostbyname() to lookup the Internet address of hplabs in /etc/hosts.

Most commands allow you to use an Internet address in place of a host name, as in the rlogin 136.4.1.22 example. Sometimes it is necessary to do this when the system you want to reach is not listed in the /etc/hosts file. Clearly, using host names is more convenient for people than trying to remember many Internet addresses. However, this requires system administrators to keep their /etc/hosts files up to date. In small, isolated networks this may not be a problem, and the **rdist** ("remote distribution") command may be helpful to keep files consistent within your administrative control. For example, the following command:

```
$ rdist
```

with the following **distfile**,

```
MACHINES = ( diamond aixtest paris )
FILES = ( /etc/hosts Makefile client.c server.c )
${FILES} -> ${MACHINES}
        install;
        special client.c "make";
        special server.c "make";
        notify  wdr@diamond;
```

would distribute copies of the `FILES` to the systems named in the `MACHINES` list. The `install` keyword instructs `rdist` to install `/etc/hosts` on the `MACHINES`, and the `Makefile` and C programs are installed in the user's home directory. In addition, the C programs are compiled by running `make` on each target system (so the machine architectures may be different), and a notification message is emailed from each system to `wdr@diamond` when `rdist` finishes.

Remote distribution does not scale up in huge, worldwide cooperating networks, where central system administration is virtually impossible. The `/etc/hosts` file would have *several thousand* lines, and it would *almost always be out of date* (every time a new host was added in France or India or Singapore or Palo Alto, `rdist` would have to be run). This doesn't even consider the problem of name conflicts, like the time we discovered an `opus` system in England after we had chosen the name `opus` for our new system in New Jersey.

So a name server was introduced with BSD 4.3. The **Berkeley Internet Name Domain** (BIND) system provides a distributed database of Internet addresses. Naming authority is decentralized among organizations in a hierarchy of Name Domains. Upon request, a Name Domain is assigned to an institution by SRI, and naming authority within that Domain is "delegated" to that institution. For example, the `opus`-naming problem could be resolved by using **opus.ukuug.uk** *(UNIX User Group, United Kingdom)* and the other would be **opus.att.com** *(New Jersey, USA)*.

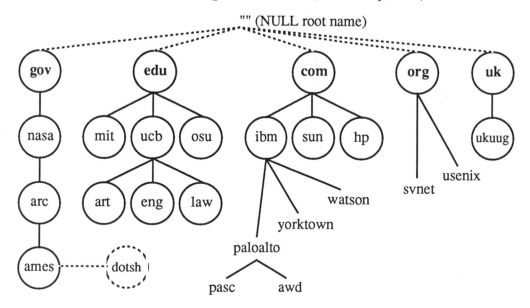

Figure 1.18 Name Domain Hierarchy

Figure 1.18 shows a typical Name Domain tree.   The top domain represents a general category, such as **government**, **education**, **commercial** businesses, nonprofit **organizations**, **military**, and two-character country codes (such as **uk** for United Kingdom, **us** for USA, or **fr** for France). The next level is also assigned by SRI-NIC. For example, NASA was assigned the name domain **nasa.gov**, and it, in turn, assigned **arc**.nasa.gov to the Ames Research Center in Mountain View, California. The host **ames** is the Internet gateway. IBM was assigned the name domain **ibm.com** and, in turn, it created internal name domains for **watson**, **paloalto**, and **cambridge**. A person at each location has authority to assign unique names for that location. The Palo Alto location was further subdivided by work groups: **pasc** (Palo Alto Scientific Center) and **awd** (Advanced Workstation Division). A person within each work group is responsible for assigning unique hostnames within their respective domain of authority.

Names are resolved by consulting systems further up in the hierarchy. For example, local names are resolved by a local name server, but an email message from Palo Alto to Cambridge is deferred to an authoritative name server for the ibm.com domain. That is, the name server at pasc.paloalto.ibm.com does not know Internet addresses at cambridge, so it forwards the name request to the authoritative paloalto name server, which sends the request to the ibm.com name server, which then asks the authoritative cambridge.ibm.com name server to look up and return the Internet address of the requested host name.

A major benefit of the Name Domain system is that a **named** daemon is executed on one or more designated **name servers**, and local gethostbyname() requests are sent to be resolved by a name server.   Instead of maintaining many copies of /etc/hosts files on each host, a primary name server is designated in a system file called **/etc/resolv.conf**. *When this file exists, library functions such as* gethostbyname() *use* **resolver(3N)** *library functions to send requests over the network to a designated name server before looking in /etc/hosts. In other words, if you change a system in your local /etc/hosts file, it may not be noticed as long as you have an /etc/resolv.conf file!*

A sample /etc/resolv.conf file is the following:

```
nameserver   129.33.192.128

nameserver   129.33.192.139

domain       pasc.paloalto.ibm.com
```

Requests to resolve a name to an Internet address are first sent to the named daemon running on 129.33.192.128. If a reply is received, all is well. Otherwise, after a timeout period, the same request is sent to 129.33.192.139. The **domain** line tells the system to append the default domain string to unqualified names. For example, telnet nautilus would become telnet nautilus**.pasc.paloalto.ibm.com** in the Scientific Center's name domain. To login to a different host named `nautilus` in the Advanced Workstation Division name domain, use the fully qualified name, as in `telnet nautilus.`**`awd`**`.paloalto.ibm.com`.

Please note that a Domain Name is not an Internet address. For example, **mtune.att.com** has only three levels, and **roid.pasc.paloalto.ibm.com** has five levels, but Internet addresses are always a four-part "dotted decimal" **number**.

The system `dotsh` in Figure 1.18 has a dialup RS-232 connection with `ames` on the Internet. The `dotsh` system is not part of the Name Hierarchy, but it can be reached by using the electronic mail address **dotsh!wdr**`@ames.arc.nasa.gov` or **wdr%dotsh**`@ames.arc.nasa.gov`. Electronic mail is normally sent by `sendmail` on the Internet and by UUCP (UNIX-to-UNIX copy) over RS-232 lines.

You can find more information on name domains in Douglas Comer's book *Internetworking with TCP/IP*, or Evi Nemeth's *UNIX System Administration Handbook*. The 4.3 BSD manuals are another excellent source of information, as well as the system manuals from your vendor.

1.6   Network Hardware

The following subsections describe network hardware architecture.

1.6.1 Ethernet and IEEE 802.3

Ethernet and IEEE 802.3 (which are almost, but not quite, identical) are two of the most popular LAN architectures used with UNIX systems. Both consist of a certain kind of cable, to which all the computers (and other devices) connect.

They use a technology called **CSMA/CD**, which stands for "Carrier Sense Multiple Access/Collision Detect." The **Multiple Access** part means that all computers (and other devices) access the media (coaxial cable or twisted pair) at the same time. This technology depends on each controller being able to sense when another station is also transmitting. This is the **"Carrier Sense"** part. First, before transmitting, each station checks the media for a carrier. If present, it does not transmit, but rather waits for a random amount of time and tries again. If no carrier is sensed, then it starts transmitting, while *continuing to check for the presence of another station's transmission.* Two stations may both check the media at the same time, sense no carrier, and begin transmitting. If two stations transmit at the same time, their signals will corrupt each other, and this is called a "collision." This is the **"Collision Detection"** part. Once detected, the colliding stations transmit a "jam signal" to make sure that all stations know what happened. Each time a collision is detected, each controller waits a random amount of time before retrying. Most controllers take a certain number of bits from a counter driven by its clock, and each iteration the number of bits they use increases by one, effectively doubling the range. Thus, for example, they first pick a random number in the range 1 to 255. If they collide twice, they pick another number in the range 1 to 511, and so on, up to a maximum at the tenth iteration. If they continue to collide, they try six more times, by using different random numbers in the same range. Two stations may collide once, even twice, but it becomes increasingly less probable that they will continue to collide with each other over time. However, it is also impossible to guarantee how long it will take to send a message, because you never know in advance how many collisions there will be. This is one reason why Ethernet is not typically used for digitized speech (although it does work) or other real-time applications. Try to keep in mind that collisions are a concern only at a microscopic level, and at the macroscopic level, Ethernet-type networks are as fast as token-rings, they work very well, and are quite reliable.

Another characteristic of Ethernet is that it does not send an acknowledgment that the receiver has received the data. To know this, it is necessary to receive some sort of reply in return. When Ethernets are used with TCP/IP, this acknowledgment comes from TCP. UDP applications must take care of this themselves.

Ethernet hardware is very reliable. A common failure is when somebody accidentally unplugs a station, that station is unreachable. If it is unplugged in the wrong way, the whole cable may be left unterminated. When this happens, there are two disconnected parts of the cable. Any energy transmitted into either end of the cable will be reflected backwards. The reflections look like collisions to the controllers, and the result is that nobody gets anything done over the LAN until the break is found. This sort of thing happens usually no more than once (due to the embarrassment factor).

Because LANs have fewer active components, they are normally much more reliable than Wide Area Networks (WANs).

1.6.2 Token-Passing Rings (IEEE 802.5)

Token-passing rings are also popular LANs. The term "token" comes from the way they handle contention. Whenever you have a media that is shared, it is necessary to control when each party transmits. Token-passing rings and busses do this by passing a token from station to station. Each station is only allowed to transmit if it has the token. An analogy would be a group of people where a microphone is passed among them and only the person holding the microphone is allowed to speak.

The "token" is a special pattern of bits that continually circulates around the ring, from station to station. When a station wants to transmit, it first acquires the token and absorbs it while it transmits. This prevents other stations from transmitting, because they will not receive the token. When the message makes a full circle, the transmitting station absorbs the message bits so they leave the loop. This means that there is no minimum nor maximum packet size required by token-ring hardware, although a maximum packet size is enforced by the software, to allow a control station to check for the token periodically.

All stations physically receive the message bits, but only the one which has the same address as in the packet header will send the message upward from the link level to the network level. One special problem that rings have is the need to deal with the loss of any part of the ring. Unlike Ethernet and other bus-type LANs, rings must always be a closed loop. If you lose a controller on a ring, the whole LAN is in trouble. If you lose an Ethernet controller, only that station is affected. When somebody turns off their computer, the ring still needs the interface board to operate. Token-ring interface boards get their power from the ring cable. If the token is lost, a designated control station generates a new one.

1.6.3 Token-Passing Busses (IEEE 802.4)

Token passing also works on a bus. One of these is defined in the IEEE 802.4 standard, which is part of the Manufacturing Automation Protocol (MAP) standards. It uses broadband media, which are different from the so-called "baseband" that Ethernet and token ring use. Baseband can handle only one signal in the cable at any one time, whereas broadband can simultaneously provide many separate and independent communication channels. Each channel operates at a different frequency band. It can have TV signals on some bands, computer data on others, and even voice data on others. This technology was developed for cable TV and has been used for many years. It is reliable, readily available, and fairly cheap. Some broadband networks use two cables, one for transmitting, and one for receiving. Other systems use just one cable, and the frequency spectrum is split into two halves. Stations transmit on one frequency band, and receive on another. Transmit and receive channels are paired, typically by a fixed number of MHz, which makes it easy to convert from the "send" channel to the "receive" channel (just add, say, 150 MHz). Broadband requires more complex, sophisticated, and expensive equipment than Ethernet, but it supports analog video and voice signals, as well as digital data.

1.6.4 Wide Area Networks

Wide Area Networks pick up where LANs leave off. The single largest difference between the two is distance. A LAN spans one or more floors of a single building, but usually not outside it. WANs tie together computers that may be hundreds, perhaps even thousands of miles apart. Another difference between LANs and WANs is that it is harder to get high bandwidth at longer distances, and it comes at a higher price. The reason is that it is harder to push a fast-moving signal through thousands of miles of copper wire. The wire makes a great antenna for picking up EM interference. Also, it has to go over (or under) land that somebody else probably owns, so there is a right-of-way factor built into the price structure, along with everything else. The growing use of fiber optics reduces the costs of high bit-rates between large urban areas, but it is expected to be many years before megabit-plus rates are as widely prevalent anywhere around the world as is POTS (Plain Old Telephone Service).

Modems convert digital signals to analog for plain old telephone wire. However, the faster you want these signals to vary (and the more bits per second you want to send down these wires) the more you need expensive modems. 1200 and 2400 bits per second are fairly easy, so modems in this speed range can be found quite inexpensively. Since they are not attempting fancy things with the signals, they can almost always get it through. As bit rates go up, though, so do the prices of the modems, and so does the rental of the telephone circuits (except with certain kinds of modems, if you want rates at 4800, 9600 or higher, you need to pay the carrier extra money to "condition" the lines in certain ways, so that the signal will be cleaner). Higher speeds cost more money, for the modems and sometimes (depending upon the modem) for the charges of the telephone circuit.

A protocol that is growing in popularity and installed base is X.25. If you wish to "talk" over the network, you can initiate a connection, called a CALL REQUEST. The network will attempt to set up a circuit for you to the destination you specified, by using an address formatted according to another standard, X.121. The circuit exists between you and your destination for a period of time, until either you, your peer, or the network itself chooses to clear it. It is called a Switched Virtual Circuit (SVC) because you can switch it later to some other destination. There also exist Permanent Virtual Circuits, which are analogous to leased lines. They are rented for a period of time from the company that is providing the network service, and they start and end at the same two physical locations.

1.6.5 Network Hardware Independence

One of the reasons why TCP/IP has become so popular is that it works very well on top of any of these hardware protocols. Although the speeds differ, there is no difference at the programming level. The speed difference means that timeout values that may be reasonable for LANs can be quite unreasonable for WANs, causing unnecessary retransmissions, or even popping of the connections unnecessarily if this isn't taken into account. Fortunately, TCP adjusts its timeouts based upon the delays that the network is exhibiting on a moment-by-moment basis (it averages the samples so that it won't be overly sensitive to short-term variations).

From a programming perspective, it is very nice not to worry about whether your data is going over X.25, 802.3, 802.4, 802.5, something else, or some combination of these. Each gives you a different set of things it does and doesn't do for you, and so a protocol like TCP which can recover from virtually anything that is recoverable alleviates a lot of problems. Even if you choose UDP, which does not recover from much of anything, you really only have to worry about whether the data failed to arrive.

Why it failed to arrive usually does not matter, unless you are the network troubleshooter and the problem is happening too often.

TCP is considered a "reliable" protocol, in the sense that it provides sequenced, once-and-only-once delivery of data. However, if the network's reliability deteriorates below a certain point, TCP will give up and you will lose your connection. What actually happens is that TCP expects to receive acknowledgments to its data, and if these are not received (for whatever reason) then it will retransmit, but it counts how many times it does this. After a while, it simply makes a decision that the network's reliability is too poor to continue. It assumes that if N consecutive messages are not acknowledged, then there must be a break in the network, separating you and the party to whom you are talking. Usually, TCP's assumption is correct, but not always. Furthermore, if a very large file transfer is almost finished, but the connection breaks just before it completes, chances are the file transfer will have to be restarted.

This brings us to another aspect of network programming, anticipating failures. All known network transmission media today are subject to periods where they are unusable. Wires and fiber-optic cables can be cut by bulldozers, and wires can pick up electromagnetic interference, even when it is shielded cable. Radio waves, microwave links, and so on are also subject to EM interference. Each has its own set of vulnerabilities, and no media is guaranteed to be able to deliver your data all the time.

Short-term interference is taken care of by the automatic retransmission property of most data-link-level protocols. The data gets through, but the time cannot be recovered. This is one reason why media bit rate is higher than network throughput.

1.7   Client/Server Model

Most network applications are implemented as clients and servers. That is, a **client process** on one system sends a **request** to a **server process** on a remote system to perform some **service**. This is very similar to normal subroutines, except a "**server daemon**" process must be running, listening for remote requests, and connecting the client to the service (subroutine) when one arrives. This analogy is illustrated in Figure 1.19.

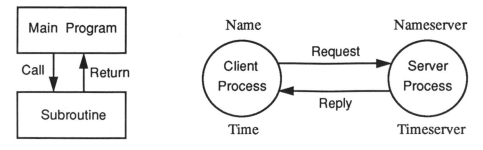

Figure 1.19   Client/Server Model

Whether a network application uses a connection (virtual circuit) or runs connectionless (datagrams) depends on the type of service provided. `Telnet` and `rlogin` use connections (TCP) while `rwho` and `ruptime` use datagrams (UDP). The basic flow of a connectionless datagram service is shown in Figure 1.19. A client sends a request message, and the server sends a reply message. If either is lost, the client simply sends the request again. The basic flow of a connection-oriented service is shown in Figure 1.20. The sequence of events is:

1.   server creates and listens on a "well-known" socket
2.   client creates a "connection" socket
3.   client sends service request to the "well-known" socket
4.   server accepts the request and creates a "service" process
5.   a "connection" socket is created for the "service" process
6.   client and server interact via the "connection" socket

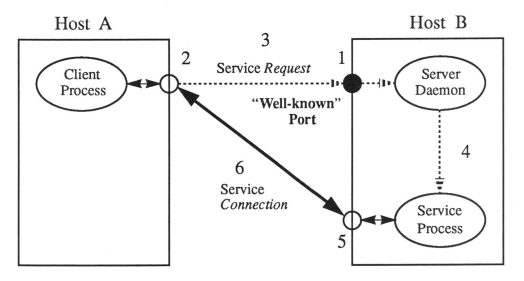

Figure 1.20   Client/Server Connections

Server daemons are started at system boot time, usually in an **/etc/rc** ("run commands") shell script, or another script invoked by it. The Internet daemon, **inetd**, is started this way. Basically, a server creates a socket endpoint at some "well-known address" and listens for requests to arrive on that socket. A client creates a new socket endpoint and tries to connect to the socket at the "well-known address," usually on some other host. "Well-known addresses" are defined in a system file called **/etc/services**. When the server "hears" the request, it creates another socket endpoint and a service process. This way, the service process can communicate with the client using the newly-created socket, and the server can continue listening for new service requests.

Note that it is not mandatory that a server create a child process to perform the requested service. In fact, most connectionless servers do not. Long-running services that require a continuous connection (such as `rlogin`, `telnet`, `ftp`) typically create a child process to manage the connection and carry out the service. Also, the **asymmetric** nature of the client/server model is based on the client being the **active** agent (such as `rlogin`) while the server is a **passive** agent (such as `rlogind`) that responds to client requests. Network applications based on a **peer-to-peer** model are **symmetric** in that a single process may initiate a request and/or perform the service.

1.8   Remote Procedure Calls

The client/server examples in the previous section involve **explicit requests** at the **command level** for remote services (such as `telnet` *hostname*). A major goal of a distributed system is to provide **transparent** access to remote resources. For example, the `man` command could access the manual pages on a remote system, and print them on the user's terminal screen, **without the user explicitly knowing which host stores the /usr/man files**. This "detour" to execute the `read()` system call on a remote system is diagramed in Figure 1.21. How the system determines that a remote call is necessary is implementation dependent, and is slightly different in NFS (Network File System), RFS (Remote File Sharing) and AFS (Andrew File System).

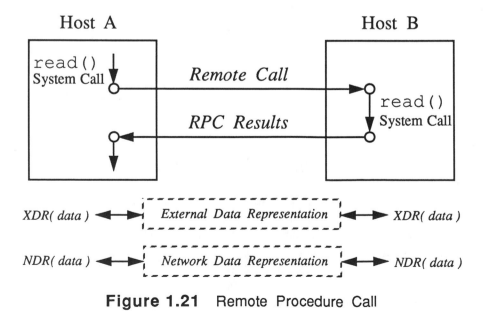

Figure 1.21   Remote Procedure Call

Remote procedure calls (RPC) are familiar to programmers. (Remember your first FORTRAN **SUBROUTINE** or BASIC GOSUB or COBOL PERFORM?) The fact that different host computers are involved requires, at least, some provision for **data conversions** between different architectures. For example, Host A may be an IBM mainframe using 8-bit EBCDIC (Extended Binary Coded Decimal Interchange Code) data representation, while Host B might be a Burroughs B5500 computer using 6-bit BCD (Binary Coded Decimal) code. The request message from Host A is converted to a machine-independent network format by XDR (Sun's External Data Representation) or NDR (Apollo's Network Data Representation) subroutines. These subroutines also run on Host B to translate in the other direction. The NDR protocol is "smart enough" to skip translation between hosts that use the same data representation and have the same byte order. Data is always converted at both ends using the XDR protocol. Add to this the potential problems introduced by the network (for example, **what if Host B crashes?**) and you see that network programmers have more choices to make than simply which subroutine library to use.

User-level transparency is provided by "**stubs**" that run on each host computer and send messages to each other at opposite ends of the "detours." The "stubs" are represented in Figure 1.21 as tiny circles: Their job is to **hide the network details** from a programmer, and make the RPC look like a local subroutine call. One choice a network application designer must make is whether to use stubs implemented in user libraries or inside the operating system kernel. The trade-offs usually center around portability versus speed issues. A more vexing problem is how to handle parameters. **Call-by-value** is easy; **call-by-reference** (address pointer) is much more difficult and usually not allowed. The problem is twofold: (1) Host A's memory addresses are not at all useful on Host B; and (2) If call-by-reference is implemented by sending values and using temporary locations on Host B, then problems may arise if the same argument is passed to two parameters.

Another issue is network reliability. How long should a request wait for a reply from a remote host that may have crashed? What if the network was overloaded during the first request, and the operation was performed on the remote host, but the reply was discarded by the busy network? What would be the effect of performing the same request more than once? Inquiries, for example, are **idempotent**—the effect of multiple executions is exactly the same as performing it only once. Debit and credit transactions, on the other hand, must not be executed more than once. (Multiple deposit credits might be acceptable, but multiple withdrawal debits would definitely be in poor taste.)

These kinds of issues are addressed by Sun's RPC and H-P/Apollo's NCS (Network Computing System). They are two popular RPC libraries available for network application programmers to use. Sun's NFS (Network File System) is implemented using the RPC/XDR protocols.

1.9   Network File System (NFS)

A major benefit of installing a network is the ability to share files among many systems. This reduces the administrative effort necessary to keep multiple copies up-to-date and consistent. It also saves disk space, but most important it ensures that everyone on the network will see the same data.

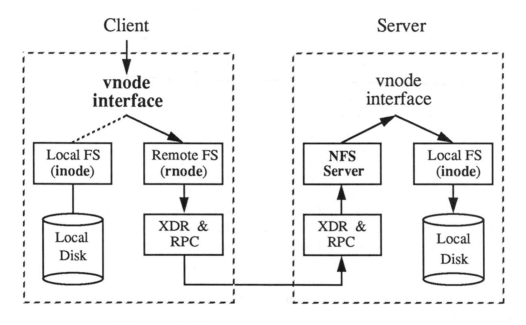

Figure 1.22 Network File System (NFS)

Figure 1.22 shows an overview of Sun's Network File System (NFS) architecture. The "vnode interface" is the code that determines whether a client request is local or remote. Vnodes are **"virtual inodes,"** so named because UNIX uses **inodes** (information nodes) to store file information such as file owner, access privileges, access times, and so on. Remote files are accessed via **rnodes** ("remote inodes"), which are used to keep information about RPC requests sent to a remote host. The NFS server is the "stub" code that handles remote requests. All file access requests go through the "vnode interface," even remote requests which are handled by the NFS server. This interface recognizes that the file requested by the NFS server is local, and therefore sends the request on to the "local FS (filesystem)" code. NFS can support non-UNIX filesystems such as VAX/VMS, VM/CMS files and even "pseudo filesystems", such as special device files (/dev) and process images (/proc), because "virtual inodes" are used to store generic information, independent of other operating system's file control blocks. NFS calls them **"Virtual** File Systems" (VFS).

NFS is a **stateless** distributed filesystem. This means that the server does not keep track of remote accesses. Only the client keeps this information in the rnode, and each read or write request is sent to the server and acted on independently. It is possible for a local user to remove a file that is being accessed by a remote user. After the file is removed, subsequent remote accesses will fail.

A few system-administration steps are necessary to use NFS. First, the server must specify which filesystems are available for remote access. This is done by listing the filesystem names in a system file called **/etc/exports**. To share a set of local utilities in /usr/local, for example, a server would have the name of that filesystem (for example, /usr/local) in /etc/exports. The **mount** command shows you which filesystems are local, and which are remote:

```
$ mount
/              on /dev/root        read/write on Tue May 07 18:09:41
/usr/local on earth:/usr/local read/write on Tue May 07 18:16:13
/students  on earth:/students  read/write on Tue May 07 18:16:14

$ uname -n
fire
```

Files in /usr/local are physically stored on a disk drive connected to the host named earth. On remote systems wind and fire, the following commands are executed in an /etc/rc script at system startup time:

```
        mount -f NFS,soft,intr -r earth:/usr/local /usr/local
        mount -f NFS,soft,intr -r earth:/students  /students
```

These commands mount the remote files in /usr/local and /students on earth over the local /usr/local and /students directories. The directory names need not be the same on both systems, although it may simplify file pathnames if they are. The "**-f** NFS" option specifies that earth:/dirname is an NFS (remote) filesystem; "soft" directs the mount command to return an error code if the server earth does not respond; and intr allows keyboard interrupts to kill a process that is waiting for a response from the server. The "**-r**" option specifies that the filesystem is mounted read-only. There are other options to the mount command, including "bg" which backgrounds the command if the server does not respond (thus allowing the system to continue, rather than hang on the mount command).

There is a system file that gives the names of filesystems that are automatically mounted at system boot time. The name of this file may be different on various vendor's systems: /etc/filesystems (AIX), /etc/vfstab (SVR4), or /etc/default/filesys (SCO Open Desktop). One problem with automatic mounts at boot time is that clients may hang (**and not boot!**) if the server is down. This can be sidestepped by testing the server before executing the mount commands:

```
if  ping earth 1 1 | grep "1 packets received" >/dev/null 2>&1
then
      echo "\tFile Server is up!"
      mount -f NFS,soft,intr -r earth:/usr/local /usr/local
      mount -f NFS,soft,intr -r earth:/students  /students
else
      echo "\tFile Server is down, down, down..."
      echo "\tSorry, no compiles today."
fi
```

Except for this extra system administration, the actual use of NFS (remote) files is completely transparent to users. That is, users can cd /usr/local and use files in that directory without modifying any of their programs, or UNIX file commands.

1.10 Summary

This chapter has presented a basic foundation for subsequent chapters on network application programming. Essential system administration commands such as ifconfig, netstat, arp, ping, ruptime, route, rdist, and mount were introduced, along with critical system files such as /etc/hosts, /etc/services, /etc/ethers, /etc/resolv.conf, /etc/hosts.equiv, ~/.rhosts, /etc/exports, /etc/default/filesys, /etc/fstab, /etc/vfstab, /etc/filesytems, and /etc/rc2.d/S01MOUNTFSYS. A basic understanding of these files and commands is helpful for network application development and testing.

Fundamental network concepts such as the client/server model and remote procedure calls (RPC) were introduced, as well as a popular Network File System (NFS) application that is implemented using RPC. Important distinctions were made between unreliable, connectionless, atomic datagrams (such as UDP) and reliable, continuous virtual circuit connections (such as TCP).

The very popular and widely available vendor-independent TCP/IP Internet Protocols were introduced, as well as the ISO's Reference Model for Open Systems Interconnection (OSI). Comparisons were shown how the TCP/IP layers fit in the OSI protocol levels. Network addressing was presented, along with Internet-Ethernet address mappings.

Physical network technologies such as Ethernet, IEEE 802.3, Token-rings (IEEE 802.5), token-busses (IEEE 802.4) and Wide Area Network (WAN) hardware were briefly covered.

BSD Sockets and System V STREAMS application programming interfaces (API) were introduced to provide a basis for later chapters on socket-level programming and TLI (Transport-Level Interface) programming.

2 UNIX Domain Sockets

by Bill Rieken

2.1 Introduction

This chapter introduces a very simple IPC (interprocess communication) example using Berkeley BSD sockets. To focus attention on the socket system calls, the local UNIX domain is presented first; the next chapter introduces the Internet (TCP/IP) domain. Socket concepts and system calls are introduced first, and then a connection-oriented client/server example is shown, followed by a connectionless datagram example. Finally, a UNIX domain address structure is introduced.

2.2 Socket Abstraction

As shown in Figure 2.1, a socket is just another I/O abstraction. Creating a socket is very much like opening a file, in that an integer "file handle" is returned to the caller. Your program can read and write data to or from a socket by using the integer "file descriptor" in the same way it does I/O to a file, as shown in Figure 2.2. The difference is that the data written by one process is sent directly to a buffer in the process that owns the socket at the other end. Thus, a socket connection between two processes is like a bidirectional pipe.

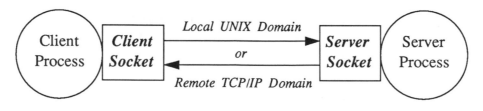

Figure 2.1 BSD Interprocess Sockets

Normally, a "client" process sends a request to a "server" process to perform some service and (usually) return the service output to the client. The service can be as simple as executing the who command on a remote system and sending the output to the client, or it can be as complex as maintaining a login session and emulating an asynchronous character terminal device over a network. Both processes can be on the same system. For example, the server process could be a line printer spooler and the client process could be one of many print requests. In the UNIX IPC protocol domain, both processes would execute on the same system. The TCP/IP or Internet protocol domain enables servers to execute on the same system or on a remote machine that is reachable from the client system.

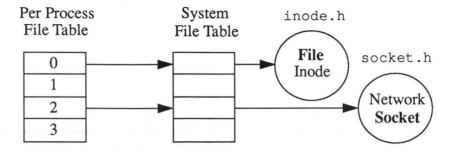

Figure 2.2 File and Socket Descriptors

2.2.1 Socket Interface Layer

The kernel code that implements the socket abstraction is called the "socket layer" and is intended to be protocol-independent. The layer of kernel code that implements UNIX domain IPC, TCP/UDP/IP (Internet), X.25, and other protocols is called the "protocol layer." Actual device I/O is done at the device driver level, as shown in Figure 2.3.

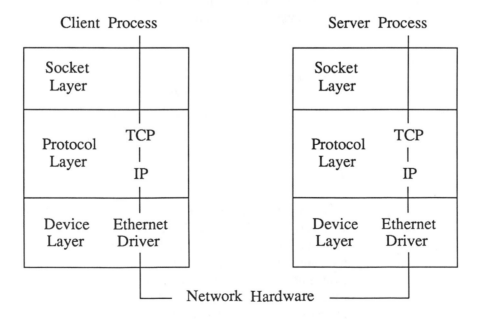

Figure 2.3 Network Software Layers

2.3   BSD Socket System Calls

The essential socket system calls are shown in Figure 2.4. Technical details are documented in Section 2 of the UNIX programmer's reference manual for your system, and you are encouraged to read the manual pages for more specific details. The examples presented in this book are intended to supplement the manual pages, not replace them. For now, the basic flow is described: a client creates a socket with the **socket()** system call, and then attempts to **connect()** to a server. Server daemons also create a socket and then **bind()** a "well-known" address to it. "Well-known addresses" are listed in a system file called **/etc/services**, and library functions are available to look them up. Servers then **listen()** on the "well-known" port, and the **accept()** system call accepts connection requests and (silently) *creates a new socket* for communication with the client. Typically, the new accept() socket is given to a child process, which performs the requested service, although quick services might be done directly by the parent daemon.

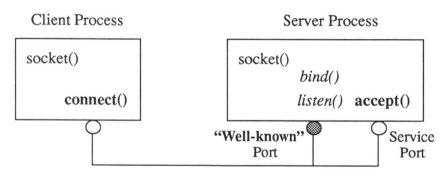

Figure 2.4   Socket System Calls Overview

The socket() system call returns an integer "socket descriptor," which, like the file descriptor returned by an open() system call, indexes an internal array of open file pointers. The pointer indexed by a file descriptor points to an internal file table entry which, in turn, points to a file "information node," or inode for short. The pointer indexed by a socket descriptor points to an internal socket control block, as shown in Figure 2.2.

The header file **socket.h** must be #included in all programs that use the socket system calls. Another header file, **types.h**, is needed to define some of the data types (such as u_short and u_long) used in the socket header file. Both of these header files are in **/usr/include/sys**.

2.3.1   The `socket()` System Call

The socket control block stores state information about an endpoint of a network communication path. Some of the state information you must specify when creating a socket are an **address format** (name) **domain** and communication **semantics**, as shown in Figure 2.5.

The domain parameter specifies the format of a protocol address used by the socket. For example, processes using the UNIX domain communicate with each other through sockets bound to the same UNIX filename. Address format symbolic constants are defined in `socket.h`:

```
/*  Address families, real and imagined ...                   */
#define AF_UNSPEC     0   /* unspecified                      */
#define AF_UNIX       1   /* local to host (pipes, portals)   */
#define AF_INET       2   /* internetwork:UDP, TCP, and so on */
#define AF_IMPLINK    3   /* arpanet imp addresses            */
#define AF_PUP        4   /* pup protocols, such as BSP       */
#define AF_CHAOS      5   /* mit CHAOS protocols              */
#define AF_NS         6   /* XEROX NS protocols               */
#define AF_NBS        7   /* nbs protocols                    */
#define AF_ECMA       8   /* european computer manufacturers  */
#define AF_DATAKIT    9   /* datakit protocols                */
#define AF_CCITT     10   /* CCITT protocols, X.25, and so on */
#define AF_SNA       11   /* IBM SNA                          */
#define AF_DECnet    12   /* DECnet                           */
#define AF_DLI       13   /* Direct data link interface       */
#define AF_LAT       14   /* LAT                              */
#define AF_HYLINK    15   /* NSC Hyperchannel                 */
#define AF_APPLETALK 16   /* AppleTalk                        */
#define AF_NIT       17   /* Network Interface Tap            */
#define AF_802       18   /* IEEE 802.2, also ISO 8802        */
#define AF_OSI       19   /* umbrella for all families used   */
#define AF_X25       20   /* CCITT X.25 in particular         */
#define AF_OSINET    21   /* AFI = 47, IDI = 4                */
#define AF_GOSIP     22   /* U.S. Government OSI              */
#define AF_MAX       23
```

The most widely used socket domains are `AF_UNIX`, for local IPC, and `AF_INET`, for remote IPC. Other address families, such as `AF_X25`, `AF_DATAKIT`, and `AF_OSI`, may be provided, depending on the vendor and the options bought.

The second parameter specifies the communication semantics and, indirectly, the protocol. For example, `SOCK_STREAM` specifies a byte-stream transfer, much like reading and writing a file or a terminal. It specifies **TCP** in the `AF_INET` (Internet) domain. SOCK_**DGRAM** sockets transfer datagram packets, much as the Postal Service delivers letters in envelopes. SOCK_**DGRAM** specifies **UDP** in the AF_INET domain. Both can be used in the UNIX domain; stream semantics make the socket behave like a bidirectional **pipe**, while datagram semantics make the socket behave like a **message queue**. Symbolic constants for communication semantics are defined in socket.h:

```
/* Types of sockets                                                     */
#define  SOCK_STREAM    NC_TPI_COTS    /* stream socket                 */
#define  SOCK_DGRAM     NC_TPI_CLTS    /* datagram socket               */
#define  SOCK_RAW       NC_TPI_RAW     /* raw-protocol interface        */
#define  SOCK_RDM       5              /* reliably delivered message    */
#define  SOCK_SEQPACKET 6              /* sequenced packet stream       */
```

Raw sockets are used by system programs that talk directly to the IP level. For example, the ping command uses raw sockets. "Reliably delivered" messages and sequenced packet stream semantics are not implemented for the UNIX or Internet (TCP/IP) domains.

The third parameter specifies which protocol to use to implement the desired semantics. Either the second or the third parameter can be defaulted, because one usually implies the other. Internally, the protocol parameter is used to index a protocol table, while the type parameter is used in a sequential search of the table (actual implementation, of course, may vary among vendors). Although there *could* be two implementations for SOCK_DGRAM semantics in the AF_INET domain, in practice only one is provided on a system, so the third parameter is often left as zero.

$$sd = socket(\ \textbf{domain, type,}\ protocol\ )$$

	Address Format		Communication Semantics
AF_UNIX	(UNIX filename)	**SOCK_STREAM** (TCP)
AF_INET	(32-bit Internet address)	**SOCK_DGRAM** (UDP)
AF_X25	(10-byte X.25 address)	SOCK_RAW
AF_DATAKIT	(DATAKIT address)	SOCK_SEQPACKET
AF_STARLAN	(STARLAN address)	SOCK_RDM

Figure 2.5 The socket() System Call

SOCK_STREAM is a reliable byte-stream flow, where bytes are received by the remote application in the same order as they were sent. File transfers and terminal emulation for remote logins are typical applications that require this kind of communication semantics. SOCK_DGRAM preserves message boundaries; SOCK_STREAM does not. Applications that exchange client request messages and server response messages are good candidates to use datagram communication semantics.

Let's consider a simple example to illustrate the difference between the communication semantics. Suppose your peer has written 200 bytes into its end of the socket, and you read 100 bytes. If the socket was created as SOCK_STREAM, the remaining 100 bytes are still in kernel buffers, and you can get them with another read. However, the data remaining in the same message would be discarded if you had used SOCK_DGRAM semantics!

Suppose the peer sends two messages, "The quick brown fox jumped over the lazy dog" and "Now is the time for all good computers to come to the aid of their users." Consider two read()s, each of four bytes. With a SOCK_STREAM socket, the read() calls will place "The " in the user's buffer the first time and "quic" the second time. A SOCK_DGRAM socket would cause the first read to put "The " in the buffer, but the second read would return "Now ". The rest of the two messages would be lost!

SOCK_STREAM sockets require your application to count the number of bytes received and **to continue a read loop until the entire application message is received.** SOCK_DGRAM sockets, on the other hand, send messages as complete units, which you can send and receive using the send(), sendto(), sendmsg(), recv(), recvmsg(), and recvfrom() system calls.

The protocol characteristics of a socket are frozen when it is created. You cannot change a stream socket to a datagram socket, or vice versa. Also, it is very important for both sides to have sockets with the same domain and protocol. Otherwise, one side might try to send datagrams while the other side sends byte-streams, and data could get lost in the kernel buffers. The connect() and accept() system calls check that socket endpoints are the same type.

Not all combinations of domain, type, and protocol are allowed. For example, a socket() call with domain AF_INET, type SOCK_DGRAM, and protocol TCP would be rejected. A quick compile of a simple C program with just a socket() call asking for the combination you want will tell you if it's supported on your system. For example, opening an AF_X25 socket will fail if that package has not been installed.

Figure 2.6 illustrates the important difference between UNIX sockets and Internet sockets. AF_UNIX is used for interprocess communication between processes running on the same system. AF_INET is used for interprocess communication between processes that may be on different computers connected by a LAN or WAN. Over a network, SOCK_STREAM is normally TCP and SOCK_DGRAM is usually UDP. When the AF_INET client and server happen to be on the same system, data is transferred in kernel buffers between the two processes, without sending any packets to or from a network device driver. In this special case, AF_INET and AF_UNIX behave the same, except that one uses Internet addresses and the other uses UNIX filenames.

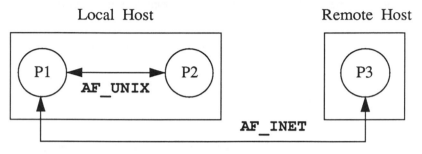

Figure 2.6 Local UNIX and Remote INET Domains

2.3.2 The connect() System Call

After a socket endpoint is created, a client process will normally try to connect() to the server. The meaning of connect() is very different for connection-oriented byte-stream sockets than it is for connectionless, message-oriented datagram sockets. With a connection-oriented socket, the system attempts to "dial a phone number" and connect with the server's socket, much like a telephone call. The connection is maintained for the life of the socket and is usually not changed. In fact, an **EISCONN** (socket is already connected) error occurs if you try to connect() a second time on a SOCK_STREAM socket. A datagram socket, on the other hand, can be associated with another socket via a connect() system call and then later connected to a different socket. All datagrams will be addressed to the same socket, and only datagrams from that socket will be accepted at this end while the connect() call is still in force.

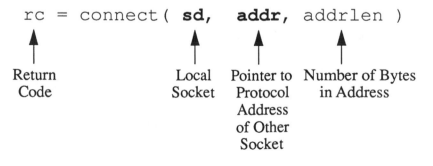

Figure 2.7 The connect() System Call

The format of a connect() system call is shown in Figure 2.7. The first argument is a local socket descriptor returned from a successful socket() system call.

The second argument is the address of the socket with which you wish to be connected. The format of this address varies depending on the communication domain (i.e., protocol) in which the socket was created. A *generic* socket address is defined in `socket.h`:

```
/* Generic structure used by kernel to store most addresses.    */

struct sockaddr {
    u_short  sa_family;   /* protocol address family            */
    char     sa_data[14]; /* up to 14 bytes of direct address   */
};
```

The first two bytes of every address structure contain a "type code" that defines how to interpret the address field (i.e., `sa_data`). Each protocol has a *protocol-specific* socket address structure which defines the format of an address in that protocol family. For example, `sockaddr_un` defines an AF_**UNIX** address in the `sa_data` area, and `sockaddr_in` defines an AF_**INET** address (Internet domain). These structures are defined in the header files, **un.h** and **in.h**, respectively, and they will be shown later, as they are needed.

To help make `connect()` "protocol-independent", a third argument tells the system call the size in bytes of an address in this domain. Notice that the generic address is 16 bytes. A return code of zero means the system call succeeded, while a -1 indicates an error was encountered, and the reason is stored in `errno`.

2.3.3   The `bind()` System Call

Addresses are assigned to sockets with the `bind()` system call. This is done in the server. An address data structure is allocated, initialized, and then bound to the socket. Figure 2.8 shows the basic format of a `bind()` system call.

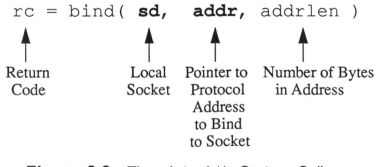

Figure 2.8   The `bind()` System Call

The kernel remembers which addresses have been bound to which sockets, and an error will be returned if the address has already been bound to another socket or if this socket has already been bound to a different address. This address must somehow be "advertised" for clients to find it and connect() to it.

2.3.4 The listen() System Call

The listen() system call applies only to connection-oriented sockets. It marks the socket as a passive "answer-mode-only" endpoint, so that outgoing requests are prevented from using this "listen" socket, but incoming requests can be accepted on this socket. As shown in Figure 2.9, this call specifies a "backlog" limit for a queue to hold incoming requests while the server is busy servicing a current request. This backlog limit is necessary to protect the system from using all its resources to hold pending requests for a (buggy) server that never finishes the current request.

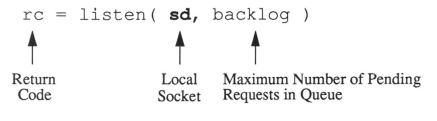

Figure 2.9 The listen() System Call

2.3.5 The accept() System Call

A connection is established on the server's side with an accept() system call, which creates a new socket that is connected to the socket used in the client's connect() call. The format of accept() is shown in Figure 2.10. The network address of the calling side's socket is returned in the second argument. The size of the storage in bytes

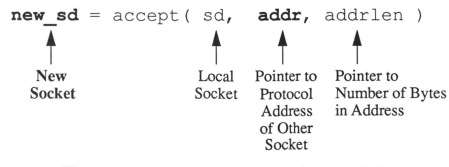

Figure 2.10 The accept() System Call

allocated for the address is placed in the third argument; after the call its value is changed to the number of bytes in the address received. This call normally blocks if an incoming connection request is not immediately available. However, a nonblocking option can be set in the socket, in which case `accept()` would return -1 with `errno` set to **EWOULDBLOCK** if no requests were queued at the time of the call. The server could do something else for a while and return to the `accept()` call later, or it could use a `select()` call (see Chapter 4) on one or more sockets and `accept()` on any ready socket returned by `select()`.

2.4   Connection-mode SOCK_STREAM Example

Our first example is a UNIX domain stream socket connection. This type of connection behaves very much like a bidirectional duplex pipe between the processes at the two ends. The client sends a message to the server, and the server sends a message back to the client. Here's the client code:

```
/* client.c -- UNIX Domain SOCK_STREAM duplex pipe          */
#include <sys/types.h>
#include <sys/socket.h>
```

The header file **socket.h** is required in every program that uses socket I/O. It `#defines` symbolic constants such as AF_UNIX, AF_INET, and SOCK_STREAM, and it defines data structures for generic socket addresses (`sockaddr`). It uses some data types defined in **types.h**, which must be included before `socket.h`. Both of these files are in the directory **/usr/include/sys,** and you can browse them if you want to know more about them.

2.4.1   SOCK_STREAM Client Code

```
main( argc, argv )
char *argv[];
{
      int   sd;               /* socket descriptor            */
      char  buf [256];        /* your basic buffer            */

      if ( (sd = socket( AF_UNIX, SOCK_STREAM, 0 )) < 0 )
         { perror( "UNIX Domain Socket" );   exit(1); }

      if ( connect( sd, " pipename", sizeof(" pipename") - 1 ) < 0)
         { perror( "UNIX Domain Connect" );   exit(2); }

      write ( sd, "This is easy!", sizeof("This is easy!") );
      read  ( sd, buf, sizeof( buf ) );
      printf( "\n\t\t%s: %s\n", argv[0], buf );
      write ( sd, "Yeah!", sizeof("Yeah!") );
}
```

Notice that the **socket ()** system call returns an integer socket descriptor, **sd**, which is used in subsequent read() and write() statements, like a file descriptor returned from an open() system call. Most system calls return -1 if they fail, and an error code is returned in the external integer **errno**. You should always test to make sure each system call succeeds and notify the user of any failures. The library routine **perror ()** is a handy utility for reporting errors. It uses errno to index an error message table and print a descriptive message. The **exit ()** system call is used when there is no point in continuing. In this example, exit() is called if a socket cannot be opened (exit(1)) or if we cannot connect to the server's socket (exit(2)). Callers can find the exit return code, 1 or 2, in **$?** (*sh/ksh*) or in **$status** (*csh*) or in the value returned by the wait() system call (C program).

The socket() system call creates a UNIX domain socket with a byte-stream protocol (SOCK_STREAM). The third parameter is zero because there is only one SOCK_STREAM implementation in the UNIX domain, and the type specification is sufficient to specify it. The **connect ()** system call attempts to make a connection between the newly created socket (sd) and a "well-known" server socket. **UNIX domain sockets use file pathnames as addresses.** In this example, both the client and server must run in the same current directory, because " pipename" is relative to the process's current directory. The name was chosen to suggest the similarity with named pipes in System V. Unrelated processes can use a common UNIX filename (for example, /usr/spool/lp/FIFO) for communication. For the two spaces in front of " pipename," see Section 2.4.3.

2.4.2 UNIX Domain Names

One of the side-effects of UNIX domain sockets is that their names stay in they UNIX filesystem until they are explicitly rmed or unlink()ed. This is what happens when the server tries to use a filename that already exists in the UNIX filesystem namespace:

```
%  ./server  &
UNIX Domain Bind: Address already in use

%  ls  -l  pipename
srwxr-xr-x 1 wdr A-team diamond Dec 22 11:15 pipename

%  rm  pipename
```

A server process is started in the background, but it fails (and exits) because it cannot bind the UNIX filename " pipename" to a socket. The filename was left in the namespace by an earlier execution of the server. A long list of " pipename" shows that the file type is **s**, for "socket," and the socket was created on a system named diamond. After the filename is explicitly rm'd, the server is able to run in the background and handle client requests:

```
%  ./server  &
%  ./client
./server: This is easy!
./client: Oh, yeah?
./server: Yeah!
```

The server sets up the "well-known" socket " pipename" and patiently waits for a
process to connect to it. This happens when the client is executed, and the output from
printf()s in the server and client are seen. The first and third lines were sent from
the client to the server with a write() to the socket. They were received in the server,
by reading the socket, and then displayed by printf() statements. When the client
finishes, the **kernel closes the client's socket** as part of the normal cleanup of an exiting
process. This causes an **EOF** condition at the server's end of the connection, and the
server exits. Unfortunately, the server doesn't remove the filename, as it should.

Another problem that might happen is the following:

```
%  ./client
UNIX Domain Connect: Connection refused
```

The connect() system call failed in the client because no process is listen()ing
on the well-known " pipename" socket. Usually, "connection refused" means that
a server daemon process is not running for the service you want.

2.4.3   SOCK_STREAM Server Code

Now, let's look at the server code:

```
/* server.c -- UNIX Domain SOCK_STREAM duplex pipe          */

#include <sys/types.h>
#include <sys/socket.h>        /* sockaddr structures        */

main( argc, argv )
char *argv[];
{
        int     ld, sd;        /* listen & service descriptors */
        char    buf [256];     /* your basic buffer          */
        struct  sockaddr from; /* client's socket address    */
        int     addrlen;       /* client's address length    */
```

The same header files are included in the server. The server uses **two** sockets: one for
listening (**ld**) and one for servicing (**sd**). The 256-character buffer buf is adequate for
our example. The sockaddr from and socket address length addrlen are used in the
accept() system call. In the Internet domain (AF_INET), it may be important to
know from where the client request is coming, and the client's address is placed in these
arguments (when non-NULL) by the accept() system call.

```
if ( (ld = socket( AF_UNIX, SOCK_STREAM, 0 )) < 0 )
   { perror( "UNIX Domain Socket" );  exit(1); }


if ( bind( ld, "  pipename", sizeof("  pipename") - 1 ) < 0 )
   { perror( "UNIX Domain Bind" );  exit(2); }
```

A UNIX domain socket is created, and the name " pipename" is given to it. A fully qualified UNIX pathname, like "/usr/spool/lp/FIFO", would allow the client and server processes to execute in different current directories. However, in this example, " pipename" is now the "well-known" service port name. The first two spaces are needed to offset over the first 16 bits of an address structure (**sockaddr**). Without the spaces, the first two characters of the UNIX filename would be truncated, leaving the socket name as "pename." **Warning: a simple character string (such as " pipename") may not work on every implementation of the AF_UNIX domain!** Later releases of the operating system require **sockaddr_un** (a UNIX domain socket address structure) and test the 16-bit "address family" field in the structure. Modified code will be shown in Section 2.5.4. Internet addresses (**sockaddr_in**) are introduced in the next chapter.

File descriptors are created and named in a single open() system call. The creation and naming of sockets, on the other hand, are two separate operations because the same socket may be reused and bound to a different name (address) later on. This is more useful in a datagram application than in a connection-oriented one.

Now that a server socket has been created and named, you must tell the operating system whether it is an active (calling) socket or a passive (listening) socket. This is done with a **listen()** system call:

```
if ( listen( ld, 5 ) < 0 ) /* mark socket a passive one  */
                            /* and allow 5 pending "holds"*/
   { perror( "UNIX Domain Listen" );  exit(3); }
```

This call sets a bit in the internal socket structure, so the kernel knows it is a "listen" socket and will disallow outgoing connect() requests through ld. Also, a waiting queue for incoming "phone calls" can grow to hold up to five connection requests that may arrive while the server is servicing a previous request. It is unlikely that that many connection requests would arrive before the server process gets back to handle the next request. The limit is set to protect the system from losing all its buffer space to incoming connection requests for a server that has gotten hung up. In fact, the kernel sets a maximum of ten waiting connections, *even if you specify a larger value in the backlog parameter to the **listen()** call.*

Now the server can **accept()** connect() requests from clients. When a connection request for ld arrives, accept() creates a *new* socket, **sd**, at this end of the connection. This new sd socket is connected to the calling side's socket and can be used to provide a long-running service, while the "well-known" socket, `ld`, is free to `accept()` new requests.

```
while (1)                  /* answer "phone calls"    */
{
    if ( (sd = accept( ld, &from, &addrlen )) < 0 )
        { perror( "UNIX Domain Accept" ); exit(4); }
```

The calling socket's address is put in **from**, and the byte length of the address is returned in **addrlen** (which is why *the third argument* must be an *address* of an integer variable, not a symbolic constant or integer value). The `addrlen` parameter is used because different protocols may use different-sized addresses, and the **accept()** system call is supposed to work with any protocol.

A child process is created, and the parent (the server daemon) immediately closes the child's socket and returns to the `accept()` call to wait for another request.

```
if ( fork() )                          /* parent = child pid > 0 */
    { close(sd); continue; }   /* parent gets next call   */
```

Note that **accept()** is the only call in the server that "blocks," or waits for something to happen. Also note that the server's time away from "`listen()`ing" is small, so a small "pending queue" is usually adequate. If the service time is short (such as in a remote request for `time`), it is possible to provide the service directly instead of creating a new process to handle it, although connectionless datagram sockets are better for quick services. Some systems offer "lightweight processes" or "threads," which can execute independently like processes, but require less system overhead to create and execute.

While the parent listens for more requests, the child proceeds. It first closes the parent's "well-known" socket, to prevent any mixups later on. Then it `read()`s and `write()`s the service socket (**sd**) connection. Here, `read()` blocks until something is received from the other end. The `printf()` prints what it received, after identifying which process (**argv[0]**) produced the output.

```
close ( ld ); /* child closes parent's listen descriptor */
read  ( sd, buf, sizeof(buf) );
printf( "\n\t\t%s: %s\n", argv[0], buf );
write ( sd, "Oh, yeah?", sizeof("Oh, yeah?") );
read  ( sd, buf, sizeof(buf) );
printf( "\n\t\t%s: %s\n", argv[0], buf );

exit(0);     /* no exit ==> child fails on accept syscall at top of loop!    */
}
```

After the "service" is finished, the child process must **exit()**. If it did not, then execution would resume at the top of the loop, and the child process would fail on the accept() system call. The error message would be "**accept: Bad file number**," because the child has closed ld.

2.5   Connectionless SOCK_DGRAM Example

The foregoing example used "virtual circuits" (SOCK_STREAM), whose **byte-stream** semantics make the connection behave like a pipe between the two processes. If you need a **message-oriented** protocol, you can use "datagram" (SOCK_DGRAM) sockets to send and receive interprocess messages. The system calls **send(), sendto(), sendmsg(), recv(), recvfrom()**, and **recvmsg()** are provided for datagrams. The sendto() call allows you to specify where to send a message, and recfrom() allows you to find out from where a message came.

A **connect()** on a datagram socket automatically "addresses" all datagrams to the address in the connect() call, and you can use send() and recv() or sendmsg() and recvmsg() without specifying a socket address and length for each datagram. **Note that message boundaries are preserved, and data might be lost if you use read()s and write()s on datagram sockets.**

2.5.1   The send() and recv() System Calls

The formats of send() and recv() system calls are shown in Figure 2.11. These system calls send messages in complete, atomic units between client and server processes. A -1 is returned, and errno is set to EMSGSIZE if an attempt is made to send() a message that is too large to be sent atomically.

The flags parameter can be set to MSG_OOB to send or receive out-of-band data, providing the underlying protocol understands the notion of out-of-band data (as in SOCK_STREAM). Clearly, MSG_OOB has little meaning in a SOCK_DGRAM protocol, where each datagram is independent of other datagrams. (The file control system call fcntl() can be used to request that a SIGURG signal be posted when any out-of-band data arrives.) Another flag, MSG_DONTROUTE, can be set at the send() side to bypass routing, but this flag is usually used only by diagnostic or routing programs. MSG_PEEK tells recv() to look at an incoming message without taking it from the kernel buffers.

The from and addrlen arguments point to the sockaddr and int that will store the protocol address and address size (in bytes) recived from the peer that sent the datagram. These can be NULL, if the receiver doesn't care from where the datagram came.

The recv() call returns the number of data bytes received, similar to the way read() returns the number of bytes read. **However, if more than len bytes are received, the extra bytes are silently discarded on datagram sockets!**

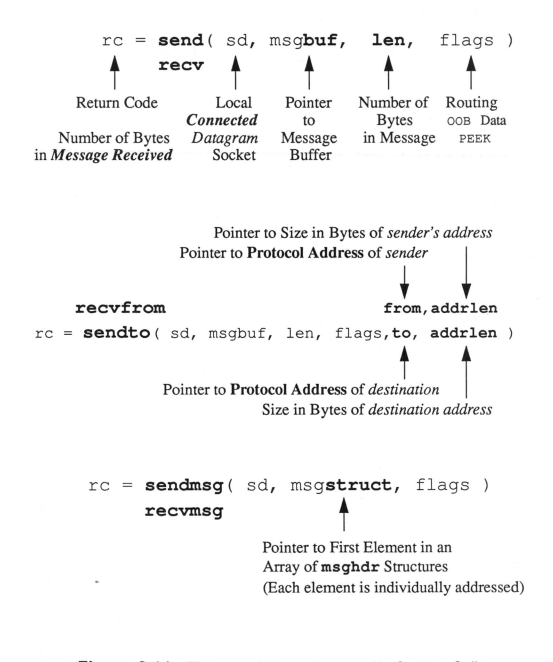

Figure 2.11 The send() and recv() System Calls

2.5.2   SOCK_DGRAM Client Code

Here is the client code using datagram sockets:

```
/* client2.c -- DATAGRAM client with connect/send            */
#include <sys/types.h>
#include <sys/socket.h>

main()
{
        int   sd;              /* datagram socket descriptor */
        char  buf [256];       /* your basic data buffer     */

        if ( (sd = socket( AF_UNIX, SOCK_DGRAM, 0 )) < 0 )
           { perror( "UNIX Domain Socket" );  exit(1); }

        if ( connect( sd, " msgfile",
                     sizeof(" msgfile") - 1 ) < 0 )
           { perror( "UNIX Domain Connect" );  exit(2); }

        send( sd, "This is easy!", sizeof("This is easy!"), 0 );
        send( sd, "Oh yeah?", sizeof("Oh yeah?"), 0 );
        send( sd, "Yeah!", sizeof("Yeah!"), 0 );
}
```

The third parameter, 0, to send() is a *flags* parameter, which could, for example, be set to MSG_OOB to send "out of band" data, such as **control-C**, on a socket.

2.5.3   SOCK_DGRAM Server Code

Here is the server code using UNIX domain datagram sockets:

```
/* server2.c -- DATAGRAM server (recv)                       */
#include <sys/types.h>
#include <sys/socket.h>

main( argc, argv )
char *argv[];
{
        int   sd;              /* datagram socket descriptor */
        char  buf [256];       /* your basic data buffer     */

        if ( (sd = socket( AF_UNIX, SOCK_DGRAM, 0 )) < 0 )
           { perror( "UNIX Domain Socket" );  exit(1); }
```

```
        if ( bind( sd,      "   msgfile",
                   sizeof("   msgfile") - 1 ) < 0 )
          { perror( "UNIX Domain Bind" ); exit(2); }

        while (1)    /* answer "phone calls" */
        {
             recv  ( sd, buf, sizeof(buf) );
             printf( "\n\t%s read: %s\n\n", argv[0], buf );
        }
}
```

Notice that `recv()` behaves like `read()`, except that **it preserves message boundaries on datagram sockets!** That is, if more than `sizeof(buf)` bytes are received, they will be discarded. Also notice that **listen()** and **accept()** are not used on datagram sockets; they are needed only for connection establishment on virtual circuit (SOCK_STREAM) sockets.

Finally, here is an example that shows three processes simultaneously using a datagram socket to communicate with the server. This kind of "multiplexing," without connection setup or teardown, illustrates a flexibility of datagram sockets that stream sockets do not have.

```
/* client3.c -- UNIX DATAGRAM client (connect/send)          */
#include <sys/types.h>
#include <sys/socket.h>
main()
{
        int   sd, i;   char  buf [256];

        if ((sd = socket( AF_UNIX, SOCK_DGRAM, 0 )) < 0 )
            { perror( "UNIX Domain Socket" );   exit(1); }
        if ( connect( sd, "   msgfile",sizeof("   msgfile")-1 ) < 0 )
            { perror( "UNIX Domain Connect" );   exit(2); }
        sprintf( buf, "%s", "Process id: " );

        for ( i=0; i < 3; i++ )
        {
          if ( fork() ) continue;   /* parent continues ...       */
          sprintf( buf+sizeof("Process id: ")-1,"%6d",getpid() );
          sprintf( buf+sizeof("Process id: ")+5,
                   "%s", " Throw me something, mister!" );
          send( sd, buf, sizeof( buf ), 0 );
          exit(0);   /* child exits */
        }
}
```

Here is the output from a sample run of the datagram server (`server2`) and the datagram clients:

```
%  ./server2  &
[1] 1042

%  ./client2

./server2 read: This is easy!
./server2 read: Oh, yeah?
./server2 read: Yeah!

%  ./client3

./server2 read: Process id: 1647  Throw me something, mister!
./server2 read: Process id: 1648  Throw me something, mister!
./server2 read: Process id: 1649  Throw me something, mister!
```

Notice that the datagram server does not exit when a client does, because no connection is broken. That is, `recv()` does not return 0 at the "end of file" ("end of connection")!

2.5.4   UNIX Domain `sockaddr_un` Address

The previous programs all compiled and executed well on early pre-releases of a UNIX-based "open system." Later versions of the software became less tolerant and required the use of a **sockaddr_un** data structure defined in `/usr/include/sys/`**un.h**. Here's the modified code:

```
/* server.c -- UNIX Domain SOCK_STREAM duplex pipe              */

#include <sys/types.h>
#include <sys/signal.h>
#include <sys/socket.h>    /* generic sockaddr  structure       */
#include <sys/un.h>        /* UNIX domain sockaddr_un structure */
        /*
         struct sockaddr_un {
                short af;          short   sun_family;
                char addr[108]; char    sun_path[108];
         };
        */
struct sockaddr_un from, here = { AF_UNIX, "pipename" };
```

For some unknown reason, the field names for address family (`af` and `sun_family`) and the UNIX domain address (`addr` and `sun_path`) were different on the desktop version of the OS and the mainframe version. This problem was noticed in a pre-release version of the OS and surely is corrected by now. However, this kind of naming problem is typical in "open system" environments. We sidestep it by initializing the **here** structure without using field names. The pathname (`"pipename"`) is used, and it is not necessary to add two blank spaces, because the name field is separated from the type field in the `sockaddr_un` structure.

```
main( argc, argv )
char *argv[];
{
        int   sd, fd;          /* socket descriptor; from descriptor */
        char buf [256];        /* your basic buffer                  */
        int   addrlen=sizeof(from); /* UNIX IPC domain name length   */

        signal( SIGCLD, SIG_IGN ); /*avoids "<defunct>" zombies */
```

The value of `addrlen` must be initialized in order for the `accept()` system call to work properly. Also, the child "servers" become defunct zombie processes without the `signal()` system call. (`SIG_IGN` tells the kernel to free the process control block used by an exiting child process, because the parent is ignoring its children, and thus will not free the child's process table entry. Without the `signal()` call, the "defunct" process stays in the process table, waiting for its parent to free it!)

```
        if ( (sd = socket( AF_UNIX, SOCK_STREAM, 0 )) < 0 )
          { perror( "UNIX Domain Socket" );  exit(1); }


        printf( "\n\tsockaddr_un af = %d\tname = %s\n",
                here.sun_family, here.sun_path );
   /*        here.af,            here.addr );                      */
        if ( bind( sd, (struct sockaddr *) &here,
                    sizeof( here )) < 0 )
          { perror( "UNIX Domain Bind" );  exit(2); }
```

Notice that the specific UNIX domain socket address (`here`) is typecast to a generic `sockaddr` pointer. This helps make the `bind()` system call protocol-independent.

The rest of the program is the same as in the earlier "character string" version and is not shown again. Only the *stream server* had to be modified! Both datagram client and server programs worked with `"  pipename"`, and the stream client code also worked as shown earlier, without any changes. Only the `bind()` system call in the `SOCK_STREAM` domain required a (`sockaddr_un  *`) pointer to a UNIX domain address structure, instead of the (`char  *`) string pointer to `"  pipename"`.

2.6   Summary

The basic system calls **socket()**, **connect()**, **bind()**, **listen()**, **accept()**, **send()**, and **recv()** were introduced in this chapter. They are summarized in Figure 2.12:

Function Purpose	Active Client	Passive Server
Create end point	socket()	
Name end point	bind()	
Connection setup (TCP)	connect()	listen()
	^-----------------------> accept()	
Send data	write(), send(), sendto(), sendmsg()	
Receive data	read(), recv(), recvfrom(), recvmsg()	
Shutdown connection (TCP)	shutdown()	
Close end point	close()	

Figure 2.12 Socket System Calls

The listen() and accept() are used only with **connection-oriented, byte-stream** SOCK_STREAM sockets, which use the TCP transport on Internet (AF_INET) sockets.   **Connectionless message-oriented** UDP (SOCK_DGRAM) sockets send and receive datagrams with the send(), sendto(), sendmsg(), recv(), recvfrom(), and recvmsg() system calls. Example programs using these system calls were shown using both stream and datagram protocol semantics in the UNIX protocol domain.   The shutdown() system call was not shown; however, it is mentioned here for completeness.   The shutdown() call can be used to prevent further data transfers while allowing data in transit to finish.   It has options to shut down further reads, writes, or both, and it may be useful to end a connection gracefully without losing data.

The UNIX filename "pipename" was used for interprocess communication, and we took advantage of a pre-release version of the operating system that did not check the "address family" field of the socket address (it allowed us to use a pointer to the character string).   A socket address structure **sockaddr_un** (UNIX) is normally required on most implementations of the UNIX IPC domain.   This leads us to the Internet (TCP/IP) domain, which requires Internet addresses to be put in **sockaddr_in** (Internet) socket address structures for interprocess communication.   A large part of TCP/IP (Internet) programming involves address structure initialization, as we'll see in the next chapter.

The client/server relationship is not symmetric; clients are active agents and servers are passive responders. They both use the same system calls to perform their part of a network application.

The **read()** and **write()** system calls can be used on byte-stream connections. Indeed, it is this fact that makes it relatively easy to extend most UNIX commands to network environments! Message-oriented (datagram) system calls include **send()**, **sendto()**, **sendmsg()**, **recv()**, **recvfrom()**, and **recvmsg()**. The main difference is that messages are sent atomically, may arrive in a different order than they were sent, and may be duplicated. Byte-streams arrive (in the application) in the same order that they were sent; duplicate packets are not given to the application; and data is kept in system buffers until it is read, much like characters typed on a terminal. Unread portions of datagram messages are simply discarded.

Two header files, types.h and **socket.h** are needed to use the socket system calls. They define a generic socket address structure (**sockaddr**) as well as symbolic constants for address families (such as **AF_UNIX**) and socket types (such as **SOCK_STREAM**). The header files introduced in this chapter are summarized in Figure 2.13.

Header File	Description
<stdio.h>	/* NULL, O_RDWR def's, etc... */
<sys/types.h>	/* u_short, u_long def's, etc... */
<sys/**socket.h**>	/* AF_INET, SOCK_DGRAM, etc... */
<sys/un.h>	/* **sockaddr_un** UNIX socket addr */
<netinet/in.h>	/* **sockaddr_in** INET socket addr */

Figure 2.13 Socket Header Files

3 *Internet Domain Sockets*

by Bill Rieken

3.1   Introduction

This chapter extends the previous chapter by focusing attention on Internet addressing. The connectionless and connection-oriented client/server examples from the previous chapter are modified to execute over a network using TCP/IP protocols. Network library functions that manipulate Internet addresses are introduced, followed by the modifications to the client/server examples from Chapter 2. Finally, a simple "socket initialization" function is used to encapsulate all the address setup code in a common function.

3.2   Internet Addresses

Internet addresses have a **network** part and a **host** part. The Internet Protocol (IP) uses only the network part of an address to route packets between independent, interconnected networks. After a packet reaches the network on which the destination host is directly connected, the host part of the address is used to get the packet to the desired host. For example, Figure 3.1 shows three interconnected networks. A packet from Host X to Host Y would be sent to Host 1, which is connected to both Networks 1 and 2. Host 1 forwards the packet to Host 2, which puts the packet on Network 3, where it will be delivered to Host Y.

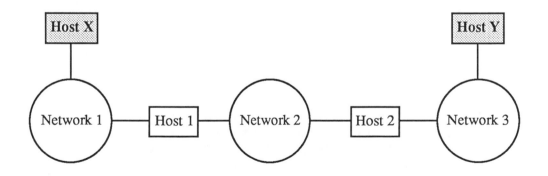

Figure 3.1   Internetwork Routing

Figure 3.2 shows a small network of 15 workstations, a file server (moon) and a printer server (fire), connected by a thin Ethernet cable, installed at the *.sh* Training Facility in Santa Clara, California.

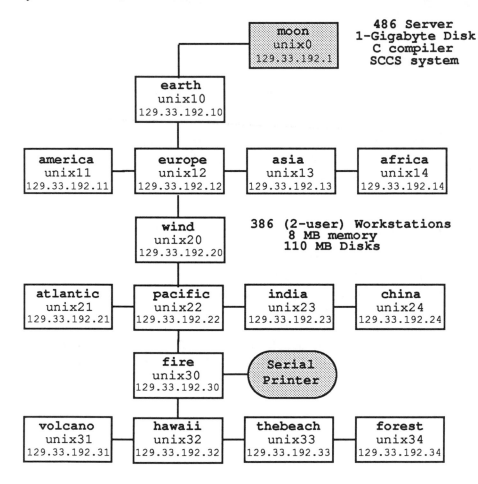

Figure 3.2 A Small Network Configuration

Each system has three names: a "user-friendly" name (such as **earth, wind, fire**), an "operations" name (such as **unix10, unix20, unix30**), and an Internet name (such as **129.33.192.10, 129.33.192.20, 129.33.192.30**). The network part of each Internet address is 129.33.192. This is what gateway hosts use to route packets between networks. When packets arrive on this network, the host part (such as 10, 20, 30) is used to deliver packets to the right destination. Actually, packets are "broadcast" on the Ethernet cable, and the Ethernet device driver on the destination host accepts packets addressed to it.

3.2.1   The `/etc/hosts` File

Users can use any of the three names to access a given system. The commands **`rlogin moon`, `rlogin unix0`,** and **`rlogin 129.33.192.1`** are all equivalent. These names are kept in a local database file called `/etc/hosts`.

Figure 3.3 shows the `/etc/hosts` file for the network shown in Figure 3.2.

```
127.0.0.1        localhost
129.33.192.1     moon       moon.dotsh.com       unix0  unix0.dotsh.com
129.33.192.10    earth      earth.dotsh.com      unix10 unix10.dotsh.com
129.33.192.11    america    america.dotsh.com    unix11 unix11.dotsh.com
129.33.192.12    europe     europe.dotsh.com     unix12 unix12.dotsh.com
129.33.192.13    asia       asia.dotsh.com       unix13 unix13.dotsh.com
129.33.192.14    africa     africa.dotsh.com     unix14 unix14.dotsh.com
129.33.192.20    wind       wind.dotsh.com       unix20 unix20.dotsh.com
129.33.192.21    atlantic   atlantic.dotsh.com   unix21 unix21.dotsh.com
129.33.192.22    pacific    pacific.dotsh.com    unix22 unix22.dotsh.com
129.33.192.23    india      india.dotsh.com      unix23 unix23.dotsh.com
129.33.192.24    china      china.dotsh.com      unix24 unix24.dotsh.com
129.33.192.30    fire       fire.dotsh.com       unix30 unix30.dotsh.com
129.33.192.31    volcano    volcano.dotsh.com    unix31 unix31.dotsh.com
129.33.192.32    hawaii     hawaii.dotsh.com     unix32 unix32.dotsh.com
129.33.192.33    thebeach   thebeach.dotsh.com   unix33 unix33.dotsh.com
129.33.192.34    forest     forest.dotsh.com     unix34 unix34.dotsh.com
```

Figure 3.3   A Sample `/etc/hosts` File

The first field on each line is the Internet address in "dotted decimal" form, and the next field is the "official" host name, followed by a list of "alias" names appropriate for your environment. In this example, each workstation is listed with both its "user-friendly" name (such as `earth`) and its "operator-friendly" name (such as `unix10`). The name **`earth.dotsh.com`** is a BIND (Berkeley Internet Name Domain) name for `earth` in the `dotsh` (*.sh*) domain in the `com` (Commercial) domain. **Name domains** distribute naming authority in a hierarchy of organizations so that names are unique within each organization and need not be unique outside of the organization. For example, **`moon.dotsh.com`** is different from **`moon.mit.edu`**, although they have the same local name, `moon`. Another system file called `/etc/resolv.conf` can be used to designate one or more nameservers (or name **resolvers**), as well as a name domain (such as `dotsh.com`) to append to every unqualified hostname. For example, `moon` becomes `moon.dotsh.com` at the **.sh** Training Center, whereas it becomes `moon.mit.edu` at the Massachusetts Institute of Technology in Cambridge.

The special name `localhost` with the special Internet address `127.0.0.1`, can be used to test Internet domain applications on a "loopback" pseudo-device whenever network hardware is unavailable.

3.2.2   The `gethostbyname()` Library Function

Life would be very tedious if network addresses were hard-coded in each application. Fortunately, there is a library function called **gethostbyname()**, which, given an ASCII host name, searches the local /etc/hosts database (or sends a request to a nameserver listed in /etc/resolv.conf), and returns a pointer to a "host entry" structure (**struct hostent**) or NULL if the host name is not found. The following example shows how this library function is used:

```
$ cc -O -o host host.c -lsocket -lnsl
```

On ESIX's SVR4, the two libraries, /lib/libsocket.**a** (socket compatibility library) and /lib/libnsl.**a** (network services library), supply the library functions gethostbyname() and inet_ntoa(). Shared object (**.so**) libraries can support **dynamic loading** of **transport-independent** name-to-address lookup routines, as we'll see in Chapter 7 on Transport-Level Interface (TLI) programming. For now, we focus on TCP/IP Internet address mapping. We check /etc/hosts to see what host names are available:

```
$ tail -3 /etc/hosts
#
127.0.0.1          localhost
129.33.192.200     dotsh3
```

Now we run the program using a few different host names:

```
$ ./host dotsh3

Host Name = dotsh3  Net Addr = 129.33.192.200

$ ./host Niners

Host Name "Niners" not found in /etc/hosts

$ ./host localhost Warriors dotsh3 CalBears

Host Name = localhost Net Addr = 127.0.0.1
Host Name "Warriors" not found in /etc/hosts
Host Name = dotsh3    Net Addr = 129.33.192.200
Host Name "CalBears" not found in /etc/hosts
```

The program listing follows. This sample program reads command line arguments and looks up their Internet addresses in /etc/hosts:

```
/*  host.c --- get IP address for host(s) on command line
 *
 *  compile:  cc -s -O -o host host.c -lsocket -lnsl
 */

#include <stdio.h>
#include <sys/types.h>
#include <sys/socket.h>

#include <netdb.h>           /* /etc/hosts data structures   */
#include <netinet/in.h>      /* Internet addresses in_addr   */
#include <arpa/inet.h>       /* inet(3N) function definitions */

main( argc, argv )
char *argv[];
{
  register struct hostent *hostp; /* ptr to static struct   */
  int i, *dum;                 /* counter and dummy pointer    */

for ( i=1; i < argc; i++ ) /* for each name on command line */
 {
 if ((hostp = gethostbyname( argv[i] )) == NULL)
      printf("\tHost Name \"%s\" not found in /etc/hosts\n",
              argv[i]);
 else
    {
      dum = (int *) hostp->h_addr ; /* not really necessary */
      printf("\tHost Name = %-12s  Net Addr = %s\n",
              hostp->h_name,
              inet_ntoa( *dum ));/* see following comments */
    }
} /* end of for loop */
}
```

The `hostent` structure is defined in `/usr/include/`**`netdb.h`**:

```
struct    hostent {
  char    *h_name;      /* official name of host       */
  char    **h_aliases;  /* alias list                  */
  int     h_addrtype;   /* host address type           */
  int     h_length;     /* length of address           */
  char    **h_addr_list; /* addresses from name server */
#define   h_addr h_addr_list[0] /* backward compatibility */
};
```

Notice that the library functions retrieve information from `/etc/hosts` (or from a nameserver), but the `hostent` container stores the information differently from the way we see it in the `/etc/hosts` file. For example, h_addr is a pointer to **an internal 32-bit Internet address, not an external "dotted decimal" character string!**

3.2.3   C Pointers to Host Addresses

The dummy pointer `(int *)` dum was not actually necessary in the program; the same results could have been accomplished by the following:

<code>inet_ntoa (* (int *) hostp->h_addr)</code>

When h_addr is typecast to **`(int *)`, all four bytes** of the internal 32-bit Internet address are sent to and interpreted properly by the library function `inet_ntoa()`. Without the typecast, only the first byte (`char *`) is used. The precedence rules of C give strange results if you pass bad pointers to `inet_ntoa()`:

```
printf( "\t* (int *) hostp->h_addr = %x, %d\n",
          * (int *) hostp->h_addr, (int *) hostp->h_addr );
printf( "\t(int *) * hostp->h_addr = %x, %d\n",
          (int *) * hostp->h_addr, (int *) * hostp->h_addr );
printf( "\t          hostp->h_addr = %x, %d\n",
          hostp->h_addr, hostp->h_addr );
```

yields the following:

```
    * (int *)   hostp->h_addr = c8c02181, -926932607
    (int *) *   hostp->h_addr = ffffff81, -127
                hostp->h_addr = 8003f674, -2147223948
```

The lone asterisk means "contents of," and if it were applied before the typecast, C would put the **contents of the byte pointed to by** h_addr on the stack frame for `inet_ntoa()`. When the call is done correctly `(*(int *)hostp->h_addr)`, the **contents of the `int` pointed to by** h_addr are put on the stack frame. The function `inet_ntoa()` expects a 32-bit Internet address as an argument, and it returns a pointer to a "dotted-decimal" string declared by the function in the static data area. Incidentally, this function and several others are documented in the **`inet (3N)`** section of the UNIX programmer's reference manual for your system.

3.2.4   The `gethostbyaddr()` Library Function

Most networking commands allow you to specify an Internet address on the command line in case the ASCII hostname is not in `/etc/hosts` and you don't have superuser authority (`root` privileges) to edit the `/etc/hosts` file. For example, the following sequence of commands allows a user to `login` to the remote system `thebeach` and execute a Motif application that opens an X-Window on the local system `earth`:

```
$  rlogin  thebeach
$  motifburger  -d"129.33.192.10:0"
```

The same results could be accomplished by the following:

```
$  rlogin  129.33.192.33
$  motifburger  -d"earth:0"
```

provided that `earth` is in the `/etc/hosts` file on `thebeach`. The `-d` option tells the application program with which **"host:server"** to establish a connection. Almost all X-Window applications allow you to use the "-d" option. The application program is the client, and the server controls one or more display screens connected to the host computer.

This section presents a new version of `host.c` that accepts Internet addresses from the command line:

```
$  ./host    129.33.192.200
Host Name = dotsh3  Net Addr = 129.33.192.200
```

The modifications to the `host.c` program are as follows:

```
for ( i=1; i < argc; i++)
    {
      unsigned long addr, inet_addr();

      if ( ( hostp = gethostbyname( argv[i] ) ) == NULL)
         {    addr = inet_addr( argv[i] );
              if((hostp = gethostbyaddr( &addr,
                        sizeof( struct in_addr ),
                                AF_INET ) ) == NULL)
         { printf("\tHost Name \"%s\" not found in /etc/hosts\n",
                        argv[i]); continue;     }
          }
    /* continue if not found; otherwise we *have* a hostent!  */
    /* and rest of code is same as before, with inet_ntoa()...*/
```

A pointer to a `hostent` structure is returned by `gethostbyaddr()`, and processing continues as in the previous version that used `gethostbyname()`. The library function has three arguments:

```
gethostbyaddr( addr, addrlen, addrtype)
```

Although it is intended to be protocol-independent by allowing for a variety of protocol addresses, this function returns only AF_INET (Internet) address types. The addr argument is declared char *addr; however, it expects a pointer to an internal 32-bit Internet address.

The conversion from the command line "dotted-decimal" character string to an internal integer is done by the following function:

$$\text{inet\_addr(char\_ptr)}$$

Like inet_ntoa(), this is another inet(3N) function; it accepts a pointer to the string and returns an unsigned long integer. These functions are tightly coupled to the TCP/IP (Internet) protocols. A set of more generic lookup functions, such as netdir_getbyname() and netdir_getbyaddr() is documented in netdir(3N). The netdir functions are described in Chapter 7 on Transport-Level Interface (TLI) programming.

3.3   Service Port Numbers

Now that we are able to deal with host addresses, the next issue is how to specify the service program you want to execute on a remote system. For example, *rlogin* hostX and *ftp* hostX both access hostX over the Internet, but they request *different service programs*. **Each different service program is identified by a unique, "well known" port number.** The port numbers must be unique to distinguish server programs, and they must be "well known" so that application programmers can request them by "name." Figure 3.4 illustrates the situation.

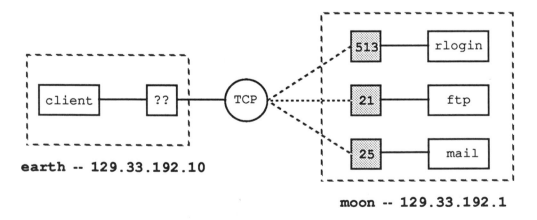

Figure 3.4   Service Port Numbers

3.3.1 The /etc/services File

It would be very tedious and error-prone for programmers and users to remember the numeric service codes for the services they want to use, so a database of service codes is maintained in a file called **/etc/services**, whose format is shown in Figure 3.5.

```
# Network services, Internet style
# name   port#/protocol  aliases   # comments...
echo       7/tcp
echo       7/udp
netstat    15/tcp
ftp-data   20/tcp
ftp        21/tcp
telnet     23/tcp
smtp       25/tcp          mail
time       37/tcp          timserver
time       37/udp          timserver
name       42/udp          nameserver
domain     53/udp
domain     53/tcp
hostnames  101/tcp         hostname
sunrpc     111/udp         rpcbind
sunrpc     111/tcp         rpcbind
#
# Host-specific functions
#
tftp       69/udp
rje        77/tcp
finger     79/tcp
nntp       119/tcp         usenet   # Network News Transfer
#
# UNIX-specific services (these are NOT officially assigned)
#
login      513/tcp
shell      514/tcp         cmd      # no passwords used
printer    515/tcp         spooler  # line printer spooler
who        513/udp         whod
talk       517/udp
route      520/udp         routed
nfsd       2049/udp                 # NFS server daemon
listen     2766/tcp                 # System V listen port
xserver0   6000/tcp
```

Figure 3.5 A Sample /etc/services File

Each line has the name of the service, followed by the "well-known" port number and the transport-level protocol (TCP or UDP) it uses. Notice that port numbers are unique within each transport protocol. That is, 513 is the "name" for `rlogin` in the TCP domain, but in the UDP domain 513 "names" the `rwho` server. Also keep in mind that the client/server model is asymmetric. The server listening on TCP port 513 is **rlogind**, and the server receiving requests on UDP port 513 is **rwhod**, where the "d" indicates "daemon" or server. The client side of these services are **rlogin** and **rwho**, respectively (no "d"). Recall that daemons are **passive** servers, which wait for incoming requests from **active** clients. That is, clients must initiate any activity; server processes remain idle, sleeping until awakened by a client request. Server daemons are normally started by command lines in **/etc/rc** shellscripts at boot time or when the system changes from single-user to multiuser mode. Client requests are issued when users execute the client commands. Both sides, client and server, use the "well-known" port numbers in /etc/services to get in touch with each other. Lookup functions use the following structure to return information on a service entry to callers:

```
struct  servent {
        char    *s_name;       /* official service name */
        char    **s_aliases;   /* alias list            */
        int     s_port;        /* port #                */
        char    *s_proto;      /* protocol to use       */
};
```

3.3.2   The `getservbyname()` Library Function

A sample program is helpful to show how servers and clients use the library function **getservbyname()** to look up the "well-known" port number for the service they provide or want to use:

```
$ ./serv login telnet ftp mail who nfs rsh rcp

Service Name = login    Port Addr = 513   Protocol = tcp
Service Name = telnet   Port Addr = 23    Protocol = tcp
Service Name = ftp      Port Addr = 21    Protocol = tcp
Service Name = smtp     Port Addr = 25    Protocol = tcp
Service Name = who      Port Addr = 513   Protocol = udp
        Service Name "nfs" not found in /etc/services
        Service Name "rsh" not found in /etc/services
        Service Name "rcp" not found in /etc/services
```

The fields printed are as follows:

```
printf("Service Name = %-8s Port Addr = %3d Protocol = %s\n",
servp->s_name,  ntohs( servp->s_port ), servp->s_proto);
```

Notice that the name `mail` is an alias for `smtp` (simple mail transfer protocol), the official ARPA name of the service, and `getservbyname()` found it by its alias name.

The utility function **ntohs()** converts a **network**-byte-order field to **host**-byte-order **short** integer and is documented in the **byteorder(3N)** section of the UNIX programmer's reference manual for your system. Service port numbers are 16-bit fields in transport-level TCP/UDP headers, and on some systems the host computer byte order is different from the network byte order. Your code may work swell for years when communicating among homogeneous hosts and then suddenly fail when run on a computer with a different byte order! So, to be on the safe side, it is best to use the `byteorder`(3N) macros, defined in `/usr/include/`**netinet/in.h**.

The code for `serv.c` is identical to that of `host.c`, except for the `for` loop:

```
/* serv.c - look up TCP/UDP "well-known" port numbers        */

#include's from host.c ...

main( argc, argv )
char *argv[];
{
   register struct servent *servp;/* ptr to static struct    */
   int i;                          /* for-loop counter        */


   for ( i=1; i < argc; i++ ) /* for each name on command line*/
   {
      if ( (  servp = getservbyname(argv[i], "tcp")) == NULL
         && ( servp = getservbyname(argv[i], "udp")) == NULL )
         printf("\tService Name \"%s\" not found in /etc/services\n",
                    argv[i]);
      else

         printf("Service Name = %-8s Port  Addr = %3d Protocol = %s\n",
            servp->s_name, ntohs( servp->s_port ), servp->s_proto);

   } /* end of for loop */
}
```

The second argument to `getservbyname()` can be **NULL**, in which case the first match in the file is returned (for example, **sunrpc/udp** would be returned and `sunrpc/tcp` would not be reached). The sample output shown for `login`, `telnet`, and so forth would be the same if the second argument were NULL. However, the `if` statement in `serv.c` checks for "tcp" before "udp", so our sample program returns **sunrpc/tcp**.

3.4   Internet Addresses and Service Ports

Two communicating processes must each know both the Internet address and the
protocol port number of the other side, as shown in Figure 3.6.

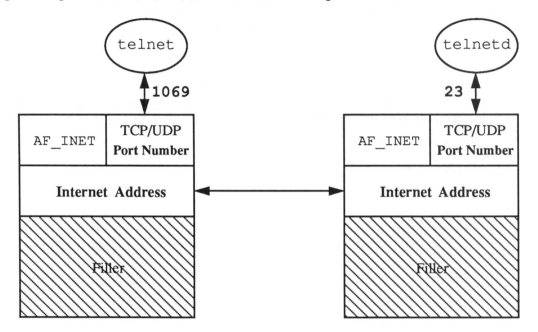

Figure 3.6   Host Address/Service Port Number Pairs

The client process (telnet) uses TCP port 1069 to communicate with the server
(telnetd), which is listening for requests on the "well-known" TCP port 23. This
information is stored in an Internet socket address structure, defined in
/usr/include/**netinet/in.h**:

```
        /*
         * Socket address, Internet style.
         */
        struct sockaddr_in {
                short      sin_family;
                u_short    sin_port;
                struct     in_addr sin_addr;
                char       sin_zero[8]; /* to match      */
        };                              /* sockaddr size */
```
where an Internet address is defined as

```
        struct in_addr { u_long s_addr };
```

The `in_addr` structure used to be a union of structures to access single bytes and halfwords of the 32-bit address.

```
union {
        struct { u_char  s_b1,s_b2,s_b3,s_b4; } S_un_b;
        struct { u_short s_w1,s_w2; } S_un_w;
        u_long S_addr;
} S_un;

#define  s_addr    S_un.S_addr
```

The range of port numbers is also defined in `in.h`:

```
/*
 * Ports < IPPORT_RESERVED are reserved for
 * privileged processes (such as root).
 * Ports > IPPORT_USERRESERVED are reserved
 * for servers, not necessarily privileged.
 */
#define     IPPORT_RESERVED             1024
#define     IPPORT_USERRESERVED         5000
```

Numbers below 1024 are reserved for "well-known" ports. For example, you would put 23 in the port field of `sockaddr_in` to request `telnet` service. On the other hand, you can put a zero in the port field, and the protocol software will assign a unique number to your port when you `bind()` the socket address. The assigned number will be greater than 1024 and less than 5000 (for example, our 1069).

An Internet address has both a network part and a host part. For very large networks, Class A addresses use one byte for the network and three bytes for the host:

```
        #define   IN_CLASSA_NET    0xff000000
        #define   IN_CLASSA_HOST   0x00ffffff
```

Class B addresses use two bytes for each part:

```
        #define   IN_CLASSB_NET    0xffff0000
        #define   IN_CLASSB_HOST   0x0000ffff
```

Class C addresses use three bytes for network and one byte for host:

```
        #define   IN_CLASSC_NET    0xffffff00
        #define   IN_CLASSC_HOST   0x000000ff
```

These classes allow three-byte network addresses and three-byte host addresses, without requiring every address to be six bytes (48 bits). This saves four bytes for the two addresses in every packet header! The first three bits of an address determine its class:

```
#define   IN_CLASSA(i)   (((long)(i) & 0x80000000) == 0)
#define   IN_CLASSB(i)   (((long)(i) & 0xc0000000) == 0x80000000)
#define   IN_CLASSC(i)   (((long)(i) & 0xe0000000) == 0xc0000000)
```

These bit masks are used by routers to determine which bits of an Internet address are the network address.

When the packet arrives on its destination network, **subnet masks** can be used to divide your local network into separate physical networks. Subnet masks can be set by the `ifconfig` (interface configuration) command:

/etc/ifconfig *<interface name>* *<hostname>* **netmask** 0x**ffffff**00

This command uses `gethostbyname()` to find the Internet address for a host name (or `inet_addr()` if an Internet address appears on the command line) and assigns it to the interface device. The optional `netmask` portion of the command effectively changes Class A (3/1) or Class B (2/2) Internet addresses to Class C (3/1) addresses inside your administrative control. External networks use the normal Internet routing to deliver packets to your Class A or B network. Outsiders are not aware that the third byte of the Internet address is used to designate a separate physical network within your organization.

Address bit masks are typically not used by application programmers; however, they are mentioned because they are important to an understanding of the underlying IP routing code. Subnetting also facilitates network administration and may even improve network performance.

Some other important constants defined in `in.h` that **are** used by application programmers are the following:

```
#define   INADDR_ANY         (u_long) 0x00000000
#define   INADDR_LOOPBACK    (u_long) 0x7F000001
#define   INADDR_BROADCAST   (u_long) 0xffffffff
```

The constant `INADDR_ANY` tells IP that you are willing to accept requests from any interface device (any network to which the host is connected). There is one `ifconfig` command per network interface device connected to your host computer. If you wish to restrict your service to a particular network, you would put the Internet address of its interface device in the `sockaddr_in` and `bind()` that address to the socket. The `INADDR_LOOPBACK` address is `127.0.0.1`, and this special address can be used to test your code without network hardware, such as on your standalone workstation at home.

Here is a simple macro function defined in `in.h` that sets the Internet address field in a `sockaddr_in` structure:

```
/*
 * Define a macro to stuff the loopback address
 * into an Internet address
 */
#define IN_SET_LOOPBACK_ADDR(a) \
{(a)->sin_addr.s_addr  = htonl(INADDR_LOOPBACK); \
 (a)->sin_family       = AF_INET;}
```

This example helps set the stage for the addressing preliminaries to use Internet sockets.

3.5   Internet Client/Server Example

A simple example will help tie together the addressing considerations presented in the previous sections. The example consists of a server that creates a socket, binds an Internet address to it, and listens for incoming messages. Whatever arrives on that socket is printed on standard output, and the server exits:

```
$ ./vcserver &
        Socket has port number: 3844

$ ./vcclient localhost 3844

        Calling socket from host 127.0.0.1
                has port number: 4100
        From hostname: localhost

Received: Dinner is ready when the smoke alarm goes off.

Closing connection...
```

The end user learns the server port number (3844) when the server prints it on standard output. Then the end user passes the port number to the client as the second argument on the command line. This simplifies our first example and allows us to introduce the Internet address setup without concerning ourselves with how a server "advertises" its port number. Although not common, there are some situations where it is reasonable to specify a service port number on the command line, and a network printer application that uses this technique will be shown in Chapter 6. Figure 3.7 illustrates our first example.

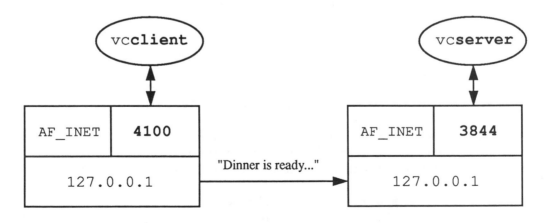

Figure 3.7   Internet Client/Server Example

3.6   TCP Server Code

Here is the source code for vcserver, a simple TCP server daemon. For further
details on the TCP connection, see Chapter 5.

```
/* vcserver.c - TCP (virtual circuit) server                 */

#include <stdio.h>        /* NULL, O_RDWR def's, etc...       */
#include <sys/types.h>    /* u_short, u_long def's, etc...    */
#include <sys/socket.h>   /* AF_INET, SOCK_DGRAM, etc...      */

#include <netinet/in.h>   /* sockaddr_in internet socket addr */
#include <netdb.h>        /* /etc/hosts table entries         */

main( argc, argv )        /* argument count, argument vector  */
char *argv[];
{
  int   rc;               /* system call return code          */
  int   sd, ld;           /* server/listen socket descriptors */
  int   addrlen, nbytes;/* sockaddr length; read nbytes req   */

  struct sockaddr_in  name;  /* Internet socket name (addr)   */
  struct sockaddr_in  *ptr;  /* pointer to get port number    */
  struct sockaddr     addr;  /* generic socket name (addr)    */

  char   buf [256];       /* your basic I/O buffer            */
  struct hostent *hp, *gethostbyaddr(); /* /etc/hosts lookup  */

  /* create a "listen" socket to receive service requests     */
  if ( (ld = socket( AF_INET, SOCK_STREAM, 0 )) < 0 )
     { perror( "INET Domain Socket" );  exit(1);  }

  /* initialize fields in an Internet address structure       */
  name.sin_family    = AF_INET; /* Internet domain            */
  name.sin_port      = 0;       /* system binds a free port#  */
  name.sin_addr.s_addr = INADDR_ANY;  /* "wildcard" accept    */

  /* bind the Internet address to the Internet socket         */
  if ( bind( ld,    &name,   sizeof( name ) ) < 0 )
     { close( ld ); perror( "INET Domain Bind" );   exit(2);  }

  /* find out the port number assigned to our socket          */
  addrlen = sizeof( addr ); /* need int to store return val   */
  if ( (rc = getsockname( ld, &addr, &addrlen ))  < 0 )
     { perror( "INET Domain getsockname" );  exit(3);  }
```

```
    /* now "advertise" the port number assigned to us          */
    ptr = (struct sockaddr_in *) &addr; /* data area has port# */
    printf( "\n\tSocket has port number: %d\n", ptr->sin_port );

    /* mark socket as a passive "listen" socket                */
    if ( listen( ld, 5 ) < 0 )/* allow 5 call "holds"          */
       { perror( "INET Domain Listen" );  exit(4); }

    while(1) /* endless loop to wait for & answer "phone calls" */
    {
      if ( (sd = accept( ld, 0, 0 )) < 0 ) /* wait & answer     */
         { perror( "INET Domain Accept" );   exit(5); }

      /* find out who's calling us...                           */
      if ( (rc = getpeername( sd, &addr, &addrlen )) < 0 )
         { perror( "INET Domain getpeername" );  exit(6); }

      /* "announce" the caller, just for our example ...        */
      printf( "\n\tCalling socket from host %s\n",
                      inet_ntoa( ptr->sin_addr ));
      printf( "\n\t    has port number %d\n",  ptr->sin_port );

      if ( ( hp = gethostbyaddr( &ptr->sin_addr, 4, AF_INET ) )
                   != NULL )
         { printf( "\tFrom hostname: %s\n\tWith aliases: ",
                      hp->h_name );
           while ( *hp->h_aliases )
                   printf( "\n\t\t\t%s", *hp->h_aliases++ );
           printf( "\n\n" );
         }
      else
         { perror( "\n\tgethostbyaddr() failed" );
           printf( "\n\th_errno is %d\n\n", h_errno );
         }
      do
      { /* bzero ( buf,    sizeof( buf ) ); /*  BSD libc func   */
           memset( buf, 0, sizeof( buf ) ); /* SYSV libc func   */
         if ( (nbytes = read( sd, buf, sizeof (buf) ) ) < 0 )
            { perror( "INET Domain Read" );  exit(7); }
        else if (nbytes == 0) printf( "\nClosing connection...\n" );
             else             printf( "\nReceived: %s\n",  buf  );
      } while ( nbytes != 0 );
    }
}
```

3.6.1   Getting Local and Remote Internet Addresses

Two library functions, **getsockname()** and **getpeername()**, were used in the foregoing code to get the local and remote Internet socket addresses, respectively. The latter can be used to authenticate or refuse service requests from remote hosts, while the former can be used to create a "rendezvous port" and send its address to the caller. The file transfer protocol, for example, uses a "control port" (21) for `ftp` commands and a "data port" (20) for the actual file transfers. The `ftp` code uses a **select()** system call to manage activity on the two TCP ports.

3.7   TCP Client Code

```
/* vcclient.c - TCP (virtual circuit) client                 */
#include <stdio.h>              /* NULL, O_RDWR def's, etc...       */
#include <sys/types.h>          /* u_short, u_long def's, etc...   */
#include <sys/socket.h>         /* AF_INET, SOCK_DGRAM, etc...     */
#include <netinet/in.h>         /* sockaddr_in internet socket addr*/
#include <netdb.h>              /* /etc/hosts table entries         */

#define DATA "Dinner is ready when the smoke alarm goes off.\n"

main( argc, argv )             /* argument count, argument vector */
char *argv[];
{ int     sd;                  /* socket descriptor               */
  struct sockaddr_in  name;    /* Internet socket addr (name)     */
  struct hostent *hp, *gethostbyname();  /* /etc/hosts lookup      */

  /* create a "client" socket to request service                  */
  if ( (sd = socket( AF_INET, SOCK_STREAM, 0 )) < 0 )
     { perror( "INET Domain Socket" );   exit(1); }

  /* initialize fields in an Internet address structure           */
  name.sin_family = AF_INET;/* Internet domain                    */
  name.sin_port   = atoi(argv[2]);        /* "advertised" port#    */

  hp = gethostbyname( argv[1] ) ;         /* "advertised" host     */
  memcpy( &name.sin_addr.s_addr,  hp->h_addr, hp->h_length );
/* bcopy ( hp->h_addr, &name.sin_addr.s_addr, hp->h_length );    */

  if ( connect( sd, &name, sizeof(name) ) < 0 )
     { perror( argv[0] );   exit(2); }
  write( sd, DATA, sizeof(DATA) );
}
```

A couple of points about the TCP client code are worth mentioning. First, there is no test for `gethostbyname()` returning **NULL** for a mistyped or unknown host name. Second, the integer returned from `atoi()` should be filtered through **htons()** (see **byteorder(3N)** in your UNIX programmer's reference manual) to convert from **host** byte order to **network** byte order. These two steps were omitted to simplify the example, but they should be part of all robust, industrial-strength programs. These omissions will serve as a good debugging example in section 3.12. The next section attempts to encapsulate socket initialization in a separate function.

The library function **bcopy()** is commonly used to copy an Internet address from the `hostent` structure to the `sockaddr_in` structure. It is a literal byte-for-byte copy and does not swap bytes or depend on a trailing NULL byte, as **strcpy()** does. However, `bcopy()` may not be included in `/lib/libc.a` on all systems; on some systems you may have to use the **memcpy()** function shown in the example.

3.8   Socket Initialization Function (`sock_init()`)

As we've seen in two programs, the code to initialize an Internet socket address is almost the same in both programs. This leads us to develop a function, **sock_init()**, to do this initialization when needed:

```
$ cc -c sock_init.c -lsocket -lnsl
$ cc -o vcclient vcclient.c sock_init.o -lsocket -lnsl
$ cc -o vcserver vcserver.c sock_init.o -lsocket -lnsl

$ ./vcserver &

    port# = 0
    Socket has port number: 8964

$ ./vcclient localhost 8964

    port# = 8964
    hostname = localhost

    Calling socket from host 127.0.0.1 has port number: 9220

Received: Dinner is ready when the smoke alarm goes off.

Closing connection...
```

The extra output of `port#` and `hostname` is due to debugging statements in the `sock_init()` function. Notice that the port number is greater than 5000 when `htons()` conversion is not done. Next, we show the new version of `vcclient.c`:

```
/* vcclient.c --  TCP (virtual circuit connection) client    */

#include <stdio.h>        /* NULL, O_RDWR def's, etc...          */
#include <sys/types.h>  /* u_short, u_long def's, etc...       */
#include <sys/socket.h> /* AF_INET, SOCK_DGRAM, etc...         */
#include <netinet/in.h> /* sockaddr_in internet socket address */

#define DATA "Dinner is ready when the smoke alarm goes off.\n"

main( argc, argv )       /* argument count, argument vector     */
char *argv[];

{
  struct sockaddr_in name;     /* Internet socket name (addr)   */
  int    sd;                   /* socket descriptor             */

  sd = sock_init( argv[1], atoi( argv[2] ),
                   AF_INET, SOCK_STREAM, &name, 0 );

  if ( connect( sd, &name, sizeof name ) < 0 )
     { perror( argv[0] );  exit(2);  }

  write ( sd, DATA, sizeof DATA );
}
```

All of the socket initialization has been encapsulated in the sock_init() function:

```
/* sock_init.c - create & initialize client & server sockets   */

#include <stdio.h>        /* NULL, O_RDWR def's, etc...          */
#include <sys/types.h>  /* u_short, u_long def's, etc...       */
#include <sys/socket.h> /* AF_INET, SOCK_DGRAM, etc...         */
#include <netinet/in.h> /* sockaddr_in internet socket address */
#include <sys/un.h>       /* sockaddr_un AF_UNIX  socket address */
#include <netdb.h>        /* /etc/hosts table entries            */

sock_init( host, port, family, type, addr, client )
char      *host;       /* hostname to bind to or connect with */
int        port;       /* port #  to bind to or connect with */
int        family;     /* address family of socket            */
int        type;       /* byte-stream or datagram socket      */
struct sockaddr *addr; /* socket address structure            */
int        client;     /* client-side(0) or server-side(1)    */
{
```

```
      struct sockaddr_in *in_name;  /* internet socket name (addr) */
      struct sockaddr_un *un_name;  /* AF_UNIX  socket name (addr) */
      struct hostent *hptr, *gethostbyname(); /* 3N lib func       */
      int    sd;                    /* socket descriptor           */

      if ( ( sd = socket( family, type, 0 )) < 0 )
         {  perror( "sock_init" );  exit(1); }

      if ( family == AF_INET ) /* Internet socket initialization   */
         {
            in_name = (struct sockaddr_in *) addr;
            in_name->sin_family = family;    /*  Adress domain      */
            in_name->sin_port = htons(port); /* "advertised" port   */
printf("\n\tport# = %d\n", htons(in_name->sin_port) ); /* test      */

            if ( host != NULL )     /* given a hostname from client */
               {
printf("\n\thostname = %s\n", host );      /*  for test only        */
                  hptr = gethostbyname( host );/* "advertised" host  */
                  memcpy( &in_name->sin_addr.s_addr, hptr->h_addr,
                                             hptr->h_length );
               }
            else
               in_name->sin_addr.s_addr = INADDR_ANY;
         }
      return( sd );               /* return the socket descriptor   */
}
```

The client parameter and the AF_UNIX socket address are not used, but they are left for future development. Client or host side can usually be determined by whether or not a host name is given as an argument.

```
/* vcserver.c -- modified TCP (virtual circuit) server          */

#include <stdio.h>       /* NULL, O_RDWR def's, etc...            */
#include <sys/types.h>   /* u_short, u_long def's, etc...         */
#include <sys/socket.h>  /* AF_INET, SOCK_DGRAM, etc...           */
#include <netinet/in.h>  /* sockaddr_in internet socket address */

main( argc, argv )       /* argument count, argument vector       */
char *argv[];
{
  int    rc;             /* system call return code               */
  int    sd, ld;         /* server/listen socket descriptors      */
  int addrlen, nbytes;   /* sockaddr length; read nbytes req      */
```

```
struct   sockaddr_in name;      /* Internet socket name (addr)   */
struct   sockaddr_in *ptr;      /* pointer to get port number    */
struct   sockaddr    addr;      /* socket name (addr)            */

char    buf [256];              /* your basic I/O buffer         */

ld = sock_init( NULL, 0, AF_INET, SOCK_STREAM, &name, 1 );

if ( bind( ld, &name, sizeof( name ) ) < 0 )
   { perror( "INET Domain Bind" ); exit(2);}
```

The rest of the server code is the same as before and is not repeated here. The same code compiles and executes on Apple's A/UX 2.0 (without `socket` and `nsl` libraries):

```
$ cc -o dgserver dgserver.c sock_init.o
$ cc -o dgclient dgclient.c sock_init.o

$ ./dgserver &

     port# = 0
     Socket has port number: 1047

$ ./dgclient localhost 1047

     port# = 1047
     hostname = localhost

Received: adidas - all day i dream about sockets.

From port: 1048
From host: 127.0.0.1
From host: localhost

$ ./vcserver &

     port# = 0
     Socket has port number: 1043

$ ./vcclient localhost 1043

     port# = 1043
     hostname = localhost
```

```
    Calling socket from host 127.0.0.1 has port number: 1045
Received: Dinner is ready when the smoke alarm goes off.
Closing connection...

        $ jobs
        [2] +  Running                   ./vcserver &
        [1] -  Running                   ./dgserver &

        $ ./vcclient localhost 1043

            port# = 1043
            hostname = localhost

    Calling socket from host 127.0.0.1 has port number: 1047
Received: Dinner is ready when the smoke alarm goes off.
Closing connection...
```

3.9   UDP Client Code

We'll use the `sock_init()` function in a datagram version of our simple service:

```c
/* dgclient.c -- UDP (datagram) client ( with sendto )    .      */

#include <stdio.h>          /* NULL, O_RDWR def's, etc...         */
#include <sys/types.h>      /* u_short, u_long def's, etc...      */
#include <sys/socket.h>     /* AF_INET, SOCK_DGRAM, etc...        */
#include <netinet/in.h>     /* sockaddr_in internet socket addr */

#define DATA "adidas - all day i dream about sockets.\n"

main( argc, argv )          /* argument count, argument vector */
char *argv[];
{
  int    sd;               /* socket descriptor                  */
  struct sockaddr_in name; /* internet socket name (addr)        */

  sd = sock_init( argv[1], atoi(argv[2]),
                AF_INET, SOCK_DGRAM, &name, 0 );

  if ( sendto( sd, DATA, sizeof DATA, 0,
                (struct sockaddr *) &name, sizeof name ) < 0 )
                        perror( "sendto failed." );
}
```

3.10 UDP Server Code

```
/* dgserver.c -- UDP (datagram) server ( with recfrom )     */

#include <stdio.h>        /* NULL, O_RDWR def's, etc...      */
#include <sys/types.h>  /* u_short, u_long def's, etc...     */
#include <sys/socket.h> /* AF_INET, SOCK_DGRAM, etc...       */

#include <netinet/in.h> /* sockaddr_in internet socket addr  */
#include <netdb.h>        /* /etc/hosts table entries        */

main( argc, argv )        /* argument count, argument vector */
char *argv[];
{
   int    ld;               /* "listen" socket descriptor       */
   int    addrlen, nbytes;  /* sockaddr length; read nbytes req */

   struct sockaddr_in  name;   /* Internet socket name (addr)   */
   struct sockaddr_in  *ptr;   /* pointer to get port number    */
   struct sockaddr addr, from; /* generic socket name (addr)    */

   int    fromlen = sizeof from;  /* address length (16 bytes) */
   char   buf [256];       /* your basic I/O buffer            */

   struct hostent *hp, *gethostbyaddr();  /* /etc/hosts entry  */

   ld = sock_init( NULL, 0, AF_INET, SOCK_DGRAM, &name, 1 );

   if (  bind ( ld, &name, sizeof( name ) ) < 0 )
      { perror( "INET Domain Bind" ); exit(2); }

   addrlen = sizeof( addr ); /* real mem int for return value  */

   if ( getsockname( ld, &addr, &addrlen ) < 0 )
      { perror( "INET Domain getsockname" );  exit(3); }

   ptr = (struct sockaddr_in *) &addr;/* data field has port no.*/
   printf( "Socket has port number: %d\n", htons(ptr->sin_port) );

   do
   {/* clear buffer to guarantee NULL byte for later printf %s */
    /* bzero( buf,  sizeof( buf ) ); /* std  BSD libc function */
    memset( buf, 0, sizeof( buf ) ); /* std SYSV libc function */
```

```
      if ((nbytes = recvfrom( ld, buf, sizeof (buf), 0,
                                 &from, &fromlen ) ) < 0 )
         { perror( "INET domain recv" );  exit(6);  }
      else
         { printf( "\nReceived: %s\n", buf );

            ptr = (struct sockaddr_in *) &from;
            printf( "From port: %d\n",      htons(ptr->sin_port));
            printf( "From host: %s\n", inet_ntoa(ptr->sin_addr));

      if ((hp=gethostbyaddr( &ptr->sin_addr, 4, AF_INET)) != NULL )
           printf( "From host: %s\n\n", hp->h_name );
      else
         { perror( "unknown host calling  ... " );
           printf( "h_error is %d\n\n", h_errno );
         }
      }
   } while (nbytes != 0);
}
```

Notice that recvfrom() returns the Internet address of the sender if you give it the address of a buffer (&from) to store it. Again, the htons() conversion is necessary on many systems (such as Intel 386 computers). The hard-coded address length, "4" passed to gethostbyaddr() should be sizeof(struct in_addr), but the intent here was to simplify the example.

   In addition to the sendto(..., &name, ...) and recvfrom(..., &from, ...) system calls, notice that sock_init() was asked to initialize **SOCK_DGRAM** (datagram) sockets in the AF_INET (Internet) domain.

3.11 A Real-World Database Application

This section describes a text retrieval application that was ported from a single processor to a client/server environment. Up to 400 users can use the system at the same time, and response time is of paramount importance. A simple program that retrieves a record from a "table of contents" file was used as the "prototype service." This greatly reduced the complexity of the sophisticated application and allowed this development effort to focus attention on distributing the application. The basic service works as follows:

```
$ ./readtc 12
Record number 12 is:
0304120 APR.1988 1.304  Agency Control and Compliance Procedures.
```

The command accepts a record number as input from the command line and it retrieves that entry from the "table of contents" file and prints it on standard output.

3.11.1 The Single Processor Code

The single processor code shown here is a function, `rtc()`, for "remote table of contents." This code was tested as a main program on the server before the networking code was added. To provide some operational flexibility without requiring a filename to be specified on the command line each time the command is used, the filename is set in a shell environment variable as follows:

```
$ RTCFILE=../AFARtc.dbs
$ export   RTCFILE
```

The `export` command can be used to see if the variable has already been set:

```
$ export | grep RTC
RTCFILE=../AFARtc.dbs
```

The `getenv()` library function is used to read the filename at runtime, as follows:

```
rtc( number )            /* remote rtc()           */
long number;             /* record number          */
{
    FILE *fp;            /* table of contents      */
    char *filename;      /* toc filename           */

    filename = getenv( "RTCFILE" );
    if ( filename == NULL )  filename = "FAR90tc.dbs";

    fp = fopen( filename, "r" );
    if ( fp == NULL )
        {
        sprintf(record, "can't open %s\n", filename );
        return -1;
        }

    fseek( fp, ( number * REC_SIZE ), 0 );
    fread( record, sizeof(char), REC_SIZE, fp );
    record[ REC_SIZE - 1 ] = '\0'; /* guarantee NULL byte */
}
```

The character buffer `record[ REC_SIZE ]` is declared a global (`extern`) variable in the common data area for `main()` and `rtc()`. The size of the buffer, `REC_SIZE`, is defined in a common header file, **rtoc.h**, which is included in both the client and server programs.

```
/* rtoc.h - header file for remote table of contents     */

#define REC_SIZE 110    /* size of "toc" record           */
#define RTC_PORT 2001   /* UDP port for our application    */
```

3.11.2 Database Client Program

The client program reads the desired record number from the command line, sends it to
the server, and waits for a reply. It uses the `sock_init()` function to create a
datagram socket and the `sendto()` system call to send a request to the `RTC_PORT`
number on the destination host. The destination host name is retrieved from a shell
environment variable named `RTCSERVER`.

```
/* rtoc.c - remote table of contents client   (Amdahl UTS)
            using  sendto/recvfrom syscalls on UDP sockets      */

#include <stdio.h>        /* NULL, O_RDWR def's, etc...          */
#include <sys/types.h>    /* u_short, u_long def's, etc...       */
#include <sys/socket.h>   /* AF_INET, SOCK_DGRAM, etc...         */
#include <netinet/in.h>   /* sockaddr_in internet socket addr    */

#include "rtoc.h"         /* REC_SIZE & RTC_PORT (2001)          */

char record[ REC_SIZE ];/* file record buffer                    */

extern char *getenv();    /* RTCSERVER environment variable
                             has hostname to call for DB query   */

main( argc, argv )        /* argument count, argument vector     */
char *argv[];
{
    int    sd;                    /* socket descriptor           */
    struct sockaddr_in addr;      /* internet socket name (addr) */
    int    addrlen = sizeof addr; /* net addr size from recvfrom */
    char *hostname;               /* name of RTC SERVER          */

    if (argc != 2){printf( "Usage: %0 record-number\n");exit(86);}

    hostname = getenv( "RTCSERVER" );
    if ( hostname == NULL )  hostname = "localhost";

    sd  =  sock_init ( hostname, RTC_PORT,
                    AF_INET,  SOCK_DGRAM, &addr, 0 );

    if ( sendto( sd, argv[1], strlen( argv[1] ), 0,
                    (struct sockaddr *) &addr, sizeof addr ) < 0 )
                                    printf( "sendto failed." );

    if ( recvfrom( sd, record, sizeof record, 0,
                    (struct sockaddr *) &addr, &addrlen ) < 0 )
                                    printf( "recfrom failed." );
    record[ REC_SIZE - 1 ] = '\0';
    printf( "\nRecord number %s is:\n%s\n", argv[1], record );
}
```

This code was initially tested on an Amdahl mainframe running UTS, and later it was ported to many other systems, including SCO Open Desktop (SVR3), ESIX SVR4, Apple A/UX, Hitachi mainframe running OSF/1, Sun workstations running SunOS 4.1, and UNISYS (Burroughs) B5000 computers. This preliminary code does not validate the record number requested, but the real application code (later encapsulated in the rtc() function) does.

3.11.3 Database Server Program

The database server waits for a datagram to arrive on the RTC_PORT. When a request arrives, it immediately fork()s a child process to carry out the request. This was done to speed up concurrency for up to 400 users. Performance is affected more by the disk access time than the network transfer time, which is about 200 Kilobytes per second.

```
/* rtocd.c - remote table of contents server (Amdahl UTS)
             using recvfrom/sendto system calls on UDP sockets */

#include <stdio.h>       /* NULL, O_RDWR def's, etc...            */
#include <sys/types.h>   /* u_short, u_long def's, etc...         */
#include <sys/socket.h>  /* AF_INET, SOCK_DGRAM, etc...           */
#include <netinet/in.h>  /* sockaddr_in internet socket addr      */

#include "rtoc.h"        /* REC_SIZE & RTC_PORT (2001)            */

char record[ REC_SIZE ];/* file record buffer                     */

extern char *getenv();   /* RTCFILE environment variable
                            has name of DataBase file to query    */

main( argc, argv )       /* argument count, argument vector       */
char *argv[];
{
  int     ld, rd;        /* listen/reply socket descriptor        */
  int     addrlen, nbytes; /* sockaddr length; read nbytes req    */

  struct sockaddr_in  addr,from;/* Internet socket name (addr)    */
  struct sockaddr_in  *ptr; /* pointer to get port number         */
  struct sockaddr     name; /* generic socket name (addr)         */

  int     fromlen = sizeof from; /* address length (16 bytes)     */
  char    buf [256];       /* your basic receive buffer           */
  long    number;          /* desired record number               */

  ld = sock_init ( NULL,      RTC_PORT,
                   AF_INET,   SOCK_DGRAM, &addr, 1 );

  if ( bind ( ld,  &addr, sizeof( addr ) ) < 0 )
     { close( ld ); printf( "INET Domain Bind" );  exit(2); }
```

```
do
{/* clear buffer to guarantee NULL byte for later printf %s */
 /*  bzero( buf, sizeof( buf ) ); /* std  BSD libc function */
 memset( buf, 0, sizeof( buf ) ); /* std SYSV libc function */

 if ( (nbytes = recvfrom( ld, buf, sizeof (buf), 0,
                                 &from, &fromlen ) ) < 0 )
     { close( ld );  printf( "INET Domain Read" );  exit(6); }
 else
     { if ( fork() ) continue;  /* parent continues ... */
       close( ld );/* child closes the service descriptor */

       rd = sock_init ( NULL,      0,
                        AF_INET,  SOCK_DGRAM, &addr, 1 );

       sscanf( buf, "%ld", &number );

       rtc( number );       /* get record from DB            */

       sendto( rd, record, sizeof record, 0,
               (struct sockaddr *) &from, fromlen );

       exit(0);             /* child exits                   */
     }
} while (nbytes != 0);
}
```

3.11.4 Application Makefile

The following `makefile` is very helpful when porting this code to various systems. No libraries are needed on Sun and Apple workstations. Amdahl UTS requires the `socket` library, and SVR3 and SVR4 require the network services library (`nsl`). The UNISYS system requires a `ddn` library. The **LIBS** macro makes it easy to change the library names on different systems. The **-g** debugging option is necessary to enable **sdb** debugging of troublesome problems, as we'll see in the next section.

```
# rtoc.mk --Makefile for remote table of contents
# usage:    make -f rtoc.mk
LIBS    = -lsocket
CFLAGS  = -g
all:    rtoc rtocd
rtoc:   rtoc.o sock_init.o rtoc.h
        $(CC) $(CFLAGS) rtoc.o sock_init.o $(LIBS) -o $@
rtocd:  rtocd.o sock_init.o rtoc.h
        $(CC) $(CFLAGS) rtoc.o sock_init.o $(LIBS) -o $@
sock_init.o:    sock_init.c
        $(CC) -c $(CFLAGS) $< $(LIBS)
```

A typical build executes as follows:

```
$ make -f rtoc.mk
   cc -g -c rtoc.c
rtoc.c: 23: warning: number unused
    cc -g  -c  sock_init.c sock_init.c  -lsocket
sock_init.c: 22: warning: sptr unused
sock_init.c: 20: warning: un_name unused
sock_init.c: 17: warning: client set but not used
    cc -g  rtoc.o  sock_init.o  -lsocket -o rtoc
   cc -g -c rtocd.c
rtocd.c: 23: warning: ptr unused
rtocd.c: 20: warning: addrlen unused
rtocd.c: 17: warning: argc set but not used
rtocd.c: 17: warning: argv set but not used
    cc -g  rtocd.o sock_init.o  -lsocket -o rtocd
```

The warning messages were heeded in `rtoc.c` and the declaration for `number` was deleted. The unused variables in `sock_init.c` and `rtocd.c` were left from the original source files used to clone `rtocd.c`. In any case, the build was successful and testing begins in the next section. Note: On some systems it was necessary to compile both source files (`rtoc.c` and `sock_init.c`) on the same command line as the **-g** (debug) option.

3.12 Socket Program Debugging

Most of the programs the authors write work correctly the first time and seldom need maintenance (:-). However, we thought it would be very helpful to readers if we contrived some bugs in our perfect code (:-) to demonstrate how you might debug your code when it does not work the way you thought it would.

Here is the first example:

```
$ ./dgserver &
[1]   29084
        Socket has port number: 1229
$ ./dgclient localhost 1229
Memory fault(coredump)
```

You were probably not expecting a coredump. One thing you should do is check that the server is still running and that the server's socket is still active:

```
$ ps -f | grep dgs
    UID    PID  PPID  C   STIME      TTY   TIME COMMAND
    tsa 29084 29062  0 11:51:02 ttyp000   0:00 ./dgserver
```

```
$ /etc/netstat -a | grep 1229
udp          0      0  *.1229                    *.*
```

Now that you know the server is still running, you should begin debugging your client code. The sdb command is used for symbolic debugging.

```
$ sdb dgclient
```

```
Warning: 'dgclient' newer than 'core'
0x14a in main:31:
    memcpy( &name.sin_addr.s_addr, hptr->h_addr, hptr->h_length );
```

The statement that caused the coredump is the first thing that sdb shows you. One of these pointers has a bad address that caused a memory fault. The sdb "w" command can be used to get a "**window**" of lines near the faulting one:

```
*w
26:name.sin_port   = atoi( argv [2] );  /* "advertised" port    */
27:
28:hptr  =  gethostbyname( argv [1] );  /* "advertised" host    */
29:
30:/*bcopy(hptr->h_addr,&name.sin_addr.s_addr,hptr->h_length);*/
31:memcpy( &name.sin_addr.s_addr, hptr->h_addr, hptr->h_length );
32:
33:  if ( sendto( sd, DATA, sizeof DATA, 0,
34:             (struct sockaddr *) &name, sizeof name ) < 0 )
35:                         printf( "sendto failed." );
```

Breakpoints are set at strategic locations (lines 28, 31, and 33) to stop execution and examine the contents of variables when they are set:

```
*28b                 ( set a breakpoint before line 28 is executed )
main:28 b
*31b                 ( set a breakpoint before line 31 is executed )
main:31 b
*33b                 ( set a breakpoint before line 33 is executed )
main:33 b
*r localhost 1229    ( run the program with command line arguments )
```

```
Breakpoint at
main:28:hptr = gethostbyname( argv [1] );/* "advertised" host */
```

```
*hptr/               ( examine hptr before line 28 is executed )
0
```

```
*c                   ( continue execution to next breakpoint )
Breakpoint at
main:31: memcpy( &name.sin_addr.s_addr, hptr->h_addr, hptr->h_length );
```

```
*hptr/                    ( examine hptr after line 28 was executed )
0                         ( still zero!   something is wrong here ...  )
*argv[1]/                 ( was hostname received from command line? )
localhost                 ( yes, it was. )
*!grep localhost /etc/hosts      ( is hostname in /etc/hosts? )
                                 ( aha!! )
*!uname -a                ( what is the local host's name? )
uts vendor systemV 2.1.3 580
*!grep vendor /etc/hosts         ( is its name in /etc/hosts?? )
192.2.13.1     vendor            ( OK!! )
*r vendor 1229            ( rerun the program with new hostname! )
Breakpoint at
main:28:hptr = gethostbyname( argv [1] );/* "advertised" host */
*hptr/                    ( examine hptr before line 28 is executed )
0
*c                        ( continue execution to next breakpoint )
Breakpoint at
main:31: memcpy( &name.sin_addr.s_addr, hptr->h_addr, hptr->h_length );
*hptr/                    ( examine hptr after line 28 was executed )
0x101a4c                  ( cool!! )
*argv[1]/                 ( was hostname received from command line? )
vendor                    ( yes, it was. )
*argv[2]/                 ( was portnumber received from command line? )
1229                      ( yes, it was. )
*c                        ( continue execution to next breakpoint )
Breakpoint at
main:33:    if ( sendto( sd, DATA, sizeof DATA, 0,
*sd/                      ( was socket sd successfully opened? )
4                         ( looks like it was ... )
*c                        ( continue execution to next breakpoint )

Client received: Hi there!          ( Success!! )
Process terminated
*q                        ( leave sdb, thank you very much! )
```

The foregoing example is a good illustration of Henry Spencer's Sixth Commandment for C programmers (see Appendix B):

If a function be advertised to return an error code in the event of difficulties, thou shalt check for that code, yea, even though the checks triple the size of thy code and produce aches in thy typing fingers, for if thou thinkest "it cannot happen to me," the gods shall surely punish thee for thy arrogance.

During very early preliminary testing it is okay to assume that unit testers will always correctly type a host name which appears in /etc/hosts, but by the production release stage of development the code should be robust enough to properly handle a user who enters gobbledegook for a host name. Again, the examples in this book focus attention on the network application calls rather than error-checking code. It is very easy to check for a **NULL** value returned by **gethostbyname()** and it will save you at least one support call for help. We hope you enjoyed this opportunity to show you how to use sdb (or your favorite debugger) to investigate and solve a runtime bug.

The next bug requires us to check an Internet address in memory. It also shows a workaround to interactively debug an executable file created from multiple source files:

```
$ sdb rtoc
Warning: 'rtoc' newer than 'core'  (recompiled with "-g" option after coredump)
0x344 in sock_init:40:    hptr->h_length );

*/recvfrom
No match

*/main:recfrom
No match

*q

$ cc -g rtoc.c sock_init.c -lsocket -o rtoc    ( recompile both .c files )

$ rm core                       ( remove the old coredump file )

$ sdb rtoc
No core image                   ( all symbols & values from a.out file )

*/recfrom                       ( find recfrom, where program hangs )
41:                     printf( "recfrom failed." );

*40
40:         (struct sockaddr *) &addr, &addrlen ) < 0 )

*39
39:    if ( recvfrom( sd, record, sizeof record, 0,

*39b               ( set a breakpoint before recvfrom is called )
main:39 b
```

```
*w
34:
35:    if ( sendto( sd, argv[1], strlen( argv[1] ) + 1, 0,
36:              (struct sockaddr *) &addr, sizeof addr ) < 0 )
37:                            printf( "sendto failed." );
38:
39:    if ( recvfrom( sd, record, sizeof record, 0,
40:              (struct sockaddr *) &addr, &addrlen ) < 0 )
41:                            printf( "recfrom failed." );
42:
43:    record[ REC_SIZE - 1 ] = '\0';
```

```
*35b                  ( set a breakpoint before sendto is called )
main:35 b
```

```
*r                    ( run to first breakpoint )
rtoc
Usage: record-number
Process terminated
```

```
*B                    ( check where breakpoints have been set )
main:35
main:39
```

```
*r 12                 ( rerun with command line argument 12 to first breakpoint )
Breakpoint at
main:35:   if ( sendto( sd, argv[1], strlen( argv[1] ) + 1, 0,
```

```
*argv[1]/             ( check that command line argument is OK )
12
```

```
*record[1]/           ( check that record buffer is empty )
^@
```

```
*c                    ( continue to next breakpoint )
Breakpoint at
main:39:   if ( recvfrom( sd, record, sizeof record, 0,

     port# = 2001        ( diagnostic output from sockinit )
     port# = 0           ( diagnostic output from sockinit )
```

```
*record[1]/           ( check that record buffer is still empty )
^@
```

```
*43b                  ( set a breakpoint after recvfrom returns )
main:43 b
*c                    ( set a breakpoint after recvfrom returns )
Breakpoint at
main:43:   record[ REC_SIZE - 1 ] = '\0';
```

```
*record[1]/          ( check the record buffer after recvfrom returns )
^@

*record[0]/          ( check the record buffer after recvfrom returns )
^@

*addr/               ( check the internet address after recvfrom returns )
*addr/
addr.sin_family/ 2                    ( AF_INET == 2 )
addr.sin_port/ 2015                   ( port # assigned by kernel )
addr.sin_addr.s_addr/ 3221359873      ( 32-bit internet address )
addr.sin_zero/

*r 12                ( rerun the program )
Breakpoint at
main:35:    if ( sendto( sd, argv[1], strlen( argv[1] ), 0,

*addr/               ( check the internet address before sendto is called )
*addr/
addr.sin_family/ 2                    ( AF_INET == 2 )
addr.sin_port/ 2001                   ( "well-known" server port # )
addr.sin_addr.s_addr/ 3221359873      ( 32-bit internet address )
addr.sin_zero/

*addr.sin_addr.s_addr/x
C0020D01                              ( 32-bit internet address in hexadecimal )

*q                   ( quit sdb )
```

The Internet address is **192.2.13.1** (C0.02.0D.01), which we recognize as the host name vendor from an earlier grep of the /etc/hosts file. Unfortunately, sdb does not have an inet_ntoa() conversion function. Still, the hexadecimal interpretation is nice. We are lucky that the Internet address field of sockaddr_in is stored in network byte order; otherwise the Internet address digits would be reversed!

This problem was caused by the server not filling the record buffer properly (it filled a buf array instead of record). After the server was modified and recompiled the text retrieval application worked correctly.

Pointer problems are common in socket-level network programming. We hope these few examples give you confidence that you can use sdb (or your favorite debugger) to troubleshoot these little buggers and kill them!

3.13 Non-BSD Sockets

Some projects require applications to run on systems that do not have the BSD socket interface to the TCP/IP protocols. Most of these systems are non-UNIX, but some are UNIX-based systems that (for whatever reasons) use a different set of functions. This section describes a project that requires the rtoc (remote table of contents) application to access a server running on an Amdahl 580 mainframe from clients running on UNISYS (formerly Burroughs) B5000 computers. The Amdahl UTS system provides a BSD socket interface but the B5000's do not. However, the computers interoperate using the TCP/IP protocols, as illustrated in Figure 3.8:

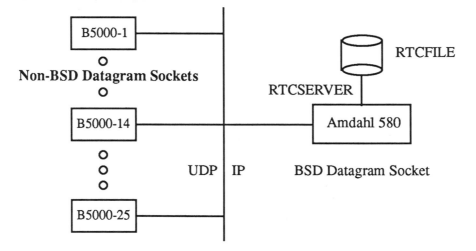

Figure 3.8 Non-BSD Sockets

The B5000-1, . . . , B5000-25 computers are UNISYS (Burroughs) B5000 computers. The makefile to build the B5000 client (fm5) and server (fm5d) is as follows:

```
#   fm5.mk -- makefile for remote table of contents
#             on UNISYS (Burroughs) B5000 computer
#   make -f fm5.mk
LIBS    = -lsocket -lsockddn    # B5000 libraries
CFLAGS  = -g
all:    fm5 fm5d
fm5:    fm5.o sock_init.o fm5.h
        $(CC) $(CFLAGS) fm5.o  sock_init.o $(LIBS)  -o $@
fm5d:   fm5d.o sock_init.o fm5.h
        $(CC) $(CFLAGS) fm5d.o sock_init.o $(LIBS)  -o $@
sock_init.o:    sock_init.c
        $(CC) -c $(CFLAGS) $< $(LIBS)
```

3.13.1 Common `sock_init()` for Non-BSD Sockets

It is helpful to isolate the non-BSD differences as much as possible in a separate function, and `sock_init()` is a good place to start. One minor difference is that B5000 implementation uses header files in a `NET-5000` subdirectory. Another minor difference is that an **rhost()** function is used instead of **gethostbyname()** to translate an ASCII host name into an Internet address. The `rhost()` function conveniently returns an Internet address instead of a pointer to a `hostent` structure from which the Internet address must be copied.

```
/* sock_init.c - create & initialize client & server sockets   */
/*               using NET-5000 TCP/IP socket syscalls          */

#include <stdio.h>       /* NULL, O_RDWR def's, etc...          */
#include <sys/types.h>  /* u_short, u_long def's, etc...        */

#include <NET-5000/sys/socket.h>/* AF_INET, SOCK_DGRAM, etc... */
#include <NET-5000/netinet/in.h>/* sockaddr_in INET sock addr  */

sock_init( host, port, family, type, addr, client )
char        *host;       /* hostname to bind to or connect with */
int         port;        /* port #   to bind to or connect with */
int         family;      /* address family of socket            */
int         type;        /* byte-stream or datagram socket       */
struct sockaddr *addr;   /* socket address structure             */
int         client;      /* client-side(0) or server-side(1)    */
{
  struct sockaddr_in *in_name; /* internet socket name (addr)   */
  int     sd;                   /* socket descriptor             */

  if ( family == AF_INET )     /* "sanity" check; must be INET */
    {
      in_name = (struct sockaddr_in *) addr;
      in_name->sin_family = family;    /* Address domain       */
      in_name->sin_port = htons(port); /* "advertised" port    */

      if ( host != NULL )    /* given a hostname from client   */
          in_name->sin_addr.s_addr = rhost( &host );
      else
          in_name->sin_addr.s_addr = INADDR_ANY;
    }
  else
    { printf( "\nsock_init: must be AF_INET family\n" );
      exit(2);
    }
```

A very major difference is that the B5000 implementation does not have a **bind()** system call! Internet addresses must be created and initialized *before* a socket is created! This causes problems when a client tries to reach a server already bound to a service address such as **FM5_PORT** (2001). This is handled in sock_init() by only initializing an Internet address structure for clients, and not trying to create a socket with the same ("well-known") service address.

```
if ( (client == 0) && (port == FM5_PORT) ) /* client gets server addr   */
      return -1;
```

The B5000 socket() library function has different parameters than the BSD socket() system call. The first parameter specifies the communication semantics (**SOCK_DGRAM** or **SOCK_STREAM**). The second parameter is a pointer to a sockproto structure, which could be used to name a specific protocol to be used with the socket. Currently only one protocol is implemented for each socket type (**UDP** or **TCP**), so the second parameter is normally NULL or zero. The third parameter is a pointer to a generic **16-byte sockaddr** socket address structure (with the same fields as those in the BSD implementation). If the port field is zero, the system assigns a port number at connection time. By specifying an Internet address in the socket() call, a separate bind() call is not necessary in the B5000 implementation. The last parameter can be used to specify options such as SO_ACCEPTCONN, SO_SMALL, SO_DEBUG, SO_DONTLINGER, and SO_KEEPALIVE which are described in the advanced socket programming chapter.

```
   if ( ( sd = socket( type, (struct sockproto *)0,
                   addr,   0 )) < 0 )
      {   perror( "sock_init" );   exit(1); }

   return( sd );                      /* return the socket descriptor */
}
```

Notice that this non-BSD implementation of sock_init() uses the same parameters as the BSD version and, if successful, returns an integer file (socket) descriptor.

3.13.2 Non-BSD Datagram Client Code

Socket creation and initialization is encapsulated in the sock_init() function, but a few other changes must be made to use this non-BSD interface to TCP/IP. The socket header files are in a NET-5000 subdirectory, and datagram transfers are done with B5000 **send()** and **receive()** library functions instead of BSD sendto() and recvfrom() system calls. Also, sock_init() is sometimes called to initialize an Internet address structure for a client, rather than actually create a socket. This address is used in a subsequent send() call to reach the server, which is waiting for requests to arrive on the "well-known" **FM5_PORT**, defined in fm5.h.

```c
/* fm5.c   remote table of contents client   (Burroughs B5000)
            using NET-5000 send/receive syscalls on UDP sockets */

#include <stdio.h>           /* NULL, O_RDWR def's, etc...            */
#include <sys/types.h>   /* u_short, u_long def's, etc...            */

#include <NET-5000/sys/socket.h>/* AF_INET, SOCK_DGRAM, etc... */
#include <NET-5000/netinet/in.h>/* sockaddr_in INET soc addr   */

#include "fm5.h"            /* REC_SIZE & FM5_PORT (2001)           */

char record[ REC_SIZE ];/* file record buffer                       */
extern char *getenv();   /* RTCSERVER environment variable
                            has hostname to call for DB query   */

main( argc, argv )        /* argument count, argument vector     */
char *argv[];
{
  int    sd, rd;                  /* send/receive sockets        */
  struct sockaddr_in serv_sock; /* server socket name (addr)   */
  struct sockaddr_in recv_sock; /* client socket name (addr)   */

  int    nbytes;                  /* number of bytes received    */
  char *hostname;                 /* name of RTC SERVER          */

  if ( argc != 2 )
     { fprintf(stderr, "Usage: %0 record-number\n" ); exit(86); }

  hostname = getenv( "RTCSERVER" );
  if ( hostname == NULL )   hostname = "localhost";

  /* bogus "sock_init" to get server's Internet address        */

  sd  = sock_init ( hostname, FM5_PORT,
                    AF_INET,  SOCK_DGRAM, &serv_sock, 0 );

  rd  = sock_init ( NULL,     0,
                    AF_INET,  SOCK_DGRAM, &recv_sock, 0 );

  if ( send( rd, &serv_sock, argv[1], strlen(argv[1])+1 ) < 0 )
                                  perror( "send failed." );

  nbytes = receive( rd, &serv_sock, record, sizeof(record) );

  if ( nbytes < 0 )  perror( "receive failed." );

  record[ REC_SIZE - 1 ] = '\0';
  printf( "\nRecord number %s is:\n%s\n", argv[1], record );
}
```

3.13.3 Non-BSD Datagram Server Code

The server is modified in similar ways as the client was modified from the BSD version. Although this version assigns a "well-known address" in the fm5.h header file, a call to the B5000 **socketaddr()** library function is made to show how it can be used in place of the BSD getsockname() system call.

```
/* fm5d.c remote table of contents server (Burroughs B5000)
          using NET-5000 receive/send syscalls on UDP sockets */


#include <stdio.h>         /* NULL, O_RDWR def's, etc...          */
#include <sys/types.h>     /* u_short, u_long def's, etc...       */


#include <NET-5000/sys/socket.h>/* AF_INET, SOCK_DGRAM, etc... */
#include <NET-5000/netinet/in.h>/* sockaddr_in INET sock addr */


#include "fm5.h"           /* REC_SIZE & FM5_PORT (2001)          */

char record[ REC_SIZE ];/* file record buffer                    */

extern char *getenv();    /* RTCFILE environment variable
                             has name of DataBase file to query */

main( argc, argv )        /* argument count, argument vector     */
char *argv[];
{
  int     ld, rd;         /* listen/reply socket descriptor      */
  int     nbytes;         /* number of bytes received            */

  struct sockaddr_in  addr,from;/* Internet socket name (addr) */
  struct sockaddr_in  *ptr;     /* pointer to get port number  */
  struct sockaddr     name;     /* generic socket name (addr)  */

  long    number;               /* desired record number       */
  char buf[256];                /* receive buffer              */

  ld = sock_init ( NULL,     FM5_PORT,
                   AF_INET,  SOCK_DGRAM, &addr, 1 );

  if ( socketaddr( ld, &name ) < 0 ) /* B5000 "getsockname()" */
    { close( ld ); printf( "socketaddr() failed.\n" ); exit(2); }

  ptr = (struct sockaddr_in *) &addr;
  printf( "\n\tServer socket has port # %d\n", ptr->sin_port );
```

```
    do
    {/* clear buffer to guarantee NULL byte for later printf %s */
     /* bzero( buf,     sizeof(buf) );/* std  BSD libc function  */
       memset( buf, 0, sizeof(buf) );/* std SYSV libc function  */

        if ( (nbytes = receive( ld, &from, buf, sizeof(buf) ) ) < 0 )
           { close( ld ); printf( "receive() failed.\n" ); exit(6); }
        else
           {  if ( fork() ) continue;  /* parent continues ...   */
              sscanf( buf, "%ld", &number );
              rtc( number );            /* get record from DB     */
              send( ld, &from, record, sizeof(record) );
              exit(0);                  /* child exits            */
           }
    } while (nbytes != 0);
}

/* fm5.h - header file for remote table of contents           */
#define REC_SIZE 110
#define FM5_PORT 2001
```

3.13.4 Non-BSD Sample Execution

First the server daemon is started on the UNISYS (Burroughs) B5000.

```
$ ./fm5d &
```

Then a few client requests are tested.

```
$ ./fm5 12

Record number 12 is:
120 0 APR.1988 1.304 Agency Control and Compliance Procedures.

$ ./fm5 10

Record number 10 is:
98 0 APR.1988 1.290 Contracting Channels and Mailing Addresses.

$ ./fm5 9

Record number 9 is:
86 0 APR.1988 1.201-90   Amendment of Army FAR Supplement.
```

A different database (with different output) was used for testing on the B5000 computer.

```
$ ls -l FAR*
-rw-r--r-- 2 tsa1 TSA 67210 Apr 22 10:53 FAR90tc.dbs
```

3.13.5 Non-BSD Socket Program Debugging

Here are some bugs that had to be removed from the B5000 code.

```
$ ./Ofm5 12
send failed.
receive failed.

$ ./fm5 12
send failed.: Bad file number
receive failed.: Bad file number

$ diff fm5.c Ofm5.c

<                    perror( "send failed." );
>                    printf( "send failed.\n" );

< if ( nbytes < 0 ) perror( "receive failed." );
> if ( nbytes < 0 ) printf( "receive failed.\n" );
```

The perror() function gives a more descriptive error message that lets the user know that the socket descriptors were not properly initialized. This leads to changes in the sock_init() calls, as we see next.

```
$ diff fm5.c Ofm5.c

<   rd = sock_init ( NULL,    FM5_PORT+1,

>   rd = sock_init ( hostname, FM5_PORT+1,

$ ./fm5 12
sock_init: Unknown error # 10048
```

The B5000 network programming reference manual documents error number 48 as **"EADDRINUSE"**, which means that FM5_PORT+1 has already been used. The code works fine when FM5_PORT+1 is changed to **zero**.

Other errors are caused by unset shell environment variables (RTCSERVER and RTCFILE).

```
$ ./fm5d &
socketaddr() failed.

$ ./fm5 12

Record number 12 is:
can't open FAR90tc.dbs
```

3.14 Summary

This chapter introduced Internet addresses and service port numbers, which are stored in system files called **/etc/hosts** and **/etc/services**, respectively. The library functions **gethostbyname()** and **getservbyname()** are provided to access and search these databases for you. These functions use **hostent** and **servent** structures, which are defined in the header file **netdb.h**. Internet socket addresses are stored in a structure named **sockaddr_in**, which is defined in the header file **/usr/include/netinet/in.h**. Internet socket address structures have a 32-bit Internet address field to specify a given host and a 16-bit port number field to identify the service you want. The port number will be assigned by the system if you initialize it to zero before binding the address to a socket. A special constant, INADDR_ANY, may be used in the address field to let the system know that your server is willing to accept requests from any network connected to the host.

Function Purpose	Function Name
Look up host name	gethostbyname(), gethostby**addr**()
Look up service port	getservbyname(), getservby**port**()
Convert ASCII to Internet	inet_addr()
Convert Internet to ASCII	inet_ntoa()
Network-to-host byte order	ntohs(16-bit port), ntohl(32-bit addr)
Host-to-network byte order	htons(16-bit port), htonl(32-bit addr)
Copy Internet address bytes	bcopy(), memcpy()
Clear bytes in I/O buffer area	bzero(), memset()
Find out assigned port number	getsockname()
Find caller's addr & port number	getpeername()

Figure 3.9   Internet Socket Functions

Figure 3.9 summarizes the functions covered in this chapter, and Figure 3.10 summarizes the header files and data structures used by those functions.

Header File	Description
`<sys/socket.h>`	`/* AF_INET, SOCK_DGRAM, sockaddr */`
`<netinet/in.h>`	`/* sockaddr_in INET socket addr */`
`<netdb.h>`	`/* /etc/hosts hostent structure`
	`/etc/services servent structure */`
`<arpa/inet.h>`	`/* inet(3N) function definitions */`

Figure 3.10 Internet Socket Header Files

Network programming libraries are listed in Figure 3.11.

Library File	Description
`libc.a`	standard C functions, including socket system calls in SunOS and Apple A/UX
`libsocket.a`	socket library functions over STREAMS in SVR4 and Amdahl's UTS
`libnsl.a`	network services library
`libnls.a`	network listener library
`libbsd.a,libucb.a`	bsd compatibility library (bzero)
`libsockddn.a`	DARPA ddn compatibility library (UNISYS B5000)

Figure 3.11 Internet Socket Libraries

A non-BSD interface to the TCP/IP protocols was shown to demonstrate protocol interoperability and illustrate a real-world situation faced by network application programmers. The non-BSD socket functions are listed in Figure 3.12.

Function Purpose	Function Name
Look up host name	`rhost()` *(returns an Internet address, not a* `hostent` *struct!)*
Look up service port	*no equivalent*
Find out assigned port number	`socketaddr()`
Create a socket	`socket()`
Bind an address to a socket	*no equivalent*
Send a datagram	`send()`
Receive a datagram	`receive()`

Figure 3.12 Non-BSD Socket Functions

This chapter also showed some debugging examples using the **sdb** (symbolic debugger) command. The `sdb` commands used in this chapter are summarized in Figure 3.13.

Command Purpose	Command Name
Run the child debuggee	`r` *<command line arguments>*
Set a breakpoint	*<line number>* `b`
Show all breakpoints	`B`
Delete a breakpoint	*<line number>* `d`
Examine a variable	*<variable name>* `/`
Set a variable's value	*<variable name>* `!` *<value>*
Continue the child's execution	`c`
Find source line with *pattern*	`/`*<pattern>*
Find next line with *same pattern*	`//`
Print a window of source lines	`w`
Quit `sdb`	`q`

Figure 3.13 Sdb (Symbolic Debugger) Commands

4
UDP Sockets

by Lyle Weiman

4.1 Introduction

This chapter builds upon the client/server pair from the previous chapter, increasing reliability and eliminating the need for the client users to supply the server's port number. As noted previously, UDP alone carries no reliability guarantees of any kind. If you use UDP, you must realize that some of the data you send **will** be lost and it may be duplicated. You must decide whether this matters, and if it does, provide whatever error recovery is needed.[1] In this chapter, we discuss methods you can use to detect when data is lost, to retransmit, and to recognize duplicated data. In Chapter 5, we will show how to use TCP, which provides several kinds of error recovery for you but does not permit you any form of control over how it operates. With UDP, you supply as much or as little recovery as you require.

4.2 Using `getservbyname()`

Our first step is to eliminate the need for users to know port numbers. As discussed in Chapter 3, the file `/etc/services` is used to map service names to port numbers. This file contains a service name, a port number, and a protocol (`tcp` or `udp`). There is also a utility procedure, `getservbyname()`, which you can use to look up mappings. It is up to the system and network administrators to ensure that the assignment is unique. For example, RFC[2] 1060, in the "PORT NUMBERS" section, specifies that port number 21 is used for `ftp`, 23 for `telnet`, and so on. You are not required to avoid using any port number in this list, but it's generally a good idea (and there are so many unused codes—port numbers are 16-bit quantities in TCP and UDP), unless you can be

---

1. Some applications can function quite well without reliable data delivery. Some could not function at all if they had it. For example, suppose you had a real-time data-delivery application, in which data has to be sent from Point A to Point B at a rate roughly equal to the average throughput for your network. There would then be no time to wait for acknowledgments, possibly time out, and retry. By then, your system could be overwhelmed with data. UDP would be a better choice than TCP in such a case, because it won't retry at all. Either the data is delivered or it isn't, so no time (or bandwidth) is "wasted" in retries.

2. RFC stands for **Request For Comments**. See the Bibliography for how to obtain them. RFC 1060 gives a listing of numbers and addresses that are "well-known" in the Internet community, such as, in this case, the TCP port number that the FTP server daemon (`ftpd`) uses.

absolutely sure that there is not, and never will be, any software in the same computer that hard-codes the same number. In most cases, it's best to code your program to look up the port number with `getservbyname()`, but keep in mind that adding entries in this file requires `root` privileges; it's therefore a good idea to provide some default port number, to be used if this lookup fails.

To add a service to the `/etc/services` file, you must first pick a port that is "suitable." There are three considerations behind "suitable." One is that the port must be unique—you wouldn't want your program to start communicating with somebody else's accidentally. The second is that in many systems the kernel enforces a convention that port numbers below a certain number, typically 1024, are reserved. Server programs cannot use reserved port numbers unless they have `root` privileges.[3] Third, within the Internet community, certain port numbers are reserved for certain services. Obtain the latest RFC index (see the "Bibliography"). Scan this for the most recent[4] RFC that lists "Assigned Numbers." Obtain the RFC for the most recent "Assigned Numbers," scan through its list of assigned port numbers, then pick one that isn't on it. Of course, if you pick one that somebody else, on some computer somewhere in the world, is already using, that's no big deal. At worst, when the software is installed, or later (for example, after the software has been installed in 50,000 nodes, and your company merges with another company that has something else installed in 75,000 nodes, and it uses the same number), the `/etc/services` file will have to be updated. Not to worry: if that indeed happens, by then you'll know enough about network programming that you can write a program, to be installed over the network, that can adjust the `/etc/services` file automatically.

Unlike the `/etc/inetd.conf` file, adding entries to the `/etc/services` file "costs" nothing more in system resources than the disk space of the file and the added time to scan and parse it each time `getservbyname()` is called. It is simply used to look up a service. There is nothing in the system that will automatically create "listen sockets" with these port numbers.

The example we shall use in this chapter provides on request, a list of events that occurred in history on the current day and month; the service will be called "This Day in History" (`TDIH`). Supposing that we've researched the matter and decided upon 31000 for a port number, we would add the following to `/etc/services`:

```
TDIH31000/udp#comment can go here
```

---

3. If the program was running with its effective user ID equal to zero when the socket was originally created, then a status bit (SS_PRIV) is set in the socket which enables certain privileges. Among these are broadcasting and binding to reserved port numbers.

4. As new RFCs are added, and as new revisions supersede old ones, they are assigned higher RFC numbers, so more recent RFCs will have numbers higher than older ones. The index lists RFCs in highest-to-lowest order, to assist you in finding the most recent version.

This line would need to be added into the `/etc/services` file at every node where either the server or the client is running, as part of the software installation procedure. The network administrator(s) may prefer to keep the same information in this file at all the nodes, to simplify their jobs. Although this makes the installation procedure for your application software slightly more cumbersome and thus subject to error, it gives the system administrators a way to change the port number your service uses, if necessary.

Returning to our example, as listed in Section 4.7, the port number is "looked up" via a call to the procedure `getserv()`, which is just a wrapper procedure for a call to the library routine `getservbyname()`. It takes two parameters, both pointers to strings. The first is the name of the service, which can be anything you like, subject to the uniqueness constraint. The second string is the name of the protocol (remember, what `getservbyname()` is really doing is looking up a port number, and port numbers are meaningful only relative to a protocol, both the service name and the protocol name are required by the lookup procedure). This protocol name is typically given in lower case: `udp` rather than UDP. We have hard-coded the service name in our example (#`defined` in `TDIH`), as well as the protocol (#`defined` in `TDIH_PROTO`) (see `dgdata.h` listed in Section 4.9). In the foregoing `/etc/services` line example, the name of the service is `TDIH`, so our program needs to look up "TDIH". Secondly, our entry in the `services` file specifies that the protocol of this service is `udp`, so we have to tell `getservbyname()` that it's a "udp" service. This is how we could code the table lookup:

```
serv_p = getservbyname("TDIH", "udp");
```

If a NULL pointer is returned, the service is not defined in `/etc/services`, so our sample program prints an error message and aborts. We could have added code to pick some default value, if we had wished for the program to be able to run even if this installation step had not been completed. Doing so would be helpful for a service, such as this one, that a casual user to the system might wish to use without having to modify `/etc/services` (casual users aren't allowed to modify that file). If a non-NULL value is returned, then it is a pointer to a `servent` structure (defined in `netdb.h`), and the port number is stored in its `s_port` field. The `servent` structure is shown in Section 3.3.1 and repeated here:

```
struct servent {
    char *s_name;              /* official name of net     */
    char **s_aliases;          /* alias list               */
    int  s_port;               /* port #                   */
    char *s_proto;             /* protocol to use          */
};
```

The port number lookup technique has to be performed by the server, before it binds the socket to this address (that is, this port number), and also by the client, before it sends out its `connect()` or `sendto()` request. This would only need to be done once per invocation of each process, since it's unlikely that the name-to-service mapping would change. Most servers look up their port numbers only once, so if it should ever be necessary to change the name-to-port mapping, the server(s) using that port name must be restarted.

The rest of the program is the same as before. The only difference is that instead of assigning the `sin_port` field to `atoi(argv(2))`, it is assigned to the return value of the procedure `getserv()`:

```
/*
 * Look up the service port number.
 */
name.sin_port = getserv(TDIH, TDIH_PROTO);
```

The procedure `getserv()` looks like this:

```
getserv(service, protocol)
char *service, *protocol;
{
    struct servent *getservbyname();
    struct servent *serv_p = getservbyname(service, protocol);
    if (serv_p == NULL)  {
        printf("Could not find %s/%s in /etc/services file.\n",
            service, protocol);
        printf("Exiting now.\n");
        exit (1);
    }
#ifdef DEBUG
    printf("getservbyname:s_name %s s_port %d s_proto %s\n",
        serv_p->s_name, serv_p->s_port, serv_p->s_proto);
#endif DEBUG
    return(serv_p->s_port);
}
```

This procedure takes two strings, the first is the name of the service, the second is the name of the transport protocol ("udp" in this case).

4.3   Recovery from Lost Messages

Our next concern is recovery from lost data. For this type of a client-server exchange it makes sense to place the responsibility for recovery on the client, since there is only one message from the client, and the service is idempotent.[5]

As noted earlier, one characteristic of the Internet Suite protocols is that if any kind of difficulty should arise during the handling of a packet as it traverses the network (and the hosts), the typical action is simply to drop it. This may be accompanied by the generation of an Internet Control Message Protocol (ICMP) packet (depending upon the circumstances). Whether generated or not, an ICMP packet has no reliability so it may or may not arrive. If you receive the reply, then you know that both the request and its reply made it. Otherwise, you can't tell which was lost. It is even possible that the packet wasn't dropped at all. It may have become caught in a routing loop and is hopping around in the network somewhere. It may eventually be delivered, or it may be dropped when its packet lifetime is exceeded. When you detect a loss, you can retransmit the request.

But what happens if the request arrived, but its reply was lost? Unless the requests are all idempotent, you do not want the server to act on this repeated request. Imagine what would happen if this was some sort of a debit/credit application handling your money!

By adding a sequence number to requests, servers can then detect when they're seeing a repeated request. They must, however, maintain "state" information for each client and keep a copy of the previous reply.

In our example, the loss either of the original request or of its reply has the same effect: the `recvfrom()` call would block forever. We need to prevent this. One way is to use `select()`'s timer mechanism, which is described a bit later. Another way is to set a timer before we call `recvfrom()`.

Timers can be set using the `alarm()` system call (see the `alarm(2)` section of the UNIX programmer's reference manual for your system). Unless the alarm is canceled (by calling `alarm(0)`), the signal **SIGALRM** will be sent to our process after the specified period of time has elapsed. This unblocks us if we happen to be blocked in the `recvfrom()`. We will cancel the alarm if we receive a response, so we don't need to worry about what happens if the alarm arrives later. As with all signals, we must define a signal handler for it.

We define how many times we will retry and the initial value for how long we will wait for the answer in MAX_RETRY and WAIT_INTERVAL, respectively. The choice of timeout interval is very important. If chosen too long, the program's response to lost messages will be too slow. If chosen too short, your program will be adding load to the network at just the wrong time, increasing network congestion (and therefore packet loss) because of the retransmissions. Due to these concerns, it is useful to make your

---

5. An **idempotent** request is one that can be repeated two or more times with the same result as if it were executed only once. Idempotent requests make recovery easy: If you don't receive an acknowledgment of the request in a reasonable period of time, you can retransmit it. If the first request was already executed, reexecuting its repetition does no harm.

timeouts start off small but increase on each retry—for example, double the value. This is sometimes referred to as "exponential backoff." The goal is to reduce network load by injecting packets into the network at ever-increasing intervals until an equilibrium is achieved.[6] If you think about the network as a whole for a moment (as a network administrator does), you would probably wish the software to reduce its "offered load" when the network is congested—the quicker the better. However, the users prefer to have the software not back off too far too fast, because the delays they experience are going up at the same rate. Exponential backoffs have been found to provide a reasonable compromise.

We have picked two seconds as the initial timeout value and have chosen to double it each retry up to a maximum (`MAX_DOUBLING`). You can use a smaller value, but it should not be smaller than twice the maximum packet lifetime in the network. (It has to be twice because you have to wait for a round trip for the reply; we assume here that the packet lifetime is the same in each direction.)

We only need a trivial `SIGALRM` signal handler, just something for the system to call. We can't set `SIG_IGN` or `SIG_DFL` for `SIGALRM`, so we need a handler to rearm the signal (for those UNIX systems that disarm it on call). It doesn't need to do anything else. Its purpose is to keep the `recvfrom()` from blocking forever if either the request or the reply is lost.

```
timeout()
{
    signal(SIGALRM,timeout);
}
```

After initializing the client, we set up the `SIGALRM` signal handler,[7] and start a `for` loop. We hope to execute the loop only once, but if we have retries, we could loop

---

6. In a larger application, it would probably be advisable to use past history on the timer value to better advantage in determining the initial value, each time.

7. It doesn't matter in this case whether we use so–called "Berkeley reliable signals" (that is, use the `sigvec()` system call) or the so-called "unreliable signals" derived from earlier AT&T UNIX releases (that is, use the `signal()` system call). Feel free to substitute `sigvec()`. The reliability of the signal handling isn't the issue here, since we won't be having any `SIGALRM` signals arrive while we are in the `SIGALRM` handler. There is a larger issue: consistency of signal handling. It may be a good idea to use reliable signals in general, when you have access to them. This is especially true if you are writing software that will be linked with a larger program that needs reliable signal handling. In some systems, for example HP-UX, mixing reliable with unreliable signal handling is virtually guaranteed to give you buggy programs, so you'd want to stick to one kind or the other. In the case where your software is linked with others', it may also be advisable to restore the signal handler address where it was before you usurped it and also restore the time remaining on the alarm clock when you reset it.

as many as MAX_RETRY times. Each time through, we build a request message and send it. We set an alarm, which is initially WAIT_INTERVAL seconds long, then we go into the recvfrom() system call. This will block the process until one of two things happen:

- The alarm goes off.
- recvfrom() returns a message.

If the alarm goes off first, recvfrom() returns -1, and errno will have been set equal to EINTR. Any recvfrom() failures other than this will cause the program to print an error message, identifying the type of failure, and exit. Otherwise, on EINTR, we continue the loop. We double the timeout value, unless we've already retried MAX_DOUBLING times.

```
alarm_interval = INITIAL_WAIT_INTERVAL;
for (retry=0; retry < MAX_RETRY; retry++) {
    .... (build and send the command)
    alarm(alarm_interval);/* Set a timer*/
    if ( (nbytes = recvfrom( sd, &reply,
                    sizeof (struct dgreply), 0,
                    &from, &fromlen ) ) < 0 ) {
        if (errno == EINTR) {
            /*
             * Timer elapsed.  We'll try again,
             * up to the maximum retry count.                  */
            if (retry < MAX_DOUBLING)
                alarm_interval = alarm_interval << 1;
            continue;
        }
        close(sd);
        perror( "INET Domain Read" );
        exit(6);
    }
}
```

The code to handle the reply is almost identical to the previous version. The only differences are that we must turn off the alarm and set a "success" flag. This is so that we can print an error message to tell the user there was no answer from the remote.

```
alarm(0);                       /* Turn off the timer.       */
++success;
```

At the bottom of the branch to handle the case where the reply arrived, there is a break, because we no longer want to keep retrying.

Finally, after the for loop exits, we check to see if we received any reply, and if not, we print an error message that there was no reply from the server, and we state how many times we tried.

```
if (!success)
   printf("No answer from server in %d retries\n", MAX_RETRY);
close( sd );
fflush(stdout);}
}
```

4.4 Using `inet_addr()`

It is sometimes useful to be able to specify just the IP address, rather than the name, of a given host. Sometimes you know the address already, but it's not in the `/etc/hosts` file. If your system is using the Domain Name Server (DNS), sometimes DNS doesn't know or has the wrong information. (Heaven forbid that a system administrator should ever make a mistake!) It also may happen that the DNS server(s) is(are) down or unresponsive to you.   Given the IP address, there's no need to go through the `gethostbyname()` routine and hence, no dependence on DNS.   Normally, `gethostbyname()` and DNS work admirably, and they provide a valuable service, but we'll now show you how to make a small addition to your program to permit users who already know the "correct" IP address to work around problem situations, should they occur. This is such a common addition in the other Internet services (Berkeley r-commands, `ftp`, `telnet`, `ping`, and so on), that people would probably notice the difference if you didn't put it in.

This technique uses the library function `inet_addr()` (see the **inet_addr(3N)** section of the UNIX programmer's reference manual for your system). It is passed a string containing an IP address either in "dot notation" or as a hexadecimal number. Dot notation is the familiar and more commonly used form for displaying and communicating IP addresses among humans; hexadecimal is sometimes also used.

The `inet_addr()` function will return -1 if the string is neither in dot notation nor hexadecimal. Consequently, you call `inet_addr()` first with whatever string you have. If `inet_addr()` returns -1, then try `gethostbyname()` to see if the string really is a node name. If this too fails, and it would if the string you've been given is just garbage, then you may wish to print an error message and either ask again for the address or node name or simply exit.

Section 4.8 lists the completed datagram client.

4.5 Using `select()`

The timer-setting method we used has several drawbacks. For one thing, you may have to set different signal handlers for `SIGALRM` at different times. For another, if your program does not otherwise have the need to provide for signal handling, its introduction can have a ripple effect throughout the code: Every interruptible system call in your program that may be executing when the alarm is active must have a test for

EINTR added to it, and repeat the system call if so, and you must make sure that the particular system call is repeatable without side effects. If you are writing code that will be in library routines and linked to a user program, then you may have the problem of which signal-handling method to use: the traditional but so-called "unreliable" ones, (such as signal()), or the more reliable BSD type (such as sigvector()). Finally, you may have another need for alarms (each process can have at most one alarm going at a time).

There is an alternative if your system supports the Berkeley select() system call. When available (and most *NIX systems have it), it's perfect for the purpose of telling us when a packet arrives on a given socket, or a time period elapses, whichever occurs first. So if you want an alternative to the timer method shown previously, check to see whether your kernel supports select(). If it does, read on.

The select() function takes three bitmaps: one for "read," one for "write," and one for "exceptional" events. By "events" we mean different things, depending on about which bitmap you're talking. Unfortunately, there are multiple meanings for the read and write bitmaps. For the "read" bitmap, an event could be the arrival of data or the death of the connection (when using connection-oriented protocols). Similarly, an event in the write map could mean that there's room in the transmission queue for at least one byte of data, or it could mean that the connection setup has been completed. This technique is used for initiating a connection (we discuss connections in the next chapter) without waiting for it to complete. If you place a socket in nonblocking mode, and then initiate a connection on it, your program does not wait. You can use select() to determine when the connection is established. Sockets also "select writable" when the connection is dead. See Section 4.6, "Cautionary Note."

The select() feature is designed to provide both a "polling" type of function and a "wait for event or maximum time" type of function. "Polling" means that you can check status without your program blocking. "Wait for event or maximum time" means exactly that: You can have the system put your process to sleep if none of the events for which you are checking is ready, and wake it when any of them occur, but wait no longer than for a specified maximum time limit. You tell the system which of these you want via the last parameter of the system call, the timeval parameter (time.h defines struct timeval).

This may be either a NULL pointer or a pointer to a timeval structure. If you want to poll, fill the timeval structure with zeros. If you want to wait as long as it takes for any one of the events you specify (in the bitmaps) to occur, specify a NULL pointer. If you want to wait, say, a maximum of 10 seconds, then load "10 seconds" into the timeval structure.

If you don't want one of the three bitmaps, it's more efficient for the kernel if you pass NULL in that parameter position, rather than a bitmap that's been filled with zeros. This tells the kernel that the bitmap is not wanted.

You can freely mix pipes, sockets, and file descriptors (regular files and device-special files) in the bitmaps, but the semantics of the system call change somewhat for each type. We are concerned here only with sockets, but it is worthwhile (and often times useful) to note that the bitmaps can be mixed in this way. The "read map" is used to see if there is any data that can be read on a given socket. You would use the "read" map if you wanted to know if you could read from any of a given set of socket descriptors without blocking (this is the polling type function).

The bitmaps are built as follows: Each descriptor you care about, say, `fd`, is related to its bit in the map by the simple rule:

```
map_bit = bit_map[fd / BITS_PER_INT] & (1 << (fd %
BITS_PER_INT))
```

For example, if `bit_map[0] == 8`, this refers to a file or socket descriptor equal to 3 ($2^3 == 8$). `BITS_PER_INT` is the number of bits in the `int`s that make up the bitmap, such as 32.

Check to see if your system supports **FD_SET** and **FD_ZERO**. If it does, then you can use `FD_ZERO(&bitmap)` to clear the bits in the bitmap, and `FD_SET(skt, &map)` to set the bit in the bitmap corresponding to the socket skt. Similarly, **FD_CLEAR** clears the corresponding bit. If they are defined to operate on the `typedef fd_set`, then declare your bitmaps that way.

That's how you set the bitmap; it's up to you whether you set the same maps for the read map as the write map. You must construct the maps prior to calling `select()`. You may wish to construct them once into another map and then copy them into "sacrificial" maps you pass to `select()`. This is faster than constructing them a bit at a time. Never forget that the contents of the maps, as returned to you, will almost *always* be different from what you passed into the kernel. What will you do if more than one bit is set on return? Always pick the first one that is set? That may be OK, but it will tend to favor one descriptor over others. An alternative is to keep track of which descriptor you serviced last, and scan for a one starting at the next higher bit position. Wrap around when you get to the highest-numbered descriptor. You'll want to code this as efficiently as possible, since the "get next item of work" section of your code will be executed for *every* element of work processed.

4.6 Cautionary Note

Strictly speaking, "select readable" only means that a `read()`, `recv()`, or `recvfrom()` issued on the socket would not block. It doesn't necessarily mean that the socket is readable. This includes error conditions. When connection-oriented sockets are used (as in TCP), the socket selects "readable" when the circuit breaks. This is because a `recv()` (or `read()` or `recvfrom()`) issued on it would not block (whatever data is queued on the socket is delivered, else `EOF` is returned). Similarly, "select writable" means that a `write()` or `send()` or `sendto()` issued on it would not block, including error conditions such as the loss of the connection. Terminology such as "select readable" makes it all too common for people to ignore these distinctions, which leads to bugs.

Bits in the "write" map are useful for telling us when we can send data. Some protocols, such as TCP, have a property called flow control, which simply means that there is a mechanism built into them to make sure that senders don't overrun receivers. In TCP's case, each packet sent carries a field that tells the other side how many bytes for which the receiver "guarantees" to have storage space. This amount is sometimes referred to as the "send window." Now, suppose that the sender has (temporarily) sent all it's allowed to. Then the send window will be "closed." This condition is detectable with `select()`. Unfortunately, all it really tells you is whether or not the flow control is closed. In most instances, what you really want to know is whether there is sufficient space in the send window to send a given number of bytes, but all `select()` is telling you is whether or not you have space for at least one byte in the window. For this reason, when we want to know if we can send, one method is just to put the socket into "nonblocking mode" (via an `ioctl`) and then test for `errno` == `EWOULDBLOCK` if the `send()` fails.

The "exceptional" map is used to see if there is a connection waiting to be accepted or cleared.

The first parameter specified in the `select()` system call must be the maximum number of descriptors to be checked; that is, the highest-numbered descriptor of all three bitmaps. In the simple case where you're only using one descriptor, you can use descriptor plus one.

The `select()` call doesn't automatically return information on all the descriptors you have open. It is not an error, on most systems, to specify a number of descriptors that is greater than the highest descriptor currently open, but there must be zeros in all maps in the bit positions corresponding to descriptors that aren't open. This is also very inefficient, so you should just specify an integer containing one greater than the highest-numbered descriptor in any of the bitmaps. The `select()` system call can be fairly high in overhead when you specify a lot of descriptors.

The value returned from the system call tells you how many descriptors are being returned. The time value (last parameter) can either be specified as a zero (`NULL` pointer)—meaning that the caller is willing to wait forever if necessary—or it can be a pointer to a `struct timeval`. In this case, store the number of seconds you are willing to wait in the `tv_sec` field (microseconds go in `tv_usec`, but the granularity of the timeout is unlikely to be smaller than milliseconds).

If the timeout arrived before any of the specified descriptors became "readable," "writable" or "exceptional," this information is returned to you in the form of a zero result from the system call.

The select () is one of the interruptible system calls. As with the others, if a signal interrupts the system call, it will return value -1 and the global integer errno will be set to EINTR.

If the return value is -1 but errno is unequal to EINTR, then something is very wrong with the system call. We won't even suggest that you might have forgotten to type the ampersand in front of the bitmaps—if you specified a single int as a bitmap, failing to put the ampersand in wouldn't be an error the compiler could flag for you— but maybe you specified too large a value for the number of descriptors. At any rate, such an error is most probably a programming one rather than a network one. Check the manual page for select () and try to figure out what's wrong from that.

From the formula in the previous sections, it's obvious that for many situations a single int (containing 32 bits) would be sufficient for the purpose. Socket descriptors are allocated in UNIX following the same rules as file descriptors, lowest available first. So, if you are coding for a situation in which the number of descriptors currently open is not known to be <= 32, then it is safest to allocate an array of unsigned ints. In this example, we have shown the use of an array of 4 ints, which means this code will work provided the socket descriptor is <= 128, but we could just as easily have chosen either a higher or lower value. In our example here, the socket descriptor is always 3 (0, 1, and 2 being already open as stdin, stdout, and stderr).

The technique shown here, despite its drawbacks in space and time, has the advantage of being generally applicable. It is (as always) up to the programmer to evaluate the situation and make the proper choice for each particular situation.

The version of the datagram client using inet_ntoa() and select() has no #include <signal.h>, and no timer routine. It is listed in Section 4.10.

4.7   Datagram Server

```
/* dgserver4.c -- UDP server ( recvfrom )                          */
/*
This server provides two kinds of services. It can look up a
message in $TDIH, where this environment variable gives the
pathnames for the "This Day In History" file.  The server returns
a message for the day in which it's running; in other words
doesn't give you Jan 1 messages in July!  Exercise for the student:
How would you modify this program so that the client and the
server may exist in different time zones, and yet the results
will still yield "today's message" (from the user's point of view)?
*/
```

```
#include <stdio.h>
#include <fcntl.h>
#include <sys/types.h>
#include <sys/socket.h>
#include <netinet/in.h> /* sockaddr_in internet socket address */
#include <netdb.h>       /* /etc/hosts table entries            */
#include <time.h>
#include "dgdata.h"
/*
 * Global Variables.
 */
FILE *TODAYFILE;/* FILE ptr for "This Day In History"database*/
FILE *fopen();

char *months[] = {
    "Jan",
    "Feb",
    "Mar",
    "Apr",
    "May",
    "Jun",
    "Jul",
    "Aug",
    "Sep",
    "Oct",
    "Nov",
    "Dec",
};

/*
 * Extern Variables.
 */
extern int errno;
extern char *sys_errlist[];
extern int sys_nerr;

/*
 * Extern procedures
 */
char *getenv();
main( argc, argv )        /* argument count, argument vector    */
char *argv[];
{
    int     ld;            /* "listen" socket descriptor         */
    int     addrlen, nbytes; int     port;
```

```
char    *cptr;
struct sockaddr_in name;    /* internet socket name (addr)   */
struct sockaddr_in *ptr;    /* pointer to get port number    */
struct sockaddr_in addr, from; /* socket name (addr)         */
int     fromlen = sizeof from;
struct hostent *hp, *gethostbyaddr();  /* /etc/hosts entry */
struct dgcmnd cmnd;
struct dgreply reply;

if ( (ld = socket( AF_INET, SOCK_DGRAM, 0 )) < 0 )
   { perror( "INET Domain Socket" );  exit(1); }

if ((cptr = getenv("TDIH")) == NULL)
   cptr = "TDIH";

TODAYFILE = fopen(cptr,"r");      /*Open "This Day In History"
                                  /* database                 */
name.sin_family= AF_INET;        /* internet domain          */
/*
 * Look up the service port number.
 */
name.sin_port   = getserv(TDIH, TDIH_PROTO);

if ( bind( ld, &name, sizeof( name ) ) < 0 )
   { close(ld); perror( "INET Domain Bind" );  exit(2); }

addrlen = sizeof( addr );  /* need a real mem location      */
if ( getsockname( ld, &addr, &addrlen ) < 0 ) {  close(ld);
   perror( "INET Domain getsockname" );
   exit(3);
}
/*
  +=========================================================+
  |                                                         |
  |  Main execution loop.                                   |
  |  This is the place where we provide the service to our  |
  |  clients.  The preceding was merely foreplay.           |
  |                                                         |
  +=========================================================+
*/

do
{
   nbytes = recvfrom( ld, &cmnd, sizeof (cmnd), 0, &from,
                      &fromlen );
   if (nbytes < 0 )  {
```

```
                close(ld);  perror( "INET Domain Read" );  exit(6); }
            else if (nbytes > 0)
                proc_cmnd(ld, &cmnd, &from, fromlen);
        } while (nbytes != 0);
        close(ld);/* close the service descriptor*/
        exit (0);
}

/*
We moved the processing of a command into a separate procedure
so that we can focus the discussion.
*/
proc_cmnd(ld, cmnd, from, fromlen)
int ld, fromlen;        /* socket descriptor, "from" addr lnth */
struct dgcmnd *cmnd;    /* Command: what service is requested? */
struct sockaddr_in *from; /* socket name (addr)                  */
{
    int lnth, i, k, error, rewind_count;
    struct dgreply reply;

#ifdef DEBUG
    printf( "From port: %d\n", ntohl(from->sin_port));
    printf( "From host: %s\n", inet_ntoa(from->sin_addr.s_addr ));
    fflush(stdout);
#endif DEBUG

    switch (ntohl(cmnd->dgcmd_type)) {
    /*
     * REQUEST_TDIH: Request "This Day In History" entry.
     * Read next entry in the file.  If it starts with todays
     * month and month-day number, use it.  If not, read the
     * next entry, and wrap around the file if necessary.
     * You can optimize this lookup if you want.
     * In this simple example, we do not check to see whether
     * we have read into "tomorrow's" entries.  We just keep
     * reading until we either reach the proper entry
     * or EOF.  In the case we hit EOF, we rewind the file
     * and start over.  This is EXTREMELY inefficient,
     * especially in two cases:  When we first start up, on,
     * say, Dec. 31st (meaning we read through the whole file),
     * and when we read an entry which is past today's date
     * (meaning this version reads through to the EOF, rewinds,
     * starts reading from Jan 1st, checking and skipping entries
     * until it gets to "today's entry" again
     */
```

```
        case REQUEST_TDIH:
           if (TODAYFILE == NULL)
              reply.dgreply_status = htonl(REPLY_NOSUCHFILE);
           else {
              char datebuf[40], *ptr;
              int slnth;
              long clock;
              struct tm *tm;
              clock = time((long *) 0);
              tm = localtime(&clock);
              sprintf(datebuf,"%s %2d",months[tm->tm_mon],
                      tm->tm_mday);
              slnth = strlen(datebuf);
              reply.dgreply_status = htonl(REPLY_OK);
              rewind_count = 0;
              while (1) {
                 clearerr(TODAYFILE);
                 ptr = fgets(reply.dgreply_msg, MSGSIZE,TODAYFILE);
                 if (ferror(TODAYFILE) != 0) {
                    reply.dgreply_status = htonl(errno);
                    if ((errno > 0) && (errno < sys_nerr))
                       strncpy(reply.dgreply_msg,
                          sys_errlist[errno], MSGSIZE);
                    else
                       reply.dgreply_msg[0] = '\0';
                       break;
                 }
                 if (feof(TODAYFILE) != 0) {
                    fseek(TODAYFILE, 0L, 0);
                    ++rewind_count;
                    if (rewind_count >=2){
                       reply.dgreply_msg[0] = '\0';
                       break;
                    }
                    continue;
                 }
                 /*
                  * Does this line start with today's date?
                  */
                 if (strncmp(datebuf, reply.dgreply_msg,slnth) == 0)
                    break;
                 else {
#ifdef DEBUG
                       printf("%s\n", reply.dgreply_msg);
```

```
                            fflush(stdout);
#endif DEBUG
                        continue;
                    }
                }
            }
            break;
        default:
            reply.dgreply_status = htonl(REPLY_GARBAGE);
    }
    /*
     * Send the reply. The structure "from" already has the
     * IP address and the port of the client process (this was
     * set in the  recvfrom() system call, which we used to read
     * the command).
     */
#ifdef DEBUG
    printf( "Sending to port: %d\n", from->sin_port );
    printf( "to host: %s\n", inet_ntoa( &from->sin_addr.s_addr ));
    fflush(stdout);
#endif DEBUG
    error = sendto( ld, &reply, sizeof (struct dgreply), 0,
            (struct sockaddr *) from, sizeof (struct sockaddr );
    if(error < 0 )
        perror( "sendto failed.");
}
getserv(service, protocol)
char *service, *protocol;
{
    struct servent *getservbyname();
    struct servent *serv_p = getservbyname(service, protocol);
    if (serv_p == NULL)   {
        printf(
"Could not find %s/%s in /etc/services file.  Exiting now.\n",
        service,protocol);
        exit (1);
    }
#ifdef DEBUG
    printf("getservbyname:s_name %s s_port %d s_proto %s\n",
        serv_p->s_name, serv_p->s_port, serv_p->s_proto);
#endif DEBUG
    return(serv_p->s_port);
}
```

4.8   Datagram Client

```
/* dgclient4.c -- UDP client ( sendto )                        */
/*
 * This client contacts its server with a message, indicating
 * service is wanted, what type, and so on.  The server performs
 * that service, and responds with a message in reply.
 */

#include <stdio.h>
#include <sys/types.h>
#include <sys/socket.h>
#include <netinet/in.h>
#include <netdb.h>
#include <signal.h>
#include <errno.h>
#include "dgdata.h"
/*
 * Global Variables.
 */
#define MAX_RETRY 20      /* How many times to retry            */
#define INITIAL_WAIT_INTERVAL 2
#define MAX_ALARM_INTERVAL 30
/*
 * Externs
 */
struct hostent *gethostbyname();      /* 3N lib func           */
unsigned long inet_addr();            /* 3N lib func           */
extern int errno;
extern char *sys_errlist[];
extern int sys_nerr;
/*
 * Forward declarations.
 */
void process_reply();
/*
 * timeout -- this routine is called when a SIGALRM signal is
 * sent to our process.
 */
timeout()
{
   signal(SIGALRM,timeout);
}
/*
```

```
 * Main program.
 */
main(argc, argv)/* argument count, argument vector*/
int  argc;
char *argv[];
{
    struct sockaddr_in name;    /* internet socket name (addr)  */
    struct dgcmnd cmnd;
    struct dgreply reply;
    int   nbytes;               /* read nbytes req              */
    int   sd, rslt;             /* socket descriptor            */
    int   retry, success = 0;
    int   alarm_interval;

    sd = client_init(argv[1], &name); /* Initialize          */
    signal(SIGALRM,timeout);
    alarm_interval=INITIAL_WAIT_INTERVAL;
    for (retry=0; retry < MAX_RETRY; retry++) {
       cmnd.dgcmd_type = htonl(REQUEST_TDIH);
       rslt = sendto(sd,cmnd, sizeof cmnd,0, &name, sizeof name);
       if (rslt < 0)
          {perror( "sendto failed."); exit(1); }
       /*
        * We now read the reply.
        */

       nbytes = get_reply(sd, &reply, sizeof(struct dgreply),
       alarm_interval);
       if (nbytes == 0) {
          /*
           * Timer elapsed.  We'll try again, up to the
           * maximum retry count.
           */
#ifdef DEBUG
          printf("Timeout. retry=%d\n", retry);
#endif DEBUG
          alarm_interval = alarm_interval <<1;
          if (alarm_interval > MAX_ALARM_INTERVAL)
             alarm_interval = MAX_ALARM_INTERVAL;
          continue;
       }
       /* We got an answer.  Set "success" flag.            */
       ++success;

       /* Handle the response.                              */
```

```
        (void) process_reply(&cmnd, &reply);
        break;/* No point in retrying now.*/
    }
    if (!success)
        printf("No answer from server in %d retries\n", MAX_RETRY);
    close( sd );
    exit(0);
}
/*
 * Initialize the client side.
 * Returns socket descriptor.
 */
client_init(host, name)
struct sockaddr_in *name;        /* internet socket name (addr)   */
char *host;
{
    int    sd, addrlen;          /* socket descriptor             */
    struct hostent *hptr;
    struct sockaddr_in addr;
    struct sockaddr_in *ptr;     /* pointer to get port number    */

    if ( (sd = socket( AF_INET, SOCK_DGRAM, 0 )) < 0 )
        { perror("");  exit(1); }

    name->sin_family = AF_INET;/* internet domain                 */
    name->sin_port = 0;          /* system assigns a free port    */
    name->sin_addr.s_addr = INADDR_ANY; /* "wildcard" accept
                                                       address     */
    if ( bind( sd, name, sizeof( struct sockaddr_in)) < 0)
        { close(sd); perror( "INET Domain Bind" );  exit(2); }
#ifdef DEBUG
    addrlen = sizeof( addr );
    if ( getsockname( sd, &addr, &addrlen) < 0)  { close(sd);
        perror( "INET Domain getsockname" ); exit(3);}

    printf( "Local socket has port number: %d\n", addr.sin_port );
#endif DEBUG

    name->sin_family = AF_INET;        /* internet domain         */
    if ((name->sin_addr.s_addr = (unsigned long) inet_addr
         (host)) == -1) {
        hptr = gethostbyname( host ); /* host                     */
        if (hptr == NULL) {
            printf("Cannot find %s in /etc/hosts\n", host);
            exit(7);
```

```
        } else
          memcpy(&name->sin_addr.s_addr, hptr->h_addr,
              hptr->h_length );
    }
    /*
     * Look up the service port number.
     */
    name->sin_port = getserv(TDIH, TDIH_PROTO);
    return(sd);
}

getserv(service, protocol)
char *service, *protocol;
{
    struct servent *getservbyname();
    struct servent *serv_p = getservbyname(service, protocol);

    if (serv_p == NULL)  {
       printf("Could not find %s/%s in /etc/services file.\n",
             service,protocol);
       printf("Exiting now.\n");
       exit (1);
    }
#ifdef DEBUG
    printf(
       "getservbyname returns s_name %s s_port %d s_proto %s\n",
       serv_p->s_name, serv_p->s_port, serv_p->s_proto);
#endif DEBUG
    return(serv_p->s_port);
}

/*
** Get the reply, or tell our caller there was a timeout.
** This example provides timeout-based recovery in case the
** datagram message we just sent was lost.
*/
get_reply(sd, reply, reply_size, alarm_interval)
int sd;                          /* Socket                       */
struct dgreply *reply;           /* Struct for reply.            */
int reply_size;                  /* Sizeof(reply structure)      */
int alarm_interval;
{
    struct sockaddr_in from;     /* socket name (addr)           */
    int fromlen, nbytes;

    fromlen = sizeof (from);
```

```
    alarm(alarm_interval);              /* Set a timer            */
    nbytes = recvfrom(sd,reply,sizeof(struct dgreply),0,&from,
        &fromlen);
    alarm(0);                           /*  turn off the timer.   */
    if (nbytes < 0 ) {
        if (errno == EINTR) {
            /*
             * Timer elapsed.  We'll try again, up to the maximum
             * retry count.
             */
            return(0);              /* Return zero for timeout       */
        }
        close(sd);
        perror( "INET Domain Read" );
        exit(6);
    }
     return(nbytes);                /* Return # bytes read           */
}
/*
** Handle the reply.
*/
void process_reply(cmnd, reply)
struct dgcmnd   *cmnd;
struct dgreply *reply;
{
    int error;

    if (ntohl(reply->dgreply_status) == REPLY_OK) {
        /*Good answer. Print it.                                  */
        printf( "%s\n", reply->dgreply_msg );
    } else if ((error = ntohl(reply->dgreply_status)) > 0) {
        /* Some error in system-call on server side.
         * Print it.
         */
        printf("Server error (%d): %s\n",ntohl(error),
            reply->dgreply_msg);
    } else switch (ntohl(error))   {
        case REPLY_GARBAGE:
            printf( "Server did not recognize request type %d\n",
                ntohl(cmnd->dgcmd_type));
            break;
        case REPLY_NOSUCHFILE:
            printf("Server could not open data file\n");
            break;
```

```
            default:
                printf("Server error: %d (don't know what this means)
                    \n", ntohl(reply->dgreply_status));
        }
    return;
}
```

4.9 **dgdata.h**

```
#define MSGSIZE 256

/*
 * Define Service Types
 */

#define REQUEST_TDIH 0          /* This Day In History              */

/*
 * Define Reply Status values
 */
#define REPLY_OK 0
#define REPLY_GARBAGE -1        /* Request code was unrecognized */
#define REPLY_NOSUCHFILE -2     /* No such file for request      */

/*
 * Structure of Datagram Server Command Message.
 */
struct dgcmnd {
    int dgcmd_type;
};

struct dgreply {
    int  dgreply_status;
    int  dgreply_lnth;
    char dgreply_msg[MSGSIZE];
};

#define TDIH "TDIH"
#define TDIH_PROTO "udp"
```

4.10 Datagram Client with **select()**

```
/* dgclient5.c -- UDP client ( sendto )*/

/*
 * This client contacts its server with a message, indicating
 * service is wanted, what type, etc.  The server performs
 * that service, and responds with a message in reply.
```

```
 */
#include <stdio.h>
#include <sys/types.h>
#include <time.h>               /* Needed for struct timeval defns */
#include <sys/socket.h>
#include <netinet/in.h>
#include <netdb.h>
#include <errno.h>
#include "dgdata.h"

#define MAX_RETRY 20            /* How many times to retry         */
#define WAIT_INTERVAL 5         /* No. of secs to wait for reply   */
/* Global Variables.
 */
/*
 * Externs
 */
struct hostent *gethostbyname();    /* 3N lib func                 */
unsigned long inet_addr();          /* 3N lib func                 */
extern int errno;
extern char *sys_errlist[];
extern int sys_nerr;
/*
 * Forward declarations.
 */
void process_reply();

/*
 * Main program.
 */
main(argc, argv)               /* argument count, argument vector */
int argc;
char *argv[];
{
    struct    sockaddr_in name; /* internet socket name (addr)    */
    struct    dgcmnd cmnd;
    struct    dgreply reply;
    int       nbytes;          /* read nbytes req                 */
    int       sd;              /* socket descriptor               */
    int       retry, success = 0;

    sd = client_init(argv[1], &name);      /* Initialize          */
    for (retry=0; retry < MAX_RETRY; retry++) {
        cmnd.dgcmd_type = htonl(REQUEST_TDIH);
```

```
        if (sendto(sd, cmnd, sizeof cmnd, 0, &name, sizeof name ) < 0 )
            {perror( "sendto failed."); exit(1); }
        /*
         * We now read the reply.
         */
        nbytes = get_reply(sd, &reply, sizeof(struct dgreply));
        if (nbytes == 0) {
            /*
             * Timer elapsed.  We'll try again, up to the
             * maximum retry count.
             */
#ifdef DEBUG
            printf("Timeout. retry=%d\n", retry);
#endif DEBUG
            continue;
        }
        /* We got an answer.  Set "success" flag.              */
        ++success;
        /* Handle the response.                                */
        (void) process_reply(&cmnd, &reply);
        break;               /* No point in retrying now.      */
    }
    if (!success)
        printf("No answer from server in %d retries\n", MAX_RETRY);
    close( sd );
    exit(0);
}
/*
 * Initialize the client side.
 * Returns socket descriptor.
 */
client_init(host, name)
struct sockaddr_in *name;     /* internet socket name (addr)  */
char *host;
{
    int    sd, addrlen;       /* socket descriptor            */
    struct hostent *hptr;
    struct sockaddr_in addr;
    struct sockaddr_in *ptr;  /* pointer to get port number   */

    if ( (sd = socket( AF_INET, SOCK_DGRAM, 0 )) < 0 )  {
        perror("");
        exit(1);
    }
```

```
    name->sin_family = AF_INET;/* internet domain              */
    name->sin_port = 0;         /* system assigns a free port  */
    name->sin_addr.s_addr = INADDR_ANY;
    if ( bind( sd, name, sizeof( struct sockaddr_in)) < 0)
        { close(sd); perror( "INET Domain Bind" ); exit(2); }
#ifdef DEBUG
    addrlen = sizeof( addr );
    if ( getsockname( sd, &addr, &addrlen) < 0)   {
        close(sd);
        perror( "INET Domain getsockname" );
        exit(3);
    }
    printf( "Local socket has port number: %d\n", addr.sin_port );
#endif DEBUG

    name->sin_family = AF_INET;         /* internet domain      */
    if ((name->sin_addr.s_addr =(unsigned long) inet_addr(host))
            == -1)  {
        hptr = gethostbyname( host ); /* host                 */
        if (hptr == NULL) {
            printf("Cannot find %s in /etc/hosts\n", host);
            exit(7);
        } else
            memmove(&name->sin_addr.s_addr, hptr->h_addr,
                    hptr->h_length );
    }
    /*
     * Look up the service port number.
     */
    name->sin_port = getserv(TDIH, TDIH_PROTO);
    return(sd);
}

getserv(service, protocol)
char *service, *protocol;
{
    struct servent *getservbyname();
    struct servent *serv_p = getservbyname(service, protocol);

    if (serv_p == NULL)  {
        printf("Could not find %s/%s in /etc/services file.\n",
            service,protocol);
        printf("Exiting now.\n");
        exit (1);
    }
```

```
#ifdef DEBUG
   printf("getservbyname returns s_name %s s_port %d s_proto %s\n"
      ,serv_p->s_name, serv_p->s_port, serv_p->s_proto);
#endif DEBUG
   return(serv_p->s_port);
}

/*
** Get the reply, or tell our caller there was a timeout.
** This example provides timeout-based recovery in case the
** datagram message we just sent was lost, but differs
** from dgclient4.c in that it uses timers in the select(2)
** system-call.
*/
get_reply(sd, reply, reply_size)
int     sd;                     /* Socket                        */
struct dgreply *reply;          /* Struct for reply.             */
int     reply_size;
{
   struct sockaddr_in from;   /* socket name (addr)              */
   struct timeval tval, *tv_p;
   int i, fromlen, nbytes;
   fd_set read_map;

   fromlen = sizeof (from);
   nbytes = sizeof(struct dgreply);
   FD_ZERO(&read_map);
   FD_SET(sd, &read_map);
   tval.tv_sec = WAIT_INTERVAL;
   tval.tv_usec = 0;
   /* We are only interested in when the socket "selects
    * readable." We don't care about anything else.  It is
    * more efficient to pass NULL instead of bitmaps
    * containing all zeros.
    */
   i = select(sd + 1, &read_map, NULL, NULL, &tval);
   if (i < 0) {
      if (errno == EINTR) {
         /*
          * Timer elapsed.  We'll try again, up to the maximum
          * retry count.
          */
         return(0);             /* Return zero for timeout       */
      }
      perror("select failed");
```

```
         exit(1);
    }
    if (i == 0)
        return(0);                    /* Return zero for timeout        */
    nbytes = recvfrom(sd,reply, sizeof(struct dgreply), 0,
                            &from, &fromlen);
    if (nbytes < 0)
        {close(sd); perror( "INET Domain Read" ); exit(6); }
    return(nbytes);/* Return # bytes read*/
}
/*
** Handle the reply.
*/
void process_reply(cmnd, reply)
struct dgcmnd  *cmnd;
struct dgreply *reply;
{
    int error;

    if (ntohl(reply->dgreply_status) == REPLY_OK) {
        /*Good answer. Print it.                                */
        printf( "%s\n", reply->dgreply_msg );
    } else if ((error = ntohl(reply->dgreply_status)) > 0) {
        /* Some error in system call on server side.
         * Print it.
         */
        printf("Server error (%d): %s\n", ntohl(error),
        reply->dgreply_msg);
    } else switch (ntohl(error))  {
        case REPLY_GARBAGE:
            printf( "Server did not recognize request type %d\n",
                ntohl(cmnd->dgcmd_type));
            break;
        case REPLY_NOSUCHFILE:
            printf("Server could not open data file\n");
            break;
        default:
            printf("Server error: %d (don't know what this means)\n",
                ntohl(reply->dgreply_status));
    }
    return;
}
```

5 TCP Sockets

by Lyle Weiman

5.1 Introduction

You have already encountered Transmission Control Protocol (TCP) sockets in Chapter 3 with the "Dinner is ready when the smoke alarm goes off" client/server pair reviewed in this chapter and listed in Sections 5.6 and 5.7. This chapter also shows how the "This Day In History" client/server pair from Chapter 4 would be modified if you wanted to use TCP. But first, why is the programming different?

Programming to use TCP is very different from programming to use UDP. TCP is connection-oriented, so you cannot begin until you have set up sockets that are connected. There are (at least) three sockets involved, one at the client and two at the server. In contrast, UDP only requires one socket at the client and one socket at the server, and there is no need (and no ability) to set up a connection.

The server code begins by creating a socket, just as before, but the second parameter is **SOCK_STREAM**, rather than **SOCK_DGRAM** as in Chapter 4. The third parameter is **IPPROTO_TCP** (zero will do, as in Chapter 3, because the default is TCP). These signify that TCP is to be used. It is common to specify zero for the third parameter, since TCP is almost invariably the only byte-stream protocol implemented in the **AF_INET** domain; however, specifying **IPPROTO_TCP** can make clear to the reader that the TCP protocol is desired.

During the socket() system call processing, the kernel scans the available domains. When it finds the AF_INET domain, it scans the list of protocols until it finds either a match to the protocol (third parameter in the socket() call), or if this is zero, it will simply take the first one it finds.

The primary difference when dealing with TCP or for that matter any connection-oriented protocol based on sockets, is the need to call listen(), after bind()ing an address to the socket. The nature and form of this "address" varies, depending on the particular connection-oriented protocol. In the case of TCP, it is actually a "TCP port number." These port numbers are just like UDP port numbers, and you can use getservbyname() to look them up, just as with UDP. TCP port numbers are independent of UDP port numbers. For example, you could have two servers, one using TCP port number 2000 and another using UDP port number 2000, and there would be no ambiguity. This is because the kernel keeps the "listen" sockets for the different protocols in separate lists. If you create your socket as SOCK_DGRAM, then the UDP list will be used; similarly, if you create it using SOCK_STREAM, the

TCP list will be used. When a packet arrives, the kernel "knows" which list to use based on the packet type, which is kept in a field in the IP header.

After creating the socket, you must use the `bind()` system call to bind an address to it. This call was discussed in Chapter 2 for UNIX domain sockets. In this chapter, we're using it for Internet domain sockets, and the details are somewhat different, as you will see shortly. For TCP and UDP, `bind()` is concerned with "addresses" consisting of two parts: a port number and an Internet Protocol (IP) address. If you specify zero for the port number, then `bind()` will choose an unused port number for you. We used this property in Chapter 3 in the server example. If you specify zero, or `INADDR_ANY`, for the IP address, this tells the kernel you will accept connections on any of the attached interfaces (more accurately, any of the network interfaces that support the Internet Protocol). Normally, servers don't care which interfaces there are, and so they specify zero for the address. The symbol `INADDR_ANY` is often used instead, as this is equivalent but clearer to readers of the code.

If, however, you want to accept connections that arrive on a particular network interface, you can specify this by setting its IP address, instead of `INADDR_ANY`, into the `s_addr` field. What if you wanted to accept connections over more than one interface, but not all of them? You would have to create a different socket for each interface you wanted to use, `bind()`ing one interface address to each of the sockets. For simplicity, you might specify the same port number for each socket, or you may choose to bind different port numbers to the different sockets. It is illegal to bind to any IP address that is not equal to any of the addresses of the attached interfaces (other than `INADDR_ANY`).

In the first example program in this chapter, we will let the system choose a port number for us. The server will print it out, and we will use that number when we run the client.

After the socket has been created and bound, you must call `listen()` to tell the kernel that the socket is a listen socket. The order must be `socket()`, `bind()`, `listen()`. The `listen()` call tells the kernel that this socket is a place where it can queue inbound connection requests that match its address. You specify this listen socket when you wish to await new connection requests, using another system call, `accept()`. Connection requests are queued by the kernel as a convenience to the programmer, up to a fixed limit, which is specifiable in the `listen()` call. Listen sockets cannot be used for sending or receiving data.

The `select()` call can be used with listen socket descriptors, along with other kinds of descriptors (such as connected sockets or special device files. When a "listen" socket "selects readable," this means that there is a connection waiting.

In the following example, we set up a listen socket:

```
unsigned char  *rd_ptr;
struct servent *getservbyname();
struct servent *serv_p, *getservbyname();

if ( (ld = socket( AF_INET, SOCK_STREAM, IPPROTO_TCP )) < 0 )   {
   perror( "INET Domain Socket" );
   exit(1);
   }
name.sin_family = AF_INET;     /* internet domain                */

/* Look up the service port number.                              */
serv_p = getservbyname("TDIH", "tcp");
if (serv_p == NULL)   {
   fprintf(stderr,
   "No service for %s defined in /etc/services.  Goodbye.\n");
   exit(1);
   }
name.sin_port = serv_p->s_port;

if ( bind (ld, &name, sizeof( name ) ) < 0 )   {
   close(ld);
   perror( "INET Domain Bind" );
   exit(2);
   }
if (listen( ld, 5 ) < 0 ) {   /* wait for a "phone call"     */
                              /* allowing 5 pending "holds"  */
   close(ld);
   perror( "INET Domain Listen" );
   exit(4);
   }
```

The listen socket only has to be created once, unless you close() it. Normally, you don't want to close the listen socket. Conceivable reasons for doing so include denying the service for a period of time. We aren't talking about cases where a parent process uses fork() to produce a child, and either the parent or the child (but not both) closes the listen socket. Child processes "inherit" open sockets, just as with files, pipes, and so on. The close() call on sockets works analogously to files: Only the last process to close() the descriptor actually closes it. Normally, when a parent produces a child process, each process will close() all descriptors except the ones it will use. Failing to do so can result in program bugs, because the socket, the associated connection (if any), and other resources remain allocated until all of the processes close() it.

The server's main service loop usually begins with an accept() call. Our example will follow this common practice. The accept() normally puts the server to sleep until a client connect()s to it (more accurately, until an incoming TCP connection request that specifies the same port number arrives over one of the computer's attached IP interfaces).

The first parameter of the `accept()` system call specifies the listen socket. The address information in the listen socket specifies which of many incoming connection requests this server cares about. There may be several listen sockets in existence at the server's computer. They are distinguished by their binding address (port number) and protocol.

The `accept()` call has two other parameters, which may both be zero if you do not care to know the client side's Internet address. The second parameter is a pointer to a `sockaddr` structure. No initialization is necessary, because it will be created and initialized by the kernel when a connection request is received.

The third parameter is a **pointer** to an `int`. This integer must be initialized to the size of the second parameter, in bytes (that is, `sizeof (struct sockaddr)`). It must be initialized before you call `accept()`, because the kernel will copy the connecting side's Internet address and port number into the second parameter, and therefore the kernel must know how much space you have reserved to hold this information.

For example, assume that `ld` is the listen socket descriptor, obtained by the foregoing code.

```
struct sockaddr addr;        /* socket name (addr)          */
int     addrlen;
addrlen = sizeof( addr );  /* need a real mem location     */

if ( (sd = accept( ld, &addr, &addrlen )) < 0 )  {
    close(ld);
    perror( "INET Domain Accept" );
    exit(5);
    }
```

When the `accept()` system call returns successfully, it returns a nonnegative integer. This integer is the descriptor of a socket (`sd`, in the preceding example). This socket is in the connected state and may be used immediately for the transfer of data. If the second and third parameters of the `accept()` system call are specified as shown, the port number being used by the client will be stored in `addr.s_port`, and the client's IP address will be stored in `addr.s_addr`. Normally, you would not be interested in the requestor's port number, since the only port number you need to know is that of the listen socket. Sometimes, however, the requestor's port number may be useful. For example, if you are troubleshooting and using a protocol analyzer on the data communications link, you need to know both port numbers in order to understand the traces. Or you may not care about the port number but be interested in the IP address of the client, perhaps for security reasons: You may wish to program your server to deny service or provide only restricted services to certain IP addresses (see also the manual pages for `inetd.sec`). There is always the possibility an intruder may masquerade as one of the "privileged service" IP addresses, so it would be unwise to base any serious security protections on such an easily circumvented scheme. This information is relatively inexpensive to obtain and thus suitable for some minimally secure applications.

Almost all Berkeley-socket TCP/IP implementations provide automatic acceptance of the connection before the user process gets a chance to run. Berkeley-derived TCP/IP implementations in the kernel build the TCP segment that accepts the connection and queues it for transmission back to the initiator even before the server process is rescheduled from its sleep. You may notice, for example when running `telnet`, that the program says "Connected to..." before the remote system begins sending you its login message. This can be contrasted with TLI (System V's "Transport Layer Interface," which is described in Chapter 6), which need not automatically respond to the connection request and thus gives the server a chance to reject it. You will also see, in Chapter 9, how X.25 can be programmed not to automatically accept connections.

Automatic acceptance of the connection from within the kernel gives quick response and can improve overall performance of your application, because the client may be able to execute in parallel while the server begins to execute. However, this also means that the other side "knows you're there" (listening on a given port) even if you don't want it to know. This has obvious implications in the case where you want only certain people to know you are there.

As an aside, if your `connect()` system call fails for any reason and you wish to provide a retry at a later time, be sure to `close()` the socket and recreate it. You are not permitted to reuse the socket for a new connection.

The example shown here passes two addresses in the second and third parameter of the `accept()` system call. The second parameter contains the address of a `struct sockaddr`. The third parameter contains the address of an `int` containing `sizeof (struct sockaddr)` (or, more properly, `sockaddr_in` see Chapter 3). The kernel returns in these (respectively) the address (IP address and TCP port number) of the requestor, and a length. You can also obtain this information using the `getpeername()` call.[1] Since this information will be the same for the duration of the connection, it is more efficient to obtain it with the same system call that first establishes the connection.

Digressing for a moment to contrast with UDP, notice that the `getpeername()` system call would not be very useful with UDP, since the information could change

---

1. `getpeername()` returns address information on the peer socket. `getsockname()` returns address information on the local socket. For Internet domain sockets, the address information returned by both of these system calls consists of a port number and an IP address.

from message to message. If you want the address information associated with a given sender, it's best to use the `recvfrom()` system call, so that you can get that information from the same system call.

Upon return from `accept()`, we have a connected socket. In our example, the client will send a message to the server, containing the ASCII string "Dinner is ready when the smoke alarm goes off." The server reads it into a buffer with the `read()` system call and prints it. After printing the message, the server closes the socket and exits. This causes the TCP connection to be released and resources to be restored to the system.

The TCP port number pair does not immediately become free for reuse upon being `close()`d. It is necessary for TCP to keep it around for twice the maximum lifetime of a packet in the network. This is because portions of messages, sent on this connection before it was closed, may still exist in the network. Recall that TCP doesn't really **know** when a message is lost. It guesses that if too much time has elapsed since it sent one, and no acknowledgment has been received, the message was "probably" lost. So it's possible that any message that it sent may have copies floating around in the network somewhere, perhaps because they were caught in "routing loops." Normally, the network routing protocols detect and eliminate routing loops quickly,[2] but they can exist for short periods of time.

What does this mean for you? It means you won't be able to restart the server for this period of time (unless you used the `setsockopt()` system call to set the `SO_REUSEADDR` option on the listen-socket after you created it; for a detailed description of the options which can be set in your system, see the `setsockopt()` manual page).

By keeping the port number around for a period of time after the connection is closed, TCP has a ready answer for any message that may arrive for this same port number: an RST segment, which is TCP-ese for "This connection is aborted." It doesn't matter whether the sender still has the connection open or not; if it doesn't, no harm is done, and if it does, then this error condition is immediately corrected (assuming that the RST segment makes it back to the other side). If it doesn't, no harm is done then, either. The sender may retransmit a few times, with the same result each time. If any of the RST responses arrive, the sender will close the connection. If none arrive, then the connection will be closed because of the timeout mechanism.

TCP has a built-in "graceful close" mechanism, which means that when you close your end, any data that is still in transit to the other end will still flow through to the other side. This is in contrast to the "abrupt close" (sometimes also called "abortive close," or "graceless close"), which means that if either side decides to abort the

---

2. An Internet Control Message Protocol (ICMP) message is generated by some implementations; this is how `traceroute` can be used to trace a path through a network.

connection, any data in transit can be dropped. If your process is aborted for any reason, the TCP connection will be aborted (abortive close), but if you call `close()` on an open socket descriptor, you get a graceful close. If you want an abortive close, set the **SO_LINGER** option with `setsockopt()`; set the "linger time" to zero, then close the socket.

We show now the first example of the "server" code from Chapter 3. The salient differences from the UDP code in Chapter 4 shown in **bold** type.

5.2   A TCP Server

```
    < #include's, #define's, externs, function def'ns >
main( argc, argv )
char *argv[]
{
    int   rc;               /* system call return code        */
    int   sd, ld;           /* server/listen socket descriptors */
    . . .
    struct  sockaddr  addr;      /* client's IP addr & port    */
    addrlen = sizeof( addr );    /* need a real mem location   */
    if ( (ld = socket( AF_INET, SOCK_STREAM, IPPROTO_TCP )) < 0){
        perror( "INET Domain Socket" );
        exit(1);
    }
      . . .
    bind( ld, &name, sizeof( name ) ) ...
      . . .
    if ( listen( ld, 5 ) < 0 ) {   /* wait for a "phone call"    */
                                   /* allowing 5 pending "holds" */
        close(ld);
        perror( "INET Domain Listen" );
        exit(4);
    }
```

The `accept()` is the server side's analog to the `connect()` call. Both produce a connection-oriented socket in the connected state, ready for the transfer of data. The `accept()` call takes a listen socket as one of its parameters, and it normally blocks the caller until a client connects to the address that was bound to the listen socket. It returns immediately if a connection request is already waiting. If the listen socket has been put in the **non blocking** state (`ioctl(2)` and `fcntl(2)` can be used for this purpose), then the caller will not be blocked; `accept()` will return immediately with either a connected socket (just as it does in the blocking case) or -1, with `errno` set to **EWOULDBLOCK**.

```
    while (1)                    /* answer "phone calls"                */
    {
       if ( (sd = accept( ld, &addr, &addrlen )) < 0 ) {
          close(ld);
          perror( "INET Domain Accept" );
          exit(5);
          }
    ...
```

TCP also differs from UDP in that once a TCP socket is connected, it remains bound to the same addresses (local port, foreign port, local IP address, foreign IP address). With UDP, there is a "local address" part but no fixed "foreign" address part.

We illustrate this in the following example.

```
/*
** This example tries to find the requestor's official host name
** in the hosts file. If found, its name is printed.
** We could equally well have taken some other action if the
** lookup failed, such as closing the socket (sd) and
** continuing the main service loop.
*/
    hp = gethostbyaddr(&ptr->sin_addr, sizeof(struct in_addr),
         AF_INET);
    if (hp  != NULL ) {
       printf("\tFrom host: %s\n\tWith aliases: ", hp->h_name );
       while ( *hp->h_aliases )
          printf("\n\t\t\t%s", *hp->h_aliases++ );
       printf("\n\n");
       } else {
          perror("\n\tgethostbyaddr failed" );
          printf("errno is %d\n\n", errno );
    }
```

We're now at the point in the code where we have a connected socket. We can use it to send or receive data. Since we're looking at the server now, and this particular server doesn't do anything before the client sends it a message, we need to wait for the message. We can use read(), we can use recv(), or we can even use recvfrom(). That's not to say these are all identical, just that we have our choice in this situation. We'll use read() because it's the most familiar to most readers.

```
    do {
       if ( (nbytes = read( sd, buf, sizeof (buf) )) < 0 ) {
          close(sd);
          perror( "INET Domain Read" );
          exit(6);
```

```
        } else if (nbytes == 0)
          printf("\nClosing connection...\n\n" );
      else
          printf("\nReceived: %s\n", buf);
    } while (nbytes != 0);

  close(sd);              /* close the service descriptor      */
```

This server services all requestors. By remaining in the loop, reading message data from the client, we consume all the data the other side has sent. When the connection is closed (from the other end), TCP takes care of shepherding the data to the server end; this is its "graceful close" feature. Execution continues in the main service loop (while(1)) and we wait for a new connection in the accept() system call. This continues for the process's notion of "forever" (that is, until the server is aborted or the system crashes or is shut down).

The client side is very similar to the UDP example shown in the previous chapter, except that the socket is created as **SOCK_STREAM** (rather than **SOCK_DGRAM**) and uses protocol **IPPROTO_TCP**. It converts a host name to an IP address via gethostbyname(), copies the address bytes to the name (a sockaddr structure), then attempts to connect() to it. The port number is taken from argv[2]. The connect() will fail if there is no listen socket at the specified host (or if that host is down or the network is broken). If connect() returns an error, examine errno. **ENETUNREACH** means that the IP level can't reach the specified destination network. **EHOSTUNREACH** means it can't reach the specified host; in some implementations, these mean essentially the same thing. Check the routing level tables, and make sure that there is a valid route to the destination host. **ECONNTIMEDOUT** can mean that there is a valid route to the destination, but its notion of a route back to you is incorrect (for instance, it sends back to you all packets destined to a gateway that is down).[3] **ECONNREFUSED** means the net is up and the remote node is responding, the routes in each direction are working, but either there is no listen socket with that port number or the pending queue of connections exceeds the limit specified in the listen() system call (the backlog parameter).

The first example of the client program is listed completely in Section 5.7.

---

3. If the nodes are running a reasonable gateway information protocol, such as /etc/gated, this sort of problem, if it occurs, should not persist more than a few minutes.

5.3   A TCP Client

```
/* vcclient1.c -- TCP client     */
    ...
#define DATA "Dinner is ready when the smoke alarm goes off.\n"
main( argc, argv )
char *argv[];
{
    struct sockaddr_in  name;
    struct hostent      *hptr, *gethostbyname();
    int     sd;
    if ( (sd = socket( AF_INET, SOCK_STREAM, IPPROTO_TCP ) ) < 0 ) {
        perror( argv[0] );
        exit(1);
        }
    ...
    if ( connect( sd, &name, sizeof name ) < 0 ) {
        close(sd);
        perror( argv[0] );
        exit(2);
        }
```

At this point, sd is a connected socket, ready to send data to the server at the IP address in name. The server was waiting for a connection request in the accept() system call. Now we send data to the socket created by the accept() system call on the server.

```
    write( sd, DATA, sizeof DATA );
    close( sd );
}
```

5.4   TCP "This Day in History"

Now, let's move on to our "This Day in History" example and recode it to use TCP.

As in the "Dinner" example, we create a SOCK_STREAM socket, which will specify TCP. We call getserv(), which was introduced in the previous chapter; it is the same, but the "protocol" parameter with which we will be calling it will be tcp in this chapter.

The server specifies INADDR_ANY in the IP address field, meaning the "wild card" address. The IP address and port number comprise the address information that is bound to the socket via the bind() system call. The server calls listen() to signify that this is a listen socket, and then the program goes to sleep until a connection comes in. This is inside a "forever" loop, so this daemon will accept connections as long as it's running.

When a remote machine requests a connection, the server daemon wakes up from the `accept()` system call, and `sd` will contain the descriptor for the socket that represents the connection.

From here, the rest of the daemon is the same as the UDP version. A message is read and decoded (only one request type is implemented), and a "history snippet" is looked up from the TDIH file and returned to the sender. Upon return from `proc_cmnd()`, the daemon will attempt to read another message, but our client sends only the one message. The chances are that the daemon will reach the second `read()` system call before the "history snippet" message has arrived at the remote. Although the result is the same either way, it is poor practice to code in such a way that you depend upon this. If the `read()` is reached before the connection dies, the process will be awakened and zero length returned. If the connection is closed before the `recv()` call is executed, then the `recv()` call will return zero length, with the same result. We `close()` our socket descriptor (to free the descriptor-to-socket mapping slot as well as the resources used by the connection) and continue, whereupon we repeat the `accept()` system call. As with the "Dinner" example, the server loops, serving all requestors until it is aborted or the system goes down. If there happens to bc a connection request already waiting for it, the server will return almost immediately with a new connection socket in `sd`. Otherwise, we must wait until somebody wants to connect to us. If your application is such that you don't want it to wait, then either put the listen socket in nonblocking mode before calling `accept()` or else use `select()`.

The data structures are shown in Section 5.8. The salient differences in a TCP-based server are shown below in **bold** type.

```
/* vcserver2.c -- TCP server */
   ...
#include "vcdata.h"
   ...
main( argc, argv )
char *argv[];
{
    int    ld, sd;         /* listen & service socket descriptors */
    ...
    struct vccmnd  cmnd;
    struct vcreply reply;
    ...
    if ( (ld = socket( AF_INET, SOCK_STREAM, IPPROTO_TCP )...
    ...    bind ( ld, &name, sizeof( name ) ...
    ...    listen( ld, ...
    /*
      Main execution loop.
    */
```

```
   while (1)                /* answer "phone calls"              */
   {
      addrlen = sizeof( addr);
   ...   sd = accept( ld, &addr, &addrlen ) ...
   do  {
      if ( (nbytes = recv( sd, &cmnd, sizeof (cmnd),0)) < 0)   {
   ...
         close(sd);
         break;
      } else if (nbytes > 0 )
         proc_cmnd(sd, &cmnd, &from, fromlen);
      } while (nbytes != 0);
   }
   /* NOTREACHED                                                 */
}

   ...
```

Now, we turn our attention to the TDIH client. As in our "Dinner" example, we need to create a socket, look up a service port number and a destination IP address, place that information in a sockaddr structure, and issue the connect() system call. If there is a daemon waiting for our connection, our call will be answered, and connect() will return zero.

As with our UDP example, we set up a message and send it. With UDP, we used sendto(), but with TCP we'll use send(), because the address information is already set, the connection having been established. Similarly, instead of using recvfrom() as with UDP, we use recv().

The rest of the code is without the lost-packet-recovery code that we needed when using UDP. This is because TCP already provides considerable lost-packet recovery. We check the response and print either an error message or the "history snippet," according to what we received. As with UDP, it is a good idea to use ntohl() and htonl() when decoding and coding data that may have different representations on different machines (the choice of transport protocol has nothing to do with the data format and representation).

5.5   Using Fixed-Size Messages with TCP

There is a very important difference between the way TCP and UDP treat the data they carry; this difference has nothing to do with the fact that TCP is connection-oriented and UDP is connectionless. UDP is a **message-oriented** transport, which means that all the data that is passed in a send() or sendto() will be copied as a **single unit** into the corresponding recv() or recvfrom() buffer, **with message boundaries preserved**. If the recv(), read(), or recvfrom() specifies a buffer length which is less than the message size, the first part of the message will be copied into the user's buffer, but the rest will be discarded.

TCP, on the other hand, provides a **byte-stream** type of service, much like files in UNIX. As with files, any structure in the data that TCP is carrying is entirely irrelevant to TCP. However, with TCP, unlike files, it is possible to have your "receive" buffer filled with less data than you asked for, even if there is more data to come. With TCP, you get however much has arrived now. If there's no data now, normally (unless the socket is in nonblocking mode) you will wait until at least one byte has arrived. If there's more data, you can ask for it later. It will be there, waiting for you to ask for it.

For example, suppose there are two communicating programs, **A** and **B**. **A** sends 100 bytes to **B** as a datagram (UDP), and assume no data is lost in transit. Suppose **B** calls `recv()`, specifying 50 bytes (this discussion also applies if `recvmsg()` or `recvfrom()` is called). When this 100-byte message arrives, the first 50 bytes of the message that **A** sent will appear in **B**'s buffer, and the rest will be discarded. If **B** tries to read more, it will wait forever (Simon didn't say **A** sent more data, did he?).

On the other hand, if there is a TCP connection between **A** and **B**, **A** might send only 50 bytes per write, and **B** must count the bytes received in each read inside a loop such as a `while` loop until all 100 bytes are received.

Besides message boundaries, TCP and UDP differ in their control of the flow of data. UDP provides no control of data flow. What happens if **A** can send data faster than **B** can read it? **B** has a certain amount of buffering available to it, but when that is used up, there is no way for the UDPs on either side to warn each other of this flow control problem. The sending side will just keep sending, and the receiving side will either queue the data, if there is buffer memory available, or drop it. This is why it is advisable to code your UDP retry loops, if you have any, so that the retries back off a little bit more each time. After all, if **B** has already queued more data than it can handle, it doesn't make much sense for **A** to keep sending more, does it? There are exceptions. You should use good judgment when you code these loops, because otherwise you can adversely affect the network as well as both the sending and the receiving sides.

Now let's consider the foregoing situation, but this time suppose we use TCP. **A** sends 100 bytes, and **B** calls `recv()` specifying 50 bytes. As above, the first 50 bytes of **A**'s buffer will appear in **B**'s buffer. Now, suppose **B** calls `recv()` again, specifying another 50 bytes. Now, the second half of **A**'s buffer data will appear in **B**'s buffer. The rest of the data isn't lost. It just waits for the program to get around to reading it.

What happens if **A** can send data faster than **B** can read it? **B** has a certain amount of buffering available to it, but, when that is used up, then **B**'s TCP will tell **A**'s TCP to stop sending. TCP has flow control; UDP has none. TCP can and does decide how much data to send and when to send it. Other than presenting the data for transmission, the user has little or no control over when the data is sent. TCP has some very sophisticated algorithms for balancing its responsibility to the network (not consuming too much of the overall bandwidth at times when bandwidth is in short supply) with the user's desire to get the job done quickly. If you want more details, you should read *Internetworking with TCP/IP, Volume I* (Second Edition) by Douglas Comer, specifically, Chapter 12. Referring again to our "A sending data to **B**" example earlier, **A** might send, say, 3000 bytes, but **A**'s TCP might send this in smaller amounts, say, two segments of 1460 bytes each, wait for an acknowledgment, and then 80 bytes. **B**'s `recv()` might specify 2000 bytes, but **B**'s TCP might deliver only 1460 on the first `recv()`. **There is no relationship whatsoever between how many bytes you send and how many bytes are delivered to the buffer of any given `recv()` call.** Moreover, let's consider what happens if the `recv()` specifies **too much** data. Suppose two messages happen to arrive back-to-back and that your `recv()` specifies a length that is larger than the first message. In this case, the first `recv()` will deliver the first message and at least part of the second to the buffer. In short, it is quite dangerous to assume that TCP will preserve the boundaries of the messages you send. In a request–reply type of application protocol, the fact that the messages are so short that they never have to be fragmented by IP or segmented by TCP will work most of the time, but should not be relied upon.

In other words, *with TCP, you **don't** have to **worry about mismatches in the speeds** of producing and consuming data in either direction. You do, however, have to **provide your own message-boundary preservation mechanism** (that is, if your application protocol deals with messages).*

Let's upgrade our TDIH examples to handle these problems. We can get around the message-boundary problem by providing our own convention that clients' and servers' messages always begin with an integer containing the length of the message. This integer specifies the length of the entire message, including the integer itself. We could choose any sized integer we want, but, for reasons that will be explained later, we choose a full 4-byte `int`. We code our `recv()` inside a loop that continues until we've received a complete message. We have to have a pointer that is initialized to the start of our buffer (`cmnd`). This pointer will be incremented with each chunk of the message that we get. We have to keep decrementing the length-to-be-received parameter, in order to avoid reading part of any subsequent message. Although our example sends only one message in each direction, in a more realistic application you would need to deal with multiple messages, so we show you how. In cases where it can't happen, then you can save the loop overhead. If you have the case where most of the messages that are exchanged are of a fixed size, with a few message types that are larger, then you might wish to code all your `recv()`s to specify a length of the smallest message type. Then, check the message type (the type must be included in the "chunk" of data you've just read). If its type says all of the message has been read, then you're done, and you've only taken one system call to do it.[4] If not, then you already have the message length (from the first portion of the message), so you can read the rest of it.

For example:

```
/* Stay in this loop until we get a complete message.        */
    total_read = 0;
    rd_ptr = (unsigned char *) &cmnd;
    while (1)
      {
      nbytes = recv( sd, rd_ptr, sizeof (cmnd) - total_read, 0);
      if (nbytes <= 0) {
          close(sd);
          break;
          /* Breaking out of this loop gets
          ** us to the outer loop, where we will
          ** wait for the next connection.              */
      }
      total_read += nbytes; rd_ptr += nbytes;
      if (total_read < sizeof(int)) continue;
      if (total_read >= ntohl(cmnd.vccmd_len)) break;
    }
```

We exit the loop when either an error is returned, zero length is returned (signifying the connection was aborted), or we have received the complete message.

The client needs the same surgery when reading the reply.

Also worth noting is the use of gethostbyname() with the Domain Name Service. DNS is capable of telling you when a node has multiple IP addresses, such as when there are multiple LAN (or other type of network interface) cards. To handle this, the hostent structure defines a pointer to the h_addr_list[] array. This is a null-terminated list. If there is only one IP address for the host, then h_addr_list[0] will contain its address, and h_addr_list[1] == 0. For backwards compatibility to older hostent interface definitions, netdb.h contains #define h_addr h_addr_list[0]. You can use this fact for creating higher-reliability clients. If you can't connect to h_addr_list[0], then try h_addr_list[1], and so on, until you get to the end of the list.

---

4. If the message is short enough, that is. If it's longer than the Maximum Transmission Unit (MTU) size for any of the links over which it's traveled, then it will have been fragmented into two or more smaller messages. Fragmented messages are rarely, if ever, reassembled before arriving at their destination, so if your smallest message is larger than typical MTU sizes for the links in your network, the attempt to read the whole message will more often take more than one system call. Typical MTU sizes vary widely for Wide Area Network links, but they are typically 1460 bytes for user data on Ethernets (1500 bytes of user data, less a minimum of 40 bytes of TCP/IP header), and 1457 bytes for user data on IEEE 802.3 links.

5.6   TCP Server Listing

```c
/* vcserver1.c -- TCP server                                  */
#include <stdio.h>
#include <fcntl.h>
#include <sys/types.h>
#include <sys/socket.h>
#include <netinet/in.h>
#include <netdb.h>
#include "vcdata.h"
extern int errno;

main( argc, argv )
char *argv[];
{
    /*      data declarations                                 */
    int     ld, addrlen, sd;
    struct sockaddr name;
    struct sockaddr_in *ptr;
    struct hostent *hp;
    char    buf[80];

    if ( (ld = socket( AF_INET, SOCK_STREAM, IPPROTO_TCP )) < 0 ) {
        perror( "INET Domain Socket" );
        exit(1);
        }
    name.sin_family      = AF_INET;
    name.sin_port        = 0;
    name.sin_addr.s_addr = INADDR_ANY;

    if ( bind( ld, &name, sizeof( name ) ) < 0 )  {
        close(ld);
        perror( "INET Domain Bind" );
        exit(2);
        }
    addrlen = sizeof( addr );
    if ( (rc = getsockname( ld, &addr, &addrlen )) < 0 ) {
        close(ld);
        printf("\ngetsockname return code = %d\n", rc);
        perror("INET Domain getsockname" );
        exit(3);
        }
    ptr = (struct sockaddr_in *) &addr;
    printf( "\n\n\tSocket has port number: %d\n\n", ptr->sin_port);
    fflush(stdout);
```

```
if ( listen( ld, 5 ) < 0 )   {
   close(ld);
   perror( "INET Domain Listen" );
   exit(4);
   }
while (1)
{
   addrlen = sizeof( addr );
   if ( (sd = accept( ld, &addr, &addrlen )) < 0 )   {
      close(ld);
      perror( "INET Domain Accept" );
      exit(5);
      }
   ptr = (struct sockaddr_in *) &addr;
   printf("\n\n\tCalling socket from host %s has port number:
         %d\n\n", inet_ntoa( ptr->sin_addr ),ptr->sin_port );
   fflush(stdout);
   /*
   ** This example tries to find the requestor's official host
   ** name in the hosts file.  If found, its name is printed.
   ** We could equally well have taken some other action if the
   ** lookup fails, such as closing the socket (sd) and
   ** continuing the main service loop.
   */
   hp = gethostbyaddr(&ptr->sin_addr,sizeof(struct in_addr),
         AF_INET);
   if (hp  != NULL ) {
      printf("\tFrom host: %s\n\tWith aliases: ", hp->h_name );
      while ( *hp->h_aliases )
         printf( "\n\t\t\t%s", *hp->h_aliases++ );
      printf("\n\n" );
   } else {
      perror("\n\tgethostbyaddr failed" );
      printf("errno is %d\n\n", errno );
   }

   fflush(stdout);
   do {
      if ( (nbytes = read( sd, buf, sizeof (buf) ) ) ) < 0 )   {
         close(sd);
         perror( "INET Domain Read" );
         exit(6);
      } else if (nbytes == 0)
         printf("\nClosing connection...\n\n" );
```

```
        else  printf("\nReceived: %s\n", buf );
    } while (nbytes != 0);

    close(sd);
}
}
```

5.7   TCP Client Listing

```
/* vcclient1.c -- TCP client                                 */
#include <stdio.h>
#include <sys/types.h>
#include <sys/socket.h>
#include <netinet/in.h> /*sockaddr_in: Internet socket address */
#include <netdb.h>        /* /etc/hosts entry (hostent)         */
#define DATA "Dinner is ready when the smoke alarm goes off. \n"
main( argc, argv )        /* argument count, argument vector    */
char *argv[];
{
    struct sockaddr_in name;   /*Internet socket name (addr)    */
    struct hostent *hptr, *gethostbyname();   /* 3N lib func    */
    int    sd;                     /* socket descriptor          */
    if ( (sd = socket( AF_INET, SOCK_STREAM, IPPROTO_TCP )) < 0 ) {
        perror( argv[0] );
        exit(1);
        }
    name.sin_family = AF_INET;            /* internet domain    */
    name.sin_port  = atoi(argv [2]);    /* "advertised" port   */
    hptr = gethostbyname( argv[1] );    /* "advertised" host   */
    bcopy( hptr->h_addr, &name.sin_addr.s_addr, hptr->h_length );
    if ( connect( sd, &name, sizeof name ) < 0 )  {
        close(sd);
        perror( argv[0] );
        exit(2);
        }
    write( sd, DATA, sizeof DATA );
    close( sd );
}
```

5.8   Data Structures for "This Day in History" Client–Server Pair

```
#define MSGSIZE 256

/*
```

```
 * Define Service Types
 */

#define REQUEST_TDIH 0          /* This Day In History           */
/*
 * Define Reply Status values
 */
#define REPLY_OK 0
#define REPLY_GARBAGE -1        /* Request code was unrecognized */
#define REPLY_NOSUCHFILE -2     /* No such file available for
                                   request                       */
/*
 * Structure of TCP Server Command Message.
 */
struct vccmnd {
   int vccmd_len;
   int vccmd_type;
   };

struct vcreply {
   int vcrply_len;
   int vcreply_status;
   int vcreply_lnth;
   char vcreply_msg[MSGSIZE];
   };

#define TDIH "TDIH"
#define TDIH_PROTO "tcp"
#define DEFAULT_PORT 51000
```

5.9   TCP "This Day in History" Server

```
/* vcserver3.c -- TCP server
 * This is the TCP version of the "This Day In History"
 * client-server pair for Chapter 4.
 */

#include <stdio.h>
#include <fcntl.h>
#include <sys/types.h>
#include <sys/socket.h>
#include <netinet/in.h>   /* sockaddr_in Internet socket addr  */
#include <netdb.h>        /* /etc/hosts table entries          */
#include <time.h>
#include "vcdata2.h"
/*
```

```
 * Global Variables.
 */
FILE *TODAYFILE = NULL;   /* FILE ptr for "This Day In History"
                            data                                */
char *months[] = {
      "Jan",
      "Feb",
      "Mar",
      "Apr",
      "May",
      "Jun",
      "Jul",
      "Aug",
      "Sep",
      "Oct",
      "Nov",
      "Dec",
};

/*
 * Extern Variables.
 */
extern int  errno;
extern char *sys_errlist[];
extern int  sys_nerr;

/*
 * Extern procedures
 */
char *getenv();

main( argc, argv )           /* argument count, argument vector    */
int    argc;
char *argv[];
{
   int ld;              /* "listen" socket descriptor           */
   int sd;              /* Current TCP connection skt descr     */
   int nbytes;          /* read nbytes req                      */
   int port;
   int addrlen;
   int total_read;
   char    *cptr;
   unsigned char * rd_ptr;
   struct sockaddr_in name;   /* Internet socket name (addr)    */
   struct sockaddr_in *ptr;   /* pointer to get port number     */
```

```
struct sockaddr_in addr, from;    /* socket name (addr)       */
struct hostent *hp, *gethostbyaddr();
struct vccmnd cmnd;
struct vcreply reply;
if((ld = socket( AF_INET, SOCK_STREAM, IPPROTO_TCP )) < 0 )  {
   perror( "INET Domain Socket" );
   exit(1);
   }
if ((cptr = getenv("TDIH")) == NULL) {
   cptr = "TDIH";
}
/* Open "This Day In History" database                        */
TODAYFILE = fopen (cptr, "r");
name.sin_family = AF_INET;     /* internet domain            */
/*
** Look up the service port number.
*/
name.sin_port   = getserv(TDIH, TDIH_PROTO);

if ( bind( ld, &name, sizeof( name ) ) < 0 )  {
   close(ld);
   perror( "INET Domain Bind" );
   exit(2);
   }
if ( listen( ld, 5 ) < 0 ){   /* wait for a "phone call"    */
                              /* allowing 5 pending "holds" */
   close(ld);
   perror( "INET Domain Listen" );
   exit(4);
   }

/*
Main execution loop.                                       |
*/
while (1)  {
   /* "ld" is our "listen socket".  If accept() returns a non-
    * negative value, then it is a socket descriptor for an
    * already-accepted connection.  We can read and/or write
    * data on it.
    */
   if ( (sd = accept( ld, 0, 0 )) < 0 )  {
      close(ld);
      perror( "INET Domain Accept" );
      exit(5);
      }
```

```
      do
      {
         /*
         ** Stay in this loop until we've got a complete message.
         */
         total_read = 0;
         rd_ptr = (unsigned char *) &cmnd;
         while (1) {
             nbytes = recv( sd, rd_ptr, sizeof(cmnd) - total_read,
                                   0);
             if (nbytes <= 0)   {
/*
** The remote end has closed the connection, or perhaps our own
** TCP has been unable to get back acknowledgements for the data
** in the message that proc_cmnd() has sent back, in a previous
** iteration thru this loop.  Either way, this connection is
** unusable, so we must close() the descriptor, to free up its
** resources.  If we did not, then the next incoming connection
** we receive will take up a new slot in the descriptor-to-skt
** mapping table (kept in the u-area, meaning, available to the
** kernel but not to us). Eventually, if this keeps up, then we
** will have used up all available slots in this table.  This
** is the same limit on total number of open files—the total
** number of open files plus open sockets can't be more than a
** certain constant, which is implementation-specific.  At any
** rate, by closing our end, we free up that slot, and avoid
** the problem entirely.                                      */
                 close(sd);
                 break;
/* Breaking out of this loop gets us to the outer loop, where
** we will wait for the next connection.
*/
             }
             total_read += nbytes;
             rd_ptr += nbytes;
             if (total_read < sizeof(int)) continue;
             if (total_read >= ntohl(cmnd.vccmd_len)) break;
         }
         if (nbytes > 0)
             proc_cmnd(sd, &cmnd, &from);
      } while (nbytes > 0);
   }  /* while(1) loop, answering phone calls                  */
   /* NOTREACHED                                               */
}
```

```
proc_cmnd(sd, cmnd, from)
int     sd;
struct vccmnd *cmnd;
     struct sockaddr_in *from;
{
   int lnth, i, k, error;
   struct vcreply reply;

#ifdef DEBUG
   printf( "From port: %d\n", from->sin_port );
   printf("From host: %s\n",inet_ntoa(from->sin_addr.s_addr));
   fflush(stdout);
#endif DEBUG
   switch (ntohl(cmnd->vccmd_type)) {
/*
   * REQUEST_TDIH: Reqest "This Day In History" entry.
   * Read next entry in the file.  If it starts with
   * today's month and month-day number, use it.  If not,
   * read the next entry, and wrap around the file if
   * necessary. You can optimize this lookup if you want to.
   * In this simple example, we do not check to see
   * whether we've read into "tomorrow's" entries.  We
   * just keep reading until we reach either the proper
   * entry or EOF. In the case we hit EOF, we rewind the
   * file and start over. This is EXTREMELY inefficient,
   * especially in two cases: when we first start up, on,
   * say, Dec.31st (meaning we read through the whole
   * file) and when we read an entry which is past
   * today's date, meaning this version reads through to
   * the EOF, rewinds, starts reading from Jan 1st,
   * checking and skipping entries until it gets to
   * "today's entry" again.
   */
   case REQUEST_TDIH:
      if (TODAYFILE == NULL)
         reply.vcreply_status = htonl(REPLY_NOSUCHFILE);
      else {
         char datebuf[40], *ptr;
         int slnth;
         long clock;
         struct tm *tm;

         clock = time((long *) 0);
         tm = localtime(&clock);
         sprintf(datebuf,"%s %2d",months[tm->tm_mon],
```

```
                    tm->tm_mday);
              slnth = strlen(datebuf);

              reply.vcreply_status = htonl(REPLY_OK);
              while (1) {
                 clearerr(TODAYFILE);
                 ptr = fgets(reply.vcreply_msg, MSGSIZE,
                    TODAYFILE);
                 if (ferror(TODAYFILE) != 0) {
                    reply.vcreply_status = htonl(errno);
                    if ((errno > 0) && (errno < sys_nerr))
                       strncpy(reply.vcreply_msg,
                          sys_errlist[errno], MSGSIZE);
                    else reply.vcreply_msg[0] = '\0';
                    break;
                 }
                 if (feof(TODAYFILE) != 0) {
                    fseek(TODAYFILE, 0L, 0);
                    continue;
                    }
                 /*
                  * Does this line start with today's date?
                  */
                 if(strncmp(datebuf,reply.vcreply_msg,slnth)==0)
                    break;
                 else {
              #ifdef DEBUG
                    printf("%s\n", reply.vcreply_msg);
                    fflush(stdout);
              #endif DEBUG
                    continue;
                    }
              }
           }
        break;
     default:
        reply.vcreply_status = htonl(REPLY_GARBAGE);
   }
   /*
    * Send the reply.
    * The structure "from" already has the IP address and
    * the port of the client process (this was set in the
    * recvfrom() system call, which we used to read
    * the command).
```

```
    */

    #ifdef DEBUG
        printf( "Sending to port: %d\n", from->sin_port );
        printf( "to host: %s\n",inet_ntoa(&from->sin_addr.s_addr));
        fflush(stdout);
    #endif DEBUG

    /* We send the reply, and rely on TCP to shepherd the data
     * thru the network.  If TCP can't get it thru, we'll take
     * that as meaning the network is broken, and we do not
     * supply any further recovery.
     */
    reply.vcrply_len = ntohl(sizeof(struct vcreply));
    send(sd, &reply, sizeof (struct vcreply), 0);
}
getserv(service, protocol)
char *service, *protocol;
{
    struct servent *getservbyname();
    struct servent *serv_p = getservbyname(service, protocol);

    if (serv_p == NULL)  {
        printf("Could not find %s/%s in /etc/services file.\n",
                service, protocol);
        printf("Defaulting to %d.\n", DEFAULT_PORT);
        return (DEFAULT_PORT);
    }
    #ifdef DEBUG
        printf("getservbyname rtns name %s port %d proto %s\n",
                serv_p->s_name, serv_p->s_port, serv_p->s_proto);
    #endif DEBUG
    return(serv_p->s_port);
}
```

5.10 TCP "This Day in History" Client

```
/* vcclient4.c -- TCP client
 *
 * This is the TCP client version of the This Day In History
 * client-server pair.
 */
#include <stdio.h>
#include <sys/types.h>
#include <values.h>
#include <time.h>
#include <sys/socket.h>
#include <netinet/in.h> /* sockaddr_in Internet socket address */
#include <netdb.h>       /* /etc/hosts entry (hostent)         */
#include <errno.h>
#include "vcdata2.h"
/* Global Variables.                                           */
/*
 * Externs
 */
extern int errno;
extern char *sys_errlist[];
extern int sys_nerr;
struct hostent *gethostbyname();   /* 3N lib func              */
unsigned long inet_addr();         /* 3N lib func              */
/*
 * Forward declarations.
 */
void process_reply();
/*
 * Main program.
 */
main( argc, argv )      /* argument count, argument vector     */
int   argc;
char *argv[];
{
   struct sockaddr_in name;   /* Internet socket name (addr)   */
   struct vccmnd cmnd;
   struct vcreply reply;
   struct timeval tval;
   int   nbytes;              /* read nbytes req               */
   int   sd;                  /* socket descriptor             */
   int   i;
```

```
sd = client_init(argv[1], argv[0]); /* Initialize         */
/* We have our socket set up and the connection is
** established with the server.
*/
cmnd.vccmd_type = htonl(REQUEST_TDIH);
cmnd.vccmd_len  = htonl(sizeof (struct vccmnd));
if (send(sd, &cmnd, sizeof cmnd, 0) < 0){
   perror( "send failed.");
   exit(1);
   }
/* We now read the reply.  */

/*
** Stay in this loop until we've got a complete message.
*/
total_read = 0;
rd_ptr = (unsigned char *) &reply;
while (1) {
   nbytes = recv( sd, rd_ptr,
                     sizeof(struct vcreply) - total_read, 0);
   if (nbytes <= 0) {
      close(sd);
      perror(
         "INET Domain Read, connection with remote broken");
      exit(6);
      }
   total_read += nbytes;
   rd_ptr += nbytes;
   if (total_read < sizeof(int)) continue;
   if (total_read >= ntohl(reply.vcrply_len)) break;
}
/* We got an answer.  What was it?                          */
if (nbytes > 0) {
   if (ntohl(reply.vcreply_status) == REPLY_OK)
      /*Good answer. Print it                               */
      printf( "%s\n", reply.vcreply_msg);
   else if ((error = ntohl(reply.vcreply_status)) > 0) {
   /* Some error in system call on server side. Print it.   */
      printf("Server error (%d): %s\n", ntohl(error),
                            reply.vcreply_msg);
   } else
      switch (ntohl(error))  {
         case REPLY_GARBAGE:
            printf(
```

```
                            "Server did not recognize request type %d\n",
                            ntohl(cmnd.vccmd_type));
                     break;
                 case REPLY_NOSUCHFILE:
                     printf( "Server could not open data file\n");
                     break;
                 default:
                     printf(
                     "Server error: %d (don't know what this means)\n",
                         ntohl(reply.vcreply_status));
             }
     }
     close( sd );
}
/*
 * Initialize the client side.
 * Returns socket descriptor.
 */
client_init(host, mycmndname)
char *host, *mycmndname;
{
    int     sd;                    /* socket descriptor           */
    struct hostent *hptr;
    struct sockaddr_in addr;
    struct sockaddr_in *ptr;   /* pointer to get port number   */
    struct sockaddr_in name;   /* internet socket name (addr)  */

    if ( (sd = socket( AF_INET, SOCK_STREAM, IPPROTO_TCP )) < 0 )  {
        perror("");
        exit(1);
        }
    name.sin_family = AF_INET; /* internet domain              */
    if ((name.sin_addr.s_addr =(unsigned long) inet_addr(host) ) ==
            -1){
        hptr = gethostbyname( host );        /* host             */
        if (hptr == NULL) {
            printf("Cannot find %s in /etc/hosts\n", host);
            exit(7);
        } else {
    /*
    bcopy( hptr->h_addr, &name.sin_addr.s_addr, hptr->h_length );
    */
            if (hptr->h_addr_list[1] != NULL)
                memmove(&name.sin_addr.s_addr, hptr->h_addr_list[1],
```

```
                                     hptr->h_length );
              else
                 memmove(&name.sin_addr.s_addr, hptr->h_addr,
                              hptr->h_length );
              printf("addr_list[0]= %x\n",hptr->h_addr_list[0]);
              printf("addr_list[1]= %x\n",hptr->h_addr_list[1]);
         }
    }
    /*
     * Look up the service port number.
     */
    name.sin_port   = getserv(TDIH, TDIH_PROTO);
    /*
     ** Attempt to connect with the remote server.
     ** When we return from this call, the TCP
     ** connection will either have been established,
     ** or it was never established.
     */

    if ( connect( sd, &name, sizeof name ) < 0 )   {
       close(sd);
       perror( mycmndname );
       exit(2);
       }

    return(sd); /* Return socket descriptor, connection is made */
}
getserv(service, protocol)
char *service, *protocol;
{
    struct servent *getservbyname();
    struct servent *serv_p = getservbyname(service, protocol);

    if (serv_p == NULL)   {
       printf( "Could not find %s/%s in /etc/services file.\n",
                        service, protocol);
       printf( "Defaulting to %d.\n", DEFAULT_PORT );
       return (DEFAULT_PORT);
       }
    #ifdef DEBUG
       printf( "getservbyname returns s_name %s s_port %d s_proto
          %s\n", serv_p->s_name, serv_p->s_port, serv_p->s_proto);
    #endif DEBUG
    return(serv_p->s_port);
}
```

5.11 Exercises

1. We discussed in this chapter what happens when a UDP-using sender overruns a receiver's ability to keep up. Is it possible for a UDP-using sender to overrun its own transmitter (send faster than its drivers can deliver bits to the wire)? If so, what should senders and receivers do about this, if anything?

2. TCP already provides considerable recovery for lost packets. However, if the network "goes down" for more than a few minutes, and assuming there are no alternate paths through the net, TCP may abort the connection. This may not be acceptable in some situations, as in a file transfer that takes hours. You wouldn't want to restart it if the connection died after an hour, would you? How could you add recovery, without losing context, and in such a way that the client and server could resume from where they left off when the network is repaired?

3. Modify the server to handle multiple requests simultaneously. Why doesn't TCP get confused and deliver packets to the wrong process, since the child and parent will be using the same port number?

 **6**

STREAMS Programming

by Bill Rieken

6.1   Introduction

The STREAMS feature of System V Release 3 and later provides a framework to stack network protocol layers on top of each other.   Just as pipes allow application programmers to combine commands easily, STREAMS allow system programmers to build **protocol stacks** easily.   For example, a TCP/IP protocol stack can be built by opening a network device, pushing an IP module on top of the network device driver, and then pushing a TCP module on top of the IP module.   In Figure 6.1, the protocol module could be TCP/IP.   Connectionless service can be provided by pushing a UDP module on top of a different stack over the same IP module, thus allowing the IP code to be shared by two protocol stacks.

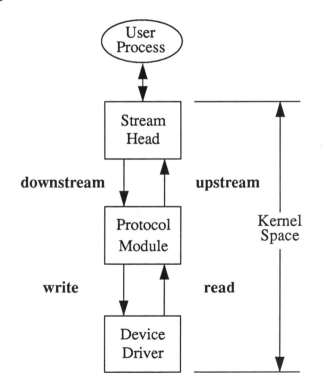

Figure 6.1   STREAMS   Modules

The device driver for a STREAMS **device** must be able to interface with a STREAMS **module** above (upstream from) it. The upstream direction flows toward the user (that is, a read system call), and the downstream direction flows toward the device (that is, a write system call). The module closest to the user is called a **stream head**, whose purpose is to move data between user space and internal messages that flow through the STREAMS modules. Protocol modules are pushed between the stream head and the device driver module. The order of pushing modules is important, as the next one will be placed on top of the last one.

Each STREAMS module consists of two **queue**s: an upstream (read) queue and a downstream (write) queue. The queues can communicate with each other when necessary. For example, the upstream queue can echo data immediately to the downstream queue. They are called queues because they can queue messages for later service processing.

Modules can be added to the top of a stack by using the **ioctl()** system call with an **I_PUSH** command. Modules can be removed by using an ioctl() with an **I_POP** command. Modules are pushed just below the stream head, and the module nearest the stream head is the one that gets popped from the stack. The code that implements a module must reside in kernel space, and it is located by searching for a character-string name in a kernel table.

Only the stream head and the device driver module are created when a STREAMS device is first opened. It is the application's responsibility to push any required modules onto the stack. Here is a sample program:

```
/* stream.c - a simple stream example                       */
#include <stropts.h>        /* I_PUSH, I_POP defs            */
#include <fcntl.h>          /* O_RDWR  def'n                 */

main()
{
        char buf[ 512 ];  int fd, count;
        if ( (fd = open( "/dev/port", O_RDWR)) == -1 )
            { perror( "/dev/port" ); exit( 1 ); }

        if ( ioctl( fd, I_PUSH, "protocol") == -1 )
            { perror( "/dev/port" ); exit( 2 ); }

        while( (count = read( fd, buf, 512) ) > 0 )
            if(write( fd, buf, count ) != count )
            { perror( "/dev/port" ); exit( 3 ); }

        if ( ioctl( fd, I_POP, 0 ) == -1 )
            { perror( "/dev/port" ); exit( 2 ); }
}
```

This sample program shows the basic system calls used on STREAMS devices. Notice that you can `read()` and `write()` to a STREAMS device. Pipes that are implemented with STREAMS technology are duplex pipes. The `ioctl()` system calls will fail if `/dev/port` is not a STREAMS device. The "protocol" module is pushed and popped just below the stream head. The module is found by searching a kernel table for a character string match on the name "protocol". The header file `stropts.h` and the `I_PUSH` and `I_POP` commands are documented in the **STREAMIO(7)** manual page.

Other STREAMIO `ioctl()` commands are:

`I_FLUSH`	Flush read and write queues
`I_SETSIG`	Request asynchronous **SIGPOLL** signal
`I_GETSIG`	Get **SIGPOLL** event bitmask setting
`I_LOOK`	Get name of top module just under stream head
`I_FIND`	See if module name is in a protocol stack
`I_PEEK`	Get first message on read queue and leave on queue
`I_SRDOPT`	Set read mode (**byte-stream** or **message mode**)
`I_GRDOPT`	Get read mode setting
`I_NREAD`	Counts the number of data bytes in first message
`I_STR`	Send an **`ioctl()` message** downstream to device driver
`I_SENDFD`	Send a file descriptor to other end of a stream pipe
`I_RECVFD`	Receive file descriptor from other end of a stream pipe
`I_LINK`	Connect two streams via a **multiplexing driver**
`I_UNLINK`	Disconnect two `I_LINK`ed streams

We will look at an example that sets up a TCP/IP protocol stack. The IP module must **multiplex** among TCP and UDP stacks above it, and it must also multiplex among Ethernet, token-ring, and X.25 device drivers below it. The TCP and UDP stacks have the same major device number with different minor device numbers. Each time an upper stack (TCP or UDP) is opened, a separate stream head is created for that process. This is why multiplexing "modules" must actually be device drivers (modules do not have stream heads), and they are connected to lower STREAMS by using the **`I_LINK`** `ioctl()` command instead of `I_PUSH`. Descriptors for the lower devices cannot be used after they have been `I_LINK`ed below a multiplexing (pseudo) driver module. Also, a module may not be `I_LINK`ed below more than one multiplexor.

An example configuration is diagrammed in Figure 6.2.

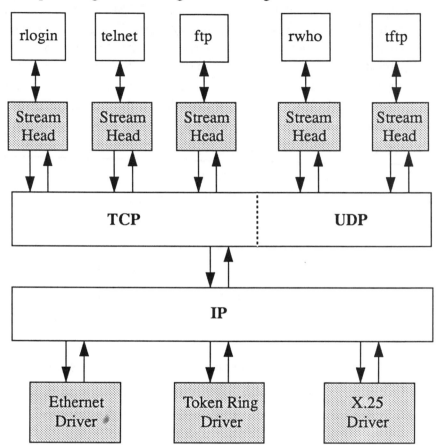

Figure 6.2   STREAMS TCP/IP Protocol Stack

The following code sets up the configuration shown in Figure 6.2.

```
/*  strmux.c - a STREAMS multiplexor example                    */
#include <fcntl.h>              /* O_RDWR definition             */
#include <stropts.h>            /* I_LINK definition             */
main()
{
    int  fd_ip, fd_ether, fd_token, fd_x25, fd_tcp, fd_tp4,
         mx_ip, mx_ether, mx_token, mx_x25, mx_tcp, mx_tp4;
    if ((fd_ether = open( "/dev/ether", O_RDWR )) == -1 )
      { perror("can't open /dev/ether");  exit(1); }
    if ((fd_ip    = open( "/dev/ip", O_RDWR )) == -1 )
      { perror("can't open /dev/ip");  exit(2); }
```

```
  if ((mx_ether = ioctl (fd_ip, I_LINK, fd_ether))  == -1 )
      { perror("can't LINK ether under ip");  exit(3); }
  if ((fd_token = open( "/dev/token", O_RDWR )) == -1 )
      { perror("can't open /dev/token");  exit(4); }
  if ((mx_token = ioctl (fd_ip, I_LINK, fd_token))  == -1 )
      { perror("can't LINK token under ip");  exit(5); }
  if ((fd_x25   = open( "/dev/x25", O_RDWR )) == -1 )
      { perror("can't open /dev/x25");  exit(6); }
  if ((mx_x25 = ioctl (fd_ip, I_LINK, fd_x25))  == -1 )
      { perror("can't LINK x25 under ip");  exit(7); }
  if ((fd_tcp   = open( "/dev/tcp", O_RDWR )) == -1 )
      { perror("can't open /dev/tp");  exit(8); }
  if ((mx_ip = ioctl (fd_tcp, I_LINK, fd_ip))  == -1 )
      { perror("can't LINK ip under tcp");  exit(9); }
  switch( fork() )
  {
    case  0:    break;       /* child (daemon) of  init    */
    case -1:    { perror( "fork failed" );  exit(10);  }
    default:    exit(0);     /* parent abandons child      */
  }
  close(fd_ip);      close(fd_ether);
  close(fd_token);   close(fd_x25);
  pause();                /* keep TCP/IP stack open forever      */
}
```

This sample code would be executed by a system daemon at startup time, usually from an **/etc/rc** shell script. For example, a "STREAMS link" (**slink**) command does the I_LINK chores on an SCO Open Desktop system. It is launched from the **/etc/tcp** script at system boot time, just before the system goes multiuser, and it runs forever while the protocol is being used. It sets up the protocol stack so that subsequent programs can use TCP by opening **/dev/tcp** (/dev/inet/tcp on SCO systems). Each client that opens /dev/tcp will do a "clone open" of the STREAMS device, and each client will have a separate stream stack. Clone opens return a different minor device number for each upper part of the protocol stack, which the multiplexing driver uses to multiplex messages above it. Lower parts have a unique **mux_id** number, which is returned by the I_LINK ioctl() system call. The multiplexing driver code uses the mux_id to multiplex messages to and from the lower STREAMS. Our sample code stores the mux_ids in mx_ether, mx_token, mx_x25, and mx_ip. Once the protocol stack is set up, the lower parts cannot be accessed directly, and therefore the /dev files are closed. SVR4 has an **autopush** command to automatically push protocol modules onto STREAMS devices such as /dev/tcp and **/dev/udp**.

6.2   Network Printer Example

Before we write a STREAMS module and add it to the kernel, it will be helpful to see a simple STREAMS application. Workstation users want to share a printer attached to an RS-232 port on a terminal server. There is an entry in /etc/services for remote printing (515/tcp), which is fine for host-to-host service. However, the terminal server is not a host computer and thus does not have the capability to run a line printer (lp) spooler daemon. Therefore, the workstation's lp spooler daemon is configured to send its output to a **pseudo-terminal device** (/dev/pts/4) instead of a physical RS-232 device port (/dev/tty??). A daemon is started in the background to read the pseudo-terminal device file and write the data to a TCP port on the terminal server.

The terminal server unit has an Internet address, and each physical RS-232 port is accessed by a TCP port number. For example, TCP port 7001 is the address of RS-232 port 1, TCP port 7002 is the address of RS-232 port 2, and so on. Some people prefer to assign an Internet address to each RS-232 port, but this depends on whether or not the terminal server unit allows you to do this. The main advantage of using a different IP address for each port is that you can modify /etc/hosts or your Domain Name Server's files when you move a printer, and not worry about TCP port numbers. On the other hand, these files may be outside of your control, and you, as printer administrator, may find it easier (more "politically correct," perhaps) to modify a printer configuration file such as /etc/lp/**printer.config**:

#	*Printer name*	*Internet address*	*TCP port number*
	printer1	129.33.192.200	**7001**
	printer2	129.33.192.200	**7002**

These issues are administrative rather than technical, and we'll leave them for you to decide how to handle them. The sample code will simply read a host name and a TCP port number from the command line. The situation is illustrated in Figure 6.3.

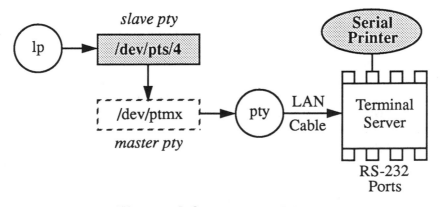

Figure 6.3   Network Printer

Please keep in mind the two problems we are solving:

(1) The terminal server is not a host computer, and **it cannot execute an LP spooler daemon.** This problem is solved by modifying the `vcclient.c` TCP program from Chapter 3 to open a virtual circuit connection to the terminal server and transfer the print file. TCP guarantees that data is printed in the same sequence in which it was sent from the client's workstation. The code executes on the client's workstation.

(2) The network daemon that solves Problem 1 does not provide terminal (`tty`) semantics (such as **mapping newlines into carriage return/linefeed character pairs**). This is solved by using "pseudo-terminal" modules in the kernel. These modules provide the line discipline semantics that are part of the UNIX `tty` device drivers. They are stacked as shown in Figure 6.4.

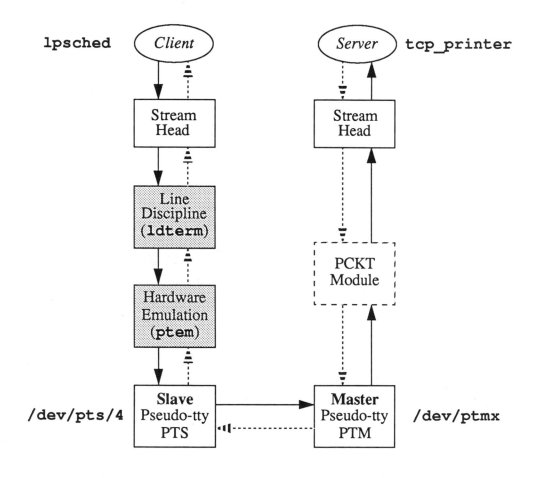

Figure 6.4 Pseudo-terminal STREAMS Modules

6.2.1   Network Printer Program

The next program was developed in two stages:

1. Code and test the STREAMS pseudo-tty interface.
2. Merge and test the `vcclient.c` code from Chapter 3.

This allowed us to test the separate parts, and it helped very much when the program
was ported to a different system. The final working version is as follows:

```
/* tcp_printer.c - remote printer (to a dumb terminal server) */
/*              client daemon                                  */
/*---------------------------------------------------------- */
/* lp -d tcp_printer file -> pseudo-tty -> tcp_printer daemon */
/*   tcp_printer -> tcp socket connection -> terminal server  */
/*     terminal server RS-232 port -> RS-232 serial printer   */
/*---------------------------------------------------------- */
/*  Usage:   # tcp_printer  printer  7001  &  (host name/port number) */
/*           Pseudo-tty is: /dev/pts/4                         */
/*           # lpadmin -d  -v /dev/pts/4  -p tcp_printer \      */
/*                                        -m standard          */
/*           # accept tcp_printer                              */
/*           # enable tcp_printer                              */
/*           # alias print='lp -d tcp_printer'                 */
/*           # print /etc/hosts                                */
/*---------------------------------------------------------- */
/* cc -O tcp_printer.c -o tcp_printer -l nsl -l socket \       */
/*                              /usr/ucblib/libucb.a           */
/* cc -O tcp_printer.c -o tcp_printer -l nsl -l socket -l net  */
/*---------------------------------------------------------- */
/* libnet.a (Wollongong WIN TCP) and                          */
/* /usr/ucblib/libucb.a (SVR4) have:                          */
/*         getdtblsize.o  bcopy.o  (note: memcpy is ANSI C std) */
/*---------------------------------------------------------- */
#include <fcntl.h>       /* O_RDWR def'n                      */
#include <stdio.h>       /*   NULL def'n                      */
#include <stropts.h>     /* I_PUSH, I_LIST def's              */
#include <sys/types.h>
#include <sys/socket.h>
#include <netinet/in.h>  /* sockaddr_in internet address      */
#include <netdb.h>       /* /etc/hosts entry (hostent)        */
```

```
main( argc, argv )
char *argv[];
{
  struct sockaddr_in name;     /* internet socket name (addr)  */
  struct hostent *hptr, *gethostbyname();    /* lib functions */
  int    n, nbytes, sd; /* TCP socket descriptor, byte counts */
  int    fd_master, fd_slave; /* master/slave pseudo-tty's    */
  char   *slavename;          /* slave pty pathname            */
  extern char *ptsname();     /* lib func gets pseudo-tty name */
  char   buff[ 256 ];         /* your basic line buffer        */

  if ( (sd = socket( AF_INET,  SOCK_STREAM , 0 )) < 0 )
     { perror( argv[0] );  exit(1); }
  name.sin_family = AF_INET ;
  name.sin_port   = htons( atoi( argv[2] ) ); /* printer port# */
  hptr = gethostbyname( argv[1] );  /* terminal server address */
  bcopy(hptr->h_addr, &name.sin_addr.s_addr, hptr->h_length );

  if ( connect ( sd, &name, sizeof name ) < 0 )
     { close(sd); perror( argv[0] );  exit(2);}

  fd_master = open( "/dev/ptmx", O_RDWR ); /* open master pty  */
                                           /* gives slave pty  */

  grantpt ( fd_master );      /* change permissions on slave   */
  unlockpt( fd_master );      /* unlock slave pty              */

  slavename = ptsname( fd_master ); /* get slave pathname      */

  fd_slave  = open( slavename, O_RDWR ); /* open slave pty     */

  ioctl( fd_slave, I_PUSH, "ptem" );      /* tty   emulation   */
  ioctl( fd_slave, I_PUSH, "ldterm" );    /* line discipline   */

  printf( "\n\tPseudo-tty is: %s:\n", slavename );

/* lp spooler writes to slave pty, which sends data to the read
   side of the master pty.  This daemon patiently waits for a
   print file to arrive on the master pty and then sends it out
   the TCP socket connected to the terminal server's printer. */

  while( 1 )
    { n = read ( fd_master, buff, sizeof(buff) );
      if ( n > 0 )   nbytes = write( sd, buff, n );
      if ( nbytes != n || n == -1 )
        { perror( "read/write loop" ); exit( 255 ); }
    }
  close( sd );
}
```

6.2.2   A Mounted Stream Filename

The library functions `grantpt()`, `unlockpt()`, and `ptsname()` are standard interfaces to the STREAMS pseudo-terminal subsystem. The master pseudo-tty device, `/dev/ptmx`, is a **clone device**, which means that each `open()` creates a new *pair* of master/slave pseudo-terminals with a unique minor number. The slave side can be accessed by opening a device file such as `/dev/pts/4`. The minor number 4 is assigned when the master side is opened. Writes to the slave device become input to the master side and, likewise, writes to the master device become input to the slave side.

Notice that the slave device minor number is not known until the master device is opened! In many cases, such as logging in over the network, this is not a problem, as the controlling terminal is assigned at login time and most users don't care which slave pseudo-tty device they are using.

On the other hand, our network printer daemon creates a pseudo-terminal device which the `lp` spooler daemon needs to know before opening it for output. The previous version requires an operator to start the network printer daemon in the background, read the slave device name printed (such as **/dev/pts/4**) and then establish an `lp` spool queue for that device by using the **-v** (device) option of the `lpadmin` command. This is acceptable for preliminary testing but not for daily operation. It is better to use a name in the UNIX filesystem name space and attach the filename to the slave pseudo-terminal device whenever the `tcp_printer` daemon is started. This is exactly what the **fattach()** library function does for us, as shown in the following code segments:

```
#define PRT1 "/usr/spool/lp/fifos/printer1"

rmspool( signum )
{
    unlink( PRT1 );              /* remove printer spool file    */
}   ...    ...    ...
for ( i=1; i<20; i++) /* risky; really should set by sig names */
                      /*   1) system may not have 20 signals    */
                      /*   2) previous settings are not saved!   */
    signal( i, rmspool );    /* remove printer spool file        */
    ...    ...    ...
/*  create the pseudo-terminal STREAMS device pair              */
    ...    ...    ...
/*  create the spool file "printer1"                            */
    spool = open( PRT1, O_RDONLY | O_CREAT | O_EXCL, 0666 );
    if ( spool == -1 )  { perror( PRT1 ); exit( 255 ); }
/*  mount pseudo-tty over the spool file "printer1"             */
    n = fattach( fd_slave, PRT1 );
    if ( n == -1 )  { perror( "fattach" ); exit( 255 ); }
/*  create a socket for TCP connection to terminal server       */
    ...    ...    ...
```

A spool file is created by our `tcp_printer` daemon. The `O_EXCL` and `O_CREAT` flags ensure that the `open()` system call will fail if the spool file already exists. This prevents a second daemon from launching if one is already running or if there were some problems with an earlier execution. When our daemon exits or catches any signal an `rmspool()` function is executed to remove the spool file. This will cause the `lp` spooler daemon to save print files in a spool directory until the spool file is available for writing. That is, only when the `tcp_printer` daemon is running will the `lp` spooler daemon resume "printing." It automatically stops whenever a `write()` to the printer "device" file (`/usr/spool/lp/fifos/printer1`) fails.

The `fattach()` function "mounts" the slave pseudo-tty STREAMS device over the UNIX file. That is, `write()`s to the file before the `fattach()` call will fill disk blocks of the UNIX file. After the `fattach()` call, `write()`s to the file will take a "detour" to the write side of the slave pty stream head. This is very similar to the way the `mount` command covers a directory with a filesystem root node. In fact, these are called **mounted STREAMS** in the system documentation. Figure 6.5 illustrates our mounted stream.

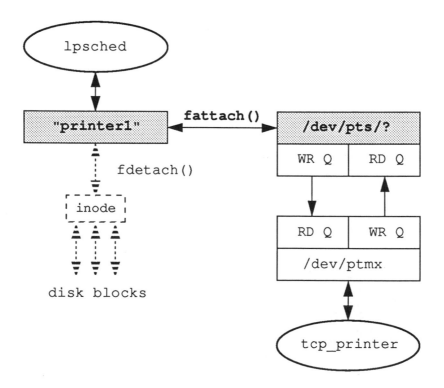

Figure 6.5 A Mounted Stream

6.2.3   Network Printer Testing

This section describes a few of the commands used to unit test the `tcp_printer` daemon. For example, the mounted stream can be seen with the `ls` command.

```
# cd /usr/spool/lp/fifos
# ls -l /dev/pts/0 printer1
c---------  2 root    tty     12, 0 Jun  2 07:38 /dev/pts/0
crw-r--r--  1 lp      other   12, 0 Jun  2 07:34 printer1
```

Both filenames refer to the same character STREAMS device with major device number 12 and minor device number 0. They have separate inodes, as evidenced by different owners, groups, access permissions, and time stamps. The pseudo-tty device file has a link count of two because it is also linked to the filename /dev/pts000. Its permissions were set as follows:

```
if ( chmod( slavename, 0 ) < 0 )
   { perror(slavename); exit(88); }
```

This is an attempt to prevent direct access to the pseudo-tty itself and force access through the "mounted on" name, /usr/spool/lp/fifos/printer1. Another `chmod( slavename, 0620 )` is needed in the signal handler `rmspool()` to restore the pty's normal permissions.

When the `printer1` file exists, we are quite sure the `tcp_printer` daemon is running in the background. The next command verifies that our code will not try to establish a second connection to the network printer.

```
# ./tcp_printer termserv 7001
        Pseudo-tty is: /dev/pts/2:
        Continue, s'il yous plait? y
/usr/spool/lp/fifos/printer1: File exists
```

The "... `File exists`" message was printed by `perror(PRT1)` just before this execution of `tcp_printer` called `exit(255)`. We use the `ps` command to see if the daemon was already running.

```
# ps -ef | grep tcp
root 1700 1636 07:45:59 pts/1   grep tcp
root 1501  793 07:33:52 console ./tcp_printer termserv 7001
```

Now kill the daemon and verify that the signal handler `rmspool()` removes the "mounted on" filename.

```
# kill 1501     (sends SOFTERM signal #15 to tcp_printer)
# ls -l printer1 /dev/pts/0
printer1: No such file or directory
crw--w----  2 root    tty     12, 0 Oct  2 07:38 /dev/pts/0
```

We configured two printers into our system: one for the "mounted on" filename, and one for a pseudo-tty device. The −v option of the lpstat command shows you which device is configured for a printer.

```
# lpstat -v printer0 -v printer1
device for printer0: /dev/pts/0
device for printer1: /usr/spool/lp/fifos/printer1
```

A simple test to check accessibility of our "printers."

```
$ cat /etc/passwd >/dev/pts/0
/dev/pts/0: cannot create
```

```
$ cat /etc/passwd >/usr/spool/lp/fifos/printer1
/usr/spool/lp/fifos/printer1: cannot create
```

Note that these commands were executed by an ordinary user. After **su**-ing to root (superuser), the behavior is as follows:

```
# cat /etc/passwd >/dev/pts/0
/dev/pts/0: cannot create
```

```
# cat /etc/passwd >/usr/spool/lp/fifos/printer1
```

The superuser was disallowed access to /dev/pts/0 because the tcp_printer daemon is not running, and therefore no process has the file open for reading, so the open() call in cat fails with EPIPE (broken pipe). The second cat creates an ordinary file, as shown by the ls command:

```
# ls -l /dev/pts/0 printer1
crw--w----  2 root    tty    12, 0 Jun  2 07:38 /dev/pts/0
-rw-r--r--  1 root    other     964 Jun  2 08:53 printer1
```

Now let's try the lp interface to these "devices". The −d (destination) option of the lp command can be used to direct your file to a specific printer. We first test output to the "mounted on" filename.

```
# lp -d printer1 /etc/passwd
request id is printer1-108 (1 file)
# lp -d printer0 /etc/passwd
request id is printer0-109 (1 file)
```

The lpstat command shows you the status of your lp print requests:

```
# lpstat
printer1-108      root    964    Jun  2 09:19 on printer1
printer0-109      root    964    Jun  2 09:19
```

The "on printer1" message means that print request printer1-108 is *now printing* on printer1! *How can that be? The tcp_printer daemon is not running!*

The −p option of lpstat shows the status of a printer:

```
# lpstat -p printer0
printer printer0 waiting for auto-retry. available.
        stopped with printer fault
```

This is what we expect. Without the tcp_printer daemon running, the lp spooler daemon cannot open the pseudo-tty device, so it keeps the print file is a spool directory and periodically tries to open the device file every five minutes or so.

However, this is not what we expect:

```
# lpstat -p printer1
printer printer1 is idle. enabled since ... available.
```

This is explained by the following:

```
# ls -l printer1
-rw-r--r--  1 root    other   1928 Jun  2 09:04 printer1
```

The regular file printer1 still exists after the previous cat command, and the lp spooler daemon is able to open the file in append mode and write to it! After removing the file, everything works as we expect:

```
# rm printer1

# lp -d printer1 /etc/passwd
request id is printer1-110 (1 file)

# lpstat -p printer1
printer printer1 waiting for auto-retry. available.
        stopped with printer fault

# lpstat
printer0-109        root    964    Jun  2 09:19
printer1-110        root    964    Jun  2 10:12
```

These files will be printed after the daemon is started:

```
# ./tcp_printer termserv 7001 &
        Pseudo-tty is: /dev/pts/0:
```

These files will automatically print when the lp spooler daemon retries to open the device file, or you can initiate an immediate retry with the enable command:

```
# enable printer1
printer "printer1" now enabled
```

Notice that both printers are using the same pseudo-tty device /dev/pts/0! This should be avoided by using mounted STREAMS rather than pseudo-tty device names.

6.2.4 Network Printer Connection Control

The previous testing assures us that print files will not be lost if something goes haywire on the host and the `tcp_printer` daemon stops running. However, other problems could arise at the terminal server end. What if somebody turns the printer off? Or what happens if the Ethernet cable is disconnected between the host and the LAN? If the terminal server is able to disconnect by sending a TCP reset packet, a subsequent `write()` to the socket will fail, causing the `tcp_printer` daemon to exit. This, in turn, will cause `write()`s to the pseudo-tty device to fail, and the `lp` spooler daemon will automatically save the print files in a spool directory.

Our programming task is to find out as quickly as possible whenever the TCP connection is broken and kill the `tcp_printer` daemon so the `lp` spooler can do its part. One option is to use TCP **"keep-alive"** packets. This socket option causes the protocol to send a packet periodically to the far end to make sure it is still alive. These packets are *only sent when normal data transfers are not taking place*, as normal data transfers will be acknowledged by the far end.

```
/* set socket options to detect "quickly" a break in the TCP connection     */
  n = 1;
/* toggle value: 1 = "on", zero 0 = "off"                                    */
  if ( setsockopt( sd, SOL_SOCKET,
                   SO_KEEPALIVE, &n, sizeof(int)) < 0 )
    { perror( "setsockopt KEEPALIVE" );  exit(1); }
```

If the terminal server fails to respond to a "keep-alive" packet, a `SIGPIPE` signal is sent to our `tcp_printer` daemon, which then executes `rmspool()` and exits. Print requests will then be queued in a spool directory while the terminal server is down.

However, data in transit may get "lost" in kernel buffers, as shown by the following `netstat` command (we could have `grep`ped for socket number 1045):

```
# netstat -a | head -3
Active Internet connections (including servers)
Proto Recv-Q Send-Q  Local Address  Foreign Address    (state)
tcp       0   2364   att.1045       termserv.7001      ESTABLISHED
```

To minimize the amount of data at risk in kernel buffers, the size of the socket's send queue can be reduced by setting another socket option:

```
/* Keep send buffers small, so less data is lost, and less chance of losing a print file*/
  n = 256;          /* send buffer size is only 256 bytes         */
  if ( setsockopt( sd, SOL_SOCKET,
                   SO_SNDBUF, &n, sizeof(int)) < 0 )
    { perror( "setsockopt SNDBUF" );  exit(1); }
```

The lp spooler daemon maintains a spool copy until the file has finished printing. Unfortunately, write()s to a socket are successful if they are able to append data to the socket's send queue. Therefore, very small print files (ones that fit entirely on a socket's send queue) can potentially be lost.

It may take some time for TCP to recognize that the terminal server is down. Application programmers have no control over how long it takes TCP to timeout waiting for an acknowledgment packet from the terminal server. There are, however, two system calls, **select()** and **poll()**, which can be used to set an application-defined timeout. The select() system call originated from the socket-oriented BSD 4.2 release, while the poll() system call came from the STREAMS-oriented System V Release 3.0.

The poll() system call can be used as follows to set a timeout:

```
#include <sys/poll.h>        /* to "poll" for timeouts        */

struct pollfd pollfds; /* file descriptor(s) to poll          */
int     timeout = 200; /* 200 milliseconds = .2 second timeout */

pollfds.fd = sd;               /* poll the TCP socket "sd"       */
pollfds.events = POLLOUT;  /* return when socket can send data */

while( (n = read (fd_master, buff, sizeof(buff))) > 0 )
{
  if ( poll( &pollfds, 1, timeout ) == 0 )  /* 0 means timeout! */
      rmspool( 88 );          /* remove spool file and exit      */

  printf("\n\tPoll returned: %d\n", pollfds.revents); /* test */

  switch ( pollfds.revents )
      {
      case POLLOUT:     /* socket can send data w/o blocking   */
      case POLLWRNORM: /* socket can send data w/o blocking   */
            if ( write( sd, buff, n ) != n )
                { perror( "Socket write" );   exit(3);}
            break;

      case POLLIN: case POLLRDNORM: case POLLPRI: break;

      case POLLERR: case POLLHUP: case POLLNVAL: rmspool( 88 );
      }
}
```

The pollfd structure has three fields: **fd** has the file descriptor being polled, **events** is a bitmask of the events of interest on the file, and **revents** is a bitmask *returned* to let you know which event(s) occurred on the file. If you wish to poll more than one file you would build an array of pollfd structures, one for each file of interest, and pass the array to the poll() system call. In this example, we only have one file of interest (the TCP socket), so we pass it the address of a single `pollfd` structure.

We are only interested in the **POLLOUT** event, which indicates that **normal data can be sent without blocking**. If the terminal server goes off line for any reason, print data will accumulate in kernel buffers and the `tcp_printer` process will soon block trying to write to the TCP socket. If that should happen, the `poll()` system call returns a value of zero, which means the nonzero timeout limit was reached. Two-tenths of a second (200 milliseconds) is ample time for a TCP packet to be sent to and acknowledged by an interface directly connected to the same Ethernet cable as the host. That is, no bridges or gateways or long-haul wide-area networks are involved.

Other events are `POLLIN` (non-priority input data is available for reading), `POLLRDNORM` (normal data can be read without blocking), `POLLPRI` (high priority data may be read without blocking) and **POLLWRNORM** (same as `POLLOUT`!). These events are "neutral" as far as our application is concerned. Serious events are `POLLERR` (an error occurred on the device file), `POLLHUP` (a hangup has occurred on the stream) and `POLLNVAL` (the specified `fd` value is not an open file). These events cannot be requested; they are returned whenever such a serious abnormal event occurs on an `fd` being polled.

Incidentally, the second argument to the `poll()` system call is the number of file descriptors being polled. A positive return value is the number of file descriptors that have a nonzero `revents` field. A return value of zero means the `poll()` call timed out. A return value of minus one means the system call failed, and the value of `errno` has the error code. A timeout value of minus one (or `INFTIM`) would cause the `poll()` call to block indefinitely, until an event occurs or until it is interrupted.

The `select()` system call uses a bitmask instead of an array of `pollfd` structures. Each bit represents a file descriptor of interest. For example,

```
    bitmask |= 1 << sd;      /* set bit for socket sd        */
```

is a logical "or" of a 1-bit in the `sd`-bit position, with the current value of `bitmask`. A `timeval` structure defined in `/usr/include/sys/time.h` is used to specify timeout limits. For example,

```
        timeout.tv_sec  = 5;    /* timeout in five seconds...   */
        timeout.tv_usec = 0;    /* ... and zero micro-seconds   */
        select( 32, &bitmask, NULL, NULL, &timeout);
```

would return if data is ready for reading from one or more of the descriptors set in `bitmask`, or five seconds elapsed without any data arriving on the descriptors of interest. Unfortunately, `bitmask` is overwritten by `select()` with a bit set for each descriptor with data ready for reading. A timeout is indicated by returning all zeros in `bitmask`. The first argument is the number of bits in the bitmask. The third and fourth arguments are the addresses of bitmasks for descriptors ready for writing or those with errors, respectively. Consult the manual for more information on these system calls.

6.2.5   Network Printer Debugging

A little trial-and-error was needed to get the master/slave pseudo-terminal
communication to work properly. The trick is to open the slave side for writing by client
processes such as `lp`. Our daemon, however, reads the **master** side of the PTS/PTM
pseudo-device pair. This subset of the whole program was handy when we began
porting our daemon to a customer's system. The smaller program, `pty.c`, writes to
standard out, instead of a TCP socket, and was tested as follows:

```
$  ./pty  &
[1]    1628
       Slave pty is /dev/pts/4

$  echo  "Hi there, Gorby!"  >/dev/pts/4
pty read: Hi there, Gorby!

$  cat  pty.c >/dev/pts/4
pty read: /* pty.c - pseudo-tty example ...
```

When this smaller `pty.c` program compiled and executed on the customer's machine,
we knew that their STREAMS pseudo-terminal subsystem was configured and working
properly.

However, the `tcp_printer` daemon didn't work. It would hang somewhere, and
never do any I/O. The SVR4 **truss** (**tr**ace **u**ser **s**ystem calls and **s**ignals) command
is an ideal tool to find out what a program is doing. SunOS has an almost identical
command called (oddly enough) **trace**. Output from these commands show you the
execution sequence of system calls, the value of input arguments to the system calls, and
values returned by the system calls. From this trace we learned that the library function
`gethostbyname()` wound up in an endless loop on the customer's system!

Here is a trace of a normal SVR4 execution that does not hang. (The **-o** option
could have been used to send output to a file, instead of the IO redirection, and the **-f**
option tells `truss` to follow all child processes created by the `fork()` system call.)

```
$ truss ./tcp_printer localhost 7001 >tcpprnt.truss 2>&1 &
execve("./tcp_printer", 0x08047E18, 0x08047E28)  argc = 3
open("/dev/zero", O_RDONLY, 020000547744)            = 3
mmap(0x00000000, 4096, PROT_READ|PROT_WRITE,
               MAP_PRIVATE, 3, 0)      = 0x8002F000
```

The kernel `exec()`s our `tcp_printer` daemon with both a command line
argument pointer (`0x08047E18`) and an environment pointer (`0x08047E28`). Then
it opens a special **/dev/zero** device (**file descriptor 3**) and memory maps a 4K
zero-filled area at virtual address `0x8002F000`. `/dev/zero` is a pseudo-device that
simply generates zeros and, by using the `mmap()` system call to map this device file
into the program's address space, it effectively creates a 4K zero-filled area.

The next system calls simply get our effective user id (0, or *root*) and our effective group id (3, or *sys*).

```
getuid()                                     = 0  [ 0 ]
getgid()                                     = 3  [ 3 ]
```

Next, the network services shared object (**.so**) library is opened (file descriptor 4) and 308 bytes of **ELF header** information is read into memory. ELF stands for "Execution and Linking Format", an object file format that supports **dynamic linking** of object and executable files.

```
open("/usr/lib/libnsl.so", O_RDONLY, 020000547744)    = 4
read(4, "7F E L F010101\0\0\0\0\0".., 308)             = 308
```

A 224K area is zero-filled from /dev/zero (file descriptor 3), and 186K of the nsl library (file descriptor 4) is memory-mapped into the process' address space, followed by a 17K area and a 16K area. The 186K area is executable code, the 17K area is initialized data, and the 16K area is uninitialized data (as **size libnsl.so** shows).

```
mmap(0x00000000, 224112, PROT_READ,
                MAP_PRIVATE, 3, 0)    = 0x80031000

mmap(0x80031000, 186456, PROT_READ|PROT_EXEC,
                MAP_PRIVATE|MAP_FIXED, 4, 0) = 0x80031000

mmap(0x8005F000, 17432, PROT_READ|PROT_WRITE|PROT_EXEC,
                MAP_PRIVATE|MAP_FIXED, 4, 184320) = 0x8005F000

mprotect(0x80064000, 16384, PROT_READ|PROT_WRITE|PROT_EXEC)=0
close(4)                                               = 0
```

The nsl library is closed, and another library is mapped into the process' address space:

```
open("/usr/lib/libsocket.so", O_RDONLY, 020000547744) = 4
read(4, "7F E L F010101\0\0\0\0\0".., 308)             = 308

mmap(0x00000000, 59224, PROT_READ,
                MAP_PRIVATE, 3, 0)    = 0x80069000

mmap(0x80069000, 45996, PROT_READ|PROT_EXEC,
                MAP_PRIVATE|MAP_FIXED, 4, 0) = 0x80069000

mmap(0x80075000, 3620, PROT_READ|PROT_WRITE|PROT_EXEC,
                MAP_PRIVATE|MAP_FIXED, 4, 45056) = 0x80075000

mprotect(0x80076000, 8192, PROT_READ|PROT_WRITE|PROT_EXEC) = 0
close(4)                                               = 0
close(3)                                               = 0
```

The socket library is closed, and so is the /dev/zero device file, now that it is no longer needed.

The next system call is platform dependent. It reports how floating-point arithmetic is supported on this machine.

sysi86(SI86**FPHW**,0x8002D4C0,0x8002CFE4,0x8000C185)=0x00000000

A system file named /etc/netconfig has a list of network protocols, devices and libraries available on the host. Some typical file entries are as follows:

```
tcp  tpi_cots_ord  v inet  tcp /dev/tcp        /usr/lib/tcpip.so
udp        tpi_clts  v inet  udp /dev/udp        /usr/lib/tcpip.so
starlan  tpi_cots  v osinet  -   /dev/starlan /usr/lib/straddr.so
```

where the tcp protocol is accessed by opening the /dev/tcp STREAMS device and using the library functions in /usr/lib/tcpip.so, while the starlan protocol would open /dev/starlan and use functions in /usr/lib/straddr.so. This file is part of the SVR4 **Network Selection** Facility and, together with dynamic shared libraries provided by ELF, it allows application programs to be truly transport independent. These will be discussed in the TLI Programming chapter.

To establish a TCP socket connection to the terminal server printer, the SVR4 ELF executable opens the **network configuration database** (/etc/netconfig), searches for the tcp protocol, opens the /dev/tcp STREAMS device and pushes a "**sockmod**" module onto the stream. The module is necessary to emulate socket behavior over a STREAMS stack implementation. Notice that an I_FIND ioctl request is done to find out if sockmod is already on the STREAMS stack before it is I_PUSH'd onto the stack. A return value of zero means the module was not found.

```
open("/etc/netconfig", O_RDONLY, 0666)          = 3
read(3, " #\n #\t T h e    N e t w".., 1024)     = 568
read(3, 0x0804ED70, 1024)                       = 0
lseek(3, 0, 1)                                  = 568
lseek(3, 0, 0)                                  = 0
read(3, " #\n #\t T h e    N e t w".., 1024)     = 568
brk(0x08050D68)                                 = 0
brk(0x08051D68)                                 = 0
read(3, 0x0804ED70, 1024)                       = 0
close(3)                                        = 0
open("/dev/tcp", O_RDWR, 020001656014)          = 3
ioctl(3, I_FIND, "sockmod")                     = 0
ioctl(3, I_PUSH, "sockmod")                     = 0
ioctl(3, I_SETCLTIME, 0x08047C84)               = 0
ioctl(3, I_SWROPT, 0x00000002)                  = 0
sigset(SIGPOLL, SIG_HOLD)                       = SIG_DFL
ioctl(3, I_STR, 0x08047BFC)                     = 0
sigset(SIGPOLL, SIG_DFL)                        = SIG_HOLD
ioctl(3, I_GETSIG, 0x08047C38)                  Err#22 EINVAL
```

Next, the **tcpip.so** library functions are mapped into the process' address space:

```
open("/etc/netconfig", O_RDONLY, 0666)              = 4
read(4, " #\n #\t T h e   N e t w".., 1024)         = 568
close(4)                                            = 0

access("/usr/lib/tcpip.so", 0)                      = 0

open("/dev/zero", O_RDONLY, 020000547744)           = 4

open("/usr/lib/tcpip.so", O_RDONLY, 020000547744)   = 5
```

Note: it is generally faster to open(path) and then fstat(fd), rather than access(path) and then open(path), because fstat() saves the pathname conversion to an inode done by access(). This probably has a very marginal (if any) effect on the performance of this particular program, but it is worth noting that truss (or trace) does show you what is going on "under the hood."

```
read(5, "7F E L F010101\0\0\0\0\0".., 308)          = 308
mmap(0x00000000, 16640, PROT_READ,
                MAP_PRIVATE, 4, 0)      = 0x80079000
mmap(0x80079000, 12076, PROT_READ|PROT_EXEC,
              MAP_PRIVATE|MAP_FIXED, 5, 0) = 0x80079000
mmap(0x8007C000, 4320, PROT_READ|PROT_WRITE|PROT_EXEC,
              MAP_PRIVATE|MAP_FIXED, 5, 8192) = 0x8007C000
close(5)                                            = 0
close(4)                                            = 0
```

Next the hosts file is read by gethostbyname(), and the services file is read by getservbyname(). **It was here that an infinite loop of opening and reading /etc/hosts was observed on the customer's system.** Our workaround was to give a dotted decimal Internet address on the command line to avoid the hosts file lookup.

```
open("/etc/hosts", O_RDONLY, 0666)                  = 4
fxstat(2, 4, 0x08047AB8)                            = 0
```

The function fxstat() is an internal version of stat() for different size inodes.

```
ioctl(4, TCGETA, 0x08047A8A)               Err#25 ENOTTY
read(4, " # i d e n t\t " @ ( # )".., 1024)         = 108
close(4)                                            = 0

open("/etc/services", O_RDONLY, 0666)               = 4
fxstat(2, 4, 0x08047B08)                            = 0
ioctl(4, TCGETA, 0x08047ADA)               Err#25 ENOTTY
read(4, " # i d e n t\t " @ ( # )".., 1024)         = 1024
close(4)                                            = 0
```

The pseudo-tty master device is opened.

```
open("/dev/ptmx", O_RDWR, 020000547744)             = 4
```

A child process is created and exits, sending a SIGCLD signal to the parent (this process). You could use the -f option to follow the child process after the fork()!

```
fork()                                                      = 1409
Received signal #18, SIGCLD [default]
siginfo: SIGCLD CLD_EXITED pid=1409 uid=0 status=0x0000
```

The siginfo structure is a new feature of SVR4 that allows you to receive more information than the plain old signal() system call. By setting the SA_SIGINFO flag in the sigaction() system call your signal handler will receive *three* arguments: the signal number, a pointer to a **siginfo** structure, and a pointer to a **ucontext** structure. The siginfo structure contains a signal-specific error code (or a child's exit status) and the process id of the sender, if the signal came from a kill() system call. The ucontext structure stores the context of a thread of control within an executing process. The next wait() system call returns zero because process 1409 has finished.

```
waitsys(0x00000000, 1409, 0x08047C00, WEXITED|WTRAPPED) = 0
```

A couple of stream ioctl()s are sent downstream on the master side of the pseudo-tty device (/dev/ptmx):

```
ioctl(4, I_STR, 0x08047CA4)                     = 0
ioctl(4, I_STR, 0x08047C18)                     = 0
```

The ioctl()s create the slave side of the pseudo-tty pair, and retrieve the pathname assigned to the slave pty. Access to the slave pty is verified:

```
access("/dev/pts/0", 0)                         = 0
```

The slave side is opened (file descriptor 5) and the physical terminal emulation and line discipline modules are pushed onto the slave's stream stack.

```
open("/dev/pts/0", O_RDWR, 020000547744)        = 5
ioctl(5, I_PUSH, "ptem")                        = 0
ioctl(5, I_PUSH, "ldterm")                      = 0
```

Standard output (file descriptor 1) has been redirected to a file, and therefore is not a tty.

```
ioctl(1, TCGETA, 0x08047A52)              Err#25 ENOTTY
read(4, 0x08047CD0, 256)          (sleeping...)
```

The program is sleeping on input from file descriptor 4, the PTM (master side) module of the pseudo-terminal pair. This is what we want!

On a faulty system, an endless loop executed open()s of /etc/hosts, so the call to gethostbyname() was removed and the function worked! The terminal server's IP address was typed on the command line, and its dotted-decimal ASCII format was converted by the library function **inet_addr(argv[2])**. This was just a temporary workaround to finish our testing. However, we hope this example gives you confidence to use the SVR4 **truss** command or the SunOS **trace** command to help troubleshoot problems in your network application program development!

6.3   User/Kernel Interfaces to STREAMS

Now we turn our attention to writing a STREAMS driver. A driver has both a stream head to interface with user system calls, and a driver module to interface with the device control and status registers. A STREAMS module can be pushed onto a stream (just below the stream head) to insert a service procedure between the user (stream head) and the device (driver module). The top STREAMS module can be popped from the stack when the module's processing is no longer needed. Each module has a read queue and a write queue to hold pointers to data as it flows upstream (read) and downstream (write). Figure 6.6 illustrates the basic structures.

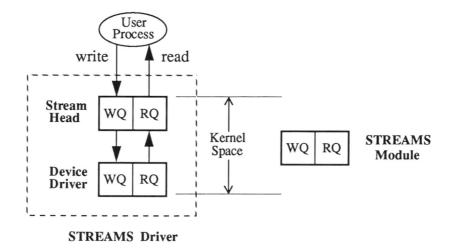

Figure 6.6   STREAMS Device Driver and Module

Each queue structure has a pointer to the next (upstream or downstream) queue. Thus, a stream stack is a linked list of STREAMS queue pairs. By pushing a module on the top of a stack, the stream head's downstream pointer is simply changed to point to the new module's write queue, and the new module's read queue pointer is initialized to point to the read queue of the stream head. The new module's write queue is initialized to point to the device driver's write queue, and the device driver's read queue pointer is changed to point to the new module's read queue. A second module would be inserted the same way, except its downstream module would be the previous module pushed on the stack, rather than the device driver module. Popping a module from the stack always removes the top module underneath the stream head (except the device driver, of course). In this way a STREAMS stack is a LIFO (last in, first out) queue of STREAMS modules.

Before we begin the STREAMS driver example, it is helpful to know how the kernel finds STREAMS drivers and modules. STREAMS **devices** are character devices, which are accessed by using the **major device number** to index an array of pointers to character device driver routines. This table is called the **cdevsw** for "character **device** switch" table. The major device number is stored in the inode (such as /dev/tcp) for the device. You can find the major and minor device numbers by getting a long ls of the device file.

```
# cd /dev
# ls -l *mem* null zero console tty tcp udp
cr--r----- 1 sys   sys    2,  0  Apr  4  1991   mem
cr--r----- 1 sys   sys    2,  1  May  3  1991   kmem
crw-rw-rw- 1 root  sys    2,  2  Jun  6 23:45   null
crw-r----- 1 root  sys    2,  3  May  3  1991   pmem
crw-rw-rw- 1 root  sys    2,  4  Apr  4  1991   zero
crw--w---- 1 wdr   tty    5,  0  Jun  7 14:03   console
crw-rw-rw- 1 bin   bin   16,  0  Jun  7 13:59   tty
crw-rw-rw- 1 root  root  12, 36  May 27 10:15   tcp
crw-rw-rw- 1 root  root  12, 37  May 27 10:15   udp
```

The major/minor numbers appear in the size field, since special device files have no data blocks. Notice that memory is accessed by the same device driver (mem.c in **row 2 of cdevsw**) and the minor number is used to distinguish among kernel memory (kmem), physical memory (pmem), virtual memory (mem), /dev/null and /dev/zero. Also notice that /dev/tcp and /dev/udp use the same STREAMS device driver, and the protocols are distinguished by different minor device numbers (36 and 37, respectively). The console driver is accessed from row 5 of cdevsw, and the special device /dev/tty is accessed from row 16. Figure 6.7 illustrates the device switch table.

u_file ——————▶ file ——————▶ inode (with **major** and minor numbers)

2	mem.open	mem.close	mem.read	mem.write	mem.ioctl	mem.d_str
5	cons.open	cons.close	cons.read	cons.write	cons.ioctl	cons.d_str
16	tty.open	tty.close	tty.read	tty.write	tty.ioctl	tty.d_str
12	tcp.open	tcp.close	tcp.read	tcp.write	tcp.ioctl	tcp.d_str

Figure 6.7   Character Device Switch Table

The open, close, read, write and ioctl fields are pointers to kernel functions that perform the desired operation on the requested device. The **d_str** field points to a **streamtab** structure if the device is a STREAMS device and is NULL for a non-STREAMS device. You cannot tell from the ls of a device file whether or not it is a STREAMS device. However, you can use the SVR4 **strconf** (STREAMS configuration) command to find out indirectly. This command shows which modules have been pushed on the stream, and fails if the device is not a STREAMS device.

```
$ strconf </dev/console
ttcompat
ldterm
ansi
char
cmux

$ strconf </dev/zero
I_LIST: No such device
strconf: I_LIST ioctl failed
```

Modules, on the other hand, do not have external filenames. They can only be accessed by a character string name given as an argument to an ioctl() on a STREAMS device. The name is used to search a kernel "**module switch**" table, **fmodsw**. Figure 6.8 shows that all roads to a module go through a streamtab structure.

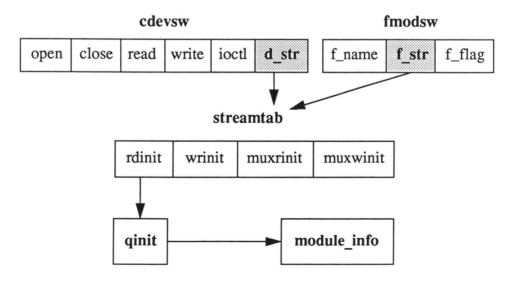

Figure 6.8   User/Kernel STREAMS Interfaces

6.3.1   Finding Installed STREAMS Drivers and Modules

This section shows a simple program that prints the names of all STREAMS modules in the kernel and the major device number of all STREAMS devices. A sample execution gives the following output:

```
$ ./strmods
fmod: d009f680              cdev: d009f140
fmodcnt = 8                 cdevcnt = 42

cdev maj #  2               d_str = d00a82a8
cdev maj #  5               d_str = d00a8308
cdev maj # 12               d_str = d00a8998
cdev maj # 16               d_str = d00a8b54
cdev maj # 19               d_str = d00a8c78
cdev maj # 20               d_str = d00a8fec
cdev maj # 21               d_str = d00a9f8c
cdev maj # 24               d_str = d00b11ac
cdev maj # 41               d_str = d00a3e9c

module name: timod           addr = d00a8380
module name: tirdwr          addr = d00a8600
module name: ldterm          addr = d00a87a4
module name: ptem            addr = d00a88b8
module name: ld0             addr = d00b1318
module name: ntty            addr = d00b1fa0
module name: consem          addr = d00b27e4
module name: vfog            addr = d00b3420
```

The pseudo-terminal subsystem is configured into this kernel, as you can see by the `ptem` and `ldterm` modules. The Transport Independent (**ti**) STREAMS modules are the kernel components that support the Transport Level Interface (TLI) library functions we'll see in the next chapter. Actually, the `timod` STREAMS module supports the TLI functions, and `tirdwr` is pushed on a transport endpoint when you want to use `read()` or `write()` system calls on the endpoint.

This program finds the character device switch table (`cdevsw`) and the module switch table (`fmodsw`) described in the previous section. The number of entries in each table is stored in an integer field in the kernel; `fmodcnt` for `fmodsw` and `cdevcnt` for `cdevsw`. The library function **nlist()** is used to find the address of these variables, followed by **lseek()**s to their virtual addresses in **/dev/mem**. Every entry in `fmodsw` is printed, but only those character devices with non-NULL `d_str` pointers are printed.

Later in this chapter we will add our own module and STREAMS device driver to the kernel. This program will help in understanding how STREAMS modules and drivers are accessed inside the kernel.

```
/* strmods.c - find STREAMS devices and modules in kernel    */
#include <errno.h>        /* perror(3) message defn's         */
#include <stdio.h>        /* NULL definition                  */
#include "sys/types.h"
#include "nlist.h"        /* a.out symbol table (namelist)    */
#include "sys/conf.h"     /* cdevsw and fmodsw definitions    */
```

The `conf.h` header file has the storage definitions for variables that access the STREAMS information we want. Another way to get the STREAMS information is described next. However, it is specific to System V 3.2 or SCO UNIX on a 386, and it only gathers static (compile-time) information.

```
# /etc/conf/bin/idconfig
# grep cnt /etc/conf/cf.d/conf.c

/*   int fmodcnt = 8;     /* no of STREAMS modules           */
/*   int cdevcnt = 42;    /* no of char device drivers       */
    int fmodcnt, cdevcnt; /* modules & char dev drivers      */
```

A UNIX system build requires you to configure a kernel with a `config` command which reads an ASCII system description file and generates a `conf.c` file which you can search for the tunable parameter values in which you are interested. The `config` command may have a different name on your system, such as `uxgen`, `mkunix` or `idbuild`, or even (gasp) a menu selection to configure and build a new kernel. However, keep in mind that the ASCII `conf.c` file stores **compile-time** information, not information extracted from your running kernel. **Beware of kernels that were built on a different system or from a different configuration file!**

To access information in the kernel (or any `a.out` executable file) you can use the **nlist**() library function. It works like the **nm** command, which gives you the namelist (symbol table) in a compiled (binary) executable file. You normally filter the nm output by `grep`ping for the symbols in which you are interested. In a C program, you specify the symbol names in an `nlist` structure, defined in the `nlist.h` header file.

```
struct nlist nl[] = {
"cdevsw", (long)0, (short)0, (unsigned short)0, (char)0, (char)0,
"fmodsw", (long)0, (short)0, (unsigned short)0, (char)0, (char)0,
"cdevcnt", (long)0, (short)0, (unsigned short)0, (char)0, (char)0,
"fmodcnt", (long)0, (short)0, (unsigned short)0, (char)0, (char)0,
        0, (long)0, (short)0, (unsigned short)0, (char)0, (char)0
};
```

The `nlist` structure is defined in the `nlist.h` header file and described in the `nlist(3)` manual page. If the symbol in field one is found in the namelist, its address is returned in field two, along with other information such as the symbol type and whether it is in the data, text, or bss segment. The value remains zero if the symbol is not found. The end of the request list is indicated by an entry of zero in the first field.

Now we define the local variables our program needs: a pointer to the base of the character device switch table (`cdev_ptr`) and a pointer to the STREAMS module table (`fmod_ptr`). We will open `/dev/kmem` to read values from inside the running kernel, using `lseek()` to position the read pointer at the right place in memory given to us by the second field returned by the `nlist()` call.

```
struct cdevsw cdev, *cdev_ptr;     /* cdevsw table start       */
struct fmodsw fmod, *fmod_ptr;     /* fmodsw table start       */
int     memfd, rc;                 /* kernel memory (/dev/kmem) */
long    lseek();                   /* seek to place in kmem    */

main(argc, argv)
char *argv[];
{
        int     k;                 /* cdevsw table counter     */
        nlist("/unix", nl);        /* get table addresses      */
        cdev_ptr = (struct cdevsw *) nl[0].n_value;
        fmod_ptr = (struct fmodsw *) nl[1].n_value;
        printf( "\n\tfmod: %x  cdev: %x\n",
                  fmod_ptr, cdev_ptr );
```

The preceding code filled the address fields (`n_value`) in our `nlist` structure and printed the base addresses of the kernel tables in which we are interested. The name of the kernel file may be different on your system (such as `/hpux` or `/vmunix`), but it is usually found in the root (`/`) directory. The other values we need (such as the number of installed modules) are not given to us by `nlist()` but must be read from memory:

```
        /* Now read parameter values from kernel memory          */

        if ( (memfd = open ("/dev/kmem", 0) ) < 0)
           { perror ("/dev/kmem"); exit (1); }

        if ( (rc = lseek (memfd, nl[2].n_value, 0) ) == -1 )
           { perror ("/dev/kmem"); exit (4); }
        if ( (rc = read (memfd, &cdevcnt, sizeof(int)) ) < 0)
           { perror ("/dev/kmem"); exit (5); }

        if ( (rc = lseek (memfd, nl[3].n_value, 0) ) == -1 )
           { perror ("/dev/kmem"); exit (4); }
        if ( (rc = read (memfd, &fmodcnt, sizeof(int)) ) < 0)
           { perror ("/dev/kmem"); exit (5); }
```

```
        printf( "\n\tfmodcnt = %d\tcdevcnt = %d\n\n",
                    fmodcnt,        cdevcnt );
```

Next, the character device switch table (cdevsw) is scanned, printing the major device number for STREAMS devices. STREAMS devices are those with a non-NULL d_str pointer to a streamtab control block.

```
        /* Now advance to start of char devsw table in kmem     */

        if ( (rc = lseek (memfd, (long) cdev_ptr, 0) ) == -1 )
            { perror ("/dev/kmem"); exit (4); }

        for ( k=0;   k < cdevcnt;   k++, cdev_ptr++)
          {
            if ( (rc = read (memfd, &cdev, sizeof(cdev)) ) < 0)
                { perror ("/dev/kmem"); exit (5); }

            if ( cdev.d_str == NULL)  continue; /* not a STREAM */

            printf ("\tcdev maj # %d\td_str = %x\n",
                        k,   cdev.d_str);

          }
        printf( "\n" );
```

Finally, the STREAMS module table is scanned and the name of each module installed in the kernel is printed.

```
        /* Now go to the STREAMS module table in kmem            */

        if ( (rc = lseek (memfd, (long) fmod_ptr, 0) ) == -1 )
            { perror ("/dev/kmem"); exit (4); }

        for ( k=0; k < fmodcnt; k++, cdev_ptr++)
          {
            if ( (rc = read (memfd, &fmod, sizeof(fmod)) ) < 0)
                { perror ("/dev/kmem"); exit (5); }

            printf ("\tmodule name: %s\taddr = %x\n",
                    fmod.f_name, fmod.f_str);

          }
}
```

This example may be helpful in other situations where you need to examine or modify values in a running kernel (or other executable file). For now, it has served as a good introduction to kernel data structures used to implement the STREAMS facility in System V Release 3 and 4.

6.3.2   Modules and Drivers

Figure 6.9 illustrates the difference between a STREAMS module and driver. A module is a single pair of queue structures, while a driver has an upper ("head") part and a lower ("driver") part. This enables a pseudo-device driver to multiplex lower STREAMS that are **I_LINK**ed below it, while upper stream heads (created by "**clone opens**") can be multiplexed among the upper stream queues. Modules are inserted at the top (just below the head) of a linked list of queue structures between the user and a device.

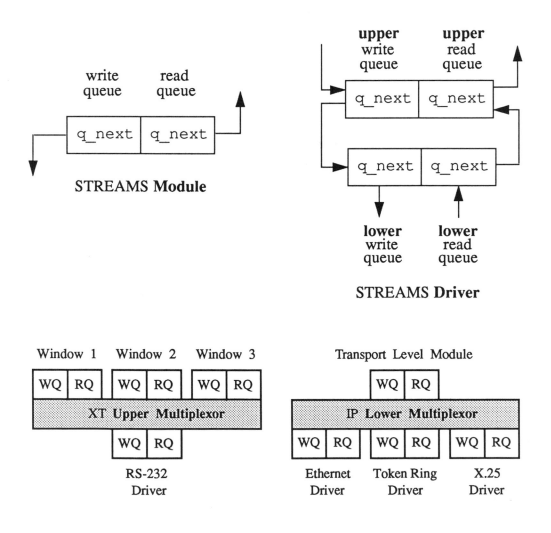

Figure 6.9   STREAMS Multiplexor Drivers

6.3.3   Queue Structure

Each module has an "upstream" queue and a "downstream" queue. Each queue has a pointer to data used to initialize the queue when it is created and another pointer to a private data area, used to store local values when the queue is active. Stream service procedures are scheduled inside the kernel, independent of processes, and thus have no "user context" to store data. The header file /usr/include/sys/**stream.h** has the definition of a queue structure which is illustrated in Figure 6.10.

```
struct  queue {
        struct    qinit  *q_qinfo;    /* procs and limits      */
        struct    msgb   *q_first;    /* first data block      */
        struct    msgb   *q_last;     /* last data block       */
        struct    queue  *q_next;     /* Q of next stream      */
        struct    queue  *q_link;     /* next Q for scheduling */
        caddr_t   q_ptr;              /* private data          */
        short     q_count;            /* no of blocks on Q     */
        unsigned short q_flag;        /* queue state           */
        short     q_minpsz;           /* min packet size       */
        short     q_maxpsz;           /* max packet size       */
        short     q_hiwat;            /* high water mark       */
        short     q_lowat;            /* low water mark        */
        char      *q_pad;             /* pad field             */
};
typedef struct queue queue_t;
```

As data flows through a stream, only the pointers to message blocks (msgbs) are passed to "move" messages to the next (upstream or downstream) queue accessed by the **q_next** pointer. This is done by the "put procedure," accessed by the **qi_putp** pointer in a qinit structure.

```
struct qinit {
        int    (*qi_putp)();          /* put procedure         */
        int    (*qi_srvp)();          /* service procedure     */
        int    (*qi_qopen)();         /* called on startup     */
        int    (*qi_qclose)();        /* called on finish      */
        int    (*qi_qadmin)();        /* for 3bnet only        */
        struct module_info *qi_minfo; /* module information    */
        int    *qi_dummy;             /* pad field for FS changes*/
};
```

The service procedure, accessed by the **qi_srvp** pointer in a qinit structure, is invoked by a STREAMS scheduler subroutine inside the kernel. The STREAMS scheduler is called from the (clock) interrupt level, and therefore service procedures have no "user context." That is, fields in **user.h** are not likely to be associated with the stream currently being serviced by the service procedure. In particular, **service procedures cannot block or sleep, and they should obey the rules of interrupt-level service routines!**

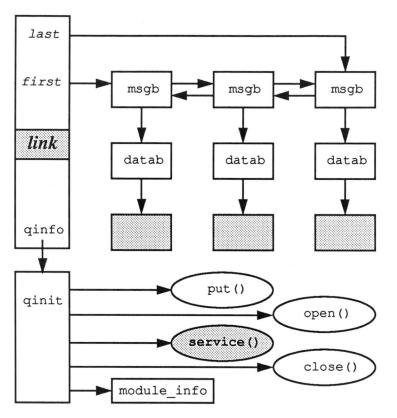

Figure 6.10 Queue Data Structure

The put procedure removes message blocks from the current queue and adds them to the linked list of the next (upstream or downstream) queue. Flow control is possible by having the put procedure examine the **q_flag** field of the next queue:

```
/* Queue flags */
#define  QENAB     01    /* Queue is already enabled to run    */
#define  QWANTR    02    /* Someone wants to read queue         */
#define  QWANTW    04    /* Someone wants to write queue        */
#define  QFULL     010   /* Queue is considered full            */
#define  QREADR    020   /* This is the read side queue         */
#define  QUSE      040   /* This queue in use (allocated)       */
#define  QNOENB    0100  /* Don't enable queue via putq         */
```

If the next queue has the **QFULL** bit set, the put procedure does not advance the message blocks, and (unless the QNOENB bit is set) it sets the **QENAB** bit of the next queue and uses the **q_link** field to add the next queue to the STREAMS scheduler's "run queue." The service procedure will be executed the next time the STREAMS scheduler notices that a queue is "ready" for service, which happens at the next return from an interrupt. The worst case wait would be for a clock interrupt.

Perhaps you noticed the intermediate **datab** control block in Figure 6.10 between the msgb and the actual data. This allows two or more queues to share the same data without copying or duplicating it. For example, the TCP module maintains a copy of the data in a TCP segment until it receives an acknowledgment from the other end, so msgbs in the IP module point to the same TCP datab control blocks while IP transmits the datagrams. A reference count is maintained in datab, which is incremented each time another msgb points to it and decremented each time a msgb dereferences the datab. When the datab reference count becomes zero, it is put back on a free list and the actual data is dereferenced as well.

The module information structure contains the initial packet size and flow control limits, as well as the module identification used to find the module in the module switch table (see Figure 6.8). These values are copied into the stream head queue structures, when a STREAMS device is opened, or into the module's queue structure when it is pushed onto a stream.

```
struct module_info {
        short    mi_idnum;         /* module id number          */
        char     *mi_idname;       /* module name               */
        short    mi_minpsz;        /* min packet size accepted  */
        short    mi_maxpsz;        /* max packet size accepted  */
        short    mi_hiwat;         /* hi-water mark             */
        short    mi_lowat;         /* lo-water mark             */
        char     *mi_pad;          /* pad field in case FS changes */
};
```

Each instance of a module is initialized with values from the module_info structure. The module_info structure is accessed via a qinit structure accessed by a streamtab structure, which has pointers to upstream and downstream qinit structures. A STREAMS device driver has pointers for both the upper and lower STREAMS modules. Lower stream queue pointers are NULL in a simple module streamtab structure. These streamtab structures are pointed to by an entry in fmodsw (module) or cdevsw (driver). See Figure 6.8 for a picture.

```
struct streamtab {
        struct qinit *st_rdinit;   /* upper read  queue   */
        struct qinit *st_wrinit;   /* upper write queue   */
        struct qinit *st_dummy1;   /* lower read  queue   */
        struct qinit *st_dummy2;   /* lower write queue   */
};
```

6.3.4 Stream Heads

Every STREAMS stack has a "head module" at the top that is the primary interface
between a user process and the stream. It maintains some state information and moves
user data to and from message blocks, which travel through the stream. Each stream's
state information is stored in an `stdata` control block, which is defined in
`/usr/include/sys/`**`strsubr.h`**:

```
struct stdata {
        struct  queue     *sd_wrq;    /* write queue              */
        struct  msgb      *sd_iocblk;/* return block for ioctl */
        struct  vnode     *sd_vnode;  /* backptr, for hangups   */
        struct  streamtab *sd_strtab;/* stream's streamtab     */
        long    sd_flag;              /* state/flags            */
        long    sd_iocid;             /* ioctl id               */
        ushort  sd_iocwait;           /* # of procs waiting
                                         to do ioctl            */
        short   sd_pgrp;              /* process group,
                                         for signals            */
        ushort  sd_wroff;             /* write offset           */
        unchar  sd_error;             /* hangup or error
                                         to set in u.u_error    */
        unchar  sd_wait;              /* time to timeout        */
        unchar  sd_min;               /* min chars for input    */
        struct  proc *sd_rsel;        /* Read select            */
        struct  proc *sd_wsel;        /* Write select           */
        struct  strevent *sd_siglist;/* pid linked list to
                                         rcv SIGSEL signal      */
        struct  strevent *sd_sellist;/* pid linked list to
                                         wakeup select()        */
        int     sd_sigflags;          /* logical OR of all
                                         siglist events         */
        int     sd_selflags;          /* logical OR of all
                                         sellist events         */
        char    sd_pktstat; /* status for tty_pty packet mode */
};
```

Once a STREAMS device is opened, the device **vnode** points to this `stdata`
structure, and `sd_wrq` points to the downstream side of the head module. A macro,
RD(`sd_wrq`), can be used to access the upstream (read) side. If a HANGUP occurs on
a stream, the device driver will send a HANGUP message to the stream head. If the
stream is the controlling terminal for a login session, a **SIGHUP** signal is sent to every
process in the controlling terminal's process group (`sd_pgrp`).

Note that **POSIX** *sessions* require modifications to this **SVR3** data structure, and
the `stdata` structure has been modified in **SVR4**. Readers are advised to avoid using

it in code, as the `stdata` structure is **system-dependent**. In fact, the equivalent data structure in OSF/1 is called **sth** ("stream head") defined in an `sth.h` header file which is only available to OSF/1 source license holders. STREAMS module and driver code is portable when it limits itself to *queue*, *qinit*, *module_info*, and *streamtab* structures. Study your vendor's documentation for their specific installation directions.

The basic connections for open STREAMS devices are shown in Figure 6.11. Once opened, a STREAMS device is accessed by its `vnode` (virtual `inode`). At open time, a pair of `queue` structures are allocated for the stream head and initialized with values accessed from the `streamtab` structure. The (pseudo) device driver's `queue` structures are also allocated and initialized at open time.

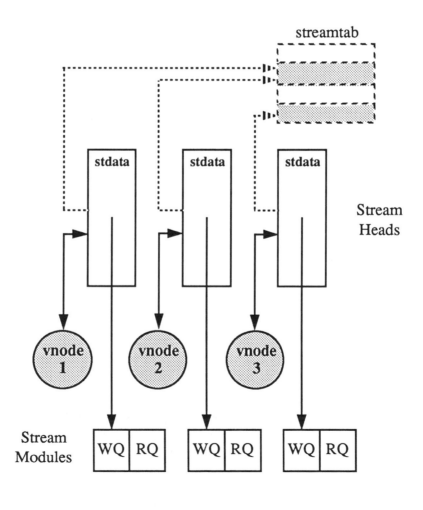

Figure 6.11   Stream   Heads

6.3.5 Kernel Control Blocks

The System V **crash** command can be used to examine kernel control blocks:

```
# crash
dumpfile = /dev/mem, namelist = /stand/unix, outfile = stdout
```

Without any arguments, `crash` reads `/dev/mem` (the running kernel) and uses `/stand/unix` to find symbols. It prompts you with "**>**" for commands.

The `stream` command asks `crash` to display the "stream table." The "stream table" consists of the `stdata` structures diagrammed in Figure 6.11.

```
> stream
  STREAM TABLE SIZE = 15
  ADDRESS     WRQ        IOCB      VNODE    PUSHCNT  RERR/WERR  FLAGS
  d10f0980  d10b7640  d00c7cc0  d10ef600      0       0/0      ondel
  d10f0a00  d10d5a40  d00c7cc0  d10ef780      0       0/0      ondel mnt
  d10b7500  d10d4d40  d00c7cc0  d10f0c00      0       0/0      rslp ondel
  d10efa00  d10d4840  d00c77dc  d10d4904      4       0/0      istty mnds
  d10f0e00  d10efc40  d00c7cc0  d10dad00      0       0/0      rslp ondel
  d10d9600  d10d9340  d00c1948  d10d9404      0       0/0      plex
  d10d9880  d10d9940  d00c1948  d10d9a04      0       0/0      plex
  d10d9e80  d10d9f40  d00c1948  d10d8204      0       0/0      plex
  d10d8900  d10d8640  d00c1948  d10d8704      0       0/0      plex
  d10d8b80  d10d8c40  d00c1948  d10d8d04      0       0/0      plex
  d10d7600  d10d7340  d00c1948  d10d7404      0       0/0      plex
  d10d7880  d10d7940  d00c1948  d10d7a04      0       0/0      plex
  d10d6300  d10d7e40  d00c1948  d10d7f04      0       0/0      plex
  d10d6580  d10d6640  d00c1948  d10d6704      0       0/0      plex
  d10b7d00  d10b7c40  d00c7cc0  d10b7d80      0       0/0      mdis ondel
```

Note that "**plex**" streams have been **I_LINK**ed below a multiplexor and can no longer be accessed directly. We are interested in the one with four modules pushed on it (because we want to follow the linked list with `crash` commands). We note that it is a tty STREAMS device (`istty` flag), and its `vnode` is located at address `0xd10d4904` in the kernel. The `vnode` command allows us to investigate fields in that control block.

```
> vnode d10d4904
  VCNT VFSMNTED VFSP  STREAMP  VTYPE  RDEV   VDATA   VFILOCKS  VFLAG
   2      0       0  d10efa00    c    5,0   d10d4900     0        0
> !ls -l /dev/* | grep " 5,  0"
crw--w----  1 root   tty    5,  0 Aug 17 10:57 /dev/console
crw--w--w-  2 bin    bin    5,  0 Apr  4 00:01 /dev/syscon
crw--w--w-  2 bin    bin    5,  0 Apr  4 00:01 /dev/systty
crw-rw-rw-  1 root   tty    5,  0 Aug 17 10:18 /dev/vt00
```

One field in the `vnode` structure has the major and minor device numbers (**5, 0**), if the `vnode` happens to represent a device file. The exclamation point (**!**) can be used to "bang out" of `crash` to run a command in a subshell. We execute a long `ls` on the `/dev` directory and `grep` for the major and minor device numbers (**5, 0**). *(Be sure to leave two spaces after the comma!)* This shows the name of the STREAMS device we picked is `/dev/console`. (Other names are `/dev/syscon`, `/dev/systty`, and `/dev/vt00`, because they have the same major and minor device numbers.)

The VDATA field (`v_data`) points to a special **character device** (`specfs`) node. A virtual filesysem `vnode` can point to a System V filesystem inode (`s5_inode`) or a BSD "fast" filesystem inode (`ufs_inode`), or even a `/proc` filesystem (`procfs`) object to open an executing process image!

The STREAMP (`v_stream`) field is non-NULL, which means our character device is a STREAMS device and its `stdata` control block is located at virtual address `0xd10efa00` in the kernel. The `queue` command formats and prints a STREAMS queue structure, allowing us to follow the NEXT (**q_next**) pointers to visit all the modules on the stream's stack.

```
> queue    d10efa00          <stdata>
  QUEADDR    INFO     NEXT      LINK       PTR   RCNT FLAG
  d10efa00 d10d4840 d10d4840  4010280        ce    0 us
> queue    d10d4840          <strhead>
  QUEADDR    INFO     NEXT      LINK       PTR   RCNT FLAG
  d10d4840 d00bdea4 d10ef840        - d10efa00    0 us
> queue    d10ef840          <ttcompat>
  QUEADDR    INFO     NEXT      LINK       PTR   RCNT FLAG
  d10ef840 d00bf690 d10d4340        - d10ef980    0 wr us ol
> queue    d10d4340          <ldterm>
  QUEADDR    INFO     NEXT      LINK       PTR   RCNT FLAG
  d10d4340 d00bf06c d10d5940        - d10ef500    0 wr us
> queue    d10d5940          <ansi>
  QUEADDR    INFO     NEXT      LINK       PTR   RCNT FLAG
  d10d5940 d00bf118 d10d4540        - d10b7940    0 wr us
> queue    d10d4540          <char>
  QUEADDR    INFO     NEXT      LINK       PTR   RCNT FLAG
  d10d4540 d00bf19c d10d4740        - d10f0c80    0 wr us
> queue    d10d4740          <cmux>
  QUEADDR    INFO     NEXT      LINK       PTR   RCNT FLAG
  d10d4740 d00c7788        -        - d10daf80    0 wr us
```

The module names *<stdata, strhead, ttcompat, ldterm, ansi,* and *char>* down to the device driver module *<cmux>* were added by us for clarity. Module names could be found by following the **q_info->qi_minfo->mi_idname** pointers, but the `crash` command does not do this for us.

Another `crash` command, `strstat`, shows current utilization of STREAMS resources.

```
> strstat
ITEM              ALLOC    IN USE    FREE    TOTAL    MAX    FAIL
streams            17       17        0       104      21     0
queues             66       66        0       382      74     0
message blocks     11        4        7      8294      24     0
data blocks        11        4        7      8294      24     0
link blocks        11       11        0        11      11     0
stream events       2        2        0         2       2     0
Count of scheduled queues:    0
```

The qrun command shows you all the STREAMS queues with a service procedure enabled to run. These are on a linked list using the `q_link` field of the `queue` structure. For every `queue` on this list, the service procedure **q_info->qi_srvp()** will be called by the STREAMS scheduler after the next interrupt is handled, before the kernel returns to user mode. The service procedure may, in turn, call the put procedure **q_info->qi_putp()**, so neither of these functions should block or sleep, because they are called from interrupt level.

```
> qrun
Queue slots scheduled for service:

> q
```

The q or `quit` command causes the `crash` command to exit and returns you to your shell prompt. The `crash` command is available on most systems derived from System V. In case your system does not have this command, the next section has a C program you can use to find the names of modules pushed on a STREAMS stack.

6.3.6   Printing a Stream Module Stack

Suppose you need to know which modules have already been pushed onto a stack. The SVR4 **strconf** command could be used on the command line or in a shell script, as shown on page 187. From a programming level, the SVR4 **I_LIST ioctl()** system call could be used, as shown in the following `strstack.c` program.

```
$ strstack /dev/console
There are 4 modules on the /dev/console stack.
        ttcompat ........ module 1
        ldterm .......... module 2
        ansi ............ module 3
        char ............ module 4
        cmux ............ device driver
```

The `ttcompat` module provides compatibility for BSD and System V `ioctl()`
requests on a `tty` device. It translates Version 7, BSD, and XENIX `ioctl` commands
into System V `termio` requests. The `ansi`, `char`, and `cmux` modules are part of
SVR4 on Intel 386 machines. A similar `I_FIND` ioctl request was used on page 182
to find out if the `sockmod` module had been pushed onto the `/dev/tcp` stream.

```
/* strstack.c -- print names of modules on stream stack         */

#include <stdio.h>            /*   NULL def'n                     */
#include <fcntl.h>            /* O_RDWR def'n                     */
#include <stropts.h>          /* I_LIST def'n                     */
#include <sys/conf.h>         /* FMNAMESZ                         */
/*         defined in sys/stropts.h for I_LIST ioctl's
                struct str_list
                  {
                    int      sl_nmods;
                    struct str_mlist *sl_modlist;
                  };
                struct str_mlist
                  {
                    char l_name[ FMNAMESZ+1];
                  };
*/
main( argc, argv )
char *argv[];
{
  int      fd, count, i, rc;
  struct str_list  modnames;         /* array for module names    */
  struct str_mlist names[10];        /*clumsy, but malloc failed  */
  fd = open( argv[1], O_RDWR );      /* STREAMS device            */
  count = ioctl( fd, I_LIST, NULL );/* NULL ptr gets number       */
  printf( "\n\tThere are %d modules on the %s stack.\n",
                      count - 1, argv[1] );

  modnames.sl_nmods   = count;       /* modules + device driver   */
  modnames.sl_modlist = names;       /* array of module names     */

  rc=ioctl( fd, I_LIST, &modnames );/* non-NULL ptr gets names     */
      if ( rc == -1 ) perror( "I_LIST ioctl" );
  for( i=0; i < count; i++ )         /* print the module names    */
      printf( "\n\t\t%s", modnames.sl_modlist++ );
  printf( "\n" );
}
```

6.4   A STREAMS Driver Source Program

With the introduction presented in the preceding section, we will now write a
STREAMS driver and add it to a System V 3.2 (and 4.0) kernel. To keep it simple, the
driver will simply **echo** data sent to its write queue onto its read queue. Although the
processing is trivial, the driver can be useful in applications that need a **FIFO queue** to
batch schedule long-running or resource-heavy jobs.

```
/*  echo_.c ------- echo driver for STREAMS IPC            */

/*   +---------+          +--------+          +---------+   */
/*   | process |--Write-->|  echo  |---Read-->| process |   */
/*   |         |          |        |          |         |   */
/*   |    1    |<--Read---| driver |<--Write--|    2    |   */
/*   +---------+          +--------+          +---------+   */

/*  A sample execution:  $ cat </dev/echo &                */
/*                       $ echo "Da bears!" >/dev/echo     */
/*                       Da bears!                         */
#include "sys/types.h"
#include "sys/param.h"
#include "sys/errno.h"
#include "sys/dir.h"
#include "sys/seg.h"
#include "sys/page.h"
#include "sys/stream.h"   /* queue, qinit, module_info defs  */
#include "sys/stropts.h"  /* stream ioctl, signal options    */
#include "sys/strlog.h"   /* stream logging (trace) defs     */
#include "sys/signal.h"
#include "sys/user.h"
#include "sys/sysmacros.h"
#include "sys/log.h"
```

All STREAMS modules and drivers must:

1. Include system header files.
2. Declare external function names (for `qinit` function pointers).
3. Define the **module_info** structure.
4. Initialize two **qinit** strucures for the read and write sides.
5. Define a **streamtab** structure with addresses of the read and write `qinit` structures.
6. Define any private data structures and local flags.
7. Write the functions to implement the module or driver.

6.4.1   Driver Interface Routines

As shown in Figure 6.8, a STREAMS device driver is accessed via a **cdevsw** (character device switch table) entry which, through a **streamtab** entry, points to the driver's queues. Each `queue` structure points to a `qinit` structure, which has pointers to "open," "close," and "service" procedures. A kernel function named **stropen()** is called when a character device with a non-NULL **d_str** pointer is opened. This function allocates the `streamtab->queue->qinit` data structures with pointers to our **echo_open()** function.

```
/*   STREAMS function declarations                            */

int echo_open(), echo_close(), echo_srv();
```

STREAMS modules and drivers have only three externally-known interface routines. Read and write requests travel through **strread()** or **strwrite()** kernel routines, which effectively put user data in a message appended to the write side of our driver, and get user data from a message queue on the read side. The service procedure, `echo_srv()`, is called from the STREAMS scheduler function within the kernel.

6.4.2   Module Name

To guarantee correct access, driver function names must begin with a unique two, three or four-character prefix that "names" the driver. On SVR3 a four-character "echo" prefix worked, but there was a naming conflict in SVR4, so a five-character **"echo_"** prefix was used successfully. This prefix identifies the kernel interfaces to our driver, and we put it in the kernel's module switch table, via our `module_info` structure.

```
/*   STREAM structure declarations        */

static struct module_info echo_m_info = {
    97,         /* module ID number        */
    "echo_",    /* module name             */
    0,          /* min packet              */
    256,        /* max packet              */
    512,        /* hi-water mark           */
    256         /* lo-water mark           */
};
```

The module ID number is only used for logging messages, and has nothing to do with normal STREAMS operations. Recall that modules are found by character-string searches for the module name. The minimum and maximum packet sizes can be examined and changed (in `qinit`) for network devices or other requirements. The hi- and lo-water marks are for flow control. If a put procedure notices that the hi-water mark has been reached, the message is put back on the queue and the service procedure is scheduled to run (and hopefully make room for more messages!).

6.4.3   Kernel Configuration Files

The module's prefix name is used to make the driver known to the system via a **system description file** in **/etc/conf/sdevice.d**/echo_:

```
echo_   Y   1   0   0   0   0   0   0   0
```

The **device name** is echo_, and the **Y** tells the configuration program "yes" to link-edit the "echo_" routines into the kernel with one subdevice.   The seven zeros are place holders for this pseudo-device.   Real devices would use those fields to specify the hardware device's interrupt vector address(es), device control registers, and status registers in physical memory.

A system **master file** (/etc/conf/cf.d/**mdevice**) would have an entry such as the following:

```
echo_   oci   icS   echo_   0   97   1   32   -1
```

where echo_ is the device name, and **oci** specifies that the device has an o**pen**(), a **c**lose(), and an **i**octl() routine.   The characteristics field, **icS**, says that the device is an **i**nstallable, **c**haracter, **S**TREAMS device.   The **handler prefix**, echo_, is prepended to standard STREAMS interface routines open(), close(), and srv().   The next zero is the **block device** major number, and the **97** is the **character device major number**.   This tells you to use the following command:

```
# mknod /dev/echo c 97 0
```

to access your STREAMS device driver.   The 1 and 32 are minimum and maximum number of devices that can be configured into your kernel (via an sdevice file).   The minus one tells the configuration program that this device does not use a DMA channel.

This source program is in the file /etc/conf/**pack.d/echo_**/echo_.c. The following **makefile** in the same directory:

```
CFLAGS=-Olt -Gs -DCMERGE -DINTRINSICS \
       -DM_S_UNIX -DVPIX -DINKERNEL
LDFLAGS=-r -Ms

SRC= echo_.c
OBJ= echo_.o

Driver.o: $(OBJ)
        mv $(OBJ) Driver.o

debug:
        $(CC) -E $(CFLAGS) echo_.c

clean:
        -rm $(OBJ)
        -rm Driver.o
```

The **make** command executes the first target-dependency rule in the `makefile`, which compiles `echo_.c` with `$(CFLAGS)` and `$(LDFLAGS)` options and renames the object file **Driver.o**. The system build command, `/etc/conf/bin/`**idbuild**, combines all the installable drivers (`Driver.o`'s) in each subdirectory of `/etc/conf/pack.d` and link-edits a new kernel in `/etc/conf/cf.d/`**unix**. The new kernel is installed with the following commands:

```
# mv /stand/unix /stand/unix.B4          <save bootable kernel>
# cp /etc/conf/cf.d/unix /stand/unix     </unix is symbolic link to /stand/unix>
# init 6                                 <reboot system with new kernel>
```

You can use the namelist (**nm**) command to see the routines linked into your new kernel. (Note that nm on the old kernel should not have these routines.)

```
$ nm /unix  | grep echo

echo_.c      |            | file |          |    |
echo_open    |3489740640|extern| int ( ) 144|    |.text
echo_close   |3489740784|extern| int ( )  52|    |.text
echo_srv     |3489740836|extern| int ( ) 264|    |.text
echo_ioctl   |3489741100|extern| int ( ) 588|    |.text
echo_m_info  |3490320732|static|          |    |.data
echo_rinit   |3490320748|static|          |    |.data
echo_winit   |3490320776|static|          |    |.data
echo_info    |3490320804|extern|          |    |.data
echo_dev     |3490415480|extern|          |    |.bss
echo_cnt     |3490320820|extern|          |    |.data
```

Our driver has an I/O control (`ioctl`) routine which is not explicitly called from outside, and hence the name need not be defined external. STREAMS messages have a message type. The `strwrite()` function copies user data into a linked list of **M_DATA** message blocks. An **M_IOCTL** message is allocated to carry an `ioctl()` system call request downstream. M_DATA messages are serviced by `echo_srv()`, which calls `echo_ioctl()` to handle M_IOCTL messages. Remember that both of these routines must return without blocking, as they are called from interrupt level, without any user context.

The `module_info` and `qinit` structures are known in the external symbol table, as are some integer constants which define the number of `echo_` devices configured into this kernel. The `crash` command could be used to read these values from the running kernel.

6.4.4   STREAM Initialization Structures

The upstream (read) and downstream (write) queues of the stream head module have separate initialization structures:

```
/*  STREAMS initialization for the read QUEUE.            */
/*  No putq because the write side echos it back.         */
static struct qinit echo_rinit = {
     NULL,              /* put procedure (none)            */
     echo_srv,          /* service procedure               */
     echo_open,         /* called on each open or push     */
     echo_close,        /* called on last close or pop     */
     NULL,              /* reserved for future use         */
     &echo_m_info,      /* module information structure    */
     NULL               /* statistics structure            */
};
/*  STREAMS initialization for the write QUEUE.           */
static struct qinit echo_winit = {
     putq,              /* put procedure                   */
     echo_srv,          /* service procedure               */
     echo_open,         /* called on each open or push     */
     echo_close,        /* called on last close or pop     */
     NULL,              /* reserved for future use         */
     &echo_m_info,      /* module information structure    */
     NULL               /* statistics structure            */
};
```

Notice that both the read and write sides use the same open, close, and service routines. *This means that* **each routine needs to test from which side it is being called.** Normally, only one side calls the open and close routines. The service routine could be different on each side, as is the putq() routine in this example.

The **putq()** routine is a "standard" utility function provided in the kernel for use by STREAMS module and device driver developers. It appends a message (**m**) to a message queue (**q**) and enables the queue's service procedure. It is usually accessed by the q_next field in the preceding queue to move a **message m,** up or downstream. A macro, putnext() hides the function pointers:

```
#define putnext(q, m) \
        (*(q)->q_next->q_qinfo->qi_putp)((q)->q_next, m)
```

The macro variable m is a pointer to the first msgb in a linked list of msgbs that comprise a message. The stream head copies user data into a message, and then calls the write side put procedure. In our driver, data sent to the write queue will be put on the read queue. *Note that an endless loop would begin if the read queue put data on the write queue!*

STREAMS kernel code must define the **streamtab** entry for the module or driver. The `streamtab` structure is known externally, as seen in the `nm` output. A driver will have two pairs of pointers: one for the read and write queues of the upper (head) module and another pair for the lower (driver) module. Our pseudo-device driver will have no lower (driver) `queues`. The `streamtab` entry points to the `qinit` structures, which in turn access the module's interface routines (refer to Figure 6.8 and Figure 6.10):

```
/*   STREAMS table entry for our echo driver                */

struct streamtab echo_info = {
    &echo_rinit,            /* read  QUEUE initialization */
    &echo_winit,            /* write QUEUE initialization */
    NULL,                   /* multiplexing READ   queue  */
    NULL                    /* multiplexing WRITE queue   */
};
```

There could be multiple instances of this module, and developers use the private data field to point to local (private) data for each instantiation:

```
/*   Private data structure, one per minor dev.            */
/*   Used by "clone opens" for separate streams            */

struct echo {
    unsigned echo_state;    /* driver state flag           */
    queue_t *echo_rdq;      /* read queue pointer          */
};
```

Macros are provided to find the other side of a queue. Given a pointer to the read side, **WR**(echo_rdq) will give you a pointer to the write side, and **RD**(wq_ptr) will give you the matching read `queue` pointer from a write `queue` pointer. **OTHERQ**(q) gives a pointer to the mate `queue`.

We define our echo_state flags as follows:

```
/*   Driver states                                          */

#define  ECHOOPEN   01      /* driver is open               */
#define  ECHOFAIL   02      /* driver open failed           */
```

Other local constants are the following:

```
#define  ECHONDEV    4      /* number of clone devices      */

/*   Allocate clone device array of STREAMS                 */

struct echo echo_dev[ ECHONDEV ];   /* "minor" devices      */

/*   Integer field to check number of clone devices         */

int echo_cnt = ECHONDEV;   /* this field can be examined    */
```

The echo_dev[] array is used to keep track of multiple instances of the same module. More than one process can share access to a given /dev/echo pseudo-device. However, if different applications need exclusive access to their own /dev/echo, a "clone open" is done, and each application (up to echo_cnt) will get its own /dev/echo. Clone opens are implemented in specfs ("special device filesystem") code in SVR4. Clone opens save the system from cluttering the filesystem namespace with many different device files (as is done for BSD /dev/pty's), each with the same major number but a different minor device number. The integer field echo_cnt can be examined in the kernel's memory, while the symbolic constant ECHONDEV cannot.

Our driver will support the following I/O control (ioctl()) commands:

```
/*  Driver ioctl requests                                         */

#define  I_NOARG    20    /* no arg, just ack                     */
#define  I_INTARG   21    /* return int, free blk                 */
#define  I_ERRNAK   22    /* return NAK with err                  */
#define  I_ERROR    23    /* return ACK with err                  */
#define  I_SETHUP   24    /* ACK, then M_HANGUP                   */
#define  I_SETERR   25    /* ACK, then M_ERROR                    */
```

These commands are presented to illustrate the ioctl mechanisms in a STREAMS device and are not necessarily useful. For example, I_SETHUP and I_SETERR are intended to test the hangup and error-handling facilities.

The kernel converts an ioctl() system call into an M_IOCTL message and sends it downstream. Each intermediate module may examine the request, and act on it if the request is recognized, or simply pass it on downstream if not. If the request reaches the driver it is acted on (if recognized) or negatively acknowledged with an M_IOCNAK message sent back up the read side (I_ERRNAK tests this case). Recognized requests are acknowledged with an M_IOCACK message (and results) sent back up the read side (all our requests except I_ERRNAK will do this).

Note that M_IOCTL, M_IOCACK, and M_IOCNAK are high priority control messages and are not subject to normal data flow control. That is, a queue's hi-water mark will not stop the ioctl message's progress through a stream.

6.4.5 Driver Open Routine

A common kernel routine named stropen() allocates a queue pair for the stream head and initializes the vnode pointer (**v_stream**) to point at the stream head. It also allocates a queue pair for the driver's top module and passes a pointer to the read queue to our echo_open() routine. A second open of the same device is recognized by a non-NULL v_stream pointer. Modules must also provide an open() routine which is called whenever the module is pushed on a stream. A flag is passed to the open () routine to indicate whether a device (DEVOPEN), a module (MODOPEN), or a clone device (CLONEOPEN) is being opened. This permits the same code to be used as a module or a driver, if this makes sense for your application.

```
/*  echo_open routine is called on open and I_PUSH             */
echo_open( q, dev, flag, sflag )
queue_t    *q;
{
    struct echo *echoptr;   /* ptr to echo_dev entry            */

    dev = minor( dev );     /* peel off minor dev num from arg2 */

    /* If CLONEOPEN, find a minor dev to use                    */

    if ( sflag == CLONEOPEN )
        for( dev = 0; dev < echo_cnt; dev++ )
            if ( !( echo_dev[ dev ].echo_state & ECHOOPEN ) )
                break;              /*  dev is available         */

    /* Check to see if dev is a good number                     */

    if ( dev < 0 || dev >= echo_cnt )
        return( OPENFAIL );

    echoptr = &echo_dev[ dev ];       /* arg2 or clone device   */

    /* Check to see that state flag is ok                       */

    if ( echoptr->echo_state  &  ECHOFAIL )
        {
        echoptr->echo_state &= ~ECHOFAIL;   /* clear it         */
        return( OPENFAIL );
        };

    /* Initialize the new clone                                 */

    if ( !( echoptr->echo_state & ECHOOPEN ) )/* first open      */
        {
            echoptr->echo_rdq = q;
                q->q_ptr = (caddr_t) echoptr;
            WR(q)->q_ptr = (caddr_t) echoptr;
            return( dev );
        }
    else
        if ( q != echoptr->echo_rdq )            /* second open  */
            return( OPENFAIL );
}
```

6.4.6   Driver Close Routine

The close routine basically "undoes" what the open routine did. It changes the device state flags and disconnects from the STREAMS read queue. It flushes all message blocks on the queue, and it clears the private data pointer to our local state structure.

```
echo_close( q )
queue_t      *q;
{
    /*  Change state, flush read queue,                        */
    /*  and erase the queue pointers.                          */

    ((struct echo *) (q->q_ptr))->echo_state &= ~ECHOOPEN;

    ((struct echo *) (q->q_ptr))->echo_rdq = NULL;

    flushq( WR(q), FLUSHALL ); /* flushall (data & ctrl) msgs */

    q->q_ptr = NULL;          /* break private data pointer to us  */
}
```

6.4.7   Driver Service Routine

The strwrite() function calls putq() to append messages to our write queue. Another utility function, **canput (q)**, tests the queue's hi-water limit and returns true (1) or false (0), depending on whether or not there is room to append a message to the queue. Messages can only be enqueued on queues with a service procedure, so canput () follows the q_next pointers to the next queue with a service procedure. If the queue is full, **putbq(q, m)** can be called to put a message back at the beginning of the starting queue and enable the starting queue's service procedure. *Be careful not to put a priority (control) message back onto its own queue from a service procedure or an infinite loop will begin! (Putbq() also enables the queue's service procedure.)*

   Our driver will queue messages on the write side and send them upstream by calling the function **qreply (q, m)** to send a message in the reverse direction on the mate queue. Figure 6.12 shows the data flow through our driver.

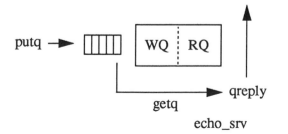

Figure 6.12   STREAMS Data Flow

```
echo_srv ( q )
queue_t   *q;
{
/*  Service procedure takes messages off the write        */
/*  queue and sends them to the read queue                */
    mblk_t *bp;             /* local ptr to an mblk buffer     */

/*  If called from read side, WR(q) switches to write q.  */
q = ( (q)->q_flag & QREADR ? WR(q) : q );     /* QREADR=read q */

/*  If next stream queue is full, put back on this q       */
while ((bp = getq(q)) != NULL )  /* get 1st msg & take off q  */
  { if ((bp->b_datap->db_type) < QPCTL /* not a priority msg */
        && !canput( RD(q)->q_next) )   /* & next q is full    */
      { putbq( q, bp );  return; } /* put back & schedule q */

    /*  Either canput up/downstream, or a priority ctl msg   */
    switch( bp->b_datap->db_type )
      {
        case M_DATA:    qreply(q, bp); /* send back up read q */
                        break;

        case M_IOCTL:   echo_ioctl( q, bp ); /* do ioctl stuff */
                        break;

        case M_CTL:     freemsg(bp); /* ignore device CTL msg */
                        break;

        case M_FLUSH:   if (*bp->b_rptr & FLUSHW) {
                                flushq(q,FLUSHALL);/* downstream */
                                *bp->b_rptr &= ~FLUSHW;
                        }
                        if (*bp->b_rptr & FLUSHR)
                                qreply(q,bp);         /* upstream */
                        else freemsg(bp);   /* eat FLUSH msg */
                        break;

        default:        freemsg(bp); /* ignore all other msgs */
                        break;
      }
  }
}
```

6.4.8   Driver I/O Control Routine

An IO control (`ioctl`) routine is a "catch-all" to perform one or more non-IO services on a device. It can be used to format a disk, or to toggle debugging mode, or anything the driver developer wants. Our sample driver recognizes a few simple `ioctl` requests.

```
echo_ioctl(q, bp)
queue_t    *q;
mblk_t     *bp;
{
   register s;   int i, n;   mblk_t *tmp;

   struct iocblk *iocbp;         /* IO control block structure   */
   /*                                                             */
   /*   struct iocblk {          /* for M_IOCTL message type.     */
   /*       int     ioc_cmd;     /* ioctl command type            */
   /*       ushort  ioc_uid;     /* effective uid of user         */
   /*       ushort  ioc_gid;     /* effective gid of user         */
   /*       int     ioc_id;      /* ioctl id (to compare at top)  */
   /*       int     ioc_count;   /* count of bytes in data field  */
   /*       int     ioc_error;   /* error code                    */
   /*       int     ioc_rval;    /* return value                  */
   /*   };                                                        */

   /* Each ioctl command tests the STREAMS ioctl mechanism.    */

      iocbp = (struct iocblk *) bp->b_rptr;  /* ioctl blk ptr */

      switch(iocbp->ioc_cmd) {        /* check command field    */

      case I_NOARG:    /* No args, just ACK the ioctl          */

         bp->b_datap->db_type = M_IOCACK; /* ioctl ACK msg */
         qreply(q, bp);            /* send it back upstream   */
         return;

      case I_ERROR:    /* Verify that error return works.      */

         iocbp->ioc_error = EINTR;/* interrupted syscall    */

         bp->b_datap->db_type = M_IOCACK; /* ioctl ACK msg */
         qreply(q, bp);            /* send it back upstream   */
         return;

      case I_ERRNAK:   /* Send a NAK back with an error value */

         iocbp->ioc_error = ENOSR;/* no STREAMS resources   */

         bp->b_datap->db_type = M_IOCNAK; /* ioctl NAK msg */
         qreply(q, bp);            /* send it back upstream   */
         return;
```

```
        case I_INTARG:   /* Send integer back as return value   */

            if (bp->b_cont == NULL) /* if no integer argument */
                { freemsg(bp); return; } /* free msg & return  */

            /* return value is int in next mblk of this msg       */
            iocbp->ioc_rval = *((int *)bp->b_cont->b_rptr);

            tmp = unlinkb(bp);/* unlink first mblk from msg      */
            freeb(tmp);        /* and give it back to free pool */

            iocbp->ioc_count = 0;    /* no data; ans in rval    */

            bp->b_datap->db_type = M_IOCACK; /* ACK the ioctl  */
            qreply(q, bp);              /* send it back upstream  */
            return;

        case I_SETHUP:   /* Send ACK followed by M_HANGUP msg. */

            bp->b_datap->db_type = M_IOCACK; /* ACK the ioctl  */
            qreply(q, bp);              /* send it back upstream  */

            putctl(RD(q)->q_next, M_HANGUP); /* HANGUP ctl msg */
            return;

        case I_SETERR:   /* Send ACK followed by M_ERROR msg.   */
            /* Error code is sent in second message block.      */
            tmp = unlinkb(bp);/* unlnk 1st blk; tmp -> 1st blk */
            bp->b_datap->db_type = M_IOCACK; /* ACK the ioctl  */
            ((struct iocblk *)bp->b_rptr)->ioc_count = 0;
            qreply(q, bp);              /* send it back upstream  */

            tmp->b_datap->db_type = M_ERROR;
            qreply(q, tmp);
            return;

    default:
        /*
         * NAK anything else.
         */
        bp->b_datap->db_type = M_IOCNAK; /* NAK the ioctl  */
        qreply(q, bp);              /* send it back upstream  */
        return;
    }
}
```

6.5   Echo Test Program

Here is a user-level program that tests our echo driver:

```
/* echotest.c - test the echo device driver                  */

#include <errno.h>          /* EPERM = "not owner" err msg    */
#include <fcntl.h>          /* O_RDWR definition              */
#include <stdio.h>          /* NULL, BUFSIZ definitions       */
#include <sys/stropts.h>    /* strioctl structure definition  */

struct strioctl ioc;        /* ioctl command structure        */

                            /* driver ioctl requests          */

#define  I_NOARG   20       /* no arg, just ack               */
#define  I_INTARG  21       /* return int, free blk           */
#define  I_ERRNAK  22       /* return NAK with err            */
#define  I_ERROR   23       /* return ACK with err            */
#define  I_SETHUP  24       /* ACK, then M_HANGUP             */
#define  I_SETERR  25       /* ACK, then M_ERROR              */

char buf[ BUFSIZ ];         /* IO buffer with stdio BUFSIZ    */

main()
{
   int  fd;

   if ((fd=open("/dev/echo", O_RDWR, 0777)) == -1)
      { perror( "/dev/echo open failed ... "); exit(1); }

   printf("Enter a string to write to the echo device:\n");

   if ((fgets(buf,BUFSIZ,stdin)) == NULL )
      { perror("fgets failed"); exit(2); }

   /* function calls to test the STREAMS echo device          */

   strwrite( fd, buf ); strread (fd);  /* write & read device */

   strioctl( fd, I_NOARG,   0,0,NULL); /* test ioctl commands */

   strioctl( fd, I_INTARG, 49,0,NULL);

   strioctl( fd, I_ERRNAK,  0,0,NULL);

   strioctl( fd, I_ERROR,   0,0,NULL);

   strioctl( fd, I_SETHUP,  0,0,NULL);  strwrite( fd, buf );

   strioctl( fd, I_SETERR,  0,0,NULL);
}
```

```
strwrite(fd, s)
int   fd;
char *s;
{
   printf("\nWriting to the echo device...\n");
   if ( write(fd,s,BUFSIZ) < 0)
      { perror("\nStream write failed"); exit(3); }
}

strread(fd)
int fd;
{
   printf("\nReading from the echo device...\n");
   if ((read(fd,buf,BUFSIZ)) < 0)
      { perror("\nStream read failed"); exit(4); }
   printf("String = %s\n",buf);
}

strioctl(fd,arg,time,len,s)
int   fd, arg, time, len;
char *s;
{
   int i;    char *p;
   ioc.ic_cmd    = arg;      /* ioctl command      */
   ioc.ic_timout = time;     /* timeout in secs    */
   ioc.ic_len    = len;      /* length  of arg     */
   ioc.ic_dp     = s;        /* pointer to arg     */

   switch (arg)
   {
      case I_NOARG :    p = "I_NOARG";          break;
      case I_INTARG :   p = "I_INTARG";         break;
      case I_ERRNAK :   p = "I_ERRNAK";         break;
      case I_ERROR :    p = "I_ERROR";          break;
      case I_SETHUP :   p = "I_SETHUP";         break;
      case I_SETERR :   p = "I_SETERR";         break;
      default :         p = "Unknown Ioctl";    break;
   }
   printf("\nTrying ioctl call %s # %d\n", p, arg);
   if ((i = ioctl(fd, I_STR, &ioc)) < 0) {
        perror("ioctl failed");
        printf("return code = %d ioctl cmd = %d\n",i,arg);
   }
   printf("ioctl() return code = %d\n",i);
}
```

Here is a test of the echo driver:

```
$ ./echotest

Enter a string to write to the echo device: Hi!

Writing to the echo device...
Reading from the echo device...
String = Hi!

Trying ioctl call I_NOARG # 20
ioctl() return code = 0

Trying ioctl call I_INTARG # 21
ioctl failed: Timer expired
return code = -1 ioctl cmd = 21
ioctl() return code = -1

Trying ioctl call I_ERRNAK # 22
ioctl failed: Out of STREAMS resources.
return code = -1 ioctl cmd = 22
ioctl() return code = -1

Trying ioctl call I_ERROR # 23
ioctl failed: Interrupted system call.
return code = -1 ioctl cmd = 23
ioctl() return code = -1

Trying ioctl call I_SETHUP # 24
ioctl() return code = 0

Writing to the echo device...
Stream write failed: I/O error       <HANGUP message at stream head>

ioctl failed: Invalid argument       <bad fd (if no exit after write)>
```

6.6   Summary

In this chapter we developed a Network Printer application using the STREAMS **pseudo-terminal subsystem,** and used the `truss` command to help debug it. We added a simple **"echo" STREAMS driver** to the kernel. We used the `crash` command to examine the structure of STREAMS modules, including kernel control blocks. STREAMS messages are an important part of the service interface routines in the Transport Level Interface (TLI) library functions that we'll see in the next chapter.

A STREAMS module is a pair of **queue** structures, one for the downstream (write) side, and one for the upstream (read) side. A STREAMS driver has both a stream head and a driver module, which enables a driver to multiplex multiple streams. STREAMIO `ioctl` commands are summarized in Figure 6.13.

Command Purpose	Command Name
Push a module onto a stream	I_PUSH
Pop a module from a stream	I_POP
See if module is on a stream	I_FIND
Get name of top module on stream	I_LOOK
Link a stream to a multiplexor driver	I_LINK
Unlik a stream from multiplexor	I_UNLINK

Figure 6.13 STREAMIO `ioctl()` Commands

The STREAMS pseudo-terminal subsystem facilities are summarized in Figure 6.14.

Facility Purpose	Facility Name
Line discipline module	ldterm
Terminal emulation module	ptem
Packet assembly/disassembly module	pckt
Master side of pseudo-terminal device	/dev/ptmx
Slave side of pseudo-terminal device	/dev/pts/?
Get name of slave pseudo-terminal device	ptsname()
Grant access to slave pseudo-terminal device	grantpt()
Unlock pseudo-terminal device	unlockpt()
Mount stream over a file name	fattach()

Figure 6.14 STREAMS Pseudo-terminal Subsystem

The STREAMS header files used in this chapter are summarized in Figure 6.15.

Header File	Description
`<stropts.h>`	`/* STREAMIO I_PUSH, I_POP, cmds */`
`<sys/poll.h>`	`/* pollfd struct for poll()     */`
`<nlist.h>`	`/* a.out symbol table (namelist) */`
`<sys/conf.h>`	`/* cdevsw and fmodsw definitions */`
`<sys/strsubr.h>`	`/* stream header (stdata struct) */`
`<sys/stream.h>`	`/* queue, qinit, mod_info defs   */`
`<sys/stropts.h>`	`/* stream ioctl, signal options  */`
`<sys/strlog.h>`	`/* stream logging (trace) defs   */`

Figure 6.15 STREAMS Header Files

We examined STREAMS control blocks using the **crash** (kernel debugger) command. The crash commands used in this chapter are summarized in Figure 6.16.

Command Purpose	Command Name
Show the open STREAMS devices	stream
Show an open vnode structure	vnode
Show an active queue structure	queue
Show the current STREAMS usage	strstat
Show the STREAMS scheduler queue	qrun
Quit crash	q

Figure 6.16 Crash (Kernel Debugger) Commands

The key kernel control blocks for STREAMS are summarized in Figure 6.17.

Control Block Purpose	Control Block Name
Store module link and data pointers	queue
Store pointers to open, close, put, service procs	qinit
Store module name, high and low water marks	module_info
Per class pointers to upper, lower qinits	streamtab
Per instance pointers to wqueue and vnode	stdata(stream head)
Store linked list of message blocks	msgb
Intermediate data block pointers	datab

Figure 6.17 STREAMS Kernel Control Blocks

Some key kernel-level STREAMS utility functions are summarized in Figure 6.18.

Function Purpose	Function Name
Put a message on a queue in priority order	putq (q, m)
Put a message back on a queue in same place	putbq (q, m)
Get a message from a queue, enable waiter	getq (q)
Send a message in opposite direction	qreply(q, m)
Check for room on a forward queue	canput (q)
Enable queue's service procedure	qenable (q)
Disallow enabling of queue's service procedure	noenable(q)
Allow enabling of queue's service procedure	enableok(q)

Figure 6.18 STREAMS Kernel Routines

7 Transport Level Interface (TLI Programming)

by Bill Rieken

7.1 Introduction

Transport level programming allows you to write applications that are independent of specific protocol details. This is one level higher than the physical network independence provided by network protocols. Today's popular open network protocols are TCP/IP and OSI, but there is no way to predict accurately which protocols will be in vogue a decade from now. **TLI (Transport Level Interface) programming** allows you to build applications that will run today over TCP/IP or OSI, and tomorrow they will be able to run over newer, yet-to-be-invented protocols, *without recompiling!* Figure 7.1 reviews the seven-layer OSI reference model.

Layer 7	application	`rlogin`, `telnet`
Layer 6	presentation	external/network data representation
Layer 5	session	remote procedure call
Layer 4	**transport**	**TCP, UDP, TP4**
Layer 3	network	IP, X.25
Layer 2	data link	device driver
Layer 1	physical	Ethernet, Token-ring, Starlan, 10baseT

Figure 7.1 OSI Reference Model

One example of protocol independence is network addressing. TLI allows your application to work with 32-bit Internet addresses, 15-character X.25 addresses, or variable-length string addresses. Another example is the capability to send user data (such as user id) along with a connection request. Some protocols allow you to do this, while others do not. Your application might use the user id to decide whether to accept or reject the connection request, if the underlying protocol allows you to refuse a connection request. With TLI, you can test whether or not the underlying network protocol has this capability, and then code accordingly. However, if your application **requires** any of these special capabilities, it may be **protocol independent**, but it cannot be **service independent**. That is, with TLI you specify your **service requirements**, rather than code to meet specific **protocol requirements**.

7.1.1   Transport Information (t_info) Structure

Protocol information is available in a **t_info** structure:

```
struct t_info
{
  long addr;     /* max size of transport protocol addr      */
  long options;  /* max #bytes of protocol-specific options   */
  long tsdu;     /* max size of transport service data unit   */
  long etsdu;    /* max size of expedited data tsdu           */
  long connect;  /* max amt of data with connect requests     */
  long discon;   /* max amt of data with disconnect requests  */
  long service;  /* service type supported                    */
};
```

A pointer to this structure is available to you after a **transport endpoint** is opened. The addr field, for example, lets you know how big the transport address is.

A value of −2 in any field indicates that feature is not provided by the underlying transport protocol. For example, the connect field would be −2 for both UDP and TCP, because neither protocol allows user data to accompany a connection request. As another example, the etsdu field lets you know whether the underlying transport protocol provides a capability for **expedited data** to cut in front of normal data (for example, a **control-C** character to terminate a process). Because expedited data only makes sense in a byte-stream data connection, where the sequence of data bytes is preserved, the etsdu field would be −2 if the transport provider were UDP.

A value of −1 in any field indicates that the corresponding attribute is unlimited in size. For example, the addr field would be 16 for TCP/UDP (a 2-byte address family and a 14-byte address field), 15 for X.25, and 55 for Starlan/ISO. The tsdu field is zero for the TCP byte-stream protocol because it has no logical message boundaries, while tsdu would have the maximum datagram size for a connectionless transport provider such as UDP or starlandg.

There are three values for the service type field:

T_COTS	**Connection-Oriented Transport Service** without orderly release
T_COTS_ORD	Connection-Oriented Transport Service **with orderly release**
T_CLTS	**ConnectionLess Transport Service** (datagram messages)

UDP has a T_CLTS value in the service field. TCP is a connection-oriented transport service with **orderly release**. Orderly release simply means that either side may terminate a connection and **data will not be lost**. That is, data in transit will be received by the other side (remember that the request to release a connection may arrive before some of the previously sent data packets arrive). An example of orderly release is when a remote connection is closed after reaching an end-of-file on a file transfer service. An orderly release request is sent, but you want the receiver to linger a while if the release request arrives before all the data is acknowledged. An **abortive disconnect** request breaks a connection immediately and **previously sent data may be discarded by the transport provider.** All transport providers are required to support the abortive disconnect, but graceful orderly release is an option that may or may not be provided by the transport protocol.

7.2   Basic TLI Functions

This section introduces the basic Transport Level Interface functions such as t_open(), t_bind(), t_connect(), t_listen(), t_connect(), t_close() and others. Familiarity with socket level system calls is helpful.

7.2.1   Opening a Transport Endpoint

The analog of a BSD socket is called a **transport endpoint**, and the analog of the BSD socket() system call is the **t_open**() library function, which has the format:

```
int     t_open( "devname",  openflag, info )
char    *devname; int openflag; struct t_info *info;
```

where the arguments are the following:

"devname" **/dev/tcp, /dev/udp, /dev/starlan, /dev/starlandg**
openflag   Same as open(2) option flags, (such as O_NDELAY)
info   Transport provider characteristics

A t_info structure is filled in, and a pointer to it is returned in the third parameter. If you don't care about the protocol characteristics (for example, if you open /dev/tcp and already know which services are available to you), you may send a NULL address to indicate you don't want access to the t_info structure. If you later discover that you need transport protocol information, or if you change some user-settable options, you can use the TLI function **t_getinfo**(fd, info) to access the current transport protocol information. The first argument, fd, is the integer file descriptor returned by a successful t_open() call.

TLI functions return a value of −1 upon error, and another TLI function, **t_error**("user msg"), can be called to send an error message to the standard error output. The function t_error() is similar to the standard library function perror(), except that it uses an error code in the extern int t_errno to index an array of error messages in t_errlist[]. This is necessary because a system call may fail inside the library function code, and system call error codes are stored in the extern int errno, which is defined in the standard header file errno.h.

All programs that call TLI functions must #include the TLI header file **tiuser.h**. This is the "stdio.h" of TLI programming.

7.2.2   A Simple TLI Program

This section has a simple program that introduces the basics of TLI programming. The program opens two STREAMS device files that access the TCP (/dev/tcp) and UDP (/dev/udp) transport level protocols. Then it prints the values returned in the etsdu field of the t_info structure:

```
$ cc tinfo.c -lnsl # network services library (t_open, t_bind, ...)
$ ./a.out
           TCP expedited data size is 1
           UDP expedited data size is -2
```

This is what we expect: TCP, a **byte-stream** protocol, can expedite the delivery of a single control byte ahead of normal data in the network buffers, but UDP, a **datagram-message** protocol, does not support expedited data.

```
/* tinfo.c -- transport information (t_info) structure        */
#include <fcntl.h>  /* file control  (O_RDWR)  definitions     */
#include <tiuser.h> /* standard TLI structure definitions      */
main()
{
  struct t_info udp, tcp; /* t_info structs for UDP & TCP      */
  int     fd;             /* transport endpoint                */
  if ( (fd = t_open( "/dev/udp", O_RDWR, &udp )) < 0 )
          t_error( "/dev/udp" );
  if ( (fd = t_open( "/dev/tcp", O_RDWR, &tcp )) < 0 )
          t_error( "/dev/tcp" );
  printf( "\tTCP expedited data size is %d\n", tcp.etsdu );
  printf( "\tUDP expedited data size is %d\n", udp.etsdu );
}
```

Transport level protocols are accessed via STREAMS device files:

```
$ ls -l /dev/tcp /dev/udp
crw-rw-rw-  1 root    root    12, 36 Aug 27 21:09 /dev/tcp
crw-rw-rw-  1 root    root    12, 37 Aug 27 21:09 /dev/udp
```

Other transport protocols are also accessed via device files, and, with a few changes the simple TLI program can be extended to give more information about more protocols:

name	addr	options	tsdu	etsdu	connect	discon	servtype	
/dev/tcp	16	-1	0	1	-2	-2	2	COTS_ORD
/dev/udp	16	-1	16384	-2	-2	-2	3	CLTS
/dev/starlan	55	44	-1	16	32	64	1	COTS
/dev/ticlts	232	4072	4096	-2	-2	-2	3	CLTS
/dev/ticots	240	4080	-1	-1	4072	4084	1	COTS
/dev/ticotsord	240	4080	-1	-1	4072	4084	2	COTS_ORD

The /dev/ti... devices are ISO protocols that use a "loopback" STREAMS module for local testing of application code.

```
/* tinfo.c -- transport information (t_info) structure        */

#include <fcntl.h>        /* file control (O_RDWR)  definitions */
#include <stdio.h>        /* standard I/O (  NULL)  definitions */
#include <tiuser.h>       /* standard TLI structure definitions */

struct transpt
   { char   *name;        /* /dev file of transport provider   */
     struct t_info tin;   /* transport provider information     */
     int    fd;           /* transport endpoint file descriptor */
   }
tp [] =
   {    { "/dev/tcp",       { 0, 0, 0, 0, 0, 0, 0 },   0 },
        { "/dev/udp",       { 0, 0, 0, 0, 0, 0, 0 },   0 },
        { "/dev/starlan",   { 0, 0, 0, 0, 0, 0, 0 },   0 },
        { "/dev/ticlts",    { 0, 0, 0, 0, 0, 0, 0 },   0 },
        { "/dev/ticots",    { 0, 0, 0, 0, 0, 0, 0 },   0 },
        { "/dev/ticotsord", { 0, 0, 0, 0, 0, 0, 0 },   0 },
        {    NULL,          { 0, 0, 0, 0, 0, 0, 0 },   0 }
   };

main()
{
  int    k = 0;                     /* tp array index            */
  printf( "\n%14s\t%s\t%s\t%s\t%s\t%s\t%s\t%s\n",
          "name",   "addr",     "options", "tsdu",
          "etsdu", "connect", "discon",  "servtype" );

  while( tp[k].name != NULL )
    { if((tp[k].fd=t_open(tp[k].name, O_RDWR, &tp[k].tin)) < 0 )
          t_error( tp[k].name );
      else
        { printf( "%14s", tp[k].name      );
          printf( "\t%d", tp[k].tin.addr    );
          printf( "\t%d", tp[k].tin.options );
          printf( "\t%d", tp[k].tin.tsdu    );
          printf( "\t%d", tp[k].tin.etsdu   );
          printf( "\t%d", tp[k].tin.connect );
          printf( "\t%d", tp[k].tin.discon  );
          printf( "\t%d", tp[k].tin.servtype );
```

```
/* This switch statement interprets integer service codes   */
/* and prints a mnemonic description of the service type.    */
        switch( tp[k].tin.servtype )
        {
          case T_COTS:      printf(" COTS");      break;
          case T_CLTS:      printf(" CLTS");      break;
          case T_COTS_ORD:  printf(" COTS_ORD");  break;
          default:          printf(" unknown!");  break;
        }
        printf( "\n" );
    }
    k++;
  }
  printf( "\n" );
}
```

There is a system file with the names of all network devices and transport providers available on your SVR4 system. The file is called **/etc/netconfig** and it will be used later in this chapter. There are library routines that read this file, and they could be used instead of the hard-coded tp array (as we'll do in Section 7.5.1). The main point here is to introduce the t_info structure and the capability for programmers to access protocol characteristics.

7.2.3   TLI **netbuf** Structures

The header file tiuser.h includes the definition of a netbuf structure.

```
struct  netbuf
{
  unsigned int maxlen;   /*   max  size of buffer             */
  unsigned int len;      /* actual data in buffer            */
  char         *buf;     /* protocol-dependent data          */
};
```

This structure is used for network addresses, protocol options, and user data. The maximum and actual length fields in this structure consolidate many of the arguments to BSD socket() system calls. When used to access a network address, a netbuf structure is similar to the BSD sockaddr generic address structure. It can point to protocol-specific address structures such as sockaddr_in, sockaddr_x25, and so on, as illustrated in Figure 7.2.

A TLI function **t_alloc**(fd, struct_type, fields) dynamically allocates memory for netbuf arguments to various TLI functions. It uses information from the t_info structure associated with the endpoint file descriptor fd to fill in the maxlen and len fields **appropriate for the underlying transport**. For example, a struct_type value of **T_CALL** would request t_alloc() to allocate a **t_call** structure, with correct address sizes for the **addr** netbuf. *Protocol independence*, rather than dynamic memory allocation, is the main benefit of t_alloc().

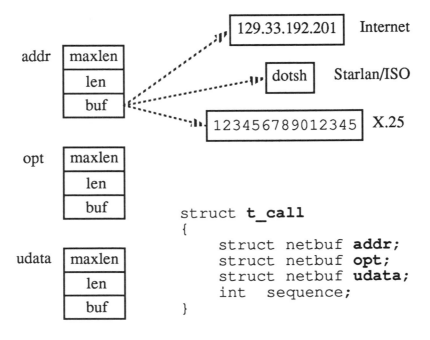

Figure 7.2 TLI netbuf Structures

Possible values for struct_type are the following:

T_CALL	t_call	structure
T_BIND	t_bind	structure
T_OPTMGMT	t_optmgmt	structure
T_DIS	t_discon	structure
T_UNITDATA	t_unitdata	structure
T_UDERROR	t_uderr	structure
T_INFO	t_info	structure

A call to t_alloc() with one of these values will return a pointer to the new memory allocated for the corresponding structure. The **t_call** structure contains the following members; the other structures, except t_info, contain a subset of these:

```
struct   netbuf   addr;
struct   netbuf   opt;
struct   netbuf   udata;
int      sequence;
```

The `addr` `netbuf` points to a protocol address, `opt` points to any protocol options, and `udata` points to any user data sent or received along with a connection request. The `sequence` field is set by `t_listen()` to keep track of multiple connection requests.

The third argument to `t_alloc()`, **fields**, can have the following values:

T_ADDR	**addr** netbuf (and addr buffer) of t_bind, t_call, t_unitdata, or t_uderr structures
T_OPT	**opt** netbuf (and opt buffer) of t_optmgmt, t_call, t_unitdata, or t_uderr structures
T_UDATA	**udata** netbuf (and udata buffer) of t_call, t_discon, or t_unitdata structures
T_ALL	**all** netbufs (and buffers) of a structure

For example, a call of `t_alloc(fd, T_CALL, T_ADDR)` would allocate a `t_call` structure (with three `netbuf` `struct`s) in which only the `addr` `netbuf` is filled in, and the **addr.buf** field points to the `addr.maxlen` bytes of newly allocated memory. A call of `t_alloc(fd, T_CALL, T_ALL)` would allocate a `t_call` structure (with three `netbuf` `struct`s), initialize each `netbuf` **maxlen** field to the appropriate size, and set each `netbuf` **buf** field to the address of the memory allocated for the corresponding field.

The first argument, `fd`, must be a transport endpoint returned by a `t_open()` call. The sizes of the allocated fields are determined from the `t_info` structure, returned by the `t_open()` or `t_getinfo()` functions. Structures whose `t_info` size values are −1 or −2 are impossible to allocate, and `t_alloc()` will fail, setting `t_errno` to `TSYSERR` and `errno` to `EINVAL`. The purpose of `t_alloc()` is to help ensure *protocol independence* and compatibility of compiled user programs with future releases of the *same or different* transport providers.

7.2.4 Naming a Transport Endpoint

The analog of the BSD `bind()` system call is the TLI library function **t_bind()**, which has the following format:

```
int t_bind  ( fd, request, return )
int fd;  struct t_bind *request,  *return;
```

where the request and reply are pointers to a `t_bind` structure:

```
struct  t_bind
{
  struct netbuf addr; /* protocol-specific addr        */
  unsigned int  qlen; /* max # of waiting  connections  */
};
```

The t_bind() function *activates* the endpoint, so it must be called for every endpoint, even those created to accept a connection request from a client. This is different from the socket accept() system call which creates a socket and automatically binds an address to it.

The qlen field sets a maximum number of waiting connect indications, similar to the qlen argument to the socket listen() system call. It is zero for client side endpoints and it is a queue limit for server side endpoints.

The return t_bind structure is filled in by the transport provider and it may have a different address than the one requested! The socket bind() system call simply fails if the kernel is unable to be bind the requested address to the socket. An application programmer can compare the address in the request structure with the one in the return structure to determine if the they are the same. Both the request and the return t_bind arguments may be a NULL pointer to indicate that the caller doesn't care about the protocol address assigned by the transport provider. For example, transport endpoints created to accept a client connection will likely use NULL pointers.

A NULL request pointer means the caller doesn't care which protocol address is used. Compare this with the socket bind() system call, where an Internet address of INADDR_ANY (zero) means the caller is willing to accept requests from any **interface device**, and an Internet port address of zero means the caller doesn't care which protocol **port number** is used.

The caller can give an address of a t_bind structure with a zero-length address field (that is, addr.len = 0). In this case, the user doesn't want to set the address but may want to set the qlen field. Keep in mind that the qlen field applies only to COTS, and the value in the return t_bind structure is the value used by the transport provider.

7.2.5 Connecting to a Transport Endpoint

The analog of the BSD connect() system call is the TLI library function **t_connect()**, which has the following format:

```
int t_connect  ( fd, request, return )
int fd;   struct t_call *request, *return;
```

where the destination address is pointed to by the addr field of a t_call structure:

```
struct  t_call
{
  struct netbuf  addr;  /* protocol-specific addr      */
  struct netbuf  opt;   /* protocol-specific options   */
  struct netbuf  udata; /* user data w/conn. req.      */
  int  sequence;        /* used with t_listen function */
};
```

and the `return t_call` structure (if non-NULL) has information on the newly established connection. For example, the `udata` in the `request t_call` structure may point to user data sent along with the connection request, and the `udata` in the `return t_call` structure would point to any data returned by the destination transport endpoint during connection establishment. The capability to send user data with a connection request depends on the transport provider, which sets the `connect` field in the `t_info` structure associated with the `fd` transport endpoint.

The `options` field of the `t_info` structure indicates whether or not the underlying transport provider supports user-settable options. A value of -2 specifies that user-settable options are not supported, in which case the **request->opt.len** field would have value of **zero**. A positive integer value gives the maximum number of bytes that can be used for user-settable options. The Transport Level Interface does not impose any structure on the protocol-specific option field pointed to by the address in `request->opt.buf`.

The `sequence` field is not used by the `t_connect()` function, but it is used by the `t_listen()` function to keep track of incoming pending connection requests.

Notice that the `t_connect()` function can set protocol options, send user data, and return the peer's address in the `return t_call` structure. The socket interface provides the `setsockopt()` and `getpeername()` system calls, and it does not allow user data to be exchanged during a connect request.

7.2.6 Receiving Connection Requests

The analogs of the BSD `listen()` and `accept()` system calls are the TLI library functions **t_listen()** and **t_accept()**, which have the following format:

```
int t_listen  ( fd, request )
int fd; struct t_call *request;

int t_accept  ( fd,   newfd,  request )
int fd, newfd; struct t_call *request;
```

where `t_listen()` fills in the `sequence` field of the `request t_call` structure with a unique integer id to identify each connection request. These functions are similar to the socket `listen()` and `accept()` system calls, except that **t_listen()** **blocks**, waiting for a connection request to arrive, and `t_accept()` decides whether to accept the request or not. Also, it is the programmer's responsibility to allocate a `newfd` by calling `t_open()` and `t_bind()` to create and name a transport endpoint when one is needed. If `newfd` and `fd` are the same, then the service is probably provided serially by the server to a single client, as `t_accept()` fails with `t_error` set to `TBADF` if other requests are pending (and `newfd=fd`). The socket `accept()` system call, on the other hand **always** creates a `newfd` socket **automatically**, and *it* is the system call that blocks, waiting for a connection request; the socket `listen()`

system call does not block. Also, the qlen parameter is set in the t_bind structure and given to the t_bind() library function; it is not an argument to t_listen(), as it is with the socket listen() system call. It is possible that the transport endpoint fd is not bound for listening (**bind.qlen=0**), in which case the t_listen() call would block forever (if the O_NDELAY flag is not set for fd). The differences between making a connection with BSD sockets and with TLI functions are as follows:

Making a connection with BSD sockets

Client	*Server*
ep2 = socket (...);	ep1 = socket (...); bind (ep1, <*server addr*>); listen (ep1, ...);
connect (ep2, <*server addr*>);	
	ep3 = accept (ep1, ...);

Making a connection with TLI functions

Client	*Server*
ep2 = t_open (...); **t_bind**(ep2, <*null addr* in t_bind>);	ep1 = t_open (...); t_bind (ep1, <*server addr*>); t_listen (ep1, ...);
t_connect (ep2, <*server addr* in t_call>);	
	ep3 = **t_open** (...); **t_bind**(ep3, <*null addr*>); **t_accept**(ep1, ep3, ...);

By blocking in the t_listen() function, TLI separates the listening and accepting functions in a way that gives the programmer an option to test the udata field of the t_call structure and refuse a connection request by calling t_snddis() instead of t_accept(). By not blocking in the listen() system call, BSD sockets require that accept() establish a connection, which may later be closed if the program decides that the connection should not have been made in the first place.

7.2.7   Connection-Oriented Data Transfer

The read() and write() system calls require that the **tirdwr** module be pushed onto the TLI STREAMS device. TLI also provides the following library functions:

```
int t_snd  ( fd, buffer, nbytes, flags )
int fd, nbytes, flags; char *buffer;

int t_rcv  ( fd, buffer, nbytes, flags )
int fd, nbytes, *flags; char *buffer;
```

where the `flags` can be the following:

```
T_EXPEDITED          expedited   (out-of-band)   data
T_MORE               there is more data in the
                     record  being sent/received
0 (zero)             normal data
```

A flag value of zero causes `t_snd()` to behave like a `write()` system call, and `t_rcv()` performs like a `read()` system call (with a flags parameter). *Be careful to give the address of an integer to hold the **received flag**, or your program will core dump!*

The `T_EXPEDITED` flag can be set for control characters. For example:

```
char CC = '\03';      /* ASCII control-C                    */
t_snd(  fd, &CC, 1, T_EXPEDITED );
```

This code segment would cause the control character `CC` to be sent as expedited data (whatever that means to the underlying transport provider).

One use of the `T_MORE` flag is to indicate that not all of the requested `nbytes` of data have been received by the transport provider. This could happen if the endpoint were opened in nonblocking mode (`O_NDELAY` or `O_NONBLOCK`) and there weren't enough kernel buffers for the transport provider to hold all `nbytes` of user data at the time the `t_rcv()` function was called. Remember that byte-stream connections have no concept of (datagram) message boundaries. Another possible use of the `T_MORE` flag is when the application message is larger than the `tsdu` field in the `t_info` structure (16K for UDP and 4K for TICLTS). The Xerox Network Services (XNS) protocol suite has a record-oriented Sequenced Packet Protocol (SPP) that sends "records" over a byte-stream connection. XNS SPP could use the `T_MORE` flag whenever a whole record could not be sent in a single `t_snd()` call.

Notice that `flags` is a **pointer to a returned integer** from a `t_rcv()` call, which lets the receiving program know whether multiple `t_rcv()` calls are needed or the data is expedited. The `flags` field is always set by `t_rcv()`, even if a zero (for normal data) is stored at that location in memory.

If there are more bytes of expedited data than requested in a `t_rcv()` call, the returned `flags` value would have both the `T_EXPEDITED` and `T_MORE` flags set:

```
nbytes = t_rcv( fd, &buf, sizeof( buf ), &flags );
if ( flags & T_EXPEDITED ) ...
if ( flags & T_MORE ) ...
```

If expedited data arrives during the processing of a sequence of normal data `t_rcv()`'s (`T_MORE` is set), then normal processing is suspended and a sequence of expedited data is returned until the expedited data has been processed (`T_MORE` is not set).

7.2.8   Connectionless Datagrams

TLI functions that can be used in datagram applications are the following:

```
int   t_sndudata  ( fd, datagram )
int   fd;   struct t_unitdata *datagram;

int   t_rcvudata  ( fd, datagram,  flags  )
int   fd, *flags; struct t_unitdata *datagram;
```

where the datagrams are accessed by t_unitdata structures:

```
struct t_unitdata
{
 struct netbuf  addr;  /* protocol-specific addr       */
 struct netbuf  opt;   /* protocol-specific options    */
 struct netbuf udata;  /* user data                    */
};
```

The fd argument is the local transport endpoint. The flags parameter is set by the transport provider to **T_MORE** to indicate that the entire datagram did not fit in the udata buffer area and another t_rcvudata() call is necessary to get the rest of the datagram. (Recall that unread data is discarded with sockets!) The addr netbuf has a pointer to the network address of the destination (in t_sndudata()) or the sender (in t_rcvudata()), and opt identifies any protocol-specific options associated with this datagram. A t_rcvudata() call returns minus one and t_errno is set to **TNODATA** if O_NDELAY or O_NONBLOCK is set and there is no data available when the call is made. A t_sndudata() call returns minus one and t_errno is set to **TFLOW** if O_NDELAY or O_NONBLOCK is set and the transport provider cannot accept any more data when the call is made.

These calls are similar to the socket sendto() and recvfrom() system calls.

Again, be sure to provide the address of an integer to hold the received flag!

7.2.9   TLI Errors and Disconnections

Error codes from TLI functions are returned in the global variable **t_errno**:

```
extern int    t_errno;          /* TLI error number        */
```

The variable t_errno is used to index an array of error messages (similar to the way errno is used):

```
extern  char *t_errlist[]; /* errmsg array indexed by t_error */
extern  int   t_nerr;      /* number of errmsg's in t_errlist */
void  t_error ( char *usrmsg );   /* like  perror(3)         */
```

The TLI function t_error() can be used like the standard library function perror() to print a TLI-specific error message. A user-supplied message (if provided) will print on standard error, followed by a colon (:), followed by the error message in t_errlist[] indexed by t_errno. If t_errno is TSYSERR, t_error() also prints the system error message that would be printed by perror().

Whenever a TLI function returns −1, you can check **t_errno** to find out if it was set to **TLOOK**, which tells you to look at the current event on the transport endpoint and respond accordingly:

```
int t_look ( fd )
int fd;
```

This function returns one of the following values:

Current Event	*Description*
T_LISTEN	connection request received
T_CONNECT	connect confirmation received
T_DISCONNECT	abrupt disconnect received
T_ORDREL	orderly release indication
T_DATA	normal data received
T_EXDATA	expedited data received
T_ERROR	fatal error indication
T_UDERR	datagram error indication

If TLOOK is set on a connectionless endpoint, the only possible value is **T_UDERR**, which tells you to call t_rcvuderr() to retrieve the event:

```
int t_rcvuderr ( fd, error )
int fd;   struct t_uderr *error;
```

The network address and protocol options in the bad datagram are returned in a t_uderr structure, along with a *protocol-specific error code* that indicates why the transport provider could not process the datagram:

```
struct  t_uderr
{
  struct netbuf  addr;   /* protocol-specific addr      */
  struct netbuf  opt;    /* protocol-specific options   */
  long    error;         /* protocol-specific error     */
};
```

Each transport provider defines the error codes for the different reasons why it might be unable to process a datagram. Unrecognizable or unsupported options are typical causes for datagram errors.

7.2.10 Orderly Release and Abortive Disconnect

There are two classes of connection-mode transport providers: those that support orderly release (T_COTS_ORD) and those that do not (T_COTS). Only T_COTS_ORD providers (such as TCP) allow either side to initiate an orderly release.

```
int t_sndrel ( int fd );        /* initiate orderly release */
int t_rcvrel ( int fd );        /* receive orderly release */
```

After t_sndrel(), you cannot send any more data on the transport endpoint, but you can drain the input data and wait for an acknowledgment from the other side. After t_rcvrel(), you cannot receive any more data from the endpoint, but you can send a closing message to the other side. Both functions can fail and set t_errno to **TNOTSUPPORT** if orderly release is not supported by the underlying transport provider. TNOREL is returned by t_rcvrel() if you call it when there is no orderly release indication on the specified endpoint. A typical use might be as follows:

```
while( t_rcv( fd, ... ) != -1 )        { /* process data ... */ }
if ( t_errno == TLOOK && t_look( fd ) == T_ORDREL )
   { t_rcvrel( fd );    t_sndrel( fd );    exit( 0 );}
```

After receiving an orderly release request with t_rcvrel(), the program sends an acknowledgment with t_sndrel(). Either of these functions may fail, and therefore they should themselves be tested in industrial-strength production code. However, the test for T_ORDREL makes it extremely unlikely that t_rcvrel() or t_sndrel() will fail. In every case, the exit() call closes the transport endpoint.

Orderly release guarantees (at the protocol level) that no data will be lost. This only ensures that data in transit that reaches the other side's protocol buffers will be sent to the user instead of being thrown away. There is no assurance that a hardware or power failure won't happen before the data reaches the application program.

Not all transport providers support orderly release, and programmers may be required to send an immediate, abrupt disconnect request. Data in transit may be discarded by an abortive disconnect. All transport providers must support abortive disconnects, and the following TLI functions can be used to handle them:

```
int t_snddis( fd, call );  /* initiate abortive disconnect */
int t_rcvdis( fd, disc );  /* receive abortive disconnect */
```

where fd is the transport endpoint and call points to a t_call structure:

```
struct t_call *call;
struct t_call {
  struct netbuf  addr;     /* protocol-specific addr      */
  struct netbuf  opt;      /* protocol-specific options   */
  struct netbuf  udata;    /* user data w/disconn. req.   */
  int  sequence;           /* used with t_listen function */
};
```

The *sequence number* in the t_call structure is used to identify which connection request is to be *rejected*. A typical usage might be as follows:

```
if ( t_listen( fd, call )  is  "ok" )
            t_accept( fd, newfd, call );
else
            t_snddis( fd, call );
```

where the *sequence number* in the t_call structure identifies the particular request to reject. The other fields (addr, opt, udata) are ignored. On the other hand, **after a connection has been established**, the **fd** parameter is sufficient to identify the connection, and a t_call structure is not necessary *unless data is being sent with the request*.

The disc parameter in **t_rcvdis()** points to a "disconnect" structure:

```
struct   t_discon    *disc;
struct   t_discon
{
  struct netbuf   udata;      /* user data w/disconn. req.   */
  int     reason;             /* protocal-specific reason code */
  int   sequence;             /* to reject a connect request   */
};
```

Here is a code segment that shows a typical usage of the connection disconnect facilities:

```
if ( t_errno == TLOOK && t_look( fd ) == T_DISCONNECT )

    if ( t_info.discon == -2 )
      { t_rcvdis( fd, NULL );       exit(77);  }
    else
      { t_rcvdis( fd, &discon ); /* process discon data   */
        exit(88);  }

/* check for T_ORDREL as shown earlier                     */

if ( t_errno != 0 )
    { t_error( "t_rcv error" );      exit(99);  }
```

The disconnect capability of the underlying transport provider is indicated by the value in the discon field of the transport's t_info structure. A positive integer value specifies the maximum amount of user data that may accompany a disconnect request. A value of −1 indicates an **unlimited** amount, while **−2** indicates that the underlying transport provider does not allow **any** user data to accompany a disconnect request. For example, neither TCP nor UDP allow user data to accompany a disconnect request, but Starlan allows up to 64 bytes of user data.

   An abortive disconnect can be initiated by either end of a connection, or the transport provider itself may abort a connection when it has a problem below the Transport Interface. In the sample code above, a disconnect request is processed by the t_rcvdis() function, but a "disconnect" structure is used only if the transport provider supports this facility. A **protocol-specific** reason code may be set in the t_discon structure, and you must check your protocol reference manual to interpret any reason codes. The sequence field is only meaningful **before** a connection is established; it is used to identify a **pending connect request** to disconnect (usually by the server, after one or more t_listen() calls).

7.2.11 Closing a Transport Endpoint

The TLI function t_close() frees any resources associated with a transport endpoint and breaks any connection that may be active. Its format is as follows:

```
int  t_close  ( int fd )
```

where fd is the transport endpoint you want to close. The only thing that can fail is if fd is not a transport endpoint. A **t_snddis()** is sent if fd is connected to a peer and this is the *last* process with fd open.

7.3   Sample TLI Programs

This section rewrites the TCP/UDP socket programs of Chapter 3 using TLI functions.

7.3.1   TLI Header Files

The header file **tiuser.h** must be #included in programs that use TLI functions. Here is a header file used in our simple TLI examples:

```
/* wintcp.h - common definitions for WIN/TCP applications    */

#include <stdio.h>              /* NULL, BUFSIZ, FILE def's    */
#include <fcntl.h>              /* O_RDWR,  O_NDELAY, etc ...  */
#include <tiuser.h>             /* standard TLI definitions    */

/* The next definitions are specific to the WIN/TCP code.     */
#include <sys/types.h>
#include <sys/socket.h>         /* WIN/TCP socket  definitions */
#include <sys/in.h>             /* WIN/TCP Internet definitions*/

#define DEV_TCP "/dev/tcp"      /* TCP Streams device          */
#define DEV_UDP "/dev/udp"      /* UDP Streams device          */

/*  The next definitions are specific to our examples.        */
#define TCP_PORT 1990           /* port number for this service*/
#define UDP_PORT 1990           /* port number for this service*/
#define HOST_ADDR "129.33.192.106"     /* server's address     */
```

7.3.2   Sample TLI Makefile

This makefile builds two simple TLI applications. Both use the Internet protocols. One uses TCP virtual circuits (vcclient/vcserver) and the other uses connectionless UDP datagrams (dgclient/dgserver):

```
MAINS = vcclient vcserver dgclient dgserver

ALL:  $(MAINS)

# Connection-mode (Virtual Circuit) Client and Server

vcclient: vcclient.o  wintcp.h
     cc  vcclient.o -o vcclient  -lnet -lnsl_s

vcserver: vcserver.o  wintcp.h
     cc  vcserver.o -o vcserver  -lnet -lnsl_s

# Connectionless (Datagram) Client and Server

dgclient: dgclient.o  wintcp.h
     cc  dgclient.o -o dgclient  -lnet -lnsl_s

dgserver: dgserver.o  wintcp.h
     cc  dgserver.o -o dgserver  -lnet -lnsl_s
```

This is not a very clever makefile, but it shows each individual command line and the library names needed to link our code with TLI functions. The file /usr/lib/libnsl_s.a is AT&T's *Network Services* (TLI) archive (shared) library, which includes t_open(), t_bind(), t_connect(), and so forth. The file /usr/lib/libnet.a is Wollongong's "socket compatibility" archive library, which includes socket(), bind(), bzero(), inet_addr(), and so forth. These programs were tested by Rowdy Rich Mayer on **AT&T 3B2/600G** computers running System V Release 3.2.2 using the following software packages:

- Wollongong Integrated Networking WIN/3B: Release 3.0
- Networking Support Utilities: Release 3.2.2 V3
- AT&T 10baseT Network Interface (NI) Package: Release 1.1

They were later run successfully on 386-based computers using System V Release 4.0.3.

7.3.3   Connectionless TLI Client

This client side uses UDP protocol to send a "Bus error - core dumped" message to the server. This message was chosen to enhance Rowdy Rich Mayer's debugging skills :-)

```
/* dgclient.c -- UDP client ( TLI t_sndudata )              */

#include "wintcp.h"   /*  TLI and WIN/TCP definitions        */
```

```
#define DATA "Bus error - core dumped.\n" /* hee hee :-)       */

main( argc, argv )    /* argument count, argument vector        */
char *argv[];
{
  struct sockaddr_in server;    /* Internet address            */
  struct t_unitdata datagram;   /* TLI datagram to send         */
  int    fd;                    /* transport endpoint           */

  if ( (fd = t_open(DEV_UDP, O_RDWR, (struct t_info *)0)) < 0 )
     { t_error( argv[0] );  exit(1); }

  if ( t_bind(fd, (struct t_bind *)0, (struct t_bind *)0) < 0 )
     { t_error( argv[0] );  exit(2); }

  bzero( (char *) &server, sizeof( server ));

  server.sin_family = AF_INET ;             /*  Internet domain */
  server.sin_port   = htons(UDP_PORT);     /* "advertised" port */
  server.sin_addr.s_addr = inet_addr( HOST_ADDR );

  datagram.addr.maxlen  =  sizeof ( server );
  datagram.addr.len     =  sizeof ( server );
  datagram.addr.buf     = (char *) &server ;

  datagram.opt.maxlen   = 0;
  datagram.opt.len      = 0;
  datagram.opt.buf      = (char *) 0;

  datagram.udata.maxlen = sizeof( DATA );
  datagram.udata.len    = sizeof( DATA );
  datagram.udata.buf    = DATA;

  if ( t_sndudata( fd, &datagram ) < 0 )
      t_error( argv[0] );

  t_close( fd );
}
```

These programs were emailed for Rich Mayer to compile and test on a 3B2 with TLI.

7.3.4 Connectionless TLI Server

```
/* dgserver.c -- UDP server ( TLI t_rcvudata )               */
#include "wintcp.h"             /*  TLI and WIN/TCP definitions */
#define BUFSIZE 1024

main( argc, argv )                 /*  arg count, arg vector     */
char *argv[];
{
```

```
int     fd, flags;              /* transport endpt, rcv flags  */
struct sockaddr_in server;      /* Internet socket name (addr) */
struct t_bind req;              /* TLI struct for bind req     */
struct t_unitdata *datagram;    /* ptr to datagram struct      */
char    buffer[BUFSIZE];        /* datagram data buffer area   */

if ( (fd=t_open( DEV_UDP, O_RDWR, (struct t_info *)0 )) < 0 )
   {  t_error( argv[0] );  exit(1); }

   bzero( (char *) &server, sizeof( server ));
   server.sin_family = AF_INET;            /* Internet domain  */
   server.sin_port   = htons(UDP_PORT); /* "advertised" port */
   server.sin_addr.s_addr=htonl(INADDR_ANY);  /* any board    */

   req.addr.maxlen = req.addr.len = sizeof( server );
   req.addr.buf    = (char *) &server;   req.qlen = 5;

   if (  t_bind ( fd, &req, (struct t_bind *) 0 ) < 0 )
      {  t_error( argv[0] );  exit(2); }

   datagram=(struct t_unitdata*)t_alloc(fd,T_UNITDATA,T_ADDR);

   if ( datagram == NULL ) { t_error( argv[0] );  exit(3); }

   datagram->opt.maxlen   = datagram->opt.len   = 0;
   datagram->udata.maxlen = datagram->udata.len = BUFSIZE;
   datagram->udata.buf    = buffer;

      if ( t_rcvudata( fd, datagram, &flags ) < 0 )
       { t_error( argv[0] );  exit(4); }
   printf( "\nReceived: %s\n", buffer );
   t_close( fd )
}
```

Notice that t_alloc() allocates memory for an Internet address (T_ADDR) but the data buffer is pre-allocated and need not be done by t_alloc(), only the datagram pointer (udata.buf) needs to be initialized with the address of our buffer.

7.3.5 Connection-mode TLI Client

```
/* vcclient.c -- TCP client ( TLI t_snd )                    */

#include "wintcp.h"             /*  TLI and WIN/TCP definitions */
#define DATA "adidas - all day i dream about streams ...\n"

main( argc, argv )             /*  arg count, arg vector       */
char *argv[];
{
  struct sockaddr_in server;  /*  Internet address            */
```

```
struct t_call *callptr;      /* TLI call request            */
char   *t_alloc();           /* TLI allocate function       */
int    fd;                   /* transport endpoint          */

if ((fd = t_open( DEV_TCP, O_RDWR, (struct t_info *)0 )) < 0)
   { t_error( argv[0] );  exit(1); }

if ( t_bind(fd, (struct t_bind *)0, (struct t_bind *)0 ) < 0)
   { t_error( argv[0] );  exit(2); }

bzero( (char *) &server, sizeof( server ));
server.sin_family = AF_INET;            /* Internet domain     */
server.sin_port   = htons(TCP_PORT); /* "advertised" port   */
server.sin_addr.s_addr = inet_addr( HOST_ADDR );

callptr = (struct t_call *) t_alloc( fd, T_CALL, T_ADDR );

if ( callptr == NULL ) { t_error( argv[0] );  exit(3); }

callptr->addr.maxlen = callptr->addr.len = sizeof(server);
callptr->addr.buf    = (char *) &server;

callptr->opt.len   = 0;   /* no special options          */
callptr->udata.len = 0;   /* no user data w/connect req.  */

if ( t_connect( fd, callptr, (struct t_call *) 0 ) < 0 )
   { t_error( argv[0] );  exit(4); }

if ( t_snd( fd, DATA, sizeof( DATA ), 0 ) < 0 )
   { t_error( argv[0] );  exit(5); }

 t_close( fd );
}
```

The Internet address of our server is initialized in the same way as we did with the socket version, a t_call structure is initialized to point at the server's Internet address, and given to t_connect(). We do not expect anything different from the server, so the received t_call structure pointer is NULL.

7.3.6 Connection-mode TLI Server

```
/* vcserver.c -- TCP server ( TLI t_rcv )                       */

exterm int t_errno ;        /*  TLI library errorcode       */
#include "wintcp.h"         /*  TLI and WIN/TCP definitions  */
#define BUFSIZE 1024
main( argc, argv )          /*  arg count, arg vector        */
char *argv[];
{
  int    fd, newfd, flags;  /*  transport endpts, rcv flag  */
  struct sockaddr_in client, server;   /* Internet addresses  */
```

```
struct t_bind    req;       /* TLI struct for bind req     */
struct t_call    *callptr;  /* TLI struct for call req     */

char   buffer[ BUFSIZE ];   /* data buffer area            */

if ((fd = t_open(DEV_TCP, O_RDWR, (struct t_info *)0 )) < 0 )
    { t_error( argv[0] );  exit(1); }

bzero( (char *) &server, sizeof( server ));
server.sin_family = AF_INET;             /* Internet domain    */
server.sin_port   = htons(TCP_PORT); /* "advertised" port     */
server.sin_addr.s_addr = htonl(INADDR_ANY);   /* any board    */

req.addr.maxlen  =  req.addr.len  =  sizeof( server );
req.addr.buf     =  (char *) &server ;  req.qlen = 5;

if ( t_bind ( fd, &req, (struct t_bind *) 0 ) < 0 )
    { t_error( argv[0] );  exit(2); }

callptr = (struct t_call *) t_alloc( fd, T_CALL, T_ADDR );

if ( callptr == NULL  )
    { t_error( argv[0] );  exit(3); }

if ( t_listen( fd, callptr ) < 0 )
    { t_error( argv[0] );  exit(4); }

if ((newfd=t_open( DEV_TCP, O_RDWR, (struct t_info *)0)) < 0)
    { t_error( argv[0] );  exit(5); }

if ( t_bind( newfd,(struct t_bind *)0,(struct t_bind *)0) < 0 )
    { t_error( argv[0] );  exit(6); }

if ( t_accept( fd, newfd, callptr )  < 0 )
    {
      if ( t_errno == TLOOK )
          {
            if ( t_rcvdis( fd, (struct t_discon *) 0 ) < 0 )
                { t_error ( argv[0] );  exit(7); }
          }
      t_error( argv[0] );  exit(8);
    }

if ( t_rcv  ( newfd, buffer, BUFSIZE, &flags ) < 0 )
    { t_error( argv[0] );  exit(9); }

printf( "\nReceived: %s\n", buffer );
t_close( fd );  t_close( newfd );
}
```

7.4   A Real-World Database Application in TLI

In this section we will convert the socket-based "remote table of contents" application from Chapter 3 to TLI. The underlying protocols will still be the Internet TCP and UDP. In the next section we will use the SVR4 Network Selection facility for transport level independence.

7.4.1   TLI Application Makefile

```
#   rtoc.mk -- Makefile for remote table of contents
#
#   make -f rtoc.mk

SOURCES = rtoc.c rtocd.c
OBJECTS = $(SOURCES:.c=.o)
TARGETS = $(SOURCES:.c=)
HEADERS = rtoc.h
LIBS    = -lsocket -lnls -lnsl
CFLAGS  = -g

all:    $(TARGETS) $(HEADERS)

rtoc:   rtoc.o sock_init.o $(HEADERS)
        $(CC) $(CFLAGS) rtoc.o  sock_init.o $(LIBS) -o $@

rtocd:  rtocd.o sock_init.o $(HEADERS)
        $(CC) $(CFLAGS) rtocd.o sock_init.o $(LIBS) -o $@

.SUFFIXES: .o .c
.c.o:   $(HEADERS)
        $(CC) $(CFLAGS) -c $*.c
```

7.4.2   TLI Application Header File

```
/* rtoc.h - header file for remote table of contents      */

#define REC_SIZE 109
#define RTC_PORT 2001

#define DEV_TCP   "/dev/tcp"            /* SVR4            */
#define DEV_UDP   "/dev/udp"            /* SVR4            */

/* #define DEV_TCP   "/dev/inet/tcp"    /* SCO Open Desktop */
/* #define DEV_UDP   "/dev/inet/udp"    /* SCO Open Desktop */
```

7.4.3 TLI Endpoint Initialization Function

```
/* sock_init.c - create & initialize client/server TLI endpts */
#include <sys/fcntl.h>   /* O_RDWR, O_NDELAY def's, etc...    */
#include <sys/types.h>   /* u_short, u_long def's, etc...     */
#include <sys/socket.h>  /* AF_INET, SOCK_DGRAM, etc...       */
#include <netinet/in.h>  /* sockaddr_in internet socket address */
#include <netdb.h>       /* /etc/hosts table entries          */
#include "rtoc.h"        /* RTC_PORT, REC_SIZE, DEV names      */
sock_init( host, port, family, type, addr, client )
    char   *host;        /* hostname to bind to or connect with */
    int     port;        /* port #   to bind to or connect with */
    int     family;      /* address family of socket          */
    int     type;        /* byte-stream or datagram socket    */
struct sockaddr *addr;   /* socket address structure          */
    int     client;      /* client-side(0) or server-side(1)  */
{
  struct sockaddr_in *in_name;  /* internet socket name (addr) */
  struct hostent *hptr, *gethostbyname(); /* 3N lib func       */
  int       tlifd;       /* TLI endpoint file descriptor      */
  char      *dev;        /* TCP (/dev/tcp) or UDP (/dev/udp)  */

  if(type == SOCK_DGRAM)
     dev = DEV_UDP;       /* /dev/inet/udp on SCO Open Desktop  */
  else
     dev = DEV_TCP;       /* /dev/inet/tcp on SCO Open Desktop  */

  if ( ( tlifd = t_open( dev, O_RDWR, (struct t_info *) 0) ) < 0 )
     {  t_error( dev );      exit(1); }

  if( t_bind(tlifd, (struct t_bind *)0, (struct t_bind *)0) < 0 )
     { t_error("bind error"); exit(99); }
  in_name = (struct sockaddr_in *) addr;
  in_name->sin_family = family;          /* Address domain     */
  in_name->sin_port = htons(port);       /* "advertised" port  */

  if ( host != NULL )          /* given a hostname from client */
     { hptr = gethostbyname( host );/* "advertised" host        */
       memcpy( &in_name->sin_addr.s_addr, hptr->h_addr,
                                    hptr->h_length );
     }
  else in_name->sin_addr.s_addr = INADDR_ANY;

  return( tlifd );        /* return the TLI endpoint descriptor */
}
```

7.4.4   TLI Connection-Oriented (TCP) Client

```
/* rtoc.c - remote table of contents client (SCO Open Desktop) */
/*          using TLI t_snd/t_rcv functions with TCP transport */

#include <sys/fcntl.h>  /* O_RDWR, O_NDELAY def's, etc...        */
#include <sys/types.h>  /* u_short, u_long def's, etc...         */
#include <sys/socket.h> /* AF_INET, SOCK_DGRAM, etc...           */
#include <netinet/in.h> /* sockaddr_in internet socket addr      */

#include <tiuser.h>     /* TLI generic definitions               */

#include "rtoc.h"       /* REC_SIZE & RTC_PORT (2001)            */

char record[REC_SIZE];  /* file record buffer                   */

extern char *getenv();  /* RTCSERVER environment variable        */
                        /* has hostname to call for DB query     */

main( argc, argv )      /* argument count, argument vector       */
char *argv[];
{
  int tlifd;            /* TLI endpoint file descriptor          */
  int flags;            /* TLI t_rcv flags received              */
  struct t_call *call;  /* TLI call structure                    */

  struct sockaddr_in addr;     /* internet socket name (addr)    */

  long  number;         /* record number                         */
  char *hostname;       /* name of RTC SERVER                    */

  if ( argc != 2 )
     { printf("Usage: %s record-number\n", argv[0]); exit(86); }

  hostname = getenv( "RTCSERVER" );
  if ( hostname == NULL )  hostname = "localhost";

  tlifd  = sock_init ( hostname, RTC_PORT,
                       AF_INET,  SOCK_STREAM, &addr, 0 );

  /* allocate TLI call structure and initialize it              */
  call = (struct t_call *) t_alloc( tlifd, T_CALL, T_ADDR );
  if( call == NULL ) { t_error( "t_call alloc" ); exit(99); };

  call->addr.maxlen = sizeof(addr);
  call->addr.len    = sizeof(addr);
  call->addr.buf    = (char *) &addr;

  call->opt.len   = 0;  call->udata.len  = 0;

  if ( t_connect( tlifd, call, (struct t_call *) 0 ) < 0)
     { t_error(argv[0]); exit(99); }
```

```
    if ( t_snd( tlifd, argv[1], strlen(argv[1])+1 ) < 0)
        { t_error(argv[0]); exit(99); }

    if ( t_rcv( tlifd, record, REC_SIZE, &flags ) < 0 )
        { t_error( argv[0] ); exit(4); }

    record[ REC_SIZE - 1 ] = '\0';
    printf( "\nRecord number %s is:\n%s\n", argv[1], record );

    t_close( tlifd );
}
```

7.4.5   TLI Connection-Oriented (TCP) Server

```
/* rtocd.c remote table of contents server (SCO Open Desktop)  */
/*            using TLI t_snd/t_rcv functions with TCP transport */

#include <stdio.h>        /* NULL, FILE def's, etc...          */
#include <sys/fcntl.h>    /* O_RDWR, O_NDELAY def's, etc...    */
#include <sys/types.h>    /* u_short, u_long def's, etc...     */
#include <sys/socket.h>   /* AF_INET, SOCK_DGRAM, etc...       */

#include <netinet/in.h>   /* sockaddr_in internet socket addr  */

#include <tiuser.h>       /* TLI generic definitions           */

#include "rtoc.h"         /* REC_SIZE & RTC_PORT (2001)        */

extern int t_errno;       /* TLI library error code            */

char record[REC_SIZE];    /* file record buffer                */

extern char *getenv();    /* RTCFILE environment variable      */
                          /* has name of database file to query */

main( argc, argv )        /* argument count, argument vector   */
char *argv[];
{
    int    tlifd, newfd;        /* TLI endpoint fds            */
    int    flags;               /* TLI t_rcv flags received    */
    struct t_bind *bind;        /* TLI bind structure          */
    struct t_call *call;        /* TLI call structure          */

    struct sockaddr_in addr,from; /* Internet socket name (addr) */
    struct sockaddr_in *ptr;      /* pointer to get port number  */
    struct sockaddr    name;      /* generic socket name (addr)  */

    long   number;                /* desired record number       */

    tlifd = sock_init ( NULL,    RTC_PORT,
                    AF_INET,  SOCK_STREAM, &addr, 1 );
```

```
if ( t_unbind( tlifd ) < 0 )    /* undo what sock_init did   */
   { t_error( argv[0] ); exit(4); }

/* allocate TLI bind structure and initialize it           */
bind = (struct t_bind *) t_alloc( tlifd, T_BIND, T_ALL );

bind->qlen = 5;          /* queue up to 5 connection requests  */
bind->addr.maxlen  = sizeof(addr);
bind->addr.len     = sizeof(addr);
bind->addr.buf     = (char *) &addr;

if ( t_bind( tlifd, bind, bind ) < 0 )
   { t_error( argv[0] ); exit(4); }

/* verify that TLI bound the "well-known" addr you gave it! */
ptr = ( struct sockaddr_in * ) bind->addr.buf;
if ( ptr->sin_addr.s_addr != addr.sin_addr.s_addr )
   { t_error( "t-bind bound wrong address" ); exit(4); }
/* this is unecessary with sockets, as bind() just fails!  */

/* allocate TLI call structure and initialize it           */
call = (struct t_call *) t_alloc( tlifd, T_CALL, T_ADDR );
if( call == NULL ) { t_error( "t_call alloc" ); exit(99); };

while(1)
{ if ( t_listen( tlifd, call ) < 0 )
     { t_error( "t_listen failed" ); exit(99); };

  newfd = sock_init ( NULL,      RTC_PORT,
                      AF_INET,   SOCK_STREAM, &from, 1 );

  if ( t_accept( tlifd, newfd, call ) < 0 )
     if ( t_errno == TLOOK )
        if ( t_rcvdis( tlifd, (struct t_discon *) 0 ) < 0 )
           { t_error( "t_rcvdis failed" ); exit(99);}
     else  { t_error( "t_accept failed" ); exit(99);}

  if ( t_rcv( newfd, record, REC_SIZE, &flags ) < 0 )
     { t_error( argv[0] ); exit(4); }

  sscanf( record, "%ld", &number );  /* get desired rec no  */
  rtc( number );                     /* get record from DB  */

  if ( t_snd( newfd, record, REC_SIZE, 0 ) < 0)
      t_error(argv[0]);

  t_close( newfd ); /* necessary to reuse newfd descriptor  */
}
t_close( tlifd );   /* not necessary; exit() will close it  */
}
```

7.4.6   TLI Connectionless (UDP) Client

Our datagram client and server programs use the same `rtoc.h` header file and the same `sock_init.c` program. The `rtoc.mk` makefile is also the same (but in a separate directory to avoid source file naming conflicts). The connectionless client and server programs use the **t_sndudata()** and **t_rcvudata()** library functions to send and receive TLI datagrams (**t_unitdata** structures). They do not need to establish connections with the `t_connect()`, `t_listen()`, and `t_accept()` library functions.

```
/* rtoc.c - remote table of contents client (SCO Open Desktop) */
/* with TLI t_sndudata/t_rcvudata functions over UDP transport */

#include <sys/fcntl.h>   /* O_RDWR, O_NDELAY def's, etc...        */
#include <sys/types.h>   /* u_short, u_long def's, etc...         */
#include <sys/socket.h>  /* AF_INET, SOCK_DGRAM, etc...           */
#include <netinet/in.h>  /* sockaddr_in internet socket addr      */
#include <tiuser.h>      /* TLI generic definitions               */
#include "rtoc.h"        /* REC_SIZE & RTC_PORT (2001)            */

char record[REC_SIZE];   /* file record buffer                    */

extern char *getenv();   /* RTCSERVER environment variable        */
                         /* has hostname to call for DB query     */

main( argc, argv )       /* argument count, argument vector       */
char *argv[];
{
  int tlifd;                 /* TLI endpoint file descriptor */
  int flags;                 /* TLI t_rcvudata flags received*/
  struct t_unitdata *datgram; /* TLI datagram structure       */
  struct sockaddr_in addr;   /* internet socket name (addr)  */
  long  number;              /* record number                */
  char *hostname;            /* name of RTC SERVER           */

  if ( argc != 2 )
    { printf("Usage: %s record-number\n", argv[0]); exit(86); }

  hostname = getenv( "RTCSERVER" );
  if ( hostname == NULL )  hostname = "localhost";

  tlifd  =  sock_init ( hostname, RTC_PORT,
                        AF_INET,  SOCK_DGRAM, &addr, 0 );

  /* allocate TLI datagram structure and initialize it         */
  datagram = (struct t_datagram *)
             t_alloc( tlifd, T_UNITDATA, T_ALL );
  if(datagram==NULL) {t_error("t_datagram alloc"); exit(99);};
```

```
datagram->addr.maxlen  = sizeof(addr);
datagram->addr.len     = sizeof(addr);
datagram->addr.buf     = (char *) &addr;

datagram->opt.maxlen   = 0;
datagram->opt.len      = 0;
datagram->opt.buf      = (char *) 0;

datagram->udata.maxlen = strlen( argv[1] ) + 1;
datagram->udata.len    = strlen( argv[1] ) + 1;
datagram->udata.buf    = argv[1];

if ( t_sndudata( tlifd, datagram ) < 0)
    t_error(argv[0]);

/* modify TLI datagram structure to receive database record */
datagram->udata.maxlen = sizeof(record);
datagram->udata.len    = 0;
datagram->udata.buf    = record;

if ( t_rcvudata( tlifd, datagram, &flags ) < 0 )
    { t_error( argv[0] ); exit(4); }

record[ REC_SIZE - 1 ] = '\0';
printf( "\nRecord number %s is:\n%s\n", argv[1], record );

t_close( tlifd );    /* not necessary; exit() will close it  */
}
```

7.4.7   TLI Connectionless (UDP) Server

```
/* rtocd.c   remote table of contents server (SCO Open Desktop) */
/* with TLI t_sndudata/t_rcvudata functions over UDP transport */

#include <stdio.h>        /* NULL, FILE def's, etc...                */
#include <sys/fcntl.h>    /* O_RDWR, O_NDELAY def's, etc...          */
#include <sys/types.h>    /* u_short, u_long def's, etc...           */
#include <sys/socket.h>   /* AF_INET, SOCK_DGRAM, etc...             */
#include <netinet/in.h>   /* sockaddr_in internet socket addr       */
#include <tiuser.h>       /* TLI generic definitions                 */
#include "rtoc.h"         /* REC_SIZE & RTC_PORT (2001)              */

char record[REC_SIZE];    /* file record buffer                      */

extern char *getenv();    /* RTCFILE environment variable            */
                          /* has name of database file to query     */
```

```
main( argc, argv )        /* argument count, argument vector    */
char *argv[];
{
  int tlifd;                /* TLI endpoint file descriptor */
  int flags;                /* TLI t_rcvudata flags received */
  struct t_unitdata *datgram; /* TLI datagram structure         */

  struct sockaddr_in addr;  /* internet socket name (addr)    */

  long  number;             /* desired record number          */

  tlifd = sock_init ( NULL,      RTC_PORT,
                    AF_INET,   SOCK_DGRAM, &addr, 1 );

  /* allocate TLI datagram structure and initialize it          */
  datagram = (struct t_datagram *)
            t_alloc( tlifd, T_UNITDATA, T_ALL );
  if(datagram==NULL) {t_error("t_datagram alloc"); exit(99);};

  datagram->addr.maxlen  = sizeof(addr);
  datagram->addr.len     = sizeof(addr);
  datagram->addr.buf     = (char *) &addr;

  datagram->opt.maxlen   = 0;
  datagram->opt.len      = 0;
  datagram->opt.buf      = (char *) 0;

  datagram->udata.maxlen = sizeof(record);
  datagram->udata.len    = 0;
  datagram->udata.buf    = record;

  if ( t_rcvudata( tlifd, datagram, &flags ) < 0 )
     { t_error( argv[0] ); exit(4); }

  sscanf( record, "%ld", &number );    /* get desired rec no  */
  rtc( number );                        /* get record from DB  */

  /* modify TLI datagram structure with database record length */
  datagram->udata.len    = strlen( record ) + 1;

  if ( t_sndudata( tlifd, datagram ) < 0)
       t_error(argv[0]);
  t_close( tlifd );   /* not necessary; exit() will close it  */
}
```

7.5   Transport-Independent Network Selection

The benefits of a Transport Level Interface have thus far been marginal due to the hard-coded TCP/UDP Internet addressing. In this section we will demonstrate the benefits described in Figure 7.2 on page 225. That is, we will code an application that uses Internet addressing or OSI addressing, depending on a shell variable NETPATH. Internet addressing is used when **NETPATH=tcp**, and OSI addressing is used when **NETPATH=ticotsord** (transport-independent connection-oriented service with orderly release). A sample execution of the "remote table of contents" application (rewritten using the Network Selection facility of SVR4) follows:

```
----------------------------------------------
$ ./rtocd &           Opened /dev/ticotsord device!
maxlen 11             len 11      addr is 134526440

$ ./rtoc 12           Opened /dev/ticotsord device!
maxlen 11             len 11      addr is 134525808

Record number 12 is:
0102010001 124 0 APR.1984 1.201-1 The two birds
----------------------------------------------
$ NETPATH=tcp
$ ./rtocd &           Opened /dev/tcp device!
maxlen 16             len 16      addr is 134526440

$ ./rtoc 12           Opened /dev/tcp device!
maxlen 16             len 16      addr is 134525808

Record number 12 is:
0102010001 124 0 APR.1984 1.201-1 The two birds
----------------------------------------------
```

The maxlen, len, and addr fields are from a netbuf structure as diagrammed in Figure 7.2 on page 225. **The beauty of this example is the program did not need a case statement to select among many transport protocols, and its behavior was changed by a different setting of a shell environment variable.**

This is possible because the SVR4 network configuration file, **/etc/netconfig**, has a list of network protocols, devices and libraries available on the host. Some typical file entries are as follows:

```
tcp     tpi_cots_ord  v  inet  tcp  /dev/tcp       /usr/lib/tcpip.so
udp          tpi_clts  v  inet  udp /dev/udp        /usr/lib/tcpip.so
starlan  tpi_cots  v osinet  -    /dev/starlan  /usr/lib/straddr.so
```

where the tcp protocol is accessed by opening the /dev/tcp STREAMS device and using the name-to-address functions in /usr/lib/tcpip.so, while starlan opens /dev/starlan using the functions in /usr/lib/straddr.so.

7.5.1 The Simple TLI Program Revisited

In this section we will introduce library functions that access /etc/netconfig by
modifying the simple TLI program of Section 7.2.2 on page 222 which introduced the
t_info structure. We call this version ns_tinfo.

```
# cc -o ns_tinfo ns_tinfo.c -lnsl
# ./ns_tinfo
```

name	addr	options	tsdu	etsdu	connect	discon	servtype
/dev/ticlts	232	4072	4096	-2	-2	-2	3 CLTS
/dev/ticots	240	4080	-1	-1	4072	4084	1 COTS
/dev/ticotsord	**240**	**4080**	**-1**	**-1**	**4072**	**4084**	**2 COTS_ORD**
/dev/tcp	**16**	**-1**	**0**	**1**	**-2**	**-2**	**2 COTS_ORD**
/dev/udp	16	-1	16384	-2	-2	-2	3 CLTS
/dev/rawip	16	-1	8192	1	-2	-2	3 CLTS
/dev/icmp	16	-1	8192	1	-2	-2	3 CLTS
/dev/starlan	**55**	**44**	**-1**	**16**	**32**	**64**	**1 COTS**
/dev/starlandg	55	44	16384	0	0	0	3 CLTS

```
        # ./ns_tinfo | cut -f1 | grep dev | xargs ls -l
        crw-rw-rw-  1 root  root  12, 28  Jun 19 16:01  /dev/icmp
        crw-rw-rw-  1 root  root  12, 35  Jun 19 16:01  /dev/rawip
        crw-rw-rw-  1 root  root  12, 55  Jun 19 16:01  /dev/starlan
        crw-rw-rw-  1 root  root  12, 56  Jun 19 16:01  /dev/starlandg
        crw-rw-rw-  1 root  root  12, 36  Jun 19 16:01  /dev/tcp
        crw-rw-rw-  1 root  root  12, 23  Jun 19 16:01  /dev/ticlts
        crw-rw-rw-  1 root  root  12, 24  Jun 19 16:01  /dev/ticots
        crw-rw-rw-  1 root  root  12, 26  Jun 19 16:01  /dev/ticotsord
        crw-rw-rw-  1 root  root  12, 37  Jun 19 16:01  /dev/udp
```

```
/* ns_tinfo.c -- network selection of t_info structure*/

#include <fcntl.h>        /* file control (O_RDWR) definitions */
#include <stdio.h>        /* standard I/O ( NULL) definitions */
#include <tiuser.h>       /* standard TLI structure definitions */
#include <netconfig.h>    /* network selection data structures */

/* struct  netconfig {                                         */
/*    char    *nc_netid;       /* tcp, udp, ti...               */
/*    ulong   nc_semantics;    /* COTS, COTS_ORD, CLTS          */
/*    ulong   nc_flag;         /* v (visible)                   */
/*    char    *nc_protofmly;   /* inet, sna, decnet, osi, x25   */
/*    char    *nc_proto;       /* tcp, udp, icmp                */
/*    char    *nc_device;      /* /dev/tcp, /dev/udp, /dev/ti   */
/*    ulong   nc_nlookups;     /* # of entries in nc_lookups    */
/*    char    **nc_lookups;    /* list of lookup directories    */
/*    ulong   nc_unused[8];                                     */
/* };                                                           */
```

```
main()
{
  int           fd;      /* file descriptor                    */
  struct t_info  tin;    /* transport provider information     */

  struct netconfig *nc;  /* network configuration database     */
  void    *handle;       /* handle to netconfig database       */

  printf( "\n%14s\t%s\t%s\t%s\t%s\t%s\t%s\t%s\n",
          "name",  "addr",    "options", "tsdu",
          "etsdu", "connect", "discon",  "servtype" );

  handle = setnetconfig(); /* initialize netconfig db pointer   */

  while( ( nc = getnetconfig( handle ) ) != NULL )
    {
      if(( fd = t_open( nc->nc_device, O_RDWR, &tin ) ) < 0 )
          t_error( nc->nc_device );
      else
        { printf( "%14s", nc->nc_device);
          printf( "\t%d", tin.addr                            );
          printf( "\t%d", tin.options);
          printf( "\t%d", tin.tsdu                            );
          printf( "\t%d", tin.etsdu                           );
          printf( "\t%d", tin.connect);
          printf( "\t%d", tin.discon                          );
          printf( "\t%d", tin.servtype);
          switch( tin.servtype )
          {
            case T_COTS:     printf(" COTS");      break;
            case T_CLTS:     printf(" CLTS");      break;
            case T_COTS_ORD: printf(" COTS_ORD");  break;
            default:         printf(" unknown!");  break;
          }
          printf( "\n" );
        }
      t_close( fd );
    }
    printf( "\n" );
}
```

The routine setnetconfig() returns a handle to the netconfig database which is needed as an argument to getnetconfig() which performs a sequential access of each entry in the netconfig database, and returns NULL at the end of the file. In this example all devices are opened, but a particular type of service could be selected using the **semantics** field of the netconfig structure, as we'll see in the next section.

7.5.2   TLI Database Application Using Network Selection

The TLI code from Section 7.4 is modified to use Network Selection. Rather than list
the whole programs again, we'll just show the changes that had to be made to rtoc.c,
rtocd.c, and sock_init.c. The old versions are in a subdirectory named **old**:

```
$ diff rtoc.c old/rtoc.c
< #include <netconfig.h> /* network selection data structures */
<                               AF_INET,  NC_TPI_COTS_ORD, &addr, 0 );
>                               AF_INET,  SOCK_STREAM, &addr, 0 );
$ diff rtocd.c old/rtocd.c
< #include <netconfig.h> /* network selection data structures */
<                               AF_INET,  NC_TPI_COTS_ORD, &addr, 1 );
>                               AF_INET,  SOCK_STREAM, &addr, 1 );
```

The only changes in the application programs were to include the **netconfig.h**
header file, and change the **type** argument in the call of sock_init() from
SOCK_STREAM to NC_TPI_COTS_ORD (defined in netconfig.h). Thus, most of
the changes were isolated in the **sock_init()** code:

```
$ diff sock_init.c old/sock_init.c
< #include <netconfig.h> /* network selection data structures */
<    int    tlifd = 0;    /* TLI endpoint file descriptor    */
<    struct netconfig *nc;/* network configuration database   */
<    void   *handle;      /* handle to netconfig database     */
---
>    int     tlifd;       /* TLI endpoint file descriptor    */
>    char    *dev;        /* TCP (/dev/tcp) or UDP (/dev/udp) */
<    handle=setnetconfig(); /* initialize netconfig db pointer */
<    while( ( nc = getnetconfig( handle ) ) != NULL )
<      {
<       if( nc->nc_semantics == type )
<        { if(( tlifd=t_open( nc->nc_device, O_RDWR, NULL ) ) < 0 )
<             t_error( nc->nc_device );
<          else
<             { printf( "\tOpened %s device!\n", nc->nc_device );
<               break;
<             }
<        }
<      }
<    if( tlifd == 0 )
<      { printf( "Sorry, no device available.\n" ); exit(99); }
```

The old `sock_init()` code used the `type` parameter to choose between the `/dev/tcp` or `/dev/udp` STREAMS devices.

```
>    if(type == SOCK_DGRAM)
>       dev = DEV_UDP;      /* /dev/inet/udp on SCO Open Desktop */
>    else
>       dev = DEV_TCP;      /* /dev/inet/tcp on SCO Open Desktop */
>    if ( ( tlifd = t_open( dev, O_RDWR, (struct t_info *) 0) ) < 0 )
>       {    t_error( dev );       exit(1); }
```

The `rtocd` daemon and `rtoc` client are built using the same `rtoc.mk` makefile shown in Section 7.4.1 on page 241:

```
$ make -f rtoc.mk
     cc -g -c rtoc.c
     cc -g -c sock_init.c
     cc -g rtoc.o sock_init.o  -lsocket -lnls -lnsl -o rtoc
     cc -g -c rtocd.c
     cc -g rtocd.o sock_init.o -lsocket -lnls -lnsl -o rtocd
```

Now we start the server in the background...

```
          $ ./rtocd &
          [1]    12572

                    Opened /dev/ticotsord device!
                    port# = 2001
```

...and try the client in the foreground...

```
          $ ./rtoc 12
                    Opened /dev/ticotsord device!
                    port# = 2001
                    hostname = localhost
          ./rtoc: System error: Protocol error
```

...oops... `ticotsord` must use different addressing, so...

```
          $ kill %1
          [1] + Terminated                   ./rtocd &
```

...and try the client in the foreground...

```
          $ NETPATH=tcp; export NETPATH
          $ ./rtocd &
          [1]    12575

                    Opened /dev/ticotsord device!
                    port# = 2001
```

Oh dear! This is getting serious.... Yet another function (described in the next section) is needed to use the secret `NETPATH` trick to change transport protocols.

7.5.3 Adding NETPATH Selection

The set/getnetconfig() functions ignore the NETPATH environment variable
and always read /etc/netconfig sequentially. This is swell for environments that
require the transports be tried in the order they appear in /etc/netconfig. The
code, of course, could test for a specific transport protocol by name (nc->nc_proto).
Another choice is to use equivalent functions **set/getnetpath()**, which serve the
same purpose as set/getnetconfig() when NETPATH is unset, but, if set, return
netconfig entries in the order specified in NETPATH. The code changes are as follows:

```
$ diff sock_init.c Osock_init.c
<    handle = setnetpath();/* initialize netconfig db pointer  */
<    while( ( nc = getnetpath( handle ) ) != NULL )
---
>    handle = setnetconfig();/* initialize netconfig db pointer */
>    while( ( nc = getnetconfig( handle ) ) != NULL )
$ make -f rtoc.mk
     cc -g -c sock_init.c
     cc -g rtoc.o sock_init.o -lsocket -lnls -lnsl -o rtoc
     cc -g rtocd.o sock_init.o -lsocket -lnls -lnsl -o rtocd
```

Notice that the code changes were isolated in the sock_init() function!

```
          $ echo $NETPATH
          tcp:ticotsord
          $ ./rtocd &
               Opened /dev/tcp device!            port# = 2001
          $ ./rtoc 12
               Opened /dev/tcp device!            port# = 2001
               hostname = localhost
          Record number 12 is:
          0102010001 124 0 APR.1984 1.201-1  The two councils.
          $ NETPATH=ticotsord:tcp
          $ ./rtoc 12
               Opened /dev/ticotsord device!    port# = 2001
               hostname = localhost
          ./rtoc: System error: Protocol error
```

Now we need some way to avoid protocol errors by allocating, initializing and using
addresses appropriate for the underlying transport. We will see how to do this in the
next section.

7.5.4   Tranport Protocol Independence

In this section we will use the SVR4 Network Selection facility to write a client/server application that will execute with TCP/IP or OSI protocols (or any new "multimedia" protocol that may become popular in the future, for that matter).   One use of this capability is shown in Figure 7.3.

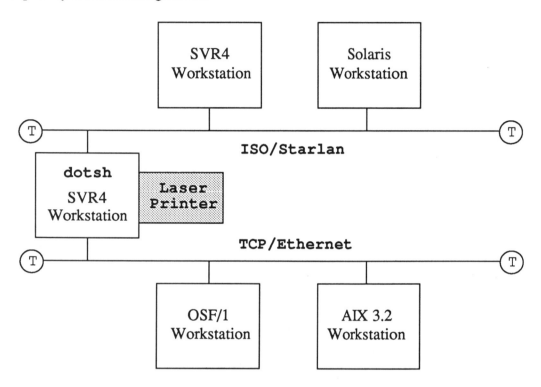

Figure 7.3   Transport Protocol Independence

The laser printer on the SVR4 workstation is reachable over two LAN cables and the printer service ought to be available over either transport. The **nlsadmin** command allows a system administrator to add services, and any user can use the **nsquery** command to see which services have been advertised in the user's RFS domain:

```
# nsquery

RESOURCE    ACCESS        SERVER        TP         DESCRIPTION
CALENDAR    read/write    dotsh.meet    starlan    Meeting info
LP          read/write    dotsh.prnt    starlan    Line printer
MAN         read-only     dotsh.manp    starlan    Man pages
LP          read/write    dotsh.prnt    tcp        Line printer
```

7.5.4.1   Network Address Independence

This section shows how to use the Network Selection facility to achieve the address independence illustrated in Figure 7.2 on page 225. Some sample output follows, with OSI addressing on the left, and TCP on the right. Both execute the same program!

```
$ NETPATH=ticosord              | $ NETPATH=tcp

$ ./rtocd &                     | $ ./rtocd &
Opened /dev/ticotsord device!   | Opened /dev/tcp device!

bind->addr.maxlen = 11          | bind->addr.maxlen = 16
bind->addr.len    = 11          | bind->addr.len    = 16
bind->addr.buf    = dotsh.rtoc  | bind->addr.buf = 127.0.0.1
                                |                     2001
$ ./rtoc 12                     |
Opened /dev/ticotsord device!   | Opened /dev/tcp device!

call->addr.maxlen = 11          | call->addr.maxlen = 16
call->addr.len    = 11          | call->addr.len    = 16
call->addr.buf    = dotsh.rtoc  | call->addr.buf = 127.0.0.1
                                |                     2001
        Record number 12 is:
        0102010001 124 0 APR.1984 1.201-1 The two birds.
```

Both processes can be running at the same time, one providing the service to OSI users, and the other providing it for TCP users. Notice that the TCP version uses the special "loopback" pseudo-device address, and thus does not attempt to access any physical network device. This changes when a hostname other than "localhost" is used.

```
        $ RTCSERVER=dotsh; export RTCSERVER

        $ ./rtocd &
         Opened /dev/tcp device!

        bind->addr.maxlen = 16
        bind->addr.len    = 16
        bind->addr.buf    = 129.33.192.200    2001

        $ ./rtoc 12
        Opened /dev/tcp device!

        call->addr.maxlen = 16
        call->addr.len    = 16
        call->addr.buf    = 129.33.192.200    2001

        t_connect: System error: Cannot assign requested address
```

This execustion tried to connect to a physical network device and it failed on a stand-alone workstation without any LAN interface for TCP.

7.5.4.2   Address-Independent Header File

The same header file is used to define a common size of database records and a common service port number for TCP/UDP users.

```
/* rtoc.h - header file for remote table of contents     */

#define REC_SIZE 109
#define RTC_PORT 2001
```

7.5.4.3   Protocol-Specific System Files

As you know, the file **/etc/services** has the entries:

```
         rtoc           2001/udp
         rtoc           2001/tcp
```

Library routines map the character-string service name "rtoc" into the TCP or UDP service port number 2001. Other protocols have similar hosts and services files in the **/etc/net** directory (on SVR4):

```
$ grep rtoc /etc/net/ticotsord/services
rtoc        rtoc

$ ls -l /etc/net/ticotsord
-rw-r--r--  1 root other 14 Aug 27  1991 hosts
-rw-r--r--  1 root other 85 Jun 28 19:26 services

$ ls -CF /etc/net
starlan/     starlandg/  ticlts/     ticots/      ticotsord/
```

These protocols use string address mapping functions in **/usr/lib/straddr.so**, while the Internet protocols use the functions in **/usr/lib/tcpip.so**   Recall that these library functions are dynamically loaded at runtime and memory-mapped into the process address space as needed. See the truss example in Section 6.2.5 on pages 180 to 184 for details.

7.5.4.4   Address-Independent Client Program

```
/* rtoc.c -- remote table of contents client (SVR4)        */
/*     using TLI t_snd/t_rcv functions with Network Selection */

#include <stdio.h>      /* NULL, FILE, stderr def's, etc...   */
#include <sys/fcntl.h>  /* O_RDWR, O_NDELAY def's, etc...     */
#include <sys/types.h>  /* u_short, u_long def's, etc...      */
#include <netinet/in.h> /* Internet address structures        */
                        /* (needed only for printing addrs)   */
```

```c
#include <tiuser.h>        /* TLI generic definitions            */
#include <netconfig.h>     /* network selection data structures  */
#include <netdir.h>        /* ns name-to-addr data structures    */

#include "rtoc.h"          /* REC_SIZE & RTC_PORT (2001)            */

char record[ REC_SIZE ];/* file record buffer                      */

extern char *getenv();     /* RTCSERVER environment variable        */
                           /* has hostname to call for DB query     */

main( argc, argv )         /* argument count, argument vector       */
char *argv[];
{
  int tlifd = 0;           /* TLI endpoint file descriptor         */
  int flags;               /* TLI t_rcv flags received             */
  struct t_call *call;     /* TLI call structure                   */

  struct nd_hostserv host;    /* Network Selection hostname        */
  struct nd_addrlist addr;    /* Network Selection addrlist        */
  struct nd_addrlist *addrp=&addr;        /* NS baloney            */

  struct netconfig *nc;    /* network configuration database       */
  void    *handle;         /* handle to netconfig database         */

  long   number;           /* record number                        */
  char *hostname;          /* name of RTC SERVER                   */

  if ( argc != 2 )
     { printf( "Usage: %s record-number\n", argv[0] ); exit(86); }

  handle = setnetpath();     /* initialize netconfig db pointer */
  while( ( nc = getnetpath( handle ) ) != NULL )
     {
       if( nc->nc_semantics == NC_TPI_COTS_ORD )
         { if(( tlifd=t_open( nc->nc_device, O_RDWR, NULL ) ) <= 0 )
              t_error( nc->nc_device );
           else
             { printf( "\tOpened %s device!\n", nc->nc_device );
               break;
             }
         }
     }
  if( tlifd == 0 )
     { printf( "Sorry, no device available.\n" );  exit(99);  }

  if( t_bind( tlifd, (struct t_bind *)0, (struct t_bind *)0) < 0 )
     { t_error("bind error"); exit(99); }
```

```
    host.h_host = getenv( "RTCSERVER" );   host.h_serv = "rtoc";

    if ( host.h_host == NULL )
        if ( strcmp( getenv( "NETPATH" ), "tcp") == 0 )
                host.h_host = "localhost";   /* Internet loopback   */
        else
                host.h_host =  HOST_SELF;   /* COTS_ORD loopback   */

    if ( netdir_getbyname( nc, &host, &addrp ) < 0 )
        netdir_perror( "name2addr" );

    /* allocate TLI call structure and initialize it             */
    call = (struct t_call *) t_alloc( tlifd, T_CALL, T_ADDR );
    if( call == NULL ) { t_error( "t_call alloc" ); exit(99); };

    call->addr.maxlen = addrp->n_addrs->maxlen;
    call->addr.len    = addrp->n_addrs->len;
    call->addr.buf    = addrp->n_addrs->buf;
    printcall( call );      /* a "debug" function to print struct */

    if ( t_connect( tlifd, call, (struct t_call *) 0 ) < 0)
        { t_error("t_connect"); exit(99); }

    if ( t_snd( tlifd, argv[1], strlen(argv[1])+1 ) < 0)
        { t_error("t_snd"); exit(99); }

    if ( t_rcv( tlifd, record, REC_SIZE, &flags ) < 0 )
        { t_error( "t_rcv" ); exit(4); }

    record[ REC_SIZE - 1 ] = '\0';
    printf( "\nRecord number %s is:\n%s\n", argv[1], record );

    t_close( tlifd );
}

printcall( call )          /* a "debug" function to print struct */
struct t_call *call;
{
struct sockaddr_in *ptr;

printf( "\n\tcall->addr.maxlen = %d ", call->addr.maxlen );
printf( "\n\tcall->addr.len    = %d ", call->addr.len     );

if ( strcmp( getenv( "NETPATH" ), "tcp") == 0 )
    { ptr = (struct sockaddr_in *) call->addr.buf;
      printf( "\n\tcall->addr.buf    = %s ",
                      inet_ntoa( ptr->sin_addr.s_addr ));
      printf( "\t %d \n\n", ntohs( ptr->sin_port ));
    }
else printf( "\n\tcall->addr.buf    = %s \n\n", call->addr.buf );
}
```

7.5.4.5 Address-Independent Server Program

```
/* rtocd.c - remote table of contents server (SVR4)        */
/*      using TLI t_snd/t_rcv functions with Network Selection */

#include <stdio.h>        /* NULL, FILE, stderr def's, etc...  */
#include <sys/fcntl.h>    /* O_RDWR, O_NDELAY def's, etc...    */
#include <sys/types.h>    /* u_short, u_long def's, etc...     */
#include <netinet/in.h> /* Internet address structures       */
                         /* (needed only for printing addrs)  */
#include <tiuser.h>      /* TLI generic definitions           */
#include <netconfig.h>   /* network selection data structures */
#include <netdir.h>      /* ns name-to-addr data structures   */

#include "rtoc.h"        /* REC_SIZE & RTC_PORT (2001)        */
char record[ REC_SIZE ];/* file record buffer                 */

main( argc, argv )       /* argument count, argument vector   */
char *argv[];
{
  int tlifd = 0;          /* TLI endpoint file descriptor      */
  int flags;              /* TLI t_rcv flags received          */
  struct t_bind *bind;   /* TLI bind structure                */
  struct t_call *call;   /* TLI call structure                */

  struct nd_hostserv host;     /* Network Selection hostname   */
  struct nd_addrlist addr;      /* Network Selection addrlist   */
  struct nd_addrlist *addrp=&addr;         /* NS baloney        */

  struct netconfig *nc; /* network configuration database    */
  void    *handle;        /* handle to netconfig database      */

  long  number;          /* record number                     */

  handle = setnetpath();   /* initialize netconfig db pointer */
  while( ( nc = getnetpath( handle ) ) != NULL )
    {
     if( nc->nc_semantics == NC_TPI_COTS_ORD )
       { if(( tlifd=t_open( nc->nc_device, O_RDWR, NULL ) ) <= 0 )
             t_error( nc->nc_device );
         else
           { printf( "\tOpened %s device!\n", nc->nc_device );
             break;
           }
       }
    }
  if( tlifd == 0 )
    { printf( "Sorry, no device available.\n" );  exit(99);  }
```

```
host.h_host = getenv( "RTCSERVER" );   host.h_serv = "rtoc";

if ( host.h_host == NULL )
   if ( strcmp( getenv( "NETPATH" ), "tcp") == 0 )
          host.h_host = "localhost";   /* Internet loopback  */
   else
          host.h_host =   HOST_SELF;   /* COTS_ORD loopback  */

if ( netdir_getbyname( nc, &host, &addrp ) < 0 )
    netdir_perror( "name2addr" );

/* allocate TLI bind structure and initialize it            */
bind = (struct t_bind *) t_alloc( tlifd, T_BIND, T_ALL );
if( bind == NULL ) { t_error( "t_bind alloc" ); exit(99); };
bind->addr.maxlen = addrp->n_addrs->maxlen;
bind->addr.len    = addrp->n_addrs->len;
bind->addr.buf    = addrp->n_addrs->buf;
bind->qlen = 3;         /* queue up to 3 connection requests  */
printbind( bind );      /* a "debug" function to print struct */

if (t_bind(tlifd,bind, bind)<0){ t_error( "t_bind" ); exit(4); }

/* allocate TLI call structure for t_listen/t_accept         */
call = (struct t_call *) t_alloc( tlifd, T_CALL, T_ADDR );
if( call == NULL ) { t_error( "t_call alloc" ); exit(99); };

while(1)
{
  if ( t_listen( tlifd, call ) < 0 )
     { t_error( "t_listen failed" ); exit(99); };

  if ( t_accept( tlifd, tlifd, call ) < 0 )
     if ( t_errno == TLOOK )
        if ( t_rcvdis( tlifd, (struct t_discon *) 0 ) < 0 )
           { t_error( "t_rcvdis failed" ); exit(99);}
     else  { t_error( "t_accept failed" ); exit(99);}

  if ( t_rcv( tlifd, record, REC_SIZE, &flags ) < 0 )
     { t_error( "t_rcv" ); exit(4); }

  sscanf( record, "%ld", &number );  /* get desired rec no  */
  rtc( number );                     /* get record from DB  */

  if ( t_snd( tlifd, record, REC_SIZE, 0 ) < 0)
       t_error( "t_snd");
  }
  t_close( tlifd );
}
```

The "remote table of contents" "doit" function from Chapter 3 is shown again for completeness of this example. Please keep in mind that you can change this function to meet your application requirements, while everything else for TLI/Network Selection remains unchanged.

```
rtc( number )              /* remote rtc() vers 1  */
long number;               /* record number        */
{
   FILE *fp;               /* table of contents    */
   char *filename;         /* toc filename         */

   filename = getenv( "RTCFILE" );
   if ( filename == NULL )  filename = "FAR90tc.dbs";

   fp = fopen( filename, "r" );
   if ( fp == NULL )
      {
         sprintf(record, "can't open %s\n", filename );
         return -1;
      }

   fseek( fp, ( number * REC_SIZE ), 0 );
   fread( record, sizeof(char), REC_SIZE, fp );
   record[ REC_SIZE - 1 ] = '\0'; /* guarantee NULL byte */
}
```

The next function is very similar to the printcall() function, and by using a union of t_bind and t_call structures, one function could print either data structure. Please keep in mind that this is the only place that the format of an Internet address (sockaddr_in) is needed, and this is for pedagogical purposes only.

```
printbind( bind )
struct t_bind *bind;
{
struct sockaddr_in *ptr;

printf( "\n\tbind->addr.maxlen = %d ", bind->addr.maxlen );
printf( "\n\tbind->addr.len    = %d ", bind->addr.len    );

if ( strcmp( getenv( "NETPATH" ), "tcp") == 0 )
   { ptr = (struct sockaddr_in *) bind->addr.buf;
      printf( "\n\tbind->addr.buf    = %s ",
                        inet_ntoa( ptr->sin_addr.s_addr ));
      printf( "\t %d \n\n", ntohs( ptr->sin_port ));
   }
else
      printf( "\n\tbind->addr.buf    = %s \n\n", bind->addr.buf );
}
```

7.6   Summary

This chapter introduced Transport Level Interface (TLI) programming and the protocol independence of Network Selection. The TLI functions are summarized in Figure 7.4.

Function Purpose	TLI Function	Socket System Call
Create an endpoint	t_open	socket
Name an endpoint	t_bind	bind
Unname an endpoint	t_unbind	
Connect to an endpoint	t_connect	connect
Listen for connection requests	t_listen	listen
Accept a connection requests	t_accept	accept
Send a byte-stream of data	t_snd	write, send
Receive a byte-stream of data	t_rcv	read, recv
Send a datagram unit of data	t_sndudata	sendto, sendmsg
Receive a datagram unit of data	t_rcvudata	recvfrom, recvmsg
Close an endpoint	t_close	close
Disconnect from an endpoint	t_snddis	
Acknowledge disconnect request	t_rcvdis	
Orderly release from an endpoint	t_sndrel	shutdown
Acknowledge orderly release request	t_rcvrel	
Get information about provider	t_getinfo	getsockopt
Set protocol options	t_optmgmt	setsockopt
Get protocol address	t_getname	getsockname
Allocate protocol address	t_alloc	
Free protocol address	t_free	
Check state of an endpoint	t_look	
Print error message	t_error	perror

Figure 7.4 TLI Programming Functions

The Network Selection functions are summarized in Figure 7.5.

Function Purpose	Function Name
Open network configuration database	setnetconfig, setnetpath
Read network configuration database	getnetconfig, getnetpath
Translate host/service name to network address	netdir_getbyname

Figure 7.5 Network Selection Functions

The TLI and Network Selection header files used in this chapter are summarized in Figure 7.6.

Header File	Description
`<tiuser.h>`	`/* generic TLI structures        */`
`<netconfig.h>`	`/* network selection structures */`
`<netdir.h>`	`/* ns name-to-addr structures   */`

Figure 7.6 TLI and Network Selection Header Files

The key data structures for TLI and Network Selection programming are summarized in Figure 7.7.

Struct Contents	Struct Name
Protocol characteristics	`t_info`
Pointer to protocol address (and queue size)	`t_bind`
Pointer to protocol address, options, & data	`t_call`
Pointer to protocol address, options, & data	`t_unitdata`
Pointer to protocol device & name library	`netconfig`
Network Selection host & service names	`nd_hostserv`
Transport provider addresses of servers	`nd_addrlist`

Figure 7.7 TLI and Network Selection Data Structures

This chapter began by introducing the basic TLI functions, and then presented a simple connectionless datagram and connection-mode virtual circuit example using the functions. The socket-based "remote table of contents" application from Chapter 3 was converted from socket system calls to TLI functions over the TCP/IP transport. Finally, the TCP/IP-based solution was generalized to be transport independent by using the Network Selection facility of SVR4. The beauty of Network Selection is the transport provider can be changed by modifying the shell environment variable **NETPATH** or by modifying the system's network configuration file **/etc/netconfig**, and the application will run over a different transport provider *without recompiling!*

Interfacing to the Internet Server Daemon

by Lyle Weiman

8.1 Introduction

In this chapter we show you how to interface to inetd, the Internet Server Daemon. The examples in previous chapters required someone to start the server daemon before anyone could access its services. You may have wondered why this wasn't necessary for the standard network daemons, such as ftpd (file transfer daemon) and telnetd (telnet daemon). The answer is, because these services interface to inetd.

Consider the disadvantages of explicitly starting up every server:

1. Each server in the system remains active, occupying system resources, even when it isn't being used.

2. Each server ties up swap space and process table space.

3. If the client is run before the server has been started, the server will receive ECONNREFUSED errors.

4. If the system were to be rebooted, it would be necessary to make sure that the server was restarted (for example, start the server /etc/rc).

5. The kind of servers we've shown thus far were incapable of performing services in parallel. Whichever client was first to get the server's attention occupied that server until it was finished, to the exclusion of all other clients. For the quickie services shown so far, that was a reasonable design choice.[1] What about servers that might take considerable time to complete their task, such as file transfers?

Interfacing your server to inetd eliminates these problems. It also adds a degree of security to the system, through the inetd.sec file (inetd can screen out unwanted

---

1. We could have added a fork() after the accept(), and had the child process handle the request and the parent wait for new requests. This would have provided as much parallelism. This method would also have given us a way to control how much of a "load" can be placed on the system by our servers: If the parent counts the number of child processes created, decrementing this counter when SIGCHLD signals arrive, it could refuse to call accept() when that counter reaches some threshold number. It could call sigblock() or wait() instead, waiting for at least one child process to terminate.

callers for you; for further details, see the manual page for the `inetd.sec` file). The `inetd.sec` file is available in HP-UX but not in many other systems.

The `inetd` creates a socket for each server specified in the `inetd.conf` file, binds the port number corresponding to this service (from the `/etc/services` file) to this socket, and calls `listen()` for it, thereby creating listen sockets for all the servers in the system. It then waits for incoming messages on those sockets (connection requests, in the case of messages for the TCP-based servers). When they arrive, `inetd` starts the server. In the case of TCP, `inetd` also `accept()`s the connection and `fork()`s a child process. The child process closes `stdin`, `stdout`, and `stderr`, `dup()`s the socket into descriptors zero, one, and two, and then `exec()`s the server. Socket descriptors, like file descriptors, are inherited across `fork()`s, and can be `dup()`ed. Thus, when the server begins execution, descriptors zero, one, and two all refer to a socket. In the case of TCP-based services the socket is already connected to the client. This skips the `socket()`, `bind()`, `listen()`, and `accept()` steps.

If you use `fork()` with sockets, remember that `close()` follows the same rules as any regular or special device files: `close()` always removes the mapping between descriptor and the system file table of the process, but it only actually **closes** the file (or socket) when there are no other processes currently existing with that file (or socket) open. In other words, when you call `fork()`, the child inherits all files and all sockets of the parent. In the case of sockets, the socket is not closed until the parent and all children (and their children, and so on) have closed their descriptors to that socket. This is why a remote shell (`rsh` or `remsh`) seems to be "busy" even after its script is completed; if the script invokes a process in the background, that process inherits the TCP socket as its `stdin`. The remote shell does not terminate until its TCP connection in the socket is closed.

Having noted the salient advantages of using `inetd`, it is only fair that we mention the drawbacks:

1. It can take a little longer to get started. First, `inetd` has to be scheduled—perhaps paged or swapped in; then it must `fork()` a child, and the child must `exec()` the server.

2. If several clients request service at the same time, multiple copies of the server daemon are created.[2] When you code your server to be started explicitly, you do not have to deal with multiple instances of your server unless you choose to (by `fork()`ing your server). Depending upon the nature of the server, there may be race

---

2. This can also be an advantage. It provides better service to the clients because the different servers execute in parallel.

conditions to be guarded against. Updating a shared database is one such case. The example in this chapter maintains a database, so it has to deal with this problem.

3. It complicates installation of the server daemon.

Interfacing to `inetd` is simple, but it places an installation burden on the system administrators. The administrator must add an entry to the `/etc/services` file as well as to the `/etc/inetd.conf` file. We have already mentioned the `/etc/services` file. The `/etc/inetd.conf` file contains one entry per server, of the following form:

```
s_name type protocol wait_flag user prog args
```

The `s_name` is the service name, which is case-sensitive. This same name must appear in `/etc/services`. The `type` is the socket type, either `"stream"` or `"dgram"`. Use the former for SOCK_STREAM (TCP), the latter for SOCK_DGRAM (UDP). The `protocol` is the protocol, and this name must appear in the `/etc/protocols` file;[3] for example, `"tcp"` or `"udp"`.

The `wait_flag` only applies to datagram sockets. Stream sockets should specify `"nowait"`. The `wait` function tells `inetd` to execute only one datagram server at a time, thus serializing the access and protecting against possible race conditions in the servicing of the requests. The `nowait` function tells `inetd` not to wait for the server to finish.

The `user` is the name of a user on the system (that is, the first field in its line in the `/etc/passwd` file). `inetd`'s child process will adopt the permissions for this "user"[4] before `exec()`ing the server. Caution: Make sure the server has "execute" permissions for the "user"; if it doesn't, then the `exec()` will fail, and your client will "see" a dropped connection. Typically, the "user" field is `"root"`, which implies the server has "root privileges" when it runs. This imposes the burden of avoiding security breaches on the server writer when it is used.

The `prog` entry is the absolute pathname for the server. The `inetd` will `exec()` the server using this pathname; it must be executable, and all parent directories must be searchable by user (`inetd` is started when the system is booted up, and it runs as `"root"`).

The `args` are the arguments to the server program, as you want them to appear. The first argument is the name of the server.

For example, the entry for `ftp`'s daemon (`ftpd`) is typically the following:

---

3. This file lists the protocols, by number. For more details, see the manual page.

4. A process normally runs with the same permissions as the process that `fork()`ed it, but there are exceptions. For more details on how one process can adopt the permissions of another user, see the manual page for `setuid()`.

```
ftp    stream  tcp  nowait root /etc/ftpd ftp
```

See the `inetd.conf` manual page for more information.

As an illustration, we developed the following example, which is useful when you have a pool of resources that are used by one person at a time, on a sign-up basis, such as test equipment or computer systems used for software development and testing. Resources have to be paid for, and there is inevitably somebody in the organization who wants to know when the resources are being used, which department to charge, and so forth. They typically put sign-up sheets next to the equipment, and they expect the people who use the resources to sign them out and sign them back into the pool when they're finished. This primitive system also lets people know when a resource is in use (by checking the sign-up sheets), but it is useful only when everybody uses the sign-up sheets.

A chief disadvantage of this method is that the sign-up sheets always seem to be placed in an inconvenient spot. You have to walk over to where they are in order to sign them. What we want is a server that will manage the sign-up sheets for us, or in other words, maintain a simple database (what a fancy title for a file). Since we have interfaced our server to `inetd`, there may be multiple instances of the server accessing our database. We will have to manage this contention.

It is convenient to use the same name for the file as for the resource being managed. By default, we will store the files corresponding to the set of resources being managed in `/usr/spool`, in a new subdirectory, named for the application (`rlock`). For flexibility, there is a section of `rlock.h` that is configurable, and users can change the default path. This can also be overridden by a run-time parameter. For each resource, this "database" is just a single-line ASCII file, containing the following fields:

- The status of the resource (locked or unlocked)

- The login name of the person who locked it (valid only when the resource is locked)

- The time-stamp when it was locked (so we can later compute how long it was used)

- The cumulative amount of time the resource has been used (so we can print reports for the accountants)

In large organizations, it's possible that the login name isn't enough to identify the person. Consequently, we'll include the name of the computer from which they locked it and the **gecos** field[5] of the `/etc/passwd` entry. This field is sometimes set up by the administrators to specify the account more completely. When the account is used by a person, the **gecos** field may include the person's full name and phone number and

---

5. See **passwd(4)** in your system's UNIX programmer's reference manual.

sometimes other information. This provides would-be lockers with information that they can use to contact the person presently holding the resource and negotiate who should have a higher priority for the resource. We can't arbitrate, but we can provide location information.

As mentioned, the servers need to guard against race conditions. Any race condition protection they need is normally up to the servers to provide (inetd does provide a "wait" option for UDP servers, but not TCP servers). Since everything about a resource is stored in this one file, we can simply call lockf()[6] to lock byte zero of this "database" file; only one server can do so at one time, so we have the atomicity of database updates that we require. This also protects the other files related to this resource. If, as would often be the case, only one server is active at a time, or if there are several, but they are interested in different resources, the overhead of locking the file is fairly low, so the choice to do so is inexpensive. If your system doesn't have lockf(), you could use lock files, but those are higher in overhead and harder to clean up in the event of an abort.

This server uses TCP. If we had chosen UDP, we'd have needed to make our transactions idempotent, so that if we had to retransmit a request that the server had already seen, it could recognize the repetition. Using TCP eliminates this problem.

When inetd starts your server, you already "know" the descriptor of the socket: zero (one or two would also do). You don't need to call socket(), nor bind(), nor listen(), because inetd already did this for you.

As previously mentioned, server processes that are started by inetd have no "real" stdout (or stdin or stderr for that matter). This is because the file descriptors zero through two all refer to your socket. This means that the typical debugging trick of using printf()s to show progress or state of variables isn't going to work (try it; what happens?). If you wish to use printf()s, you'll need to open() or fopen() a log file. You probably will want this to be conditional—say, on a "verbose" run-time argument. This allows troubleshooters to switch on the logging capability only when they need to. Scanning argv[] is still possible (arguments are as set in the inetd.conf file), but to get the "verbose" option turned on there are more steps. It is necessary to change the inetd.conf file to provide the "verbose" argument and then to restart inetd. For example, if you use -v as the "turn on verbose mode" indicator, then you would change the /etc/inetd.conf file from

```
rlock      stream tcp  nowait  root /etc/rlockd     rlock
```

to

```
rlock      stream tcp  nowait  root /etc/rlockd     rlock    -v
```

---

6. The database should be kept in the same computer where the server is running. The database may be NFS-mounted only if lockf() is supported over NFS.

We're calling this server `rlockd` (you may have noticed the convention is to add the letter "d" as a suffix to the name of server daemons). We're going to put it in `/etc`, with the others. We could equally well have put it in `/foo/bar`, or anywhere else. The essential step, however, is that we tell the `inetd.conf` file where it is and make the directories in this path (and the server) executable by the `user` field in the `inetd.conf` file.

It can be somewhat more difficult to develop the application with a source-code debugger when you rely on `inetd` to create the listen socket. You can't run it by itself. To solve this problem, either `#ifdef` the `socket()`/`bind()`/`listen()` portions or put them under a run-time parameter check. Better still, execute them but check for `EADDRINUSE` errors in the `bind()` system call. If this happens, assume that `inetd` has the socket—though that doesn't have to be true. The server in this chapter uses this latter method.

Our server is message-oriented, like the previous examples shown. It loops to read a complete message, because `recv()` isn't obligated to return as many bytes as were requested—only a number between zero (if the circuit died) and the requested number. Outside of this is another loop, because we want the server to be able to service multiple requests when necessary. This is generally true of servers and will give us the most flexibility in handling requests of various kinds. If, during any of these loops, `recv()` returns an error, then the daemon will simply exit. If there happened to be a partial message read, we make no distinction: If we don't have a complete message, we can't process it, and if the connection is dead, we can't reply anyway.

In this example, we defined the message header with two fields for the version number. We need one version number in the header so that we have some way to detect when client and server are dealing with different definitions of either the request or reply message formats. For this method to work, we must be careful to change the version number every time we change the format of our headers. In a distributed environment, subject to software modifications, upgrades, and bug fixes, version mismatches can happen more frequently than you might at first imagine. We placed one version number field near the front of the header.

8.2   Detecting Structure Alignment Mismatches

We put the other version number field at the very end of the structure. We put it there so that it can also detect structure alignment mismatches: Situations in which the C compiler used for the client has allocated storage for the fields at different offsets from that of the server. Some machine architectures restrict how data of different sizes may be stored. For example, on some machines 32-bit integers must be stored at an address whose least-significant two bits are zero (sometimes called "four-byte aligned"). If a programmer mixes the storage for different types of data (such as `char`, `int`, and `short`), the compiler will automatically adjust the addresses of these variables to fit the storage alignment restrictions of the machine architecture. Different compilers may adjust the offsets differently. In a structure that is communicated between different processes and which may be running on different machine architectures, different offsets present problems. Fortunately, we can avoid them if we are careful in our choice of the placement of the fields. That is, if we make sure everything fits the alignment restrictions of all machines of interest, there is nothing for the compiler to adjust. In today's machine architectures, where 32-bit architectures are the most common, this means using four-byte integers where two-byte `shorts` would be sufficient to hold the largest data value. It means padding out `char` arrays to multiples of four.[7]

To see how structural misalignment problems may arise, consider the following example:

```
struct example1 {
    char a;
    int  b;
    char c;
    short d;
};
```

Let's suppose, for the moment, that `sizeof(int) == 4`, `sizeof(short) == 2`, and `sizeof(char) == 1`. Some machines may be able to pack these into a structure whose size is equal to `sizeof a + sizeof b + sizeof c + sizeof d = 1 + 4 + 1 + 2 = 8` bytes. Other machines may store a in the first byte of the structure and leave either one or perhaps three bytes of unused space, so that b will fall on a multiple-of-four-byte boundary. Similarly, there may be one byte of fill space between c and d. Lastly, there may be fill space following d.

We made `char` arrays multiples of four in size, so there'd be no need for the compiler to generate fill space. As an additional precaution, putting the version field last means that we'll match the version only if the structure alignments between client

---

7. Communications involving the transfer of messages in C `structs` is obviously more convenient than, for example, filling `char` arrays one field at a time. This method presents no difficulties when used between machines with the same alignment characteristics. It can create problems in more general interoperability cases. This simple scheme works (or, with padding fields, can be made to work) in many cases, but it can't work for all computer architectures. In fact, it relies upon the prevalence of 32-bit `int` fields in most of the computers available today. If you have such radically dissimilar architectures, or need to code for the completely general case (and your application can stand the performance penalty), then you must either load `unsigned char` arrays one field at a time, or you'll have to encode the format for the data fields as well as the data fields themselves. Rather than invent your own mechanism, you should consider using Sun Microsystems's XDR mechanism or the OSI presentation schemes, such as ASN.1. These mechanisms impose overhead and add constraints to your programming, so you may wish to use the simple method shown here when you can.

and server machine architectures are identical. We don't have to worry about the more common difference in machine architectures: data representation of integers. We'll just use `ntohl()` and `htonl()` (introduced in Chapter 3).

With these two (seemingly redundant) version number fields, we can print meaningful error messages—when necessary—to the user. We will take the simplistic view that either the versions match exactly or our daemon will refuse to play.

8.3   `rlock.h`

In this example, we have a message format structured as follows (from `rlock.h`):

```
#define MAX_RESOURCE_NAME 16 /* max # chars in a resource name */
#define MAX_GECOS       32
#define VERSION         12
#define L_CUSERID       16 /* Must be >= L_cuserid on each system */
struct rqst_msg {
    int msg_len;              /* Message length, in bytes          */
    int version_num;
    int request_type;/*Request type, defined following this struct */
    char resource_2_lock[MAX_RESOURCE_NAME];
    char locker_name[L_CUSERID];      /* login name of locker      */
    char locker_gecos[MAX_GECOS];
    char locker_locn[MAXHOSTNAMELEN];/* location of locker         */
    char locker_mailname[MAXHOSTNAMELEN+L_CUSERID];/*mail name of
                                                         locker     */
    int version_num_check;
};
/*
** Request Types
*/
#define LOCK_RESOURCE                1
#define UNLOCK_RESOURCE              2
#define CHECK_LOCK_STATUS            3
#define CHECK_LOCK_STATUS_NO_INFO    4
#define SHOW_RESOURCES               5
#define LIST_LOCK_USAGE              6
#define LIST_LOCK_USAGE_AND_CLEAR    7
#define UNQUEUE_ME                   8
#define LOCK_RESOURCE_QUEUE          9
```

We also have replies structured as follows:

```
struct reply_msg {
    int msg_len;                      /* Message length, in bytes  */
    int version_num;
```

```
    int result;                    /* Result of the request, defined
                                       following this struct        */
    char locker_name[L_CUSERID];   /* Login name of locker          */
    char locker_gecos[MAX_GECOS];
    char locker_locn[MAXHOSTNAMELEN];/* location of locker          */
    char resource_2_lock[MAX_RESOURCE_NAME];
    unsigned long locked_timestamp;
    int version_num_check;
};
/*
** Reply result codes
*/
#define UNKNOWN_REQUEST_TYPE        0
#define RESOURCE_IS_ALREADY_LOCKED 1 /* Means somebody has it        */
#define RESOURCE_IS_NOW_LOCKED     2 /* Means you have it now        */
#define NO_SUCH_RESOURCE           3 /* Means there is no database
                                      /* for the named resource      */
#define RESOURCE_NOT_LOCKED_TO_YOU 4 /* Means resource not locked
                                        to you.                      */
#define RESOURCE_WAS_NOT_LOCKED    5 /* Means what it says           */
#define RESOURCE_IS_NOW_UNLOCKED   6
#define RESOURCE_NAME_RETURNED     7
#define RESOURCE_LOCK_QUEUED       8
/*
** Return Codes from rlocksub (must be unique from the
** result reply codes above)
*/
#define RTN_CANT_REACH_DB_SERVER        10
#define RTN_NO_RESPONSE_FROM_DB_SERVER  11
#define RTN_RESPONSE_UNRECOGNIZABLE     12
#define RTN_CANT_FIND_YOUR_UID          13
```

You can customize the following portion of rlock.h to fit your taste:

```
/*
** Customize section:  Change the following strings to fit your
** requirements.  These definitions are overridden if there is
** an environment variable (having the same name) defined;
** otherwise the defaults shown below are used.
*/
/* You must customize this file.  Set DBASE_HOME to the name of
** the node where you have installed the daemon rlockd.
*/
#define DBASE_HOME "nowhere"    /* name of node on which the
                                   resource database resides.  */
```

```
#define DBASE_PATH "/usr/spool/"/* Base pathname for the resource
                             database files.Subdirectories underneath
                             this path should be: rlock rlock_info
                             (optional) and rlock_queue.              */
/*
** For /etc/services lookups
*/
#define RLOCK_SERVICE_NAME      "rlock"
#define RLOCK_SERVICE_PROTO     "tcp"
#define RLOCK_DEFAULT_PORT      31347   /* Default port to use
                                        until /etc/services is set   */
#define RLOCK_DEFAULT_PORT_NAME "RLOCK_PORT_NUM"
```

We now turn to the server daemon.

8.4   `inetd` Version of a TCP Server Daemon (`rlockd`)

```
/*
** Resource Locker Daemon
*/
#include <stdio.h>
#include <errno.h>
#include <fcntl.h>
#include <sys/types.h>
#include <unistd.h>
#include <signal.h>
#include <sys/socket.h>
#include <netinet/in.h> /* sockaddr_in Internet socket address */
#include <netdb.h>       /* /etc/hosts table entries            */
#include <time.h>
#include <sys/utsname.h>
#include <sys/param.h>
#include "rlock.h"
/*
** MACROS and SYMBOLIC CONSTANTS
*/
#define RESOURCE_FORMAT "%d %s %s %ld %ld %s\n"
#define MAX_BUF 256
#define RLOCK_DB "/rlock/"
FILE *fopen();
/*
 * Global Variables.
 */
char   dbase_pathname[MAXPATHLEN] = DBASE_PATH;
char   qbuffer[2048];
```

```
char    *dbase_path = dbase_pathname;
int     log_flag = 0;
int     port = -1;
FILE    *dbptr;
/*
 * Extern Variables.
 */
extern int errno;
extern char *sys_errlist[];
extern int sys_nerr;
/*
 * Extern procedures
 */
char *getenv(), *strrchr(), *mktemp();
/*
** Forward Declarations
*/
char *get_my_host_name();
main( argc, argv )       /* argument count, argument vector     */
int argc;
char *argv[];
{
    struct sockaddr_in addr;    /* Internet socket name (addr)  */
    struct sockaddr_in *ptr;    /* pointer to get port number   */
    struct rqst_msg rqst;
    struct reply_msg reply;
    int     listen_skt;
    int     skt;            /* Current TCP connection socket descr */
    int     nbytes;             /* read nbytes req                 */
    int     rc;
    int     addrlen;
    int     total_read;
    int     i;
    int     I_am_son_of_inetd = 0;
    unsigned char *rd_ptr;
    struct sockaddr_in name;
    signal(SIGHUP, SIG_IGN);
```

We want our server to have some configurability. We should give the user the ability to decide whether or not there's a log file kept; this will be the −v option. Turning this option on permits some degree of troubleshooting: If somebody complains that it isn't working properly, we edit inetd.conf, add the −v option, restart inetd, and ask them to try again. Then, when the problem reoccurs, we can check the file and find out about which error the daemon was complaining.

We also need to give the user some degree of control over where the database file is kept. This will be the −D option. Lastly, we'll provide the ability to control which port number to use (the −p option). This is of no use whatsoever when inetd starts the daemon, but it can be used when the daemon is started manually. Both this option and the −D option allow the daemon to be set up on a system for which we don't have root access (though it will need to be restarted every time the system is shut down and brought back up again).

```c
for (i = 1; i < argc; i++) {
    if (argv[i][0] != '-')  goto badargs;
        switch (argv[i][1]) {
            case 'p':                    /* -p : port number          */
                if (++i >= argc) {
                    if (log_flag)
                        fprintf(dbptr, "-p parameter requires an
                                        argument\n");
                    exit(1);
                }
                port = atoi(argv[i]);
                break;
            case 'v':                  /* -v : verbose mode          */
                ++log_flag;
                if (log_flag)
                    dbptr = fopen("/tmp/rlockd.log", "a");
                break;
            case 'D':                    /* -D : set database pathname */
                if (++i >= argc) {
                    if (log_flag)
                        fprintf(dbptr, "-D parameter requires an
                                        argument\n");
                    exit(1);
                }
                strncpy(dbase_pathname, argv[i], MAXPATHLEN);
                break;
            default:
            badargs:
                if (log_flag)
                    fprintf(dbptr, "Parameter %s not an available
                                    option\n", argv[i]);
                exit(1);
        }
}
```

Next, we'll want to put in some code which allows this daemon to be started up without **inetd**. As stated before, this allows us to use a debugger on it. We'll set the

`I_am_son_of_inetd` flag if we are one; otherwise it'll retain its initialized value, zero.

```
/*
** We don't know if we were started from inetd or not.
** Try to create a socket, binding it to our service address.
** If we get no error, then go on.  If we get EADDRINUSE, then
** assume inetd has that address in use, and change the socket
** descriptor to zero (stdin).  For all other errors, abort.
*/
listen_skt = socket(AF_INET, SOCK_STREAM, IPPROTO_TCP);
i = 1;
setsockopt(listen_skt, SOL_SOCKET, SO_REUSEADDR, &i,
                sizeof(int));
name.sin_family= AF_INET;
name.sin_addr.s_addr= INADDR_ANY;
name.sin_port = getserv(RLOCK_SERVICE_NAME,
                                RLOCK_SERVICE_PROTO);
if (bind(listen_skt, &name, sizeof(name)) < 0) {
    if (errno == EADDRINUSE) {
        close(listen_skt);
        skt = 0;
        I_am_son_of_inetd = 1;
        goto go_on;
    }
    perror("bind");
    exit(1);
    }
if (listen(listen_skt, 5) < 0) {
    perror("listen");
    exit(1);
}
```

We come here for each new client and await its connection.

```
next_client:
addrlen = sizeof(struct sockaddr);
skt = accept(listen_skt, &name, &addrlen);
if (skt < 0) {
    perror("accept");
    exit(1);
}
go_on:
```

We'll use `getpeername()` to find out the address information of the new client. This allows us to find out the IP address of every client. We'll use this for logging.

```
addrlen = sizeof( addr );  /* need a real mem location       */
if ( (rc = getpeername( skt, &addr, &addrlen )) < 0 ) {
    if (log_flag) {
        fprintf(dbptr, "\ngetpeername return code = %d\n", rc);
        fprintf(dbptr, "INET Domain getpeername %s (%d)\n",
            ((errno <= sys_nerr) ? sys_errlist[errno]: ""), errno);
        fflush(dbptr);
    }
    addrlen = 0;
}
```

We have a new connection. Read the client's request message. This has to be performed in a loop, in order to ensure that we can read it in its entirety, no matter how TCP and IP may choose to fragment and segment it.

```
/*
** Read all the messages the client sends, responding as
** appropriate to each one.
*/
while(1) {
    total_read = 0;
    rd_ptr = (unsigned char *) &rqst;
    while (1) {
        /*
        ** Stay in this loop until we've got a complete message.
        */
        nbytes = recv( skt, rd_ptr, sizeof (rqst) - total_read, 0);
```

When `recv()` returns either an error or zero bytes of data, then the connection has died. In our example, this could mean that the client doesn't want to hear from us any more and has closed its end of the connection, or it could mean that the network has failed and the connection has been aborted. Either way, the result is the same: We close our socket and (if we weren't spawned by `inetd`) await new connections. Otherwise we just exit.

```
/* The remote end has closed the connection, or perhaps our own
** TCP has been unable to get back acknowledgments for the data
** in the message that proc_cmnd() has sent back in a previous
** iteration thru this loop.  Either way, this connection is
** unusable, so we must close() the descriptor, to free up its
** resources.  If we do not, then the next incoming connection
** we receive will take up a new slot in the descriptor-to-socket
```

```
** mapping table (kept in the u-area, that is, available to the
** kernel but not to us).  Eventually, if this keeps up, then
** we will have used up all available slots in this table.  This
** is the same limit on total number of open files -- the total
** number of open files plus open sockets can't be more than a
** certain constant, which is implementation-specific.  At any
** rate, by closing our end, we free up that slot and avoid
** the problem entirely.                                        */
        if (nbytes <= 0) {
            close(skt);
            if (log_flag) {
                fprintf(dbptr, "recv error %s (%d)\n",
                        sys_errrlist[errno], errno);
                fflush(dbptr);
            }
            skt = -1;
            break;        /* Breaking out of this loop gets us
                                     to the outer loop.          */
        }
        if(log_flag) {
            fprintf(dbptr, "recv %d bytes\n", nbytes);
            fflush(dbptr);
        }
        total_read += nbytes;
        rd_ptr += nbytes;
        if (total_read < sizeof(int)) continue;
        if (total_read >= ntohl(rqst.msg_len)) break;
    }
```

At this point, if we still have a nonnegative socket, then we have a message, and we'll want to process it. proc_cmnd() is the procedure for doing that.

```
    if ((skt >= 0) && (total_read > 0))
        proc_cmnd(skt, &rqst, &addr, addrlen);
    else break;
```

The connection is terminated. We are finished processing this client's request(s). We close the socket. If we were not spawned by inetd, then we wait for the next request, otherwise we exit; inetd will spawn new daemons as necessary:

```
    }
    close(skt);
    if (I_am_son_of_inetd)
        exit(0);
    else goto next_client;
}
```

8.4.1 Processing the Lock Request Structure

We must check for any structure misalignment problems when we send `structs` back and forth between systems. As already mentioned, we do this by storing copies of the version number near the beginning and near the end of the `struct`. These should both be equal to the version number we expect to work with. If not, then the message we received is unintelligible, and so we can't proceed. If the first one is different, then there's a version number mismatch. If the second is different, then we have a structure misalignment problem. This code is found in the `proc_cmnd()` procedure:

```
if (ntohl(rqst->version_num) != VERSION) {
    if (log_flag) {
        fprintf(dbptr,"Version mismatch, I am version %d but
            remote is %d\n", VERSION, ntohl(rqst->version_num));
        fflush(dbptr);
    }
    reply.result = NO_SUCH_RESOURCE;
    goto send_bad_reply;
}
if (ntohl(rqst->version_num_check) != VERSION) {
    if (log_flag) {
        fprintf(dbptr,"Struct alignment mismatch detected.\n");
        fflush(dbptr);
    }
    reply.result = NO_SUCH_RESOURCE;
    goto send_bad_reply;
}
```

We now have a proper message, and we are ready to process it. We'll just use `ntohl()` to convert the request type into the local node's integer format, and branch to the proper procedure to process the request.

```
switch ((request_code = ntohl(rqst->request_type))) {
    case LOCK_RESOURCE:
    case LOCK_RESOURCE_QUEUE:
        result = lock_resource(rqst, &reply, request_code);
        break;
    case UNLOCK_RESOURCE:
        unlock_resource(rqst, &reply);
        break;
    case CHECK_LOCK_STATUS:
    case CHECK_LOCK_STATUS_NO_INFO:
        check_lock_status(rqst, &reply);
        break;
```

```
     case SHOW_RESOURCES:
        show_resources(socket, rqst, &reply, from, fromlen);
        return;
     case LIST_LOCK_USAGE:
     case LIST_LOCK_USAGE_AND_CLEAR:
        list_lock_usage(socket, rqst, &reply, from, fromlen,
                                        request_code);
        return;
     case UNQUEUE_ME:
        unqueue_locker(rqst, &reply);
        break;
     default:
        reply.result = UNKNOWN_REQUEST_TYPE;
     }
```

Having processed the request, we'll send the reply now. You may have noticed that some of the message types are processed completely in their associated procedures, because instead of `break;` at the end of each case statement, there is a `return;` in some cases. These are for cases where the reply is unusual in nature and has to be processed individually.

```
send_reply:
   /*
   * Send the reply.
   */
   msglen = sizeof(struct reply_msg);
   if (log_flag) {
      fprintf(dbptr,"Sending %d bytes to port: %d\n", msglen,
                         from->sin_port );
      fprintf(dbptr,"to host: %s\n",
                         inet_ntoa(from->sin_addr.s_addr ));
      fflush(dbptr);
   }
   reply.msg_len = htonl(msglen);
   reply.version_num = reply.version_num_check = htonl(VERSION);
   send(socket, &reply, msglen, 0);
```

It is sometimes helpful to be able to display extra information about the resource, such as where it's located, whom to contact regarding changes to its configuration, or topical information such as when the disk drive was repaired. If there is such information, it will be stored in the file `rlock_info/<resource_name>`. If this file exists, open it and send its contents to the requestor:

```
   /*
   ** Is there ancillary information the system manager wants the
```

```
 ** locker to know about?  This action is only performed for
 ** certain requests.  The ancillary information is stored in
 ** $DBASE_PATH/rlock_info/<resource_name>, if it exists.
 ** If this file exists, open it, and send its contents to the
 ** requestor.
 */
 switch (request_code) {
     case LOCK_RESOURCE:
     case LOCK_RESOURCE_QUEUE:
         if (result == RESOURCE_LOCK_QUEUED){
             if ((len = strlen(qbuffer)) > 0)
                 send(socket, qbuffer, len, 0);
             close(socket);
             return;
         }
```

The contents of qbuffer are set by the **lock_resource()** procedure and will contain either an empty string or the names and other information of the users in the queue. This is so we can give users some idea of how long the line is.

```
         /* Otherwise, fall into VVVV ... */
     case CHECK_LOCK_STATUS:
         proc_ancillary(socket, rqst->resource_2_lock);
         /* VVVV fall into .... */
     case UNLOCK_RESOURCE:
     case UNQUEUE_ME:
         send(socket,"\0",1,0);
     }
     return;
 send_bad_reply:
     reply.msg_len = htonl( sizeof(reply) );
     reply.version_num = htonl(VERSION);
     reply.version_num_check = htonl(0);
     /* Now the client will see the prob */
     send(socket, &reply, sizeof(reply), 0);
     close(socket);
     return;
 }
```

8.4.2 Locking the Resource

lock_resource() is the procedure to handle all the tasks associated with locking a resource. It takes two arguments, one a pointer to the rqst structure (this holds the request parameters), the other a pointer to the reply structure, which will hold the reply parameters. The steps involved are as follows:

1. Open the database file. If there is no such file, then assume that the resource specified isn't being controlled.

2. Lock the database file. This is how we protect against race conditions caused by multiple daemons spawned by `inetd`.

3. Read the database file and decide whether the resource is locked or not.

4. If the resource is locked, then tell the user so and queue his or her name, e-mail name, and such parameters in the queue file.

5. If the resource is unlocked, then lock it and tell the user so.

```
lock_resource(rqst, reply, cmnd)
struct rqst_msg *rqst;
struct reply_msg *reply;
int cmnd;
{
   char dbase[MAX_BUF], buffer[MAX_BUF];
   int fd, islocked, len, sleepy_time, result;
   /* Set to 0 to force same locker to Q                       */
   int recognize_same_locker = 0;
   unsigned long locked_timestamp, total_used;
   char locker_name[MAX_BUF], locker_locn[MAX_BUF];
   char *ccptr;
   float hours_used;
   char lockergecos[MAX_GECOS];
```

We need to build the name of the database file. This will be the database path + the name of the resource. For example, assuming our database path is /usr/spool/rlock, then the name of the file for resource **asteroid** will be **/usr/spool/rlock/asteroid**.

```
   /*
   ** Build the pathname for the resource file.
   */
   strncpy(dbase, dbase_path, MAX_BUF);
   strncat(dbase,RLOCK_DB, MAX_BUF);
   strncat(dbase,rqst->resource_2_lock, MAX_BUF);
   if (rqst->locker_locn[0] == '\0') {
      /* User didn't give me a location.  Hm.  Why was that?   */
      strcpy(rqst->locker_locn,"??????");
   }
```

Now that we have the name of the file, we will try to open it with read/write capability (O_RDWR), since we'll be changing the contents of that file. If no such file exists, this means that the system administrator for the server node has not set up the file for this resource and doesn't want rlockd controlling a resource with this name.

```
if ((fd = open(dbase,O_RDWR,0)) <0){
    reply->result = NO_SUCH_RESOURCE;
    if (log_flag) {
        fprintf(dbptr,"No such resource %s\n",
                                        rqst->resource_2_lock);
        fflush(dbptr);
    }
    return(0);
}
```

There is a file for this resource. Lock it using lockf(), thus guaranteeing that exactly one copy of rlockd is now accessing this resource database file (and all the others associated with it, more of which we'll see later).

```
lock_it(fd);
```

Now that we have exclusive access to the database, we will read the database record. It's in ASCII. The file may contain zero bytes, or it may have a complete record in it from the last time any copy of rlockd modified it. A typical way to set up the resources database is to touch the names of all the resources we want to control, as by the following:

```
cd /usr/spool/rlock; touch hydra coolidge lincoln jackson
```

If read() returns an error, then return status to the caller that there is no such resource. This could happen if the user tried to lock a resource that never existed or has been purged from the tracking system (the rlockd/<resource_name> file has been deleted). Otherwise, parse the fields in the record if more than zero bytes were read; if the file was empty, then just assume it's lockable.

```
len = read(fd, buffer,MAX_BUF);
if (len <0) {
    reply->result = NO_SUCH_RESOURCE;
    lockf(fd, F_ULOCK, 0L);
    close(fd);
    if (log_flag) {
        fprintf(dbptr,"No such resource %s\n",
                                        rqst->resource_2_lock);
        fflush(dbptr);
    }
```

```
        return(0);
    } else if (len > 0) {
        sscanf(buffer, RESOURCE_FORMAT, &islocked, locker_name,
            locker_locn, &locked_timestamp, &total_used,
                                      lockergecos);
        if (log_flag) {
            fprintf(dbptr,"total_used %ld\n", total_used);
            fflush(dbptr);
        }
        strncpy(reply->locker_name, locker_name, L_CUSERID);
        strncpy(reply->locker_locn, locker_locn, MAXHOSTNAMELEN);
    } else {
        islocked = 0;
        total_used = 0;
        if (log_flag) {
            fprintf(dbptr,"total_used %ld\n", total_used);
            fflush(dbptr);
        }
        strncpy(reply->locker_name, rqst->locker_name, L_CUSERID);
        strncpy(reply->locker_locn, rqst->locker_locn,
                                        MAXHOSTNAMELEN);
        strncpy(locker_name, rqst->locker_name, L_CUSERID);
        strncpy(locker_locn, rqst->locker_locn, MAXHOSTNAMELEN);
    }
    reply->locked_timestamp = locked_timestamp;
    strncpy(reply->locker_gecos, lockergecos, MAX_GECOS);
```

If the status of the resource is locked, then see if the requestor is the same as the original locker. This can happen if the user forgot that he or she had it locked. If this is the case, then just tell them they have it locked. The variable `recognize_same_locker` is a debugging trick, so that we can verify that lockers can queue without having to login as someone else.

```
    if (islocked){
        /*
        ** Check to see if the requestor is the same as the locker.
        */
        if (recognize_same_locker && strcmp(locker_name,
                                    rqst->locker_name) == 0) {
            /* Yes, apparently this person forgot that he or she
            ** already had it locked.  Let's be charitable, and
            ** just say it's now locked.  We don't update the
            ** database, though; we just let the clock keep on
            ** tickin'.                                          */
```

```
        reply->result = RESOURCE_IS_NOW_LOCKED;
        lockf(fd, F_ULOCK, 0L);  close(fd);
        if (log_flag) {
            fprintf(dbptr,"Resource %s is already locked to same
                locker, %s\n", rqst->resource_2_lock, locker_name);
            fflush(dbptr);
        }
        return(0);
    }
```

At this point, someone else already has this resource locked. If the original request was to "lock and queue," then try to queue this request (call `queue_lock()`; we'll show `queue_lock()` in more detail shortly). Otherwise, or if this request cannot be honored, place in the reply that the resource is locked to someone else.

```
    /*
    ** The resource is already locked.  If the request was to
    ** queue, do so;  otherwise, or if this fails, return status
    ** that the resource is locked, including the name and
    ** location of the locker.
    */
    if ((cmnd == LOCK_RESOURCE_QUEUE) && queue_lock(rqst))
                /* Can we queue this?                          */
        result = reply->result = RESOURCE_LOCK_QUEUED;
                /* Yes, tell caller                            */
    else
        result = reply->result = RESOURCE_IS_ALREADY_LOCKED;
                /* No.                                         */
```

We are finished with the database, and can unlock **it** and return status (either that the request is locked, or that it's locked but the user has been queued) to the requestor.

```
    lockf(fd, F_ULOCK, 0L);     close(fd);
    if (log_flag ) {
        fprintf(dbptr, "Resource %s is already locked to
                different locker,%s\n", rqst->resource_2_lock,
                locker_name);
        fflush(dbptr);
    }
    return(result);
} else {
```

Here, we have the situation where the resource was not locked. Since we have the database locked, we can rewrite the record after building it with `sprintf()`. The `gecos` field of the **/etc/passwd**[8] entry for the user sometimes contains more information, so we have implemented our server to include it in the request entry. We'll write it as part of the database record, but first we have to change any embedded blanks to something else, such as underscores.

```
    /*
    ** The resource was unlocked, so lock it now.  Store
    ** who has it locked, which machine they're at, and when
    ** they locked it.
    ** Make sure the "gecos" field has no blanks in it.
    ** Replace any found with underscores.  Ditto tabs.
    */
    fill_with_underscores(rqst->locker_gecos, MAX_GECOS);
    reply->result = RESOURCE_IS_NOW_LOCKED;
    lseek(fd, 0L, 0);                   /*Rewind the file       */
    time(&locked_timestamp);
    memset(buffer, " ", MAX_BUF);
    sprintf(buffer, RESOURCE_FORMAT, 1, rqst->locker_name,
    rqst->locker_locn, locked_timestamp, total_used,
     rqst->locker_gecos);
    if (log_flag) {
        fprintf(dbptr,"total_used %ld\n", total_used);
        fflush(dbptr);
    }
    write(fd, buffer, strlen(buffer));
    lockf(fd, F_ULOCK, 0L); close(fd);
    if (log_flag) {
        fprintf(dbptr, "Locking resource %s, locker, %s at %s\n",
                rqst->resource_2_lock, rqst->locker_name,
                rqst->locker_locn);
        fflush(dbptr);
    }
    reply->locked_timestamp = locked_timestamp;
    return(0);
    }
}
```

8.4.3 Unlocking the Resource

As its name implies, unlock_resource() is the procedure for handling the unlocking of a resource. It must verify that the unlocker is indeed the person who locked it; add a usage record to the resource usage file; and, if there is a queue of users

---

8. The gecos field is unused by the rest of the system for normal password-related information. System administrators will sometimes store in this field descriptive information on the user, such as the user's real name, phone number, and so forth.

waiting for it, then take one name from the head of the queue, lock the resource to him or her, lock it and e-mail that person. Otherwise, if the "waiting queue" is empty, the resource is simply unlocked.

```
unlock_resource(rqst, reply)
struct rqst_msg *rqst;
struct reply_msg *reply;
{
   char dbase[MAX_BUF], buffer[MAX_BUF], time_started[30],
             time_finished[30];
   int fd, fdrpt, islocked, len, temp, sleepy_time;
   unsigned long locked_timestamp, finished_timestamp, total_used;
   char locker_name[MAX_BUF], locker_locn[MAX_BUF];
   char lockergecos[MAX_GECOS];
   float time_used, hours_used;
   /*
   ** Build the pathname for the resource file.
   */
   strncpy(dbase, dbase_path, MAX_BUF);
   strncat(dbase,RLOCK_DB, MAX_BUF);
   strncat(dbase,rqst->resource_2_lock, MAX_BUF);
   if (rqst->locker_locn[0] == '\0') {
      /* User didn't give me a location.  Hm.  Why was that?  */
      strcpy(rqst->locker_locn,"??????");
   }
   if ((fd = open(dbase,O_RDWR,0)) <0){
      reply->result = NO_SUCH_RESOURCE;
      if (log_flag) {
         fprintf(dbptr, "No such resource %s\n",
                   rqst->resource_2_lock);
         fflush(dbptr);
      }
      return;
   }
   /*
   ** inetd will fork(2) and exec(2) a new instance of this daemon
   ** for each connection request. Each instance must have
   ** exclusive access to the database to guard against race
   ** conditions.
   */
   lock_it(fd);
   /*
   ** We now have exclusive access.  Read the database file,
   ** find out the status of the resource.
```

```
*/
if ((len = read(fd, buffer, MAX_BUF)) < 0) {
    reply->result = NO_SUCH_RESOURCE;
    lockf(fd, F_ULOCK, 0L);
    close(fd);
    if (log_flag) {
        fprintf(dbptr, "No such resource %s\n",
                rqst->resource_2_lock);
        fflush(dbptr);
    }
    return;
}
if (len > 0) {
    sscanf(buffer,RESOURCE_FORMAT, &islocked, locker_name,
     locker_locn, &locked_timestamp, &total_used, lockergecos);
    if (log_flag) {
        fprintf(dbptr,"total_used %ld\n", total_used);
        fflush(dbptr);
    }
    strncpy(reply->locker_name, locker_name, L_CUSERID);
    strncpy(reply->locker_locn, locker_locn, MAXHOSTNAMELEN);
} else {
    islocked = 0;
    total_used = 0;
    if (log_flag) {
        fprintf(dbptr,"total_used %ld\n", total_used);
        fflush(dbptr);
    }
    strncpy(reply->locker_name, rqst->locker_name, L_CUSERID);
    strncpy(reply->locker_locn, rqst->locker_locn,
            MAXHOSTNAMELEN);
    strncpy(locker_name, rqst->locker_name, L_CUSERID);
    strncpy(locker_locn, rqst->locker_locn, MAXHOSTNAMELEN);
    lockergecos[0] = '\0';
}
/*
** Check to see if the resource is still locked.
** If it wasn't, return "was not locked" status.
*/
if (!islocked) {
    reply->result = RESOURCE_WAS_NOT_LOCKED;
    lockf(fd, F_ULOCK, 0L);
    close(fd);
    if (log_flag) {
```

```
        fprintf(dbptr, "Resource %s was not locked\n",
                rqst->resource_2_lock);
        fflush(dbptr);
    }
    return;
}
/*
** Check to see if the requestor is the same as the locker.
*/
if (strcmp(locker_name, rqst->locker_name) != 0) {
    reply->result = RESOURCE_NOT_LOCKED_TO_YOU;
    lockf(fd, F_ULOCK, 0L);
    close(fd);
    if (log_flag) {
        fprintf(dbptr,
            "Resource %s was not locked to %s, it is locked to
            %s\n", rqst->resource_2_lock,
            rqst->locker_name, locker_name);
        fflush(dbptr);
    }
    return;
}
/*
** The resource was locked to this requestor, so unlock it now.
** Store who had it locked, which machine they're at, and when
** they locked it.
*/
reply->result = RESOURCE_IS_NOW_UNLOCKED;
lseek(fd, 0L, 0);/*Rewind the file */
time(&finished_timestamp);
temp = finished_timestamp - locked_timestamp;
time_used = temp / 3600.0;
total_used += (finished_timestamp - locked_timestamp);
hours_used = total_used/3600.0;
/*
** Now build an entry in the "report" file.
** If there is no report file, create one and include a heading
** showing the columns.
** Each entry shows who locked the resource, when they locked
** it, and when they unlocked it, from which we can also
** calculate how long it was used.  The "report" file has
** the same name as the resource, but with ".rpt" suffixed.
**/
strcat(dbase, ".rpt");
```

```
if ((fdrpt = open(dbase, O_APPEND|O_RDWR)) < 0){
   /*
   ** A new report file has to be created.
   ** Make a pretty header, so people can see what the fields
   ** mean, and so on.
   */
   fdrpt = open(dbase, O_CREAT|O_APPEND|O_RDWR, 0644);
   if (fdrpt >= 0) {
      sprintf(buffer,"Resource name: %s\n",
              rqst->resource_2_lock);
      write(fdrpt, buffer,strlen(buffer));
      sprintf(buffer,
              "User     Name Date Date    User    Total\n");
      write(fdrpt, buffer,strlen(buffer));
      sprintf(buffer,
              "Name                                   locked
              unlocked        Used   Used\n");
      write(fdrpt, buffer,strlen(buffer));
      sprintf(buffer, "(hrs)   (hrs)\n");
      write(fdrpt, buffer,strlen(buffer));
      sprintf(buffer,
              "======== =============================== \
      ================= ================  =====   ======\n");
      write(fdrpt, buffer,strlen(buffer));
      write(fdrpt,"\n",1);
   }
}
if (fdrpt >= 0) {
   strcpy(time_started, ctime(&locked_timestamp));
   time(&finished_timestamp);     /* Time now              */
   strcpy(time_finished, ctime(&finished_timestamp));
   len = strlen(time_finished);
   /* Strip off trailing newline and the year              */
   if (len > 10) time_finished[len-9] = '\0';
      len = strlen(time_started);
   if (len > 10) time_started[len-9] = '\0';
      sprintf(buffer,"%-8s %-32s %16s  %16s %6.2f %8.2f\n",
         locker_name, lockergecos, time_started, time_finished,
         time_used, hours_used);
      write(fdrpt, buffer, strlen(buffer));
      close(fdrpt);
}
if (!lock_4_next_in_queue(fd, rqst)){
   memset(buffer, " ", MAX_BUF);
   sprintf(buffer, RESOURCE_FORMAT, 0, locker_name,
```

```
            locker_locn, finished_timestamp, total_used,
            lockergecos);
    write(fd, buffer, strlen(buffer));
    lockf(fd, F_ULOCK, 0L);
    close(fd);
    if (log_flag ) {
        fprintf(dbptr, "Un-Locking Resource %s from %s\n",
                rqst->resource_2_lock, rqst->locker_name);
        fflush(dbptr);
    }
    return;
    }
}
```

8.4.4 Checking a Resource Lock Status

The routine check_lock_status() checks whether a resource is locked. It is used
to service requests from rislock, which in turn is used from shell scripts to find a
resource that is available for use from a group of similar ones. It is essentially just the
beginning portion of lock_resource() and does not change the status of the
resource.

```
check_lock_status(rqst, reply)
struct rqst_msg *rqst;
struct reply_msg *reply;
{
    char dbase[MAX_BUF], buffer[MAX_BUF];
    int fd, islocked, len, sleepy_time;
    unsigned long locked_timestamp, total_used;
    char locker_name[MAX_BUF], locker_locn[MAX_BUF];
    char lockergecos[MAX_GECOS];
    float hours_used;
    /*
    ** Build the path-name for the resource file.
    */
    strncpy(dbase, dbase_path, MAX_BUF);
    strncat(dbase,RLOCK_DB, MAX_BUF);
    strncat(dbase,rqst->resource_2_lock, MAX_BUF);

    if ((fd = open(dbase,O_RDWR,0)) <0){
        reply->result = NO_SUCH_RESOURCE;
        if (log_flag) {
            fprintf(dbptr,"No such resource %s\n",
                                    rqst->resource_2_lock);
            fflush(dbptr);
```

```
      }
      return;
   }
   lock_it(fd);
   len = read(fd, buffer,MAX_BUF);
   if (len <0) {
      reply->result = NO_SUCH_RESOURCE;
      lockf(fd, F_ULOCK, 0L);
      close(fd);
      if (log_flag) {
         fprintf(dbptr,"No such resource %s\n",
                                         rqst->resource_2_lock);
         fflush(dbptr);
      }
      return;
   }
   if (len > 0) {
      sscanf(buffer, RESOURCE_FORMAT, &islocked, locker_name,
                locker_locn, &locked_timestamp, &total_used,
                lockergecos);
      if (log_flag) {
         fprintf(dbptr,"locked %d name %s locn %s t-stamp %ld\n",
            islocked,locker_name, locker_locn, locked_timestamp);
         fflush(dbptr);
      }
      strncpy(reply->locker_name, locker_name, L_CUSERID);
      strncpy(reply->locker_locn, locker_locn, MAXHOSTNAMELEN);
   } else {
      islocked = 0;
      total_used = 0;
      if (log_flag) {
         fprintf(dbptr,"Zero-length data file\n");
         fflush(dbptr);
      }
      strncpy(reply->locker_name, rqst->locker_name, L_CUSERID);
      strncpy(reply->locker_locn, rqst->locker_locn,
                                    MAXHOSTNAMELEN);
      strncpy(locker_name, rqst->locker_name, L_CUSERID);
      strncpy(locker_locn, rqst->locker_locn, MAXHOSTNAMELEN);
      if (islocked){
         reply->locked_timestamp = locked_timestamp;
         /*
         ** Check to see if the requestor is the same as the locker.
         */
```

```
        if (strcmp(locker_name, rqst->locker_name) == 0) {
            /* Yes, apparently this person forgot that he or she
            ** already had it locked.  Let's be charitable and
            ** just say it's now locked.  We don't update the
            ** database, though; we just let the clock keep on
            ** tickin'.
            */
            reply->result = RESOURCE_IS_NOW_LOCKED;
            if (log_flag) {
                fprintf(dbptr, "Resource %s is already locked to
                    same locker, %s\n", rqst->resource_2_lock,
                    locker_name);
                fflush(dbptr);
            }
        } else {
            reply->result = RESOURCE_IS_ALREADY_LOCKED;
            if (log_flag) {
                fprintf(dbptr, "Resource %s is already locked but
                    to a different locker, %s\n",
                    rqst->resource_2_lock, locker_name);
                fflush(dbptr);
            }
        }
        lockf(fd, F_ULOCK, 0L);
        close(fd);
        return;
    } else {
        /*
        ** The resource is unlocked.
        */
        reply->result = RESOURCE_IS_NOW_UNLOCKED;
        lockf(fd, F_ULOCK, 0L);
        close(fd);
        return;
    }
}
```

8.4.5 Listing Resources

The show_resources() routine handles the request to show the lockable resources. This is simply an ls list of all the files in the resources database, sans the usage report files (these have .rpt suffixes) and the RESOURCES file (which is the redirected output of the ls command). We build this each time, so that if somebody adds a new resource, the next "show resources" request will include it.

```
/*
** Show the resources that we are administrating.
** The resources are in a file, $DB_PATH/RESOURCES, which is
** normally created by an ls > RESOURCES command.  This means that
** any name with the .rpt suffix, and the name RESOURCES itself,
** is to be ignored.
*/
show_resources(socket, rqst, reply, from, fromlen)
int socket, fromlen;
struct rqst_msg *rqst;
struct reply_msg *reply;
struct sockaddr_in *from; /* socket name (addr)*/
{
   char dbase[MAX_BUF], buffer[MAX_BUF];
   char lockergecos[MAX_GECOS];
   int len, msglen;
   FILE *fp;
   /*
   ** Build the pathname for the resource file.
   */
   strncpy(dbase, dbase_path, MAX_BUF);
   strncat(dbase,RLOCK_DB, MAX_BUF);
   sprintf(buffer, "cd %s;/bin/ls |/bin/grep -v '.rpt$'|
              /bin/grep -v RESOURCES > RESOURCES", dbase);
   strncat(dbase,"RESOURCES", MAX_BUF);
   /*
   ** We don't believe sys-admin people have the time to keep
   ** the RESOURCES file current, so we'll build a new one each
   ** time we need it.  It just involves a simple "ls" command on
   ** the database directory, so we'll use the system() routine
   ** to execute that command.
   */
   system(buffer);
   if ((fp = fopen(dbase,"r")) == NULL){
      reply->result = NO_SUCH_RESOURCE;
      if (log_flag) {
         fprintf(dbptr,"No RESOURCES file\n");
         fflush(dbptr);
      }
      return;
   }
   while (1) {
      if ( fgets(buffer, MAX_BUF, fp) == NULL)
         buffer[0] = '\0';                 /* EOF read, end of msg   */
```

```
                /*
                * Send the reply.
                */
                if (strcmp(buffer, "RESOURCES\n") == 0) continue;
                len = strlen(buffer);
                /* Take out the new-line                              */
                if ((len > 0) && (buffer[len-1] == '\n'))
                    buffer[len-1] = '\0';
                strncpy(reply->resource_2_lock, buffer, MAX_RESOURCE_NAME);
                /* We send the reply, and rely on TCP to shepherd the data
                ** through the network.  If TCP can't get it through, we'll
                ** take that as meaning the network is broken, and we do not
                ** supply any further recovery.  The client "knows" the last
                ** message is the one having a zero-length resource name in
                ** the resource_2_lock field.
                msglen = sizeof(struct reply_msg);
                reply->msg_len = htonl(msglen);
                reply->version_num = reply->version_num_check =
                            htonl(VERSION);
                reply->result = RESOURCE_NAME_RETURNED;
                send(socket, reply, sizeof (struct reply_msg), 0);
                if (log_flag) {
                    fprintf(dbptr,"Informing peer of existence of resource
                            %s\n", buffer);
                    if (fromlen > 0) {
                        fprintf(dbptr,"Sending %d bytes to port: %d\n",
                            msglen, from->sin_port);
                        fprintf(dbptr, "to host: %s\n",
                            inet_ntoa(from->sin_addr.s_addr ));
                    }
                    fflush(dbptr);
                }
                if (strlen(buffer) == 0) break;
            }
        }
```

8.4.6 Listing Lock Usage

list_lock_usage() reports the usage log files. It also can clear the time-used accrual field, as when the user is requesting a printout and wants the logs to be cleared to start accruing anew. The security issue we "finessed," based on the assumption that if the user is running as root on the same system as the database, we can allow the report files to be cleared.

The algorithm is to create a file that contains the list of files, other than itself, and read the logs they contain. We could read the directories directly, and this would be a lower-overhead solution, but directory structures are different formats, especially between AT&T and BSD-derived.

Since the report files and the RESOURCES file will also appear in the output of the `ls` command, we have code to detect and skip these cases.

```
list_lock_usage(socket, rqst, reply, from, fromlen, request_type)
int socket, fromlen, request_type;
struct rqst_msg *rqst;
struct reply_msg *reply;
struct sockaddr_in *from; /* socket name (addr)*/
{
    char dbase[MAX_BUF], buffer[4096], buf2[MAX_BUF],
        buf3[MAX_BUF];
    char sprbuf[MAX_BUF], resource_name[MAX_BUF], *cptr, *cptr2;
    int len, msglen, fd_report, fd_lock;
    int islocked, sleepy_time, nbytes, clear_DB_flag = 0;
    unsigned long locked_timestamp, total_used;
    char locker_name[MAX_BUF], locker_locn[MAX_BUF];
    char lockergecos[MAX_GECOS];
    FILE *fp;
    /*
    ** Send a dummy message, so the client knows we got something.
    reply->result = htonl(RESOURCE_NAME_RETURNED);
    msglen = sizeof(struct reply_msg);
    reply->msg_len = htonl(msglen);
    reply->version_num = reply->version_num_check =
        htonl(VERSION);
    send(socket, reply, msglen, 0);
    */
```

If this user has asked to clear the report files after we've transmitted them and clear the time-used accrual field in the database, we can let the user do so if he or she is running as root on the same system as the database. Otherwise, we'll just list the info and leave the database as is.

```
    if (log_flag) {
        fprintf(dbptr,"user %s locn %s my locn %s \n",
            rqst->locker_name, rqst->locker_locn,
            get_my_host_name());
        fflush(dbptr);
    }
    if ((request_type == LIST_LOCK_USAGE_AND_CLEAR) &&
        (strcmp(rqst->locker_locn, get_my_host_name()) == 0) &&
```

```
                (strcmp(rqst->locker_name, "root")  == 0) ||
                (strcmp(rqst->locker_name, "rootk") == 0) ||
                (strcmp(rqst->locker_name, "rootc") == 0)    )
             ++clear_DB_flag; /* We will clear the database as we go. */
        if (clear_DB_flag && log_flag) {
             fprintf(dbptr,"user wants to clear database\n");
             fflush(dbptr);
        }
        /* We don't believe sys admin people have the time to keep
        ** the RESOURCES file current, so we'll build a new one each
        ** time we need it.  It just involves a simple "ls" command on
        ** the database directory, so we'll use the system() routine
        ** to execute that command.
        */
        strncpy(dbase, dbase_path, MAX_BUF);
        strncat(dbase,RLOCK_DB, MAX_BUF);
        sprintf(buffer, "cd %s;/bin/ls > RESOURCES 2> /dev/null",
                dbase);
        if (log_flag) {
             fprintf(dbptr,"list_lock_usage cmd:\n%s\n", buffer);
             fflush(dbptr);
        }
        system(buffer);
        strncpy(buffer, dbase, MAX_BUF);
        strncat(buffer, "RESOURCES", MAX_BUF);
        if ((fp = fopen(buffer,"r")) == NULL){
             if (log_flag) {
                 fprintf(dbptr,"No RESOURCES file\n");
                 fflush(dbptr);
             }
             close(socket);
             return;
        }
        while (1) {
             if ( fgets(resource_name, MAX_BUF, fp) == NULL) {
                 /* EOF read, end of msg                         */
                 if (log_flag) {
                     fprintf(dbptr,"list_lock_usage exiting\n");
                     fflush(dbptr);
                 }
#define CLOSE_MESSAGE \"\nReport files have been cleared.\n\Total
time used accruals for these resources have also been reset.\n"
                 /*
                 ** If we cleared the database, so inform the user.
```

```
                  */
                  if (clear_DB_flag)
                     send(socket, CLOSE_MESSAGE, strlen(CLOSE_MESSAGE), 0);
                  close(socket);
                  return;
            }
            if (log_flag) {
               fprintf(dbptr,"resource: %s\n", resource_name);
               fflush(dbptr);
            }
            if (strcmp(resource_name, "RESOURCES\n") == 0) continue;
            if ((len = strlen(resource_name)) < 2) continue;
            /* Take out the new-line                              */
            if (resource_name[len-1] == '\n')
               resource_name[--len] = '\0';
            /* If this is a report file, then skip that, too.     */
            if ((len >= 4) && resource_name[len -4] == '.' &&
               resource_name[len -3] == 'r' && resource_name[len -2] ==
               'p' && resource_name[len -1] == 't' ) continue;
            if (log_flag) {
               fprintf(dbptr,"#2 resource: %s\n", resource_name);
               fflush(dbptr);
            }
            /*
            ** "dbase" contains the base pathname, resource_name
            ** contains its name.
            */
            strncpy(buf2, dbase, MAX_BUF);
            strncat(buf2, resource_name, MAX_BUF);
            if (log_flag) {
               fprintf(dbptr,"resource: %s path: %s\n", resource_name,
                     buf2);
               fflush(dbptr);
            }
            if ((fd_lock = open(buf2, O_RDWR, 0)) < 0) {
               if (log_flag) {
                  fprintf(dbptr,"no file for resource %s\n", buf2);
                  fflush(dbptr);
               }
               continue;
            }
            /*
            ** Lock the resource file (aka the lock file).  This
            ** will assure us of no changes to either this file
```

```
** or the report file while we are sending the
** contents to the client, and thus that no information
** is lost.
*/
if (log_flag) {
   fprintf(dbptr,"attempting to lock resource file %s\n",
           buf2);
   fflush(dbptr);
}
lock_it(fd_lock);
if (log_flag) {
   fprintf(dbptr,"locked resource file%s\n", buf2);
   fflush(dbptr);
}
/*
** We now have exclusive access.  Read the database file,
** find out the status of the resource.  If the file is
** empty (because this is the first time anybody's looked
** at it), just keep on going.
*/
memset(buf3, " ", MAX_BUF-2);
buf3[MAX_BUF-1] = '\0';
if ((len = read(fd_lock, buf3, MAX_BUF)) > 0) {
   sscanf(buf3, RESOURCE_FORMAT, &islocked, locker_name,
          locker_locn, &locked_timestamp, &total_used,
          lockergecos);
   if (log_flag) {
      fprintf(dbptr,"clearing total used, was %ld\n",
              total_used);
      fflush(dbptr);
   }
   /*
   ** Are we clearing the database as we go?
   */
   if (clear_DB_flag) {
      /*
      ** Yes.  We have the resource file info (islocked,
      ** locker_name, locker_locn, locked_timestamp).  We
      ** rewrite this, but we store a zero in the total_used
      ** field, so that usage times start over again.  If
      ** this resource is locked now, then when it is
      ** unlocked, the time used will appear in the report
      ** file when it is next printed.
      */
```

```
      lseek(fd_lock, 0L, 0);   /*Rewind the file          */
      memset(buf3, " ", MAX_BUF);
      sprintf(buf3, RESOURCE_FORMAT, islocked, locker_name,
         locker_locn, locked_timestamp, 0.0);
      write(fd_lock, buf3, strlen(buf3));
   }
   /*
   ** Read everything in the report file, and dump it
   ** onto our socket.  The client is waiting for this
   ** info and will report it on its own stdout.  When
   ** we read the end of file, if we are clearing
   ** the database as we go (clear_DB_flag), then we'll
   ** purge the report file.  The next time somebody un-
   ** locks the resource, a new report file will be created,
   ** with the new total-used time accruing from this
   ** moment.                                            */
   strcat(buf2, ".rpt");
   if (log_flag) {
      fprintf(dbptr,"attempting to open report file %s\n",
         buf2);
      fflush(dbptr);
   }
   if ((fd_report = open(buf2, O_RDONLY, 0)) >= 0) {
      if (log_flag) {
         fprintf(dbptr,"report file is open\n");
         fflush(dbptr);
      }
      while (1) {
         nbytes = read(fd_report, buffer, 4096);
         if (nbytes <= 0) break;
         if (log_flag) {
            fprintf(dbptr,"sending %d bytes to client\n",
               nbytes);
            fflush(dbptr);
         }
         if (send(socket, buffer, nbytes, 0) < 0) {
            nbytes = -1;
            break;
         }
      }
      if (log_flag) {
         fprintf(dbptr,"finished with report file\n");
         fflush(dbptr);
      }
```

```
                    send(socket, "\n\n", 2, 0);
                    close(fd_report);
                    /*
                    ** EOF read.  If this user has the proper privileges
                    ** and has asked to do so, purge the report file.
                    */
                    if (nbytes >= 0 && clear_DB_flag) {
                        unlink(buf2);
                        if (log_flag) {
                            fprintf(dbptr,"report file %s purged.\n", buf2);
                            fflush(dbptr);
                        }
                    }
                } else {
                    sprintf(sprbuf, "Resource %s has not been used.\n\n",
                        resource_name);
                    if (log_flag) {
                        fprintf(dbptr,"%s\n", sprbuf);
                        fflush(dbptr);
                    }
                    send(socket, sprbuf, strlen(sprbuf), 0);
                }
            } else {
                if (log_flag) {
                    fprintf(dbptr,"resource file %s is empty\n", buf2);
                    fflush(dbptr);
                }
            }
            lockf(fd_lock, F_ULOCK, 0L);
            close(fd_lock);
        }
}
```

8.4.7 Printing Resource Information

The proc_ancillary() routine looks up extra information about a given resource, if there is any, and gives it out. This extra information is kept in the rlock_info directory. Whatever is in the file with the same name, we return to our caller, constituting a shift to a byte-stream protocol here. We just send() ASCII until we get to the file EOF, then close the connection. There is no problem here, since TCP does not depend on the structure of the data it carries; we do have to make sure that our client and daemon are both expecting byte-stream, rather than message-formatted, data.

```
proc_ancillary(socket, resource)
int socket;
char *resource;
{
    int fd, nbytes;
    char *cptr, ancillary_file_name[MAX_BUF];
    char buffer[MAX_BUF], buf1[MAX_BUF];
    /*
    ** Build the name for the ancillary file.
    */
    strncpy(ancillary_file_name, dbase_path, MAX_BUF);
    strncat(ancillary_file_name,"/rlock_info/", MAX_BUF);
    strncat(ancillary_file_name, resource, MAX_BUF);
    if (log_flag) {
        fprintf(dbptr,"Sending ancillary info from file %s\n",
                ancillary_file_name);
        fflush(dbptr);
    }
    if ((fd = open(ancillary_file_name,O_RDONLY)) < 0)
        return;                               /* No info              */
    /*
    ** Info file exists.  Just read it, copying to the socket.
    */
    while (1) {
        nbytes = read(fd, buffer, 4096);
        if (nbytes <= 0) break;
        if (log_flag) {
            fprintf(dbptr,"sending %d bytes to client\n", nbytes);
            fflush(dbptr);
        }
        if (send(socket, buffer, nbytes, 0) < 0)
            break;
    }
    if (log_flag) {
        fprintf(dbptr,"finished with info file\n");
        fflush(dbptr);
    }
    gethostname(buf1,MAX_BUF);
    sprintf(buffer,
        "\nTo modify this information, edit %s\nat node %s\n\n\0",
        ancillary_file_name, buf1);
    send(socket, buffer, strlen(buffer), 0);
    close(fd);
}
```

8.4.8 Some Auxiliary Routines

```
** Get my host name (gethostname called, if that doesn't
** get an answer, try uname).
** Return char pointer to name.
static char my_host_name[MAXHOSTNAMELEN] = "";
char *get_my_host_name()
{
    gethostname(my_host_name, MAXHOSTNAMELEN);

    if (strlen(my_host_name) == 0) {
        struct utsname name;
        /*
        ** This system isn't reporting its node name to
        ** gethostname(2).  Try to get the name from uname(2).
        */
        uname(&name);
        strncpy(my_host_name, name.nodename,
            (MAXHOSTNAMELEN < UTSLEN ? MAXHOSTNAMELEN:UTSLEN));
        if (strcmp(my_host_name, "unknown") == 0)
            strncat(my_host_name," node name", MAXHOSTNAMELEN);
    }
    return(my_host_name);
}
/*
** Attempt to lock the file.  Retry certain retry-able errors,
** but fail (with diagnostic message in the log file, when logging
** is enabled) for the others.
*/
lock_it(fd)
int fd;
{
    int sleepy_time;
    sleepy_time = 1;
    while (lockf(fd, F_LOCK, 1L) <0) {
        switch (errno ) {
            case EINTR:
            case EDEADLK:
            case ENOLCK:
                sleep(sleepy_time);
                if ((sleepy_time += 2) > 30) sleepy_time=30;
                break;
            default:
                if (log_flag) {
                    fprintf(dbptr, "lockf error %s (%d)\n",(errno
```

```
                         <= sys_nerr ? sys_errlist[errno]: ""), errno);
                    fflush(dbptr);
                }
                exit(1);
            }
        }
    }
}
getserv(service, protocol)
char *service, *protocol;
{
    struct servent *getservbyname(), *serv_p;
    char *portname;
    if (port <= 0 ) {
        if (port < 0 && (portname = getenv(RLOCK_DEFAULT_PORT_NAME))
                        != NULL)
            port = atoi(portname);
        else {
            /*
            ** No -p parameter, no environment variable set.
            ** Try to look up the service in /etc/services.
            */
            serv_p = getservbyname(service, protocol);
            if (serv_p == NULL) {
                /*
                ** We can't find any override anywhere for the
                ** default port.  Just use the one in rlock.h.
                */
                port = RLOCK_DEFAULT_PORT;
                if (log_flag) {
                    fprintf(dbptr,"Could not find %s/%s in
                        /etc/services file.  Defaulting to %d.\n",
                        service, protocol, port);
                    fflush(dbptr);
                }
            } else port = serv_p->s_port;
        }
    }
    if (log_flag) {
        fprintf(dbptr, "Using port number %d.\n", port);
        fflush(dbptr);
    }
    return (port);
}
```

The `lock_4_next_in_queue()` procedure locks the resource for the next person in the waiting queue, if any. This person will be removed from the queue. In this implementation, we copy the queue (after the first person) to a temporary file, deleting the original, linking the temp file to the original name, and deleting the temp file name. A more efficient but more complex approach might be to mark the queue entry, making sure to skip entries that are so marked in the scan, and, if the EOF is reached during the scan, delete the file.

Since we allow queueing for the resource, we want to allow users to take themselves out of the queue if they wish. We'll adopt the convention that any entry beginning with a single blank character means a user who has taken herself or himself out of the queue and skip those in our scan. We could change the whole entry to blanks, but one is enough, and we may someday want to see (perhaps for debugging purposes) which users have put themselves in but changed their minds.

If we find someone's name in the queue, we'll lock the resource to that user and send him or her a message to that effect by electronic mail.

```
/*
** If there is a queue for this resource, then lock it to the
** next person in the queue.
*/
lock_4_next_in_queue(fd, rqst)
int fd;
struct rqst_msg *rqst;
{
    char dbase[MAX_BUF], buffer[MAX_BUF], buffer2[MAX_BUF],
         buffer3[MAX_BUF], *cptr, *qbptr;
    int tfd, qfd, len, k, nchars;
    unsigned long last_position;
    unsigned long locked_timestamp;
    char resource_2_lock[100];
    char locker_name[100];
    char locker_mailname[100];
    char locker_gecos[100];
    char locker_locn[100];
    FILE *popen(), *pfp;
    /*
    ** Build the pathname for the locker queue file.
    */
    strncpy(dbase, dbase_path, MAX_BUF);
    strncat(dbase,"/rlock_queue/", MAX_BUF);
    strncat(dbase, rqst->resource_2_lock, MAX_BUF);
    if ((qfd = open(dbase, O_RDONLY, 0666)) <0){
        if (log_flag) {
```

```
            fprintf(dbptr,"No such resource queue: %s\n", dbase);
            fflush(dbptr);
        }
        return(0);              /* Return "No Queue" status to caller */
    }
tryagain:
    /* Read who's next in the queue                         */
    nchars = getlin(qfd, buffer, MAX_BUF);
    if (nchars == 0)        /* Anything read?                */
        return(0);              /* No.  return to caller.      */

    /* Did the user dequeue himself or herself before we got to them? */

    if (buffer[0] == ' ')
        /* Yes.*/
        goto tryagain;

    /* We have a winner.                                     */
    sscanf(buffer,"%s %s %s %s %s\n", resource_2_lock, locker_name,
            locker_mailname, locker_gecos, locker_locn);
    time(&locked_timestamp);
    /* Convert all this info to what we need to write a locker record */
    sprintf(buffer, RESOURCE_FORMAT, 1, locker_name, locker_locn,
                locked_timestamp, 0.0);
    lseek(fd, 0L, 0);/*Rewind the file */
    write(fd, buffer, strlen(buffer));/*Now lock it for next user
*/

    /* Now send the user mail to the effect that he or she has the
    ** resource locked now.
    */
    signal(SIGCHLD, SIG_IGN);
    sprintf(buffer,"/usr/bin/mailx -s 'Resource %s is ready' %s ",
            resource_2_lock, locker_mailname);
    if ((pfp = popen(buffer,"w")) != NULL) {
        fprintf(pfp, "Resource '%s' is ready for you to use, and
                locked to you.\n", resource_2_lock);
        fprintf(pfp, "\n\nPlease unlock it when you are finished
                with it.\n\n\--The Resource Lock Manager Daemon\n");
        if (pclose(pfp) < 0) {
            if (log_flag) {
                fprintf(dbptr, "pclose error %s (%d)\n", ((errno <=
                        sys_nerr) ? sys_errlist[errno]: ""), errno);
            }
        }
    }
    /*
```

```
**  Now we want to put everything else in the queue into a
**  temporary file, remove the first one, and rename the temp
**  file to the queue file.
*/
strcpy(buffer3, dbase);
strncat(buffer3,"XXXXXXX", MAX_BUF);
cptr = mktemp(buffer3);
if ((tfd = open(cptr, O_RDWR|O_CREAT,0666)) <0){
    if (log_flag) {
        fprintf(dbptr,"No such resource %s\n",
                rqst->resource_2_lock);
        fflush(dbptr);
    }
    return(0);
}
while ((k = getlin(qfd,  buffer2, MAX_BUF)) >0) {
    if(buffer2[0] == ' ')
        continue;        /* This entry dequeued himself        */
    write(tfd, buffer2, k);
}
close(tfd);
unlink(dbase);
if (link(buffer3,dbase) < 0) {
    if (log_flag) {
        fprintf(dbptr,"Cannot rename %s\n", dbase);
        fflush(dbptr);
    }
    return(0);
}
unlink(buffer3);
return(1);
}
```

The `queue_lock()` procedure queues the user; we'll use FIFO queueing, no priorities, for simplicity. During the scan, this procedure will also add the names and other information of the users in the queue into `qbuffer[]`, which will be sent back to show the user his or her place in line.

```
/*
**  Attempt to queue this locker.
*/
queue_lock(rqst)
struct rqst_msg *rqst;
{
    int fd, maxlen, k, i;
```

```
char   buffer[MAX_BUF], buffer3[MAX_BUF], dbase[MAX_BUF];
char   *qbptr, *cptr, resource_2_lock[80], locker_name[80],
       locker_mailname[80], locker_gecos[80], locker_locn[80];
if (rqst->locker_mailname[0] == '\0')
    return(0);            /* Can't queue -- no mail name.        */
/*
** Build the pathname for the locker queue file.
*/
strncpy(dbase, dbase_path, MAX_BUF);
strncat(dbase,"/rlock_queue/", MAX_BUF);
mkdir(dbase, 0755);
strncat(dbase, rqst->resource_2_lock, MAX_BUF);
if ((fd = open(dbase,O_RDWR|O_CREAT, 0666)) <0){
    if (log_flag) {
        fprintf(dbptr,"No such resource queue: %s\n", dbase);
        fflush(dbptr);
    }
    return(0);      /* Return "Cannot Queue" status to caller */
}
*qbuffer = '\0';
i = 0;
while ((k = getlin(fd,  buffer, sizeof(buffer))) >0) {
    if (buffer[0] == ' ')
        continue;        /* This entry dequeued himself         */
    sscanf(buffer,"%s %s %s %s %s\n", resource_2_lock,
        locker_name, locker_mailname, locker_gecos, locker_locn);
    sprintf(buffer3, "%d) ",++i);
    strncat(qbuffer, buffer3, sizeof(qbuffer));
    strncat(qbuffer, locker_name, sizeof(qbuffer));
    strncat(qbuffer, " ", sizeof(qbuffer));
    strncat(qbuffer, locker_gecos, sizeof(qbuffer));
    strncat(qbuffer, "\n", sizeof(qbuffer));
}
fill_with_underscores(rqst->locker_gecos, MAX_GECOS);
sprintf(buffer,"%s %s %s %s %s\n", rqst->resource_2_lock,
    rqst->locker_name, rqst->locker_mailname,
    rqst->locker_gecos, rqst->locker_locn);
write(fd, buffer, strlen(buffer));
close(fd);
return(1); /* Return "lock is now queued" status to caller */
}
```

The unqueue_locker() procedure removes a user from the queue for a resource. It's used, for example, when the user changes his or her mind after having been queued. All we need to do is scan the file; if we find this user, then just write a single blank over the first position of the record (having saved the position of the first byte of each record). A more efficient algorithm would compact the file.

```
/*
** Remove this person from the queue of lockers awaiting
** this resource.
*/
unqueue_locker(rqst, reply)
struct rqst_msg *rqst;
struct reply_msg *reply;
{
    int fd, nchars, k;
    long posn;
    char *cptr, buffer[MAX_BUF], dbase[MAX_BUF];
    char resource_2_lock[80], locker_name[80], locker_mailname[80],
                locker_gecos[80], locker_locn[80];
    /*
    ** Build the pathname for the locker queue file.
    */
    strncpy(dbase, dbase_path, MAX_BUF);
    strncat(dbase,"/rlock_queue/");
    mkdir(dbase, 0755);
    strncat(dbase,rqst->resource_2_lock, MAX_BUF);
    if ((fd = open(dbase,O_RDWR, 0666)) <0){
        if (log_flag) {
            fprintf(dbptr,"No such resource queue: %s\n", dbase);
            fflush(dbptr);
        }
        return(0); /* Return "Cannot Queue" status to caller    */
    }
    while(1) {
        /* Read who's next in the queue                         */
        posn = lseek(fd, 0L, SEEK_CUR);      /* current position */
        nchars = getlin(fd, buffer, MAX_BUF);
        if (nchars == 0) {                        /* Anything read?    */
            reply->result = RESOURCE_IS_ALREADY_LOCKED;
            return(0);/* No.  return to caller. */
        }
        sscanf(buffer,"%s %s %s %s %s\n", resource_2_lock,
            locker_name, locker_mailname, locker_gecos, locker_locn);
        /* Found requestor ?                                    */
        if (strcmp(locker_name, rqst->locker_name) == 0) {
            /* Yes.                                             */
```

```
                lseek(fd, posn, SEEK_SET);
                buffer[0] = ' ';
                write(fd, buffer, 1);
                reply->result = RESOURCE_IS_ALREADY_LOCKED;
                close(fd);
                return;
        }
    }
}
fill_with_underscores(ccptr, len)
char *ccptr;
int len;
{
    while (*ccptr != '\0' && --len >= 0){
        if ((*ccptr == ' ') || (*ccptr == '\t'))
            *ccptr = '_';
        ++ccptr;
    }
}
getlin(qfd, buffer, len)
int qfd, len;
char *buffer;
{
    int nchars = 0, k;
    while(nchars <= len){
        if (( k = read(qfd, buffer,1)) == 0) break;
        ++nchars;
        if (*buffer == '\n') break;
        ++buffer;
        *buffer = '\0';
    }
    return(nchars);
}
```

8.5   inetd Version of a TCP Server Client (rlock.c)

The client functions of locking, unlocking, checking the lock, reporting the usage log, and so on, are all very similar in structure. We could use flag options (such as −l or −u), but remembering them all can be rather tiresome, so instead we will use the familiar trick of linking multiple names to the same inode. In the client, we will check which name was used, in those places where operation is different depending upon the command name.

The client, rlock.c, is shown in this section. The main() code begins with the familiar checking of arguments. We need the following options:

  • An option to specify the remote host name where the database (and associated daemon) resides: -h, as in many other commands

  • An option to clear the utilization timers for the resources (this is only used for the rlockadm command): -c

  • An option to specify what "mail name" to use (in case the environment variable $LOGNAME either isn't set or isn't what should be used): -m

  • A port number override: -p

  • A verbose option for debugging: -v

  • A "be silent" option (used in shell scripts that can scan through all the resources, looking for one that's available)[9]: -s

```
/*
 * Resource account/locker program
 */
#include <stdio.h>
#include <sys/types.h>
#include <values.h>
#include <time.h>
#include <sys/socket.h>
#include <netinet/in.h> /* sockaddr_in internet socket address */
#include <netdb.h>       /* /etc/hosts entry (hostent)          */
#include <errno.h>
#include <fcntl.h>
#include <pwd.h>
#include <sys/utsname.h>
#include <sys/param.h>
#include "rlock.h"
#define MAX_NAME 32
char where_I_got_host_from[80] = "default, from rlock.h file";
char user_mail_name[MAXHOSTNAMELEN+L_CUSERID] = "";
int silent_mode = 0;
int verbose = 0;
```

---

9. By placing rlock in a for loop script, whose list elements come from `cat <file>`, it is possible to build up a script that will sequentially scan all the resources of a particular kind, locking the first available one. For example, if you had a file that listed the names of all the machines having, say, a laser printer attached, you could make a script that would lock the first of these that became available. For use in scripts, it's inconvenient to have messages printed.

```
int port_number = -1;
struct rqst_msg rqst;
struct reply_msg reply;
extern char *strrchr(), *getenv();
/*
** Forward declarations.
*/
char *get_my_host_name();
char *read_ancillary_info();
main(argc, argv)
int argc;
char **argv;
{
    struct passwd *pwd;
    struct sockaddr_in name;   /* internet socket name (addr)   */
    int my_uid = getuid();
    int total_read, nbytes, sd, i;
    int clear_flag = 0;
    char *dbhome, *ptr, *cptr;
    unsigned char *uptr;
    char dbase_home[MAXHOSTNAMELEN+1];
    char my_name[MAX_NAME];
    char resource[MAX_RESOURCE_NAME+1];
    dbase_home[0] = '\0';
    resource[0] = '\0';
    if ((cptr = getenv("LOGNAME")) != NULL)
        strncpy(user_mail_name,cptr, MAXHOSTNAMELEN+L_CUSERID);
    /* Process options.                                          */
    for( i = 1; i < argc; i++ ){
        if( argv[i][0] == '-' ){
            switch( argv[i][1] ){
                case 'c': /* -c option:clear database at remote   */
                    ++clear_flag;
                    break;
                case 'h': /* -h host : specify name remote host    */
                    if (++i >= argc) {
                        fprintf(stderr, "-h parameter requires an
                                argument\n");
                        exit(14);/* 14 == user parameter error       */
                    }
                    strncpy(dbase_home, argv[i], MAXHOSTNAMELEN);
                    strcpy(where_I_got_host_from,"from -h parameter");
                    break;
                case 'm': /* -m mail_name: specify where to mail to user*/
```

```
                if (++i >= argc) {
                    fprintf(stderr, "-m parameter requires an
                            argument\n");
                    exit(14);    /* 14 == user parameter error    */
                }
                strncpy(user_mail_name, argv[i],
                        MAXHOSTNAMELEN+L_CUSERID);
                break;
            case 's':            /* -s option: set silent mode    */
                silent_mode = 1;
                if (verbose) {
                    usage(argv[0]);
                }
                break;
            case 'p':            /* -p port : specify port number */
                if (++i >= argc) {
                    fprintf(stderr, "-p parameter requires an
                            argument\n");
                    exit(14);    /* 14 == user parameter error    */
                }
                port_number = atoi(argv[i]);
                if (!silent_mode)
                    printf("Using port # %d\n",port_number);
                break;
            case 'v':            /* -v option: set verbose option */
                ++verbose;
                if (silent_mode == 1) {
                    usage(argv[0]);
                }
                break;
            default:
                usage(argv[0]);
        }
    }
    else {
        strncpy(resource, argv[i],MAX_RESOURCE_NAME);
        if (argc != i+1){
            fprintf(stderr,"Only one resource name at a time,
                        please!\n");
            usage(argv[0]);
        }
        break;
    }
}
```

Now we'll see which command name was invoked. `rlock`, `rlockq`, `rislock`, and `runlock` are all self-explanatory; `rlockadm` is used for administration functions (all that's implemented is the printout of the usage logs, with optional clearing of the usage).

```
/* How were we invoked?  As ""rlock", "runlock", or "rislock" or
** "rlockadm" or ... ?
** Make sure to strip out any leading pathname components.
** We only want to compare the last part for "runlock".
*/
ptr = strrchr(argv[0],'/');
if (ptr == NULL)
   ptr = argv[0];
else ++ptr;      /* Move pointer past the "/" character       */
strncpy(my_name, ptr, MAX_NAME);
if ((strcmp(my_name, "rlock") != 0) && (strcmp(my_name,
   "runlock") != 0) && (strcmp(my_name, "rlockq") != 0) &&
   (strcmp(my_name, "rislock") != 0) && (strcmp(my_name,
   "rlockadm") != 0)) {
   fprintf(stderr, "Can't operate under the name of
                \'%s\'\n",my_name);
   exit(11);
}
```

For all the commands except `rlockadm` we need a resource parameter. Make sure it was specified:

```
if ((resource[0] == '\0') && (strcmp(my_name, "rlockadm") != 0)) {
   fprintf(stderr,"Please specify a resource name!\n");
   usage(argv[0]);
}
```

Enforce a "no use as root" policy:

```
if ((my_uid == 0) && strcmp(my_name, "rislock")   != 0) &&
   (strcmp(my_name, "rlockadm") != 0)) {
   if (!silent_mode) {
      printf("Sorry, can't allow resources to be locked to
             super-user.\n");
      printf( "If I did, then anybody logged in as root could
             release it.\n");
   }
   exit(9);
}
/*
** Find the "home" node where the database resides.
** If we got a -h parameter, then we already have it in
```

```
** dbase_home.  Otherwise, if the environment variable
** "DBASE_HOME" is defined, then use that.  If none of the
** above, then use the default, which is set in "rlock.h."
** Save where we got the "home," so that we can tell the user,
** in case we can't contact the server.  This will help him or
** her troubleshoot.
*/
sd = -1;
if (dbase_home[0] == '\0') {
    if ((dbhome = getenv("DBASE_HOME")) == NULL)
        strncpy(dbase_home, DBASE_HOME, MAXHOSTNAMELEN);
    else  {
        strncpy(dbase_home, dbhome, MAXHOSTNAMELEN);
        strcpy(where_I_got_host_from,
               "from $DBASE_HOME environment variable");
    }
}
```

We need to give some more information on the user to the server, specifically the gecos field from the /etc/passwd entry. We look up this information using the library routine getpwuid(); if this returns an error, such as if the user-id has been deleted since the user logged on, we print an error message and quit.

```
if((pwd = getpwuid(my_uid)) == NULL) {
    if (!silent_mode) {
        fprintf(stderr, "cannot find entry in /etc/passwd for uid
                %d\n", my_uid);
    }
    exit(8);
}
sd = client_init(dbase_home,argv[0]);/* Initialize */
if (sd < 0) {
    char err_msg[256];

    sprintf(err_msg,"Could not contact database server at %s\n",
            dbase_home);
    perror(err_msg);
    exit(1);
}
/* We have our socket set up and the connection is
/* established with the server.
*/
/*
** Build request message.
*/
```

```
strncpy(rqst.locker_name, pwd->pw_name, L_CUSERID);
strncpy(rqst.locker_gecos, pwd->pw_gecos, MAX_GECOS);
strncpy(rqst.locker_locn, get_my_host_name(), MAXHOSTNAMELEN);
strncpy(rqst.resource_2_lock, resource, MAX_RESOURCE_NAME);
strncpy(rqst.locker_mailname, user_mail_name,
        MAXHOSTNAMELEN+L_CUSERID);
rqst.msg_len = htonl(sizeof(struct rqst_msg));
/*
** We must check for any structure misalignment problems when
** we send structs back and forth between systems.  The easiest
** way to do this is to store a copy of the version number near
** the beginning and near the end of the struct.  These should
** both be equal to the version number we expect to work with.
** If not, then the message we received is unintelligible, and
** so we can't proceed.
*/
rqst.version_num = rqst.version_num_check = htonl(VERSION);
if (strcmp(my_name, "runlock") == 0)
   rqst.request_type = htonl(UNLOCK_RESOURCE);
else if (strcmp(my_name, "rlockq") == 0)
   rqst.request_type = htonl(LOCK_RESOURCE_QUEUE);
else if (strcmp(my_name, "rislock") == 0)
   rqst.request_type = htonl(CHECK_LOCK_STATUS);
else if (strcmp(my_name, "rlockadm") == 0) {
   if (clear_flag && (my_uid == 0))
      rqst.request_type = htonl(LIST_LOCK_USAGE_AND_CLEAR);
   else {
      if (clear_flag) {
         printf( "You are not running as root. Clear flag will
                      be ignored\n");
      }
      rqst.request_type = htonl(LIST_LOCK_USAGE);
   }
}
else
   rqst.request_type = htonl(LOCK_RESOURCE);

/*
** Send the message.
*/
if (send(sd, &rqst, rqst.msg_len, 0) < 0){
   perror( "send failed.");
   exit(10);
}
```

```
/*
* We now read the reply.
*/

/*
** Stay in this loop until we've got a complete message.
*/
total_read = 0;
uptr = (unsigned char *) &reply;
while (1) {
   nbytes = recv( sd, uptr, sizeof (struct reply_msg) -
            total_read, 0);
   if (nbytes <= 0) {
      close(sd);
      perror( "INET Domain Read, connection with remote broken");
      exit(10);
   }
   total_read += nbytes;
   uptr+= nbytes;
   if (total_read < sizeof(int)) continue;
   if (total_read >= ntohl(reply.msg_len)) break;
}
```

Checking for a proper reply is the same for each command:

```
/* We got an answer.  What was it?                           */
if (nbytes > 0) {
   if (ntohl(reply.version_num) != VERSION) {
      if (!silent_mode)
         printf("Sorry, I am version %d but daemon is version
               %d\n", VERSION, ntohl(reply.version_num));
         exit(13);
   }
   if (ntohl(reply.version_num_check) != VERSION) {
      if (!silent_mode)
         printf( "Sorry, the version numbers check but the
               struct alignments are different.\n");
         exit(13);
   }
   if (ntohl(reply.result) == UNKNOWN_REQUEST_TYPE) {
      if (!silent_mode) {
         printf( "Sorry, remote didn't understand this
               request.\n");
         printf( "Perhaps the revisions of client and server
               are mismatched.\n");
```

```
      }
      exit(6);
   } else if (ntohl(reply.result) == NO_SUCH_RESOURCE) {
      if (!silent_mode) {
         printf( "Sorry, the remote has no such entry for %s in
                its resources database\n", resource);
      }
      exit(3);    /* Exit code 3 == no such resource in database  */
   }
```

The common reply error checking completed, we now branch off to process the different types of reply messages, based upon the original command:

```
   if (strcmp(my_name, "runlock") == 0)   {
      /* Process reply for "unlock" message                      */
      do_runlock_reply(ntohl(reply.result), resource);
   }
   else if ((strcmp(my_name, "rlock") == 0) ||
            (strcmp(my_name, "rlockq") == 0)) {
      /* Process reply for "lock" message */
      do_rlock_reply(sd, ntohl(reply.result), resource);
   } else if (strcmp(my_name, "rlockadm") == 0) { /* List usage*/
      do_rlockadm_reply(sd);
   } else {
      /* Check Lock Status */
      do_check_status_reply(sd, ntohl(reply.result), resource);
   }
   }
   if (!silent_mode)
      printf("Sorry, can't contact remote database server.\n");
   exit(5);
}
```

8.5.1 Processing the Reply

From here, the procedures for processing the reply are similar. Each one will print a message telling you if your request succeeded, or, if it failed, why it failed. In some of these, you're told the name of the person who has it locked ahead of you or the list of names in the queue ahead of you. In some, you're told the "ancillary information," if any, for the resource.

```
do_runlock_reply(result, resource)
int result;
char *resource;
{
   switch (reply.result) {
```

```
      case RESOURCE_NOT_LOCKED_TO_YOU: /* Means resource not yours*/
         if (!silent_mode) {
            printf("Sorry, resource %s is not locked to you.\n",
               resource);
            printf("It is locked to %s at %s, not you.\n",
               resource,reply.locker_name, reply.locker_locn);
         }
         exit(7);
      case RESOURCE_WAS_NOT_LOCKED:
         if (!silent_mode) {
            printf("Resource %s was already unlocked.\n", resource);
         }
         exit(0);
      case RESOURCE_IS_NOW_UNLOCKED:
         if (!silent_mode) {
            printf("Resource %s is now unlocked.\n", resource);
         }
         exit(0);
      default:
         if (!silent_mode) {
            printf("Sorry, the remote responded with code %d\n",
               ntohl(reply.result));
            printf("which I don't understand\n");
         }
         exit(4); /* Exit code 4 == weird response (not understood) */
   }
}

do_rlock_reply(socket, result, resource)
int socket, result;
char *resource;
{
   char *cptr;
   switch (result) {
      case RESOURCE_IS_ALREADY_LOCKED:
         /* Means somebody already has it */
         if (!silent_mode) {
            printf("Sorry, %s is already locked to %s at %s\n",
               resource, reply.locker_name, reply.locker_locn);
            printf("It was locked at %s",
                  ctime(&reply.locked_timestamp));
            printf( "Try finger %s from node '%s' to find where
               and how to contact.\n", reply.locker_name,
               reply.locker_locn);
         }
```

```
      cptr = read_ancillary_info(socket);
      if (strlen(cptr) > 0) {
         printf("Info about %s\n%s\n", resource, cptr);
      } else {
         printf("No ancillary info on %s provided by
            server.\n", resource);
      }
      exit(2);/* Exit code 2 == already locked */
   case RESOURCE_LOCK_QUEUED:
      if (!silent_mode) {
         printf( "Sorry, '%s' has been locked to '%s' at '%s'
            since\n\t%s\n", resource, reply.locker_name,
            reply.locker_locn,
            ctime(&reply.locked_timestamp));
         printf( "Your request has been queued, in order, and
            you will be\n");
         printf( "notified by e-mail (by the mail name: %s)
            when you have it.\n\n", user_mail_name);
         printf( "If you cannot wait for the resource, then try
            to contact them.\n");

         printf("If you don't otherwise know how to reach them,
            try\n");
         printf( "'finger %s' at '%s' to find where and how to
            contact that person,\n", reply.locker_name,
            reply.locker_locn);
         printf( "and you can argue with them over who should
            have priority.\n");
         printf( "I am just the lock manager daemon, not an
            arbitrator.\n\n");
         cptr = read_ancillary_info(socket);
         if (strlen(cptr) > 0) {
            printf( "\nThe following information will tell you
               where you are in the queue,\n");
            printf("and who is ahead of you:\n%s\n", cptr);
         } else
            printf("You appear to be first in the queue.\n");
      }
      exit(0);
   case RESOURCE_IS_NOW_LOCKED:   /* Means you have it now */
      if (!silent_mode) {
         printf("%s is now locked to you (%s at %s)\n",
            resource, reply.locker_name, reply.locker_locn);
      }
```

```
          cptr = read_ancillary_info(socket);
          if (strlen(cptr) > 0) {
             printf("Info about %s\n%s\n", resource, cptr);
          } else {
             printf("No ancillary info on %s provided by
                 server.\n", resource);
          }
          exit(0);/* Exit code 0 == now you have it */
          break;
       case NO_SUCH_RESOURCE: /* Means there is no database    */
          if (!silent_mode) {
             printf( "Sorry, the remote has no such entry for %s in
                 its database\n", resource);
          }
          exit(3);    /* Exit code 3 == no such resource in database   */
          break;
       default:
          if (!silent_mode) {
             printf("Sorry, the remote responded with code %d\n",
                 ntohl(reply.result));
             printf("which I don't understand\n");
          }
          exit(4); /* Exit code 4 == weird response (not understood) */
   }
}

do_rlockadm_reply(socket)
int socket;
{
   int nbytes;
   char buffer[4096];
   while ((nbytes = recv(socket, buffer, 4096, 0)) > 0) {
      write(1, buffer, nbytes);      /* Write on stdout        */
   }
   close(socket);
   close(1);                          /* Flush output           */
   exit(0);
}

do_check_status_reply(socket, result, resource)
int socket, result;
char *resource;
{
   char *cptr;
   switch (result) {
```

```
      case UNKNOWN_REQUEST_TYPE:
         if (!silent_mode) {
            printf( "Sorry, the remote did not understand this
               request\n");
         }
         exit(4); /* Exit code 4 == weird response (not understood) */
      case NO_SUCH_RESOURCE:
         if (!silent_mode) {
            printf( "Sorry, the remote has no such resource as
               %s", resource);
         }
         exit(2);                       /* Exit code 2            */
      case RESOURCE_IS_NOW_LOCKED:  /* Means you have it now   */
         if (!silent_mode)
            printf("resource '%s' is currently locked to you.\n",
               resource);
         cptr = read_ancillary_info(socket);
         if (strlen(cptr) > 0) {
            printf("Info about '%s'\n%s\n", resource, cptr);
         } else {
            printf("No ancillary info on %s provided by
               server.\n", resource);
         }
         exit(0);
      case RESOURCE_IS_NOW_UNLOCKED:
         if (!silent_mode)
            printf("resource %s is not currently locked.\n",
               resource);
         cptr = read_ancillary_info(socket);
         if (strlen(cptr) > 0) {
            printf("Info about %s\n%s\n", resource, cptr);
         } else {
            printf("No ancillary info on %s provided by
               server.\n", resource);
         }
         exit(0);
      case RESOURCE_IS_ALREADY_LOCKED:
         if (!silent_mode) {
            printf("%s is locked to %s at %s\n",
               resource, reply.locker_name, reply.locker_locn);
         }
         cptr = read_ancillary_info(socket);
         if (strlen(cptr) > 0) {
            printf("Info about %s\n%s\n", resource, cptr);
```

```
      } else {
        printf("No ancillary info on %s provided by
        server.\n", resource);
      }
      exit(2);            /* Exit code 2 == already locked    */
      break;
   default:
      if (!silent_mode) {
        printf("Sorry, the remote responded with code %d\n",
           ntohl(reply.result));
         printf("which I don't understand\n");
      }
      exit(4);  /* Exit code 4 == weird response (not understood) */
   }
}
```

8.5.2 Other Client Routines

```
/*
 * Initialize the client side.
 * Returns socket descriptor.
 */
client_init(host, mycmndname)
char *host, *mycmndname;
{
   int    sd;      /* socket descriptor                         */
   struct hostent *hptr;
   struct sockaddr_in addr;
   struct sockaddr_in *ptr;/* pointer to get port number*/
   struct sockaddr_in name;/* internet socket name (addr)*/
   if ( (sd = socket( AF_INET, SOCK_STREAM, IPPROTO_TCP )) < 0 ) {
      perror("could not create socket");
      exit(11);
      }
   name.sin_family = AF_INET;        /* internet domain       */
   if ((name.sin_addr.s_addr = (unsigned long) inet_addr(host)) == -1)
   {
      hptr = gethostbyname( host ); /* host                  */
      if (hptr == NULL) {
         if (!silent_mode) {
            fprintf(stderr,"Cannot find %s in /etc/hosts\n",
               host);
            fprintf(stderr, "%s is the node name I am using for
               the server daemon.\n", host);
```

```
                    fprintf(stderr, "You told me to use this via %s, but
                        that node name doesn't\n",  where_I_got_host_from);
                    fprintf(stderr, "exist in the /etc/hosts database\n");
                }
            exit(77);
        } else {
            /* Use this when available                               */
            memmove(&name.sin_addr.s_addr, hptr->h_addr,
                hptr->h_length);
            /* Else use this one                                     */
            /*bcopy( hptr->h_addr, &name.sin_addr.s_addr,
                hptr->h_length);                                     */
        }
    }
    if (port_number < 0) {
        /*
        * Look up the service port number.
        */
        name.sin_port   = getserv(RLOCK_SERVICE_NAME,
            RLOCK_SERVICE_PROTO);
    } else
        name.sin_port   = port_number;
    /*
    ** Attempt to connect with the remote server.
    ** When we return from this call, the TCP
    ** connection will either have been established,
    ** or it was never established.
    */
    if ( connect( sd, &name, sizeof name ) < 0 ) {
        close(sd);
        return(-1);
        }
    return(sd); /* Return socket descriptor, connection is made.*/
}

getserv(service, protocol)
char *service, *protocol;
{
    struct servent *getservbyname(), *serv_p;
    int port;
    char *portname;
    if ((portname = getenv(RLOCK_DEFAULT_PORT_NAME)) != NULL)
        port = atoi(portname);
    else {
```

```
        /*
        ** No -p parameter, no environment variable set.
        ** Try to look up the service in /etc/services.
        */
        serv_p = getservbyname(service, protocol);
        if (serv_p == NULL) {
            /*
            ** We can't find any override anywhere for the default
            ** port. Just use the one in rlock.h.
            */
            port = RLOCK_DEFAULT_PORT;
            if (verbose)
                printf( "Could not find %s/%s in /etc/services file.
                    Defaulting to %d.\n", service, protocol, port);
        } else
            port = serv_p->s_port;
    }
    if (verbose)
        printf("Using port number %d.\n", service,protocol,
            serv_p->s_port);
    return (port);
}

usage(cmd)
char *cmd;
{
    if (!silent_mode) {
        printf("Usage:\n");
        printf("%s <resource>\n", cmd);
        printf("or\n");
.0      printf("%s <flags> <resource>\n", cmd);
        printf("or\n");
        printf("%s -h <remote_host> <resource>\n", cmd);
        printf("or\n");
        printf("%s -p <port_number> <resource>\n", cmd);
        printf("or\n");
        printf("%s <flags> -h <remote_host> <resource>\n", cmd);
        printf("or\n");
        printf("%s <flags> -p <port_number> -h <remote_host>
            <resource>\n", cmd);
        printf("<flags> : -v or -s (mutually exclusive)\n");
    }
    exit(12);                 /* 12 == user parameter error        */
}
```

```
bcopy(fromptr, toptr, length)
unsigned char *fromptr, *toptr;
int length;
{
    while (length-- > 0)
        *toptr++ = *fromptr++;
}
/*
** Get my host name (gethostname called, if that doesn't
** get an answer, try uname).
** Return char pointer to name.
*/
static char my_host_name[MAXHOSTNAMELEN] = "";
char *
get_my_host_name()
{
    gethostname(my_host_name, MAXHOSTNAMELEN);
    if (strlen(my_host_name) == 0) {
        struct utsname name;
        /*
        ** This system isn't reporting its node name to
        ** gethostname(2). Try to get the name from uname(2).
        */
        uname(&name);
        strncpy(my_host_name, name.nodename,
            (MAXHOSTNAMELEN < UTSLEN ? MAXHOSTNAMELEN:UTSLEN));
        if (strcmp(my_host_name, "unknown") == 0)
            strncat(my_host_name," node name", MAXHOSTNAMELEN);
    }
    return(my_host_name);
}
/*
** Read any ancillary information the server may want to send us.
** The server puts this info onto the socket after it sends the
** reply to the request.  There may be nothing to read, however,
** and the old-format server sent nothing (before we added this
** great feature!), so be prepared for this.  We read this into a
** moderately large static buffer and return a pointer to it.  This
** allows our caller to printf() it or create a pop-up window for
** it.  When the circuit dies, we're done reading (may have nothing
** in this buffer, in which case buffer[0] == '\0').
*/
```

```
#define BIG_BUFFER 4096
static char big_buffer[BIG_BUFFER];
char *
read_ancillary_info(socket)
int socket;
{
    int nbytes, total_read;
    char *ptr;
    total_read = 0;
    ptr = big_buffer;
    *ptr = '\0';
    while ((socket >= 0) && (total_read < BIG_BUFFER)) {
        if ((nbytes = recv(socket, ptr, (BIG_BUFFER - total_read),
            0)) > 0) {
            ptr += nbytes;
            total_read += nbytes;
            if (big_buffer[total_read-1] == '\0') break;
        } else break;
    }
    close(socket);
    return(big_buffer);
}
```

8.5.3 Sample Client Output

Before leaving this chapter, here's a sample of the rlockadm program's output in
Figure 8.1. This program could be run from a cron script, for example, mailing the
result to whoever keeps track of the resources.

Resource name: asteroid

User Name	Name	Date locked	Date unlocked	Time Used(h)	Total Used(h)
lyle	Lyle_Weiman,43L_R10/P10,2319,	Fri Dec 21 13:56	Fri Dec 21 13:58	0.02	0.14
lyle	Lyle_Weiman,43L_R10/P10,2319,	Fri Dec 21 14:00	Fri Dec 21 14:01	0.01	0.15
lyle	Lyle_Weiman,43L_R10/P10,2319,	Fri Dec 21 14:12	Fri Dec 21 14:17	0.09	0.24
lyle	Lyle_Weiman,43L_R10/P10,2319,	Fri Dec 21 14:18	Fri Dec 21 14:19	0.01	0.25
lyle	Lyle_Weiman,43L_R10/P10,2319,	Fri Dec 21 14:28	Fri Dec 21 14:28	0.00	0.25
lyle	Lyle_Weiman,43L_R10/P10,2319,	Fri Dec 21 14:30	Fri Dec 21 14:30	0.00	0.25

Resource name: birch

User Name	Name	Date locked	Date unlocked	Time Used(h)	Total Used(h)
lyle	Lyle_Weiman,43L_R10/P10,2319,	Fri Dec 21 13:56	Fri Dec 21 13:58	0.02	0.09
lyle	Lyle_Weiman,43L_R10/P10,2319,	Fri Dec 21 14:00	Fri Dec 21 14:01	0.01	0.10
lyle	Lyle_Weiman,43L_R10/P10,2319,	Fri Dec 21 14:12	Fri Dec 21 14:17	0.08	0.19
lyle	Lyle_Weiman,43L_R10/P10,2319,	Fri Dec 21 14:18	Fri Dec 21 14:19	0.01	0.20
lyle	Lyle_Weiman,43L_R10/P10,2319,	Fri Dec 21 14:28	Fri Dec 21 14:28	0.00	0.20

Figure 8.1 Sample rlockadm Output

9

Advanced Socket Programming

by Lyle Weiman

9.1 Introduction

In this chapter, we will explore more advanced uses of sockets: how to broadcast, how to set Internet Protocol options for a socket, how to send and receive out-of-band data, and how to survive TCP disconnects.

9.2 How to Broadcast

Broadcasting means sending out a message whose destination address is the code for "all nodes." In the Internet protocol suite, if you issue a `sendto()` system call, specifying the IP address of any one of the locally attached networks capable of broadcasting (LANs are, most WAN networks are not), then the message transmitted on the network will have that network's broadcast address in its Level-2 header. This means the packet is addressed to all the computers on that network. For example, if you're using an Ethernet, and you `sendto()` using the IP address of the broadcast for that network (the command `/etc/ifconfig lan0` will tell you what the broadcast address is for `lan0`, and similarly for other attached network interfaces[1]), then the message will be sent using all ones in the destination address of the Ethernet header.[2]

There are some sorts of tasks which are best implemented using broadcast protocols. While they can be quite useful, there is the potential for overuse, with consequent effect on every node on the LAN. Broadcasts should be used with caution and very careful

---

1. If `/etc/ifconfig` doesn't tell you the broadcast address, or you need to compute the address, here is how to do it. Take the network number field (the eight most significant bits of the IP address if the address is a Class A address, 16 if it's a Class B address, 24 if it is a Class C address), plus the bits in the subnet address field, if your network is using subnet addressing; otherwise, just use the network number field. Take these bits just as as they are. The remaining bits in the IP address are the "host part" bits. The broadcast address is formed by taking the network number and the subnet number, just as they are, and using 1 for each remaining bit position. For example, suppose your network address was `192.20.15.20`. `192` is a Class C address, so the most significant 24 bits are `0xC0140f`. If we had a two-bit subnet address, starting in the next available bit position, then this leaves only six of the remaining eight bits (32 to 24 bits for Class C address, leaving eight available for "host part," two of which—in this example—are subnet address). Inclusive-ORing these six ones (`0x3F`) to the aforementioned `0xc0140f00` (notice that now the 24-bit number has been shifted to properly fit into its place in the 32-bit IP address) yields `0xc0140f3f` as a broadcast address.

planning, or not at all. Broadcasts are sent out over "the ether" without specific destination addresses (the packets contain the "addressed to all nodes" value of all 1s, rather than any one station's address), and therefore they are received by every node on that same network. Bridges cannot filter out broadcasts, so they can go out over all the attached LAN segments as well, potentially affecting hundreds of nodes. Every node on the LAN must expend CPU and memory resources to receive a broadcast packet, even if the end result will be to discard the packet. More importantly, perhaps, broadcasts used in a careless manner, combined with certain TCP/IP/LAN implementations, can result in what's sometimes called "Ethernet meltdown" or "broadcast storms." This is partially the result of a change of opinion as to whether to use zeros or ones to represent broadcasts. Between the release of Berkeley's 4.2 and 4.3 versions, the decision of whether to use zeros or ones to represent the broadcast address (at the IP level) changed, and this has led to broadcast storm problems (rwhod is one culprit). If there happens to be a mixture of 4.2-derived and 4.3-derived UNIX systems on the same LAN, and the implementations fail to recognize the two different broadcast types in use, the one kind may attempt to "forward" a packet using the other type of broadcast, which the other kinds of nodes may attempt to "forward," and so on. The end result is a flurry of packet activity on the LAN, consequent slowdowns of the computers while they process these messages, and a great deal of dissatisfaction all around.

If possible, try to avoid use of broadcast protocols at all. If you can't do that, then try to arrange your protocol so that you move to specific addresses just as soon as they are known. For example, supposing you wanted to implement some sort of "LAN Conversationalist" program (like the Berkeley talk or ntalk programs, but for group conversations), you might need to broadcast a request for others to join into the conversation. You may need to do so occasionally, since people might not be interested when you start the conversation on a topic, but become interested later. As soon as your application program receives responses to these broadcasts, it "knows" the respondent's address, and can thereafter send messages to the specific addresses. Assuming the LAN you're using is not dedicated to the purpose of holding broadcast conversations, it is probably not justifiable to maintain the whole conversation on a broadcast basis. Switching to specific addressing has one other benefit: The retransmissions don't need to be broadcast (assuming your application needs this level of reliability), and don't interrupt every host on the LAN.

---

2. There is also the concept of "directed broadcast," which means specifying the IP broadcast address of some distant LAN (that is, one which is not directly connected to the sending node). Such packets are carried through to the last gateway and broadcasted from there. Finally, there is multicasting, which is a subset of broadcasting, in which addresses are used to which only certain nodes will respond.

Having (we hope) cautioned you against carelessness, now we tell you how to use broadcasts. All you really need to do is use the `sendto()` system call, specifying the IP-level broadcast address for the LAN network to which your computer is connected. In the kernel, when the destination address is recognized as a broadcast address, the kernel will use the Ethernet broadcast address for the destination address in the LAN packet header, instead of a specific station address. How do you find out what the IP broadcast address is? You use `ioctl(skt, SIOCGIFBRDADDR, <ifreq struct ptr>)`, after having set up the `ifreq struct`.

For example:

```
struct    ifreq ifr;
struct    sockaddr_in *sin;
int       s;

    s = socket(AF_INET, SOCK_DGRAM³, 0);
    strncpy(ifr.ifr_name, "lan0", sizeof (ifr.ifr_name));

    if (ioctl(s, SIOCGIFBRDADDR, (caddr_t)&ifr) < 0) {
        perror("ioctl (SIOCGIFADDR)");
        exit(1);
    }
    sin = (struct sockaddr_in *)&ifr.ifr_addr;
    if (sin->sin_addr.s_addr != 0)
        printf("lan0 broadcast %s\n", inet_ntoa(sin->sin_addr));
    strncpy(ifr.ifr_name, "lan1", sizeof (ifr.ifr_name));
    if (ioctl(s, SIOCGIFBRDADDR, (caddr_t)&ifr) < 0) {
        perror("ioctl (SIOCGIFADDR)");
        exit(1);
    }
    sin = (struct sockaddr_in *)&ifr.ifr_addr;
    if (sin->sin_addr.s_addr != 0)
        printf("lan1 broadcast %s\n", inet_ntoa(sin->sin_addr));
```

With this method, you have to know the "name" of the interface you want to use. This "name" is the name you'll see in `netstat  -i` printouts. It's not the `/dev` special device file name (at least, it doesn't have to be). If the node has more than one attached LAN, you'll need to use this `ioctl()` on all the ones you want to use.

---

3. You must use a datagram protocol if you're going to broadcast. You certainly cannot use TCP. "Broadcast" means "send the packet with the 'all addresses' address." This gives every station the **opportunity** to receive it, but does not guarantee that every station **will** receive it. In general, you should assume that broadcast messages will be received by some, perhaps most, of the stations, but not by all of them. TCP could be used in a broadcast environment, but the implementations won't let you because of the horrible implications of broadcasting retransmissions.

Fortunately, these names will follow the sequence "lan0", "lan1", and so forth. There are no "holes" in the sequence, so you can interpret an error returned on the ioctl() as meaning that you've reached the end in your search. Alternatively, you could use popen(), fork(), and exec() of "netstat -i" to obtain them all, but that is a rather heavy-handed approach to the problem.

Now you have the IP address to use. You store this in the sin_addr field of the in_addr structure that you pass in the sendto(). Before you send anything, however, you also need to enable broadcasting on the socket. Use of broadcasting is denied[4] unless your program is running as root (effective user ID = 0). Assuming you're running as root, [5] then you enable broadcasting on your socket as follows:

```
if(setsockopt(sd_bcast_snd,SOL_SOCKET,SO_BROADCAST,&optval,
        sizeof(int)) <0){
    perror("setsockopt(SO_BROADCAST)");
    exit(1);
}
```

The sd_bcast_snd is a socket that has been created as a UDP socket, such as by sd_bcast_snd = socket(AF_INET, SOCK_DGRAM, 0).

The relative order of obtaining the broadcast address and enabling the socket for broadcasting is immaterial. Once you know what the IP broadcast is, follow these steps to send a broadcast packet:

1. Store this address in a sockaddr's sin_addr.s_addr field.

2. In a sockaddr structure, set the sin_port field. This must be the port number that the potential receiver(s) will be using for their recvfrom()s.

3. Specify a pointer to that sockaddr in a sendto() system call. If you've forgotten to enable broadcasting on the socket, the sendto() will fail.

On the receiving end, you still need to create a datagram socket, bind() it to a port number (the same port number that the broadcasting senders will be using), set the sin_addr field to INADDR_ANY (just as you would with any other UDP-based recvfrom()), and bind() this address to the socket. The socket is now capable of receiving any UDP packet with this same port number, either directed to this node with a specific address or broadcast to it. You may use recv(), read(), or recvfrom() to read the data, and select() may be used to check if any packet has arrived first, just as was shown in Chapter 5. In many cases, recvfrom() will be your best choice for obtaining the packet, since this will provide you with the IP address of the sender

---

4. Another indication of how careful you need to be when broadcasting.
5. And assuming you've taken proper security precautions for any program running as root.

(this will be the source address, which cannot be a broadcast address). Why would you want to know this? Besides the possibilities for adding a level of security (that is, refusing to respond to packets from IP addresses emanating from other than certain trusted addresses of your choosing), knowing who sent the messages gives you the option of replying to it with a specific address and thus not burdening the other computers on the network. Once the respondents have been identified (you may still wish to broadcast at — hopefully infrequent — intervals), the dialogue among peers can proceed with specific addresses, and thus reduce somewhat the hazards about broadcasts already mentioned.

Note that "capable of receiving any UDP packet with this same port number" does not mean "**will** receive..." In a broadcast environment, it's possible that **some** nodes will receive the broadcast message, but others will not. This may be contrary to what you would expect, but it can happen because the packet may be dropped by the low-level receiving mechanism at some of the nodes. When the node and LAN are lightly loaded, of course, you would expect broadcast packets to be received universally, but heavier loading can alter this picture. Building reliability on top of UDP is a "simple matter of retransmissions,"[6] but the situation is more complicated in a broadcast environment (see "Exercises" at the end of this chapter). By the way, recall the drawbacks of sending UDP packets that are larger than the LAN MTU[7] which we mentioned in Chapter 4. Such messages require fragmentation. This is even more so if you are broadcasting, since retransmissions are more costly in that every node on the LAN is slowed down by each one of them. Some implementations do not permit messages requiring fragmentation to be broadcast.

9.3   How to Set Internet Protocol Options

The Internet Protocol is defined with some interesting options (see RFC 791; see the "Bibliography" for how to obtain RFCs, if you don't already know). One of these is the Record Route option. This can be specified in any packet, but if you combine it with the `ping` packet (otherwise known as the Internet Control Message Protocol (**ICMP**) "Echo" packets), you can see how packets are being routed through the network. The ICMP "Echo" packet is frequently used to test connectivity thru the network. Most UNIX-type implementations include `/etc/ping` program for this purpose. Since the replies to these Echo request messages are generated at a very low level (inside the IP/ICMP layer), they don't depend upon any particular server or port number. If you get an answer back, then the target IP address is responsive, and you can eliminate the

---

6. Said with tongue planted firmly in cheek.

7. MTU = Maximum Transmission Unit, that is, the maximum number of bytes which can be sent in any one packet.

network as the source of your problem (or, almost; at least, you have established that some packets get through the network, and that the remote node is not "dead"). The Record Route option specifies a fixed number of bytes in the IP header, into which the intervening gateways must store their IP addresses (if they follow the RFC's, that is). When the packet returns, you can see where it has been. This helps you determine what routes are in use throughout the network.

Another interesting option is Loose Source and Record Route (LSRR). This combines the Record Route option with the concept of source routing. Source routing means that the source of the packet places information in it to direct how the packet is routed through the network. For the most part, the gateways in the network "know best" which path to take, but not always. You may know of a faster route at the moment, or you may have decided that the gateways are wrong for some reason, and you know better. With LSRR, you can specify at least some of the gateways that are to be used to route the packet.

Another interesting option is Strict Source and Record Route, which is like LSRR except that every hop of the route is specified, and if the gateways can't route as directed, they will drop the packet. There are, of course, other options, and the interested reader is directed to RFC 791, which specifies the Internet Protocol, for more information.

The example below shows one way to set the Loose Source and Record Route IP option. This example shows just two IP addresses in the source route, which are assumed to be stored in `ls_ip_address1` and `ls_ip_address2`:

```
int i, j;
char optval[MAX_IPOPTLEN];
optval[0] = (char) IPOPT_LSRR;
optval[1] = (char) 3;
optval[2] = (char) IPOPT_MINOFF;
i = IPOPT_MINOFF-1;
memcpy(&optval[i], &lsrr_ip_address1, 4); i +=4;
optval[IPOPT_OLEN] += (char) 4;
memcpy(&optval[i], &lsrr_ip_address2, 4); i +=4;
optval[IPOPT_OLEN] += (char) 4;
optval[IPOPT_OFFSET] = (char) IPOPT_MINOFF;
if (setsockopt(sd, 0, IP_OPTIONS, optval,MAX_IPOPTLEN) < 0)
    perror("setsockopt");
```

This would add the Loose Source and Record Route option to each and every IP packet that is sent out using this socket. If you're only interested in controlling which route the packets take, that's all you need to do (beyond setting up the connection or association with the peer, of course, and don't forget that the peer may need to set up the route in the reverse direction).

If you also want to explore the route information that is returned, you could do so, as in the following example (taken from the public-domain `ping.c`):

```c
#include <stdio.h>
#include <errno.h>
#include <fcntl.h>
#include <signal.h>
#include <sys/types.h>
#include <sys/stat.h>
#include <sys/socket.h>
#include <netdb.h>
#include <sys/timeb.h>
#include <time.h>
#include <sys/utsname.h>
#include <unistd.h>
#include <sys/param.h>
#include <sys/file.h>
#include <netinet/in_systm.h>
#include <netinet/in.h>
#include <netinet/ip.h>
#include <netinet/ip_var.h>
#include <netinet/ip_icmp.h>
#include <values.h>

int ident;
struct optstr {
   struct optstr *next;
   int count;
   char optval[MAX_IPOPTLEN];
} *sumopt = NULL, *curopt;

ping_it(node_addr, datalen)
struct in_addr node_addr;       /* IP address of node to ping    */
int datalen;                    /* number of bytes in PING packet */
{
   u_char outpack[MAXPACKET];
   char optval[MAX_IPOPTLEN];
   char cc;
   int err, i, j, k, hlen, this_status, fromlen, icmp_protocol;
   struct sockaddr_in from;
   struct timeval *tp = (struct timeval *) &outpack[8];
   struct icmp *icp = (struct icmp *) outpack;
   struct protoent *proto;
   u_char *datap = &outpack[8+sizeof(struct timeval)];

   /* Look up the protocol number for ICMP messages
```

```
         (should be in /etc/protocols).
   */
   if ((proto = getprotobyname("icmp")) == NULL) {
      fprintf(stderr, "icmp: unknown protocol\n");
      exit(10);
   }
   icmp_protocol = proto->p_proto;
   /* Create a raw socket, which is bound to ICMP protocol.   */
   socknbr = socket(AF_INET,SOCK_RAW, icmp_protocol);
   if (socknbr < 0) {
      perror("socket fail");
      exit(1);
   }
   /*
   ** Build IP Record Route option.  In this example,
   ** we don't care about LSRR, just Record Route.
   */
   optval[IPOPT_OPTVAL] = (char) IPOPT_RR;
   optval[IPOPT_OLEN] = (char) MAX_IPOPTLEN - 1,
   optval[IPOPT_OFFSET] = (char) IPOPT_MINOFF;
   bzero(&optval[IPOPT_MINOFF - 1], MAX_IPOPTLEN - 4);
   optval[MAX_IPOPTLEN - 1] = (char) IPOPT_EOL;
   /* Attach the IP option to the socket.                     */
   if (setsockopt(socknbr, ip_protocol, IP_OPTIONS, optval,
         MAX_IPOPTLEN) < 0)
      perror("setsockopt");
   bzero( (char *)&whereto, sizeof(struct sockaddr) );
   to->sin_family = AF_INET;
   to->sin_addr.s_addr = node_addr.s_addr;

   icp->icmp_type  = ICMP_ECHO;
   icp->icmp_code  = 0;
   icp->icmp_cksum = 0;
   icp->icmp_seq   = ntransmitted++;
   icp->icmp_id    = ident = getpid();     /* ID              */
   cc = datalen+8;                /* skips ICMP portion        */
   gettimeofday( tp, &tzp );
   for( i=8; i<datalen; i++)   /* skip 8 for time             */
      *datap++ = i;
   /* Compute ICMP checksum here.  It is necessary that the
   ** icmp_cksum field contain zeros during the computation,
   ** then we fill in the proper checksum value.              */
   icp->icmp_cksum = in_cksum( icp, cc );
```

```
    signal(SIGALRM,timeout);
    alarm(60);   /* very arbitrarily assumes round-trip time <=
                 /* 60 seconds.                                   */
    sendto(socknbr,outpack,cc,0,&whereto, sizeof(struct sockaddr));
    get_nxt:
    alarm(60);   /* very arbitrarily assumes round-trip time <=
                 /* 60 seconds.                                   */
    fromlen = sizeof (from);
    if((cc=recvfrom(socknbr, inbuf, sizeof(inbuf), 0, &from,
         &fromlen)) < 0){
      if( errno == EINTR ) continue;
      perror("ping: recvfrom");
      continue;
    }
    if (!pr_pack(inbuf, cc, &from ))
       goto get_nxt;
    this_status = STAT_UP;
    alarm(0);
    close(socknbr);
    if ((this_status == STAT_UP) && (n_returns > 0))
       return(1);
    else
       return(0);
}
/*
 *        P R _ P A C K
 *
 * Print out the packet, if it came from us.  This logic is
 * necessary because ALL readers of the ICMP socket get a copy of
 * ALL ICMP packets which arrive ('tis only fair).  This permits
 * multiple copies of this program to be run without having
 * intermingled output (or statistics!).
 */
pr_pack( buf, cc, from )
unsigned char *buf;
int cc;
struct sockaddr_in *from;
{
    struct ip *ip;
    struct icmp *icp;
    long *lp = (long *) inbuf;
    struct timeval tv, *tp;
    int ipoptlen, i, num_routes, len, n_routes, hlen, triptime;
    char *inet_ntoa(), *rtptr;
```

```
    unsigned char *ipopt;
    unsigned long time_stamp, route_file_ptr;
    from->sin_addr.s_addr = ntohl(from->sin_addr.s_addr );
    gettimeofday( &tv, &tzp );
    ip = (struct ip *) buf;
    hlen = ip->ip_hl << 2;
    if (cc < hlen + ICMP_MINLEN) {
        printf("packet too short (%d bytes) rom %s\n", cc,
               inet_ntoa(ntohl(from->sin_addr)));
        return(0);
    }
    cc -= hlen;
    icp = (struct icmp *)(buf + hlen);
    if( icp->icmp_type != ICMP_ECHOREPLY )
        return(0);

    if( icp->icmp_id != ident )
        return(0);                          /* 'Twas not our ECHO       */
    tp = (struct timeval *)&icp->icmp_data[0];
    if ((hlen > sizeof(struct ip))) {
        ipopt = buf + sizeof(struct ip);
        /* We only know how to parse RR options             */
        if (ipopt[IPOPT_OPTVAL] == IPOPT_RR) {
            ipoptlen = ipopt[IPOPT_OLEN];
            num_routes = (ipopt[IPOPT_OLEN+1]/sizeof(struct in_addr))
                     -1;
            for (curopt = sumopt; curopt; curopt = curopt->next) {
                if (ipoptlen != curopt->optval[IPOPT_OLEN])
                    continue;
                if (!memcmp(ipopt, curopt->optval, ipoptlen))
                    break;
            }
            if (!curopt) {
                curopt = (struct optstr *)
                calloc(1, (sizeof(struct optstr)));
                curopt->next = sumopt;
                sumopt = curopt;
                memmove(curopt->optval, ipopt, ipoptlen);
            }
            curopt->count++;
        }
    }
    return(1);
}
```

In order to simplify the example, no error checking is shown, and only one PING packet is sent. In a more realistic example, you would probably want to issue several packets, since one or two may be lost in the network, but the node might still be responsive. You shouldn't conclude that the node is dead just because you did not receive a response to just one packet. Also, for simplicity, some of the setup work, which could easily be done just once (such as the getprotobyname() procedure call), is done in-line here.

9.4   How to Send and Receive Out-of-Band TCP Data

You may at some point have wondered, "What do I do if I need to get a message to the peer process **fast**?" You have two choices: Open another connection and use it only for urgent messages— don't clog it up with large messages — or use "TCP urgent data."

The TCP specification allows "urgent" data, which is somewhat analogous to the out-of-band data that some other protocols support (such as ISO Transport Class 4 or X.25). You need to understand the sense in which the word "urgent" is used, and part of the implementation, before you can use TCP urgent data correctly. It isn't a true out-of-band transmission mechanism, because the data itself is transmitted in sequence and is subject to normal flow control. This means that even though there may be "urgent data" ready for transmission, if you used send() to send any other data ahead of it, then that data will be transmitted first.[8] There is no separate communications "channel" for sending TCP urgent data—it is still flow-controlled along with all normal data. However, you can use this to send some information more quickly through the network, namely, the "TCP urgent data pointer" itself. As part of its normal header, TCP carries an "urgent data pointer" and a flag indicating whether the urgent pointer is valid or not. Imagine the situation where you have just sent a rather large amount of data, and just sent an "urgent" byte of data. We'll assume that TCP has sent all of the data it can send, and must wait for an acknowledgment from the peer. Thus, it cannot send the "urgent" byte of data (yet). Even when the acknowledgment arrives, TCP cannot (necessarily) send the urgent data: It must send the (presumably "normal") data that is ahead of it in the transmission queue. When it does send data, it will set the urgent data pointer field to be the sequence number of the urgent data byte. Every byte of data in TCP is assigned a sequence number, by the way.

To obtain this data quickly (and we presume that's what you would be using "urgent" data for), it will be necessary for the recipient to read all the normal data in the data stream first. Whether the application discards this data or saves it somewhere is unimportant to TCP, but it is of prime concern to the you as application designer. One

---

8. The "urgent data" byte may of course be in the same packet as normal data, but the byte immediately prior to the "urgent data" byte will be the last byte of normal data that you sent.

particular situation deserves mention. Suppose you're only going to use TCP's urgent data to notify the peer of some change of conditions—such as "Stop doing what you're doing now." Then you could use the fact that notification of urgent data can travel through the network faster than normal data.

Before you go ahead and use "urgent data," you should consider the advantages offered by opening a second TCP connection:

1. Data you send on this second connection can flow through the network independently of the flow control of the other connection. It is separately flow-controlled. (If the network is congested or slow in delivery packets, **any** packet can be affected, no matter whether it contains urgent data or which TCP connection is belongs to. The gateways route strictly on the IP header, including the addresses, LSRR or SSRR, and sometimes on type of service. They do not consider TCP header information of any kind in their choices.)

2. You can send any amount of data on either connection (in contrast, some TCP implementations limit you to one byte for TCP urgent data[9]).

3. There is no danger of the urgent information becoming mixed in with the normal channel's data. Some TCP implementations have bugs in how they handle urgent data under severe load and with retransmissions.

4. Assuming you've decided that TCP's urgent data best meets your needs, this is how you use it:

```
send(s, &oob_byte, 1, MSG_OOB);
```

If the transmission queue for the socket is full, your program will be blocked, but otherwise the data byte will be placed at the end of the transmission queue and sent in turn and at the next opportunity.

Similarly, to receive one byte of urgent data,

```
recv(s, &oob_byte, 1, MSG_OOB);
```

If there is no urgent data to be read, recv() will return an error. If there is data, it will return the number of bytes transferred. If you need to have the system report to you asynchronously when urgent data arrives, you can use the SIOCSPGRP ioctl(), in a manner similar to that described in Chapter 10, and set up a signal handler for SIGURG.

---

9. You can use the SO_OOBINLINE socket option (setsockopt()) to specify that TCP urgent data is to be left where it is in the input data stream. With this, there can be more than one such message "in the pipe" between sender and receiver at the same time.

9.5   How to Build in TCP Disconnect Survivability

As has been stated many times, TCP provides "reliability," but this only means that in the presence of network errors it will keep trying. Suppose the network is simply broken between points A and B. Should TCP keep trying forever? There are those who argue "yes" to this question, but most implementations will eventually give up. What if this happens in the middle of a lengthy application, say, a file transfer that's taken three hours? Sure, once the network is repaired, you can restart the transfer, but it'd be nice if the transfer application didn't give up just because TCP did. To solve this problem, the server will need to create a second `SOCK_STREAM` socket (we assume the server also has a socket bound to some well-known address). Bind this second socket to `INADDR_ANY` (zero). As we saw in Chapter 3, the system will choose an unused port number for you. Now, you can send a message back to your client (on the original connection, the one that's to the well-known port number), something along the lines of "My private number is <system-assigned port number here>. Call me back on that number." Recall that `inetd` will create listen sockets for all the port number-protocol combinations listed in the `inetd.conf` file, and when new connections are established to these sockets, it will `accept()` them, `fork()`, and `exec()` the specified daemon. The daemon begins its life with this socket as its `stdin`, `stdout`, and `stderr`. So it isn't enough for the client to effect recovery simply by creating a new socket to the same well-known port, and then connect to it. This would simply start a new instance of the server, which would have no knowledge of the actions that had gone before, and therefore would find recovery somewhat complicated, to say the least.

If however, the server creates a second socket, and binds this to port number zero (`INADDR_ANY`), the kernel will choose an unused port number. We can find out what port number this is with the `getsockname()` system call. We can send this port number back to our client, on the first connection. If the connection survives at least long enough for the client to receive this information, well and good. If it doesn't, there's no important state or "prior history" to worry about, and the client can simply retry the original connection. We must provide a mechanism for the server to absent itself, in this instance. That is, if the server detects that the original connection dies before it receives a connection on the second listen socket (the one where the kernel picked the port number), then it can simply terminate itself.

With this setup, recovery is simple: Whenever the client detects that the connection has died, it should close the socket, create a new one, bind the new port number (the one the server obtained from the kernel) to it, and `connect()` to the server. Similarly, whenever the server detects that a connection has died, it should close the socket and wait for a new connection to come in on this new port number, using the `accept()` system call and specifying the second listen socket (the one whose binding address was chosen by the kernel). Communication can pick up from this point onward, as soon as the two processes reestablish synchronization with each other. In the simple case where a request/reply protocol is used, there shouldn't be more than one message "in the pipe" at the same time, so the sender should retransmit the last message it sent, once the new connection is established. Resynchronizing is easier with message-oriented protocols than with byte-stream oriented ones because you can adopt the simplifying assumption that any partially received message can be discarded, and all you need to do is make the sender retransmit it. Servers would cache replies, and sequence numbering would be used in the messages to detect lost replies.

What happens if the connection breaks when the side with recovery responsibility is listening for a reply? Some TCPs, in fact, probably most, implement **keepalives**, which are messages sent at intervals just for the purpose of seeing if the other side is listening. **Keepalives** have their disadvantages, not the least of which is the potential to take down a connection merely because the network happens to be broken between the endpoints, regardless of whether the application needs the network to be functional at that time. Imagine, for example, `telnet` connections, and suppose the user has stepped out for lunch. If the network breaks, but is repaired again before the user returns, wouldn't this person be surprised to find that the `telnet` session is gone, including whatever he or she may have been working on?

Of more direct interest, perhaps, to this discussion is the timing of the keepalives. In some implementations, they are sent at two-hour intervals, and it takes several repetitions, all unanswered, before the TCP will abort the connection. Depending on the application, you may choose to accept the fact that the network may be broken for several hours before initiating recovery procedures. After all, perhaps the repair crews will have remedied the problem, and if not, what else can you do if the gateways can't find a functional route?

You may find yourself wondering why you'd build all this recovery mechanism on top of TCP. Why not just use UDP and put the reliability on top? This may indeed be a proper choice, but consider: TCP already has built into it years of experience in dealing with network congestion, and the heuristics found in a "proper" implementation are quite good at avoiding unnecessary retransmissions, while still handling packet losses well. If you use UDP, you either forgo these advantages or reimplement them yourself.

9.6   Exercises

1. Implement reliability and data flow control using UDP, broadcast addressing, and a variable number of participating hosts.

2. Implement a "LAN Conversationalist" program, using broadcasts. There should be no inherent limit in the program design on the number of people who can participate, and the program must provide reliable delivery of each person's contributions to each of the other participants, once and once only.

3. Implement a file transfer facility that doesn't quit when TCP does.

 # X.25 Sockets

by Lyle Weiman

10.1 Introduction

This chapter describes how to program X.25 sockets. These are sockets that give you direct access to the X.25 protocol. Accessing X.25 directly is sometimes preferable to using TCP/IP. It may be the **only** protocol available and common to both platforms. It offers greater control over network bandwidth and network usage charges than TCP/IP.[1] It is available on most computer platforms. Often, it will be the only way to talk with a piece of equipment, particularly if the functionality of that equipment is too complex for simple RS-232. Finally, it makes an interesting contrast to TCP/IP.

X.25 is often used in wide area networking, although it can also be used for shorter distances. There are actually three layers in the protocol "stack":

- Physical layer
- Data link layer
- Packet layer

The physical layer deals with bits and signaling and is of little direct interest to the applications programmer. Modems handle this layer transparently to the programmer. The data link layer is connection-oriented, a variation of the high-level data link control (HDLC) protocol known as LAP–B (Link Access Protocol "B").[2] This level, too, is transparent to you when programming at the X.25 packet layer directly. It suffices to know that this layer provides for detection of data link–type errors (chiefly data corruption) and recovery through retransmission. The third layer is the one of most interest to the applications programmer when accessing X.25 directly. This layer is sometimes called the "network layer" but is more properly called the "packet layer."

The packet layer of X.25 is similar in these respects to TCP/IP:

- It is connection-oriented.

- State information is kept at both ends of the connection (in X.25, the terms "connection," "virtual circuit," and "circuit" are used interchangeably).

---

1. The concept of charging for communications services based upon usage is somewhat new to the "TCP/IP crowd," having been introduced only relatively recently. It is well established in the X.25 world.

2. A later modification of the link layer protocol, LAP–D, is sometimes used instead.

- Data in a circuit is flow-controlled separately from the other streams. This means that if one end sends faster than the other can receive, the flow control automatically stops the sender from sending any more data until the receiving side "consumes" some data. It also means that if the receiver of one stream is slow to read the data, this does not slow down the other streams. Instead, it speeds them up, because they get a larger "share" of the available bandwidth.

- Transmission is bidirectional.

- Each direction is independently flow-controlled.

- There is provision for automatic recovery from most types of communications errors, so you don't have to worry about errors (in contrast to UDP; see the discussion in the section titled "Resets" for an exception).

- There is a provision for sending "urgent" data. The X.25 Recommendation calls this INTERRUPT data.[3] INTERRUPT data is not subject to the flow control of ordinary data, so you can send an INTERRUPT data packet even if the data flow has stopped. Only one packet can be "in the pipe" at any one time, but another can be sent when the reception of the first has been acknowledged.[4]

- Separate data streams may share the same physical network facilities without interference.

- These streams may be using any higher-level protocols without interfering with each other (other than that they share the same physical-layer bandwidth limitations).

X.25 is also different in other respects from TCP/IP:

- Messages have boundaries (a property shared with UDP).

- Urgent data may overtake ordinary data in the data stream.[5]

---

3. X.25's out-of-band data is, however, designed to be able to traverse the network ahead of in-band data, which TCPs cannot.

4. Out-of-band data will be abbreviated to "OOB" in this chapter.

5. With TCP, the "urgent data" cannot proceed through the network any faster than the ordinary data that has been presented to TCP before it. X.25 networks can send "urgent data" through the network faster than ordinary data sent before it. The ability for some data to "overtake" other data can be useful in some applications. For example, consider terminal emulation. You would want the SIGINT character to cancel screen output; otherwise, if you accidentally cated the wrong file, you would have to wait for in-transit data characters to be written to your terminal's screen.

• The X.25 packet layer depends upon the data link level for reliable delivery of data (TCP/IP and UDP/IP require very little more of their lower layers than "reasonable probability of delivery").

• X.25 automatically protects data against errors on the data link by a CRC[6] code. TCP protects data too, with a checksum, but it is computed once by the sender and checked once by the receiver. X.25's CRCs are calculated (usually in hardware; TCP's checksums are usually computed in software) separately for each transmission link. This means the protection is not end-to-end, as with TCP, so the data may be corrupted anywhere in the switching equipment.

• The packet layer depends on the data link layer to tell it when delivery is not possible.

• In many implementations, HP's among them, the maximum number of virtual circuits that can be "open" at any time is limited by the amount of free buffer memory on the X.25 interface. Buffer memory in the host computer is still used, but it is not the limiting factor. In contrast, TCP's buffering is taken from a pool on the host, and so there is, practically speaking, no limit on the number of open connections. In HP's case, the number is typically in the 32–64 range, per interface, although this number depends upon the flow control parameter configuration.

Figure 10.1 depicts a typical architecture of X.25, as implemented within the kernel. As you can see from the diagram, TCP/IP and UDP/IP have access to X.25 through a module that converts between IP's connectionless networking model and X.25's connection-oriented model.[7] The programming interface for TCP/IP and UDP/IP is the same when the underlying network is X.25 as for any other communications technologies, such as LAN. Thus, when you are using TCP/IP or UDP/IP, your programs should still work, regardless of whether the packets traverse LANs, X.25 networks, or (perhaps) both. When TCP/IP or UDP/IP protocols are used, however, you are not in direct control—not in direct contact, so to speak, with the X.25 protocol. In this chapter, however, we are describing **direct** access to X.25—that is when there is no other protocol layer between you and X.25. More specifically, by "direct access to

---

6. CRC stands for Cyclic Redundancy Check, a technique easily implemented in hardware for detecting errors in transmission.

7. This means that it must open an X.25 connection whenever necessary and detect when to terminate the connection. It also must convert address formats. There is a Defense Data Network standard for conversion, but it only works for certain ranges of IP addresses. In other cases, a mapping table must be used.

X.25," we mean that you're using the path through the kernel software that goes through the box labeled "sockets interface to X.25" in Figure 10.1. You specify that you wish direct access to X.25 in the parameters to the socket() system call (we'll see how a bit later).

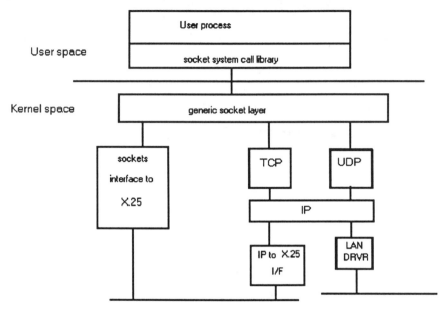

Figure 10.1 Typical Architecture

There is no capability in either 4.2BSD or 4.3BSD that provides direct access to X.25, and no industry standard or quasi-standard interface. This dictates a different approach to the subject matter. We can show **in general** how to program X.25, but generalities are no fun, so we will illustrate the specifics of one interface, that of the HP 9000 computers. This access method happens to be similar to that of Sun Microsystems (but not identical).

The contrast between X.25 and TCP will help you to see which features are generic to connection-oriented protocols and which features are unique to TCP. X.25 provides a richer variety of connection setup options, and we will describe these. Richness in functionality also brings with it complexity, and that is the case here: There are more programming steps involved in setting up a connection. We show you how the "Dinner is ready when the smoke alarm goes off" example would need to be modified if it were to be used directly over an X.25 network.

You will be much more "at the mercy of" the X.25 protocol specifics than you are when using either TCP or UDP. X.25 has so many more protocol options than TCP or UDP that few vendors implement them all. (For that matter, few providers of X.25

services offer them all, either.) You can take advantage only of protocol features and options that lie in the intersection of the set that your vendor has implemented, the network services provider has implemented, and your contract with the network services provider permits. You cannot take advantage of anything that's outside of that set. The shaded area in the middle of Figure 10.2 illustrates this intersection.

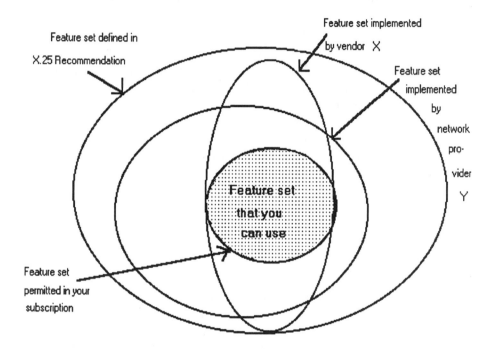

Figure 10.2 X.25 Protocol and Feature Set Intersection

The jargon is somewhat different from that used in the TCP/IP "world." To help you, we've included a glossary of terms in this chapter.

You will probably find it necessary to get a copy of the X.25 protocol specification (see the "Bibliography" at the end of this book). You may find the spec hard to read, due in part to the "standards-committee-ese" language that is used and in part to terminology from the telephone industry. See *X.25: The PSN Connection* (referenced in the Bibliography) for an overview. In addition, the spec changes because the CCITT reviews it every four years. As of this writing, the most recent revision was in 1988, but 1984, 1980, and 1976 versions exist. Fortunately, modifications to the spec tend to be evolutionary rather than revolutionary. CCITT usually introduces new features as options in any new version of the spec. In a future version, they may become mandatory. It's rare, but sometimes a newly introduced feature is dropped in the next revision (datagrams, for example). Backward compatibility is, as always, highly important, which puts a conservative slant on modifications.

Most manufacturers offer at least the 1980 version. This has pretty well become the minimum level of X.25 functionality; that is, you will usually find at least 1980-level functionality if the vendor has implemented any X.25 direct-access functionality at all. Many vendors offer some or all the 1984 features, and some offer some or all of the 1988 features.

The X.25 service is usually offered with a variety of options. It is helpful to know that the X.25 protocol specification is, technically, only a **recommendation**, not a **requirement**. Providers of the X.25 network service[8] usually have a great deal of power to choose what features to offer. Vendors, too, may choose to implement a part of the protocol feature set, although most choose to implement as much as they possibly can (for obvious reasons). Before you use of any of the optional features, you have to find out if it's available to you. Which providers will be used? Which features will they support? What switching equipment will be used? What features will it support? Sometimes the network provider represents a third party that contracts to provide the X.25 service to others. Sometimes it is a government agency. In many respects, this is very much like telephone companies. In most countries, the provider is a part of the same government agency that also provides postal, telephone, and telegraph services.

Most network providers that claim to support a given version of the X.25 specification will offer all the mandatory features for that version. Some features were optional in, say, 1980, but became mandatory in 1984. Since you can't use unsupported features, you're targeting the lowest common denominator, in a sense. An example is the amount of data that can be sent in an INTERRUPT packet. In the 1980 spec, INTERRUPT packets may contain only one byte of data. The 1984 version permits up to 32 bytes (the X.25 spec, and most communications standards, call an eight-bit unit of data an "octet"). You might be tempted to believe that if your vendor(s) implement a 1984 level of the spec, you can send 32 bytes. Did you forget that you may only use a feature that the vendor, the network, and the vendor of the equipment at the other end of your connection all support? Sometimes, you may not know in advance everything that is and isn't supported. To permit your implementation to operate over the widest variety of network implementations, and to take advantage of features as the provider and switching equipment allow, you should be prepared either to receive an error back or to have the circuit reset. With some implementations and some networks, initiating a

---

8. The services provided in X.25 networks are much more sophisticated than mere emulations of copper wires. The equipment between the computers communicating over an X.25 network provides buffering, error recovery, accounting, and numerous other services. The organization which offers this service is called the "network provider" or simply "the provider." The costs associated with servicing this equipment are usually borne by the network users.

packet type whose format or contents are disallowed by the subscription, not supported by the provider, or just illegal, triggers a DIAGNOSTIC packet response from the provider. DIAGNOSTIC packets may not be delivered to the "culprit," so to speak (as is the case in HP's implementation). They may simply be logged by the system's error-logging mechanism, in a file available for a qualified troubleshooter to find. In such cases, all you could detect from your program would be that you'd sent the packet but the other side had not received it.

10.1.1   Resets

In X.25, a "reset" does not destroy the circuit (unlike TCP's RST, which is sometimes also called "reset"). It merely empties all the data in each direction. Following a reset, you still have a circuit, but you don't know what happened to the data that was in transit at the time of the reset. How much did the peer process receive, and how much was lost? Some of the data may have been delivered, perhaps even all of it. All you know is that there's no data "in the pipe." Due to this uncertainty, it is usually necessary to design the application such that the context can be reestablished following a reset. This can be very simple if the application is essentially request–reply in nature, since there can only be one message outstanding at a time. You just put a sequence number in the message header, incrementing its value with each new message. Following a reset, you can retransmit the last message. If the receiver has seen it already, it should acknowledge the message, just as it did the first time, but not act upon it. If you designed your application such that every action is idempotent, your recovery is even simpler: Retransmit any message when your acknowledgment timer expires before you see the acknowledgment.

You can check to see whether the local provider is supporting a given feature simply by establishing a circuit to yourself (using your side's address) and trying to use it; for instance, send an INTERRUPT packet. If you ask for the feature but the provider doesn't support that option, your call will be rejected. This also may happen if you ask for a feature that your contract with the provider doesn't allow. A call rejected this way is called "cleared by the DCE," a situation described in the following paragraphs.

10.1.2   DTE and DCE

The term "DCE" stands for Data Communication Equipment. This term covers all the provider's equipment. Your equipment is called the Data Terminating Equipment (DTE). What X.25 **really** specifies is the interface between DTE and DCE. When the DCE **clears** the call, what this means is the provider popped the circuit, not the peer. The distinction is important in the troubleshooting. The CLEAR packet contains a "cause" code and usually a "diagnostic" code (some equipment may not supply this code; HP's does). You can usually figure out what went wrong from these codes. These codes are listed in the X.25 Recommendation.

There are several ways to deal with this variety. One would be to specify that your application has certain requirements of the X.25 service, such as 32-byte INTERRUPT packets. This is simplest, but it isn't foolproof. Somebody may very well try to use your application anyway and call you when it fails to work, invariably in the middle of the night. It also limits how much your application will be used.

Another method is to design your applications so that you depend only on a very small subset of X.25 protocol features and options, the 1980 version of the spec for example. To be extremely conservative, you might only depend on those features listed as mandatory in the 1980 spec, although this would be cutting yourself off from some implementation choices that could be especially advantageous to your application in some way. Those X.25 protocol options were put into the protocol for a reason, after all. Another possibility would be to design your application such that you can take advantage of these options when available, but you can scale back when necessary. This adds to program and testing complexity, but it permits your program to be used in a broader variety of environments. It can reduce support costs and angry calls from customers who bought the package only to find out it can't be used because of some dependency. For example, you could design your application so that both sides immediately begin to exercise the options that you'd like to use, in loopback mode. After each end determines which of the features your application **might** be able to use, you exchange messages that inform the peers. You can be clever and work this into the normal exchange of information that typically occurs at the start of any connection between peers. Even better, save the information in a file, so you don't have to rediscover the same things each time. This keeps the costs of using the network down.

X.25 is an international standard, and it may be used for communication not only within the same network but across different networks. In many countries there is only one network provided. Other countries, such as the United States, permit more than one provider to exist. Each will have a certain set of the X.25 protocol features and options that it supports. These networks are interconnected using another standard called X.75. This wrinkle can further reduce the set of features you can use, in the same way that switching equipment can.

The X.25 protocol defines a "packet sequence," which for our purposes is the same thing as a message. It is a clearly marked boundary in the data stream. TCP lacks message boundaries. It's up to the user of the protocol to handle this, where necessary. As we have seen, any part of a message may be delivered to the user process, even if the message hasn't completely arrived. This causes extra overhead on the recipient, as we have shown in previous chapters. X.25 automatically does this for you. When the message arrives in its entirety, then and only then will the system deliver it.[9] This feature of the protocol readily lends itself to providing a message-based user interface as HP's is, for example. This is similar to UDP in that if you "read short," unread data after the message will be discarded. With TCP, you get what you asked for (or less), but the rest will be waiting for you next time.

To set up a connection in X.25, you need to understand the packet sequences. There are three phases of a connection: setting it up, using it (transfer of data), and closing it (teardown). During setup and teardown, four packets are (normally) sent. Figure 10.3 illustrates a simple exchange of packets for establishing a connection. Packets which start a new connection are called, naturally enough, CALL packets. Those that tear it down are called CLEAR packets. The second part of the name (Request, Indication, Response, or Confirm) tells you in which stage of the exchange that packet occurs.

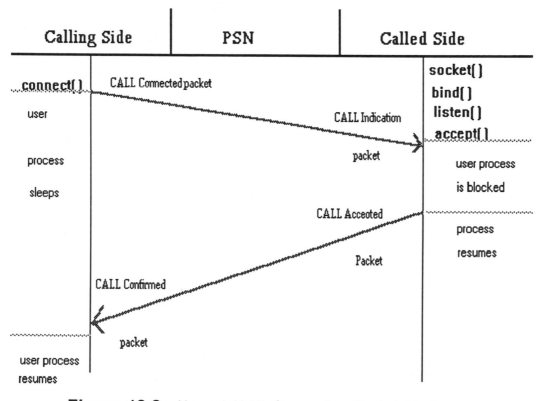

Figure 10.3 Normal X.25 Connection Packet Exchange

9. As of HP's HP-UX Release 7.0, X.25 permits the programmer to specify that message fragments are to be delivered as they arrive. This feature permits the receipt of arbitrarily-sized messages.

The diagram in Figure 10.3, and others like it shown in this chapter, follow the usual convention of indicating direction of transfer with arrows, either left to right or right to left (the arrowhead tells you in which direction the packet is traveling). The time sequence of events is shown vertically; that is, events that occur first are shown above those that occur later. This sequencing is only relative to other events in the diagram and is only approximate. It is not to scale.

A similar pattern will be seen for the teardown phase (CLEAR Request, CLEAR Indication, CLEAR Response, CLEAR Confirm).

"PSN,"[10] shown in the center of the diagrams, stands for "packet-switching network" and refers generically to all the equipment in between the communicating DTEs.

If the recipient of the call chooses to accept, it sends a CALL Response packet. When this packet arrives back at the initiating side, it is called a CALL Confirmation packet. Although the formats of the two packets are identical, these are **not** the same packets, and there is no guarantee that the same data in the CALL Request packet will appear in the CALL Indication packet. The same can be said for CALL Response and CALL Confirm, as well as CLEAR and other types of packets. This is because the switching equipment takes a more active part in the "conversation" than is the case with Internet routers.

When the vendor's interface uses sockets (as opposed to STREAMS or file I/O), you need to create a socket before you can do anything else in the protocol. The setup parameters are conveyed to the kernel through ioctl()[11] calls (called the call setup sequence). In X.25, CALL packets can specify up to 16 bytes of **call data** (in the 1980 version of the recommendation; 128 bytes are permitted in the 1984 version of the recommendation). They may carry a plethora of different options, called "facilities." You have to tell the kernel what call data, if any, and what facilities, if any, you want to use, **before** you start the connection.

The 4.2BSD and 4.3BSD implementations of ioctl() can pass data into and out of the kernel. The HP-UX implementation adds a seven-bit field in the cmd parameter that tells the kernel how much data to transfer. (The cmd also contains bits telling the kernel which direction to transfer data: in, out, both, or neither.) Thus, HP-UX can only support transfers up to 127 bytes in length for ioctl()s. In addition, the data structure contains a length byte in it, leaving room for a maximum of 126 bytes of data. So, if you want to specify either 127 or 128 bytes of call data, you have to make two ioctl() calls as part of the call setup.

---

10. No, it doesn't stand for Pretty Stupid Network.

11. The HP-UX X.25 implementation makes heavy use of ioctl() calls to carry X.25-specific information to and from the kernel which the BSD socket user interface cannot handle directly.

Two excellent places to begin your study of the X.25 protocol itself (in this order) are HP's *X.25: The PSN Connection* (see References), and the CCITT publication covering X.25 (1980, 1984, or 1988, as your needs dictate). PSN refers to the packet-switching network,—that is, the X.25 network and its associated equipment, excluding the computers that use the network to transport their data.

The specification for the 1980 version is known as "the Yellow Book"; the one for the 1984 version is called the "Red Book"; and the one for the 1988 version is called "the Blue Book." If you expect to need to use the tracing features of the product, or if you will need an X.25 protocol analyzer, then you should read *The PSN Connection* in its entirety (and keep the relevant CCITT spec handy, too). Keep in mind that the switches may affect the circuit, as can the peer process.

10.1.3   Packet Switches

In X.25, the packet-switching equipment occupies a somewhat analogous position to bridges and routers in a TCP/IP network, but it can affect the connections more directly, such as by generating resets and/or disconnects. With TCP, bridges and routers either forward the packets or they don't; if they do, the connection stays up, and if they stop for several minutes (and no alternate paths are available), the connection times out and is aborted. That's about the extent to which the routers can affect the connection. In contrast, with X.25 the DCE switches can disconnect the circuit, negotiate flow-control parameters, and permit or prohibit the use of certain facilities, such as multiple-byte INTERRUPT data or permanent virtual circuits (PVCs). Check the documentation of the switches used in your network for details.

10.1.4   Addressing: X.121 Addresses

In X.25, addresses are strings of up to 15 binary-coded decimal (BCD) digits. Their format has been defined by another CCITT specification, X.121; hence, they are sometimes called X.121 addresses. This format is different from Internet Protocol format, which is of fixed size (32 bits) and specified in binary. Addresses are assigned to an X.25 interface by the network provider. This is similar to the way the telephone company assigns telephone numbers to telephones. A telephone does not have a telephone number until it is attached to the network. When attached, it has a telephone number that is determined by the wires to which it is attached. Similarly, a piece of X.25-compatible communications equipment does not have an X.121 address until it is connected to an X.25 network. Then its address is determined by the wires to which it is connected. These addresses are unique in the world (just like telephone numbers). Contrast this with an Ethernet interface, for example. The Ethernet address is an intrinsic part of the interface, assigned at the factory, and will be the same 48 bits, no matter where it is located or attached to a network.

Sometimes several hosts will share the same network provider "wire," and they use a piece of equipment called a "packet switch"[12] to multiplex and demultiplex packets over it. Network providers do not assign addresses with the full 15 digits possible, and they will allow addresses to be longer than what they assign. This leaves room for using extra address digits for finer-grained addressing. The "extra digits" are always suffixed, never prefixed, to the provider-assigned address, and they are called "subaddress digits." Subaddressing is sometimes used for addressing a particular host when several share the X.25 point of attachment. The same technique may be used to address a particular socket within a computer. Both of these may be used, so long as the limit of 15 digits is not exceeded.

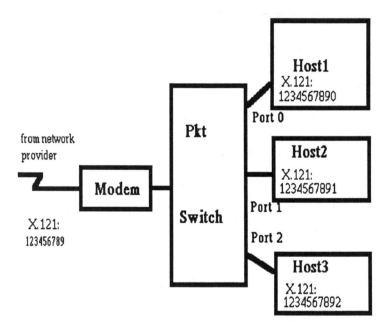

Figure 10.4   Hosts Sharing DTE Address

Figure 10.4 shows Host1, Host2 and Host3 all sharing the same DTE address (as it is known to the network provider; for example, 1234567890). To distinguish them, the system administrator has added a one- or two-digit suffix to the provider-assigned address. This suffix is the "subaddress." For example, Host1 = 12345678901, Host2

---

12. In its simplest form the "provider" of the X.25 network service, and the X.25 network itself, might be nothing more complicated than one packet switch with at least two ports. Interconnected packet switches form the basis of the X.25 network.

= 1234567890**2**, and Host3 = 1234567890**3**. The packet switch must be configured with this information, so that it "knows" which address corresponds to which port. Within each host, too, the software is configured to conspire in this link-sharing arrangement. In the figure, the address of Host1 is 1234567890**1**; Host2's address is 1234567890**2**, and so on. Note that the subaddress has no meaning to the network provider, but it is necessary that the network support more address digits than it assigns to subscribers. Host1, Host2, and Host3 aren't in any way "aware" that they are using subaddressing; to the implementation, the 11-digit numbers just "look like" ordinary X.121 addresses.

As noted, the X.121 address specifies only the "wire" coming from the provider (or, when packet switches are in use, the "wire" coming out of the packet switch). To select a particular host, you need more levels of addressing. There are three methods that could be used. The calling side has to be coded for the method that the called side is using.

One of these methods is called "Protocol-ID." This method is really just a programming convention that was started with X.25/PAD. The intended recipient (in other words, which server) of an inbound connection is addressed using bits of the call user data field (CUDF). This convention is not standardized, so you use what you need. The X.25 network doesn't care.

Another choice is to use subaddressing. This method concatenates an extra few digits to the end of the DTE address. In our example above, Application-A might be distinguished by address 1234578901**1**, Application-B by address 1234578901**2**, and so on. With some providers and some kinds of equipment, the use of subaddressing is either disallowed or precluded by other equipment (such as the packet switches). Here we showed only one-digit subaddresses, but we could have used more.

For subaddressing to work, it is necessary that the network provider supply the Called address in the INCOMING CALL packet. Some don't. Addressing by protocol-ID may be the better choice and is more generally applicable, but feel free to use whichever you need to. If you are dealing with a network that strips the X.121 address component, such as Transpac, and you want to use subaddressing, then the server side needs to bind to the subaddress part only.

The address structure for X.25 is defined in the file x25addrstr.h:

```
/* Maximum # bytes in protocol-ID                            */
#define X25_MAX_PIDLEN 8

/* Maximum # BCD digits in X.121 address                     */
#define X25_MAXHOSTADDR 15

/* X25_MAXHOSTADDR+1                                          */
#define X25_MAXHP1 X25_MAXHOSTADDR+1

/* MUST BE (X25_MAXHOSTADDR + 1) >> 1                         */
```

```
#define X25_MAX_HOST_ADDR_BYTES ((X25_MAXHOSTADDR+1) >> 1)

/* Maximum interface name length                              */
#define X25_MAX_IFNAMELEN 12
struct x25addrstr {
    u_short x25_family;   /* Must contain AF_CCITT            */
#define x25family x25_family
    u_char x25hostlen;
    u_char x25pidlen;      /* # bytes in protocol ID          */
    u_char x25pid[X25_MAX_PIDLEN];/* protocol-ID              */
    u_char x25_host[X25_MAXHP1]; /* X.121 address, BCD or ASCII*/
#define x25host x25_host
    char x25ifname[X25_MAX_IFNAMELEN + 1];
    /* Identifies X.25 card, by name                          */
};
```

The `x25_family` field must be set to `AF_CCITT`. The `x25hostlen` field must contain the number of digits in the X.121 address for the host.

For `connect()`, the `x25pid` and `x25pidlen` fields of the structure are not used. You must use the call `ioctl(X25_WR_USER_DATA)` to specify a `CUDF` prior to the `connect()`, which will be described later in this chapter.

On the call-receiving side, before binding the application program should set the first `x25pidlen` bytes of the `x25pid[]` field in the `x25addrstr` structure to be the protocol-ID desired. This information must be made known to client programs, so they can connect to it. Specify `x25pidlen == 0` if you are not using the protocol-ID convention.

You may wish to specify additional information in the call user data field. This may be done after you write the protocol-ID information, or the two writes may be done at the same time.

Not all implementations provide for the various forms of addressing available in X.25. Again, you'll need to check the vendor's documentation.

10.1.5   Example: `x25addrstr` Setup

```
#define HOST "30912345678"        /* Sample host address      */
#include <sys/types.h>
#include <sys/socket.h>
#include <x25/ccittproto.h>
#include <x25/x25.h>
#include <x25/x25addrstr.h>

struct x25addrstr addrstr;

addrstr.x25_family = AF_CCITT;   /* Set up address-family.    */
addrstr.x25hostlen = strlen(HOST);
```

```
strncpy(addrstr.x25_host, HOST, X25_MAX_HOSTADDR,
                                        X25_MAX_HOSTADDR);
strncpy(addrstr.x25ifname, "transpac1", X25_MAX_IFNAMELEN);
```

10.1.6   Creating an X.25 Socket

These are created just like any other kind of socket, except that the address family is
AF_CCITT and the protocol must be defined, or defaulted, to X.25:

```
s = socket (AF_CCITT, SOCK_STREAM, X25_PROTO_NUM);
```

The third parameter may be zero. By specifying X25_PROTO_NUM you are explicitly
telling the implementation you want X.25. This would be unnecessary and redundant
except if there were other protocols within the CCITT suite of protocols implemented on
that platform.

The socket () system call may return[13] ENOBUFS if insufficient network buffer
memory is available to support the socket. EPROTOTYPE or EPROTONOSUPPORT
will be returned if the address family or protocol or type fields are not specified as per
the above example or if the kernel was **not** built with X.25 in it.

10.2   Client Side Setup

A connection can be initiated with merely one system call: connect (). In the
simplest cases, the steps necessary to set up a connection are the same as when using
TCP: Create a socket, initialize a structure with address information, and call
connect (). If, however, you desire to make use of the X.25 protocol features
(termed "Facilities"), specify a call user data field (CUDF), or set the connection into
certain modes, you must use ioctl ()s to pass these parameters to the kernel. You
must do so **before** you call connect () if you're going to use these features. You
might, for example, wish to specify flow control parameters,[14] reverse charging (similar

---

13. For brevity, we use the expression "returns Exxxx" instead of the clumsier, "returns -1, and
errno is set to Exxxx".

14. Flow control parameters are the DATA packet size (in bytes) and the number of packets that
can be sent before requiring an acknowledgment (called the "send window," or sometimes
the W parameter). These parameters control the flow of data from the receiver's side, because
only a limited amount of data (packet size times W) can be sent until the receiver
acknowledges any of it. Flow control parameters may be fixed by the subscription, or the
subscription may permit them to be negotiated. In the latter case, the initiator of the
connection proposes values, but the DCEs and the peer application process may modify
them. Flow control and throughput class are the only parameters that are negotiable in any
real sense. The other facilities parameters are on a "take it or leave it" basis.

to calling collect with a telephone), or Fast Select (described in more detail later in this chapter). For a complete list of the possible Facilities, see the X.25 Recommendation.

Note that the request will fail if the called side has not yet created a listen socket with the specified address. This is just like TCP: If a request for connection arrives, but there is no listen socket with matching address information, the connection is cleared automatically.

10.2.1   The `connect()` System Call

Use `connect()` like this:

```
int s, addr_len, error;
struct x25addrstr addr;

s = socket (AF_CCITT, SOCK_STREAM, X25_PROTO_NUM);

addr.x25_family = AF_CCITT;/* Set up address-family.*/
addr.x25hostlen = strlen(HOST);
addr(addrstr.x25_host, HOST, X25_MAX_HOSTADDR, X25_MAX_HOSTADDR);
strncpy(addr.x25ifname, "transpac1", X25_MAX_IFNAMELEN);
addr.x25pidlen = 1;            /* 1 byte for protocol-ID      */
addr.x25pid[0] = 0x55;         /* Using Protocol ID 55        */
error = connect(s, &addr, sizeof(struct x25addrstr));
```

Notice that the `addr` parameter passed in `connect()` is not a `struct sockaddr` or `sockaddr_in`, but an `x25addrstr`, whose size is also different. The caller must know the X.121 address of the DTE, including any subaddressing and protocol-IDs that may be needed. Address and subaddress are included in the `addr` parameter. Protocol-ID must be the first portion of the call user data, which is set with an **ioctl()** call we discuss later.

Unless the socket has been placed in nonblocking mode, the user process will be blocked until the virtual circuit is set up or until a disconnect is received. X.25 specifies the maximum amount of time within which the circuit must be either confirmed or destroyed. These timers run several minutes (see the X.25 specs for details). If the socket is in nonblocking mode, then **EINPROGRESS** will be returned, and the socket **cannot** be used to send data until the virtual circuit is set up (**ENOTCONN** will be returned on **send()** and **recv()** until it is). If the connection succeeds, and the socket is in blocking mode, then `connect()` returns zero. The socket will then be in a state where **send()** and **recv()** calls may be issued on it.

If any errors were detected, then the `connect()` system call will return with the value −1, and the programmer must check `errno` to find out the cause of the error. Other than EINPROGRESS (which isn't really an error), the programmer must arrange to close the socket on errors, so that the kernel can release its resources. There may be call user data (CUD), which can be read from an `ioctl()` call, but you must close the socket eventually. Don't try to reuse it: The system attaches too much information during the initial stages of the connection setup, and it isn't reinitialized when an error occurs. The best method is to close the socket and **then** retry (if you're going to).

The following values may be returned in `errno`:

`EINPROGRESS`: `connect()` issued on a socket that's in nonblocking mode; this value means that the connection has been initiated, but is not yet complete.

`EDESTADDRREQ`: The programmer didn't specify an `x25addrstr` structure in the second parameter.

`EINVAL`: can mean any of the following:

- The third parameter's value is not `sizeof(struct x25addrstr)`.

- The X.121 address is invalid (length < one or > 15, or character in `x25_host[]` is not in the range `'0'` to `'9'`).

- A `connect()` call is issued on a socket that was connecting, but not connected (that is, the connection not fully established); this can happen if the socket was in nonblocking mode, so that the `connect()` call did not block the caller, and another `connect()` call was issued on it.

- The specified socket has been connected. For example, it was connected, it has been cleared, and now the user is attempting to reconnect with it. You're not permitted to do this. The proper way to handle such a situation is to close the old socket when the circuit dies (optionally, after reading any Facilities, and OOB or CUD data it may have); create a new socket; then `connect()` it.

`ENOTCONN`: The local side detected an error.

`ENOBUFS`: Insufficient system networking memory is available to support the connection.

`EAFNOSUPPORT`: `x25_family` does not contain `AF_CCITT`.

`ENETDOWN`: The X.25 interface specified in the `x25_ifname` field either does not exist or is not in the initialized state: It has been shut down or the link level connection has been lost, because of transitory conditions, such as unusually lengthy periods of high electrical interference in the wires, or because some equipment failed. When the interference goes away or the equipment is repaired, the link will automatically reestablish the connection. The X.25 subsystem will automatically become usable again when the link is restored, but all preexisting connections will have been terminated. This is a specified recovery procedure in X.25, when level 2 goes down. The user is not notified; therefore, you must keep trying if you want to recover.

ECONNREFUSED: A CLEAR packet arrived instead of a CALL ACCEPTED packet. This could mean that the remote DTE refused the connection, that the addresses specified lacked a matching listen socket, that the remote DTE is not responding to its DCE (system or its modem is turned off or not responding), or that the network provider cleared the call. These cases are sometimes distinguishable by reading the cause and diagnostic codes, which some networks provide in the CLEAR packets, with the out-of-band data read mechanism (see "Receiving-Out-of-Band Data" later in this chapter).

EISCONN: A connect() call was issued on a socket that was already connected.

If the socket is in a nonblocking state, the caller will resume execution, and the error EINPROGRESS will be returned. Select() can be used to determine when the connection has been set up (it will "select" for writing). Please see Section 4.6, "Cautionary Note," because it also applies to X.25 sockets.

After the call is set up, you may wish to use the X25_RD_FACILITIES ioctl() to check that the negotiated parameters (Facilities, and so forth) are acceptable. Negotiable parameters mean just that: The call initiator proposes values, and the switching equipment can change them, as can the call recipient. They are **not renegotiable**: If you don't like the parameters at this point, you cannot change them. You have only two choices: Go ahead and use the circuit anyway, or clear it.

10.3   Passive Call Setup

The passive side is set up differently, but the procedure is just the same as for TCP. You bind() an address to the socket, call listen() to specify that the socket is a "listen socket," and call accept() to get a connected socket. The general picture is the same as you've seen with TCP and UDP, but the details of the data structures are different.

The server must have completed its initialization of the socket before the client attempts to connect; otherwise, the client will get an **ECONNREFUSED** error. Recovery for that case would be to exit or else to close the socket, sleep a while, and try again later, creating a new socket. The client can't use a socket again if the connect() call failed; it has been "polluted," so to speak.

To prepare to receive incoming calls, the passive side must perform the same three system calls as when using AF_INET sockets:

1.   Create a socket.

2.   Bind the socket to an address.

3.   Make the socket a listen socket.

10.3.1 The `bind()` System Call and Address Matching

The `bind()` system call assigns an address to the socket. This address will be used to decide which incoming calls should be delivered to it (called **call matching**). The address information can be one of the following:

- an X.121 address
- an X.121 address plus a subaddress
- a protocol-ID
- any combination of the foregoing.

Addressing in X.25 is more complicated than in TCP, because of these different modes and because the different address components can have different lengths. With TCP, there is only one port number (always 16 bits), and one IP address (always 32 bits).

The simplest case would be to bind the address of the socket to the X.121 address of the interface (the DTE's X.121 address), with no subaddress and no protocol-ID. Without any further addressing, this is tantamount to saying "All incoming calls shall be delivered to this socket." If this one program is the only one that will ever receive any incoming X.25 calls, this is one way to do that. It is more practical, however, to provide more bits of addressing, so that multiple X.25 servers may exist in the computer. Just as it would be confusing to give the same telephone number to different people, it would be confusing (and therefore disallowed) if you try to `bind()` an address which is already bound to another socket. Address matching proceeds from left to right in address strings, so the leftmost portion of the string **must** be the address assigned to the DTE. For example, if your DTE address is 1234, you could `bind()` to "1234" or to any string beginning with "1234" and not longer than 15 digits. The substring appearing to the right of the DTE address is called the **subaddress**. The subaddress is ignored by the network provider's switching equipment. It is therefore available for us to use. As we saw in Figure 10.4, one possible use is to share the use of one X.25 link among several computers. Another use is to address a particular socket in the computer, distinguishing it from the others. These uses may be combined.

You specify address information to the kernel in the `x25addrstr` structure. The combinations of address, subaddress, and protocol-ID are specified in the different fields of this structure:

- The `x25_family` field must be set to `AF_CCITT`.
- The `x25ifname` field is used to specify a particular X.25 interface (names are assigned to them by the system administrator when the X.25 subsystem is configured). If this field contains a null string (an end-of-string marker in the first byte), then the `bind()` applies across all the existing X.25 interfaces. The meaning of a null string in the `x25ifname` field for `bind()` is different than for `connect()`. If

the x25ifname field contains the name of an X.25 interface, then the bind() applies only to calls arriving on that interface. The subsystem will look up that interface by name. If found, that interface's address will be used as part of the incoming call matching. If the x25hostlen field is also zero, then the subsystem will fill in the X.121 address of the specified interface.

•   The unsigned char array x25_host[] contains the X.121 address.

•   The x25hostlen field specifies the number of digits in the address. If you do not specify an X.121 address (x25hostlen = 0), then calls arriving over any of the X.25 interfaces can be matched to this socket (subject to matching on the rest of the address information, that is). If you specify an X.121 address with subaddress digits, only calls matching this address exactly can be delivered to this socket.

•   The x25pidlen field specifies the number of bytes of the protocol-ID.

•   The unsigned char array x25pid[] contains the protocol-ID.

In both the Sun and the HP implementations, the programmer only deals with addresses in ASCII. The implementation converts to and from BCD as necessary.

Here is an example of how to use bind():

```
int s, addr_len;
struct x25addrstr bind_addr;

s = socket (AF_CCITT, SOCK_STREAM, X25_PROTO_NUM);

    /* fill in the bind_addr fields                           */
error = bind(s, &bind_addr, addr_len);
```

The "fill in the bind_addr fields" part depends on what form of addressing you choose to use. These are described in subsequent sections.

If you use subaddressing, you might want to use ioctl(skt, X25_RD_HOSTADDR, &adr). This copies the X.121 address of the named X.25 interface into an x25addrstr structure (here, adr). You might, for example, want to use this ioctl() to read the address of the X.25 interface, and then append the subaddress digit(s) you want to use for your server. In this way, you can write programs that don't depend upon hard-coded X.121 addresses.

The bind() system call does not block. Control returns to the user. The socket is not in any state where **send()** or **recv()** system calls can be issued on it; doing so will return ENOTCONN errors.

The bind() system call may return the following errors:

EAFNOSUPPORT: The x25_family field does not contain AF_CCITT.

EADDRINUSE: Address is already bound for another socket.

EADDRNOTAVAIL: Address specified overlaps with an existing address.

EDESTADDRREQ: No address structure was passed in the `bind()` system call.

ENODEV: No X.25 interface with this name.

ENETDOWN: The interface so named exists, but it has been shut down, or the link level connection has been lost. You may `bind()` even if the Level 2 is down, but not if it's been shut down or never initialized.

EINVAL: The size of the structure passed in the system call was not equal to `sizeof(struct x25addrstr)`; the X.121 address was not of legal format; the user structure specified a negative address length; the user structure specified a negative protocol-ID length; either of these fields is specified too large; or the user's socket has been, at one time in the past, in the connected state.

ENOBUFS: Insufficient networking memory available.

EISCONN: `bind()` issued against a socket that is already connected.

10.3.2   Matching by Called Address Only

If at binding time the `x25hostlen` field is positive, then the only incoming calls that will be accepted on that socket are those matching the binding address. If the incoming call has an address length that is longer than the socket's bound address (as when it contains a subaddress), then the match will fail.

The following example shows how the `bind()` call should be used for this case. Only those incoming calls arriving at the specified interface, and bearing exactly its X.121 address (no subaddress digits) will be accepted on the listen socket s, because no subaddressing or protocol-ID matching is used.

```
struct x25addrstr bind_addr;
int s;

/* assume that the bind_addr.x25ifname[] field
   has been set to either an empty string, or the
   name of the X.25 interface which should handle
   the Call.  You must also set x25_family to AF_CCITT. */

error = ioctl(s, X25_RD_HOSTADR, &bind_adr);
if (error < 0) {
    perror("X25_RD_HOSTADR");
    exit(1);
}
bind_addr.x25pidlen = 0;
```

```
error = bind(s, &bind_addr, sizeof(struct x25addrstr));
```

The X25_RD_HOSTADR ioctl() stores the X.121 address of the interface named into an x25addrstr structure. The name must previously have been set in the structure by the caller. Since all arriving calls on the named interface match this socket in this method, there can be at most one socket using this form of addressing, per interface.

10.3.3   Matching by Subaddress

The method above can be extended to use subaddressing and also to a "wildcard" part of a subaddress. It is only necessary to append the subaddress, or portion thereof, to the bind() address, as shown above. If you want to have more than one server process, then you need to use one of the available forms of addressing, over and above the X.121 address of the DTE: either subaddressing or protocol-ID. Subaddressing may not be available to every host node. In the following example, subaddress 05 is used by the code fragment shown. Client programs will need to know both the X.121 address of the X.25 interface that the server is using and that this server is using subaddress 05. Note that other subaddresses that begin with 05 but contain more than two digits would not match; for instance, subaddresses 050 through 059 (inclusive) would not match. Since no protocol-ID is specified in this example (bind_addr.x25pidlen == 0), the match ignores whatever protocol-ID may exist in the CALL packet.

```
struct x25addrstr bind_addr;
int s;
/* assume the bind_addr.x25ifname[] field has been set to specify
   the interface that is wanted, or else an empty string. You must
   also set the X25_family field to AF_CCITT.                    */
error = ioctl(s, X25_RD_HOSTADR, &bind_adr);
if (error < 0) {
   perror("X25_RD_HOSTADR");
   exit(1);
}
/* Now the bind_addr structure has
   the local node's X.121 address filled in.                    */
strcat(bind_addr.x25_host, "05");
bind_addr.x25hostlen = strlen(bind_addr.x25_host);
bind_addr.x25pidlen = 0;
error = bind(s, &bind_addr, sizeof(struct x25addrstr));
```

10.3.4 Matching by Protocol-ID

Another way to identify a server is to use a protocol-ID. X.25 has a programming convention that the first part of the call user data field in the CALL Request packet can be used for addressing in the destination. This is called the protocol-ID. It can be of various numbers of bits. A length parameter, and the option of supplying a "mask," which is bitwise ANDed, are provided to handle these cases. The length specifies the number of bytes in the protocol-ID. The mask determines which bits from the protocol-ID are significant, and will be discussed in the example following this one. The default is a mask with all bits on and a length of eight bytes. The following example shows how to set a binding address for a protocol-ID without the use of a mask.

```
struct x25addrstr bind_addr;
int s;

/* assume that the bind_addr.x25ifname[] field has been
/* set to either an empty string, or the name of the X.25
/* interface which should handle the Call.                 */

error = ioctl(s, X25_RD_HOSTADR, &bind_adr);

/* Now the bind_addr structure has had
   the local node's X.121 address filled in.                */

if (error < 0) {
   perror("X25_RD_HOSTADR");
   exit(1);
}
/* Set the protocol-ID to 0x0105.                           */
/* No subaddressing is added.                               */

bind_addr.x25pidlen = 2;
bind_addr.x25pid[0] = 0x01;
bind_addr.x25pid[1] = 0x05;
error = bind(s, &bind_addr, sizeof(struct x25addrstr));
```

10.3.5 Address Matching with a Mask

Address matching with a mask applies to protocol-ID addressing. Sometimes it isn't feasible to define specific addresses, such as when you want "wildcards." Or sometimes the protocol-ID you need to use isn't an integral number of bytes. The x25_mask_data structure and the X25_WR_MASK_DATA ioctl() call are used to set a mask. The mask length must be the same as the protocol-ID length.

   The address-masking mask works as follows. Bytes from the incoming CALL packet's call user data field are masked against the x25_mask_data of the mask. The number of bytes in the mask is taken from the x25pidlen field. Bytes are bitwise

ANDed. After being masked, each byte of the address is compared to the corresponding byte in the protocol-ID field of the first X.25 listen socket. If unequal, then the comparison fails, and the operation is repeated for the next listen socket in the list. If equal, then the operation continues with the next byte of each field, until a mismatch is found or all protocol-ID bytes have been compared. The length used is taken from the x25_pidlen field of the address bound to the socket. If the protocol-IDs match, this part of the address comparison succeeds. Of course, a subaddress comparison may also be performed, as described previously. If the subaddress also matches or is not used, the incoming call matches the socket.

As indicated by the description just given, you should never specify any bit as one (1) in an address that is masked off, because then it's impossible for an inbound call to be matched to that socket. For example, a protocol-ID of 0x05 is acceptable with a mask of 0x07, but specifying a mask of 0x04 for the same protocol-ID would be a mistake.

```
This field        is ANDed with      and compared to

Call-user         x25_mask           x25_pid
data byte         data byte          data byte
---------         ---------          ---------
0                 0                   0
1                 1                   1
...
x25pidlen         x25pidlen          x25pidlen
```

For example, suppose you wish to accept all incoming calls with protocol-IDs 0xc033, 0xc133, 0xc233, ... 0xcf33. Set the bind() protocol-ID to 0xc033, and the mask to 0xf0ff, which says (with the binding-address set to 0xf033) that any value in the range 0xf033 to 0xff33 can be accepted.

```
int s;
struct x25_mask_data input_parms;

input_parms.x25_masklen = 2;
input_parms.x25_mask[0] = 0xf0;
input_parms.x25_mask[1] = 0xff;
error = ioctl(s, X25_WR_MASK_DATA, &input_parms);

/* set the binding address,
   as shown in the previous example                              */

error = ioctl(s, X25_RD_HOSTADR, &bind_adr);
if (error < 0) {
   perror("X25_RD_HOSTADR");
   exit(1);
}
/* Set the protocol-ID to 0xc033.                                */
bind_addr.x25pidlen = 2;
```

```
bind_addr.x25pid[0] = 0xc0;
bind_addr.x25pid[1] = 0x33;
error = bind(s, &bind_addr, sizeof(struct x25addrstr));
```

10.3.6   The `listen()` System Call

Also part of the precall setup, the `listen()` system call is used to establish a place for incoming calls to be queued. This system call establishes the specified socket as a "listen socket," sometimes referred to as a "call socket." The system call is used just as with TCP or UDP:

```
error = listen(s, backlog);
```

where s is a socket, created with the `socket()` system call. It must previously have been bound to an address via a `bind()` system call. The `backlog` parameter is an integer. Some BSD socket implementations silently reduce this to five, if you specify a larger value; the HP implementation will allow up to 20. This limit is intended to prevent huge numbers of incoming calls from tying up large amounts of system resources.

It is an error to attempt to send or receive data, or to `connect()`, using any socket created with address-family `AF_CCITT` and protocol X.25 that are marked as "listen sockets" (`EOPNOTSUPP` is returned). This type of socket is not capable of sending or receiving data. It has only two purposes: to provide a rendezvous point for incoming calls, and to serve for passing facilities, address-matching parameters, and other information regarding how to field incoming calls.

Incoming calls that match the address previously bound to any listen socket will be queued on that socket. Whether the kernel automatically answers that call or not depends on you. In X.25 you have the option of letting the system automatically respond to incoming calls (this is the default), or your application can do it. If you decide not to accept the call, simply `close()` the socket. This will generate the `CLEAR Request` packet. You may wish to check the caller's address and call parameters first. You might wish to reject calls that reverse the charges. If you wish to control this decision, use the `ioctl()` command `X25_CALL_ACPT_APPROVAL` on the listen socket; it cannot be "undone." When you do this, `accept()` will still yield a new socket for each invocation and incoming connection request pair, but the call will not be answered automatically. It is up to you to accept the call (see the `X25_SEND_CALL_ACPT` discussion, Section 10.8.7) or to `close()` the newborn socket. This clears the call. If you are handling your own call responses, be sure to respond within about three minutes, because the DTE that initiated the connection and the DCE that is nearest the call recipient maintain timers. Calls must be answered or rejected within this time period, typically three minutes. If not, the call will be cleared.

The `listen()` call returns `EINVAL` if made against a connected or connecting socket. `EDESTADDRREQ` is returned if no bind address has been established (including cases where the `bind()` call returned an error).

10.3.7   The `accept()` System Call

This system call causes a new socket to be created when an incoming call has arrived. If no call has yet arrived that matches the binding address of the specified listen socket, the user process blocks (if the listen socket is in blocking mode, that is; if it's in nonblocking mode, the `accept()` call returns `EWOULDBLOCK`). You may include listen sockets in the bitmasks you pass to `select()`. When a listen socket selects readable, this means that it has a connection waiting and thus that an `accept()` on it will not block.

The return value from the `accept()` system call is either −1, to indicate an error, or a new socket. The state of this socket, assuming there was no error, depends upon whether `ioctl(X25_CALL_ACPT_APPROVAL)` was issued on the listen socket or not. If not, the socket will already be in the "connected" state, as will the virtual circuit,[15] and ready for transfer of data. If the `X25_ACPT_APPROVAL ioctl()` has been issued on the listen socket, then this "newborn" socket will not be in the ready-to-transfer-data state until the `X25_SEND_CALL_ACEPT ioctl()` has been issued on it.

A socket in the connected state will remain in that state until any one of the following occurs:

- The local process or local DCE clears the call (`close()` system call) specifying that socket.

- The local process, or any other of its children or parents who also "own" the same socket (like files, they are inherited across `fork()`s), issues a `shutdown(skt, 1)` or `shutdown(skt, 2)` on the socket.

- The remote process or remote DCE clears the call.

- The remote process, or any other of its children or parents who also "own" the same socket, issues a `shutdown(skt, 1)` or `shutdown(skt, 2)` on the socket.

---

15. Whether or not the socket is in the "connected" state is somewhat independent of whether or not the circuit is in that state. For the most part, though, they do remain in the same state together.

- The system administrator at either end begins a Restart sequence[16] (this includes shutdown of the X.25 interface or reconfiguring it).
- The local or remote DCE begins a Restart sequence.
- The data link level (Level 2) connection drops.

After any of the foregoing events occurs, any `send()` system call specifying the associated socket will return an `ENOTCONN` error. Further `recv()` calls may be used to retrieve whatever data remains; otherwise, EOF status (zero length) will be returned.

If a non-NULL pointer is specified in the `from` parameter in a `recvfrom()` call, and the `fromlen` parameter is `sizeof(struct x25addrstr)`, then the `from` structure will be loaded with the address of the calling DTE. The `fromlen` will be returned with the number of bytes of valid data in `from`. All this is exactly the same as with TCP and UDP sockets, except for the structure of the address information parameter `from`. If the "Calling DTE" field in the packet was absent, then `fromlen` will be set to zero.

In conjunction with the `X25_CALL_ACPT_APPROVAL ioctl()`, you can make whatever authenticity checks you wish by using this returned information before accepting the call. Even if your server is relatively innocuous if accessed by unauthorized clients, your finance department probably will object to having to pay for the call (reversing the charges is one of the Facilities codes that can be specified). In the particular case of the HP implementation, one of the X.25 subsystem configuration parameters controls whether **any** reverse-charged calls will be accepted. Still, it's a good idea to check anyway, since there may be other applications also running in the same machine that will accept such calls.

Properties from the listen socket such as the process group ID, and the inbound and outbound message sizes, are inherited by the new socket. The "listen" socket remains allocated and will be the rendezvous point for any other calls that may arrive.

Subsequent changes in any parameter of the listen socket will affect calls that arrive later but not those that arrived before the change.

10.3.8   When a **CALL Request** Packet Arrives Example

Figure 10.3 showed the simple exchange of packets that takes place when a connection is being established and the called process is permitted the system to automatically answer calls. Figures 10.5 through 10.8 will show some other cases. The listen socket is in blocking mode in each of these cases.[17]

---

16. A Restart sequence means exactly that: The link is restarted. All SVCs are cleared; PVCs, which of course cannot be cleared, receive resets, which is how users of any circuit are informed of possible loss of data. Restart sequences occur anyway if the link level drops, as can happen, for example, if the modem loses carrier for a sustained length of time.

Figure 10.5 illustrates how the actions differ when the server process is handling its own call acceptances. The case shown is when the server chooses to accept an incoming connection. What's different about this diagram? Notice that the client side is the same, but the server ("called side" in the diagram) issues `ioctl()` with `X25_CALL_ACPT_APPROVAL` on the listen socket. This action must be taken prior to issuing the `listen()` call. Otherwise, any `CALL Indication` packets that arrive will be accepted automatically. This is because sockets are initially created in the "automatically accept calls" mode. In Figure 10.5, the server process determines to accept the call, so it issues `ioctl()` with `X25_SEND_CALL_ACPT`.

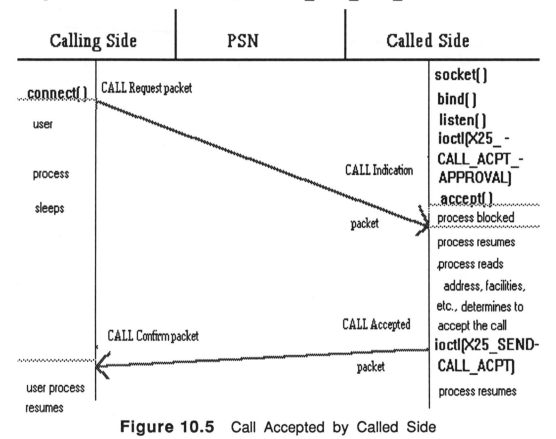

Figure 10.5 Call Accepted by Called Side

---

17. You can place any socket in nonblocking mode through the use of `ioctl()` or `fcntl()`. If you place the listen socket in nonblocking mode, then `accept()` system calls will not block. If there is a cennection pending on that socket, it will be handled in the same manner as for blocking mode, but if there is no pending connection, `accept()` returns with `EWOULDBLOCK` (or `EAGAIN`, depending upon which method you used to put the socket into nonblocking mode).

Figure 10.6 is similar to Figure 10.5, except it illustrates how the actions differ when the server process chooses to reject an incoming call. The server calls `close()` to clear the call.

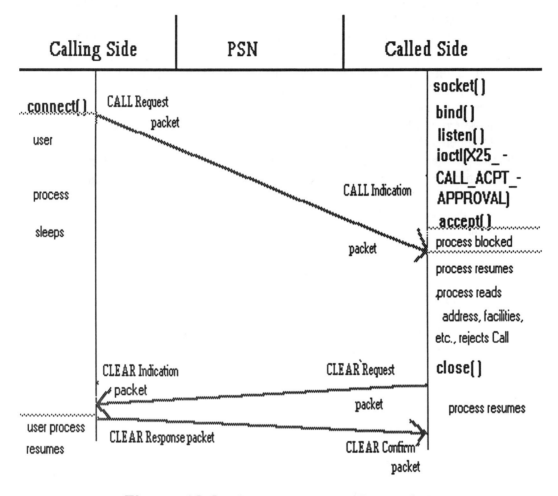

Figure 10.6 Call Rejected by Called Side

10.4   The D-bit

The "D-bit" is a bit in the X.25 DATA packet. Setting this bit requests a form of end-to-end acknowledgment. Normally, the flow-control acknowledgment packet for that DATA packet comes from the DCE closest to the sender. However, when the D-bit is set, the local DCE still passes the data along but does not send any acknowledgments. There is still an acknowledgment, but it is generated by the DCE closest to the receiver.

Thus, it would appear that if you are using the D-bit and receiving regular acknowledgments for the data you are sending, this means the peer has received the data, right? This is not always the case. In many implementations (HP's among them), microprocessors form the basis for the lower layers in the protocol stack. This raises the question, "Does the acknowledgment mean that the remote's lower layers received the DATA packet, or does it mean that the remote's application has received the packet?" The answer to this question is implementation dependent. Since in general it is best to write applications that work across a broad range of situations, many application programmers forgo the use of the D-bit, even when it's available. There is another reason for this, too: Using the D-bit reduces throughput. This is because the acknowledgment has to wait until the packet traverses the network. Longer delays in the acknowledgments slow down the data flow.

In the HP implementation, if you want the acknowledgment to signify that the remote application program actually received the data, each side must express this desire to the subsystem, but they do so differently. The side initiating the connection has the easier job: It simply issues the X25_SEND_TYPE ioctl() on the socket, any time between the socket() call and the connect() call. The called side accomplishes this in two parts: by notifying the subsystem that the application will be providing the call acceptance (X25_CALL_ACPT_APPROVAL ioctl(); you must prevent the CALL Accepted packet from being sent until after you've set the D-bit mode on the new socket), and also by issuing the X25_SEND_TYPE ioctl(), with the D-bit set, on the newly-created socket. This must be done prior to accepting the call (with the X25_ACCEPT_CALL ioctl()). These ioctl()s are explained later (see Section 10.8.6, "How to Control Which Calls You Accept," and Section 10.8.7, "How to Accept a Call").

10.5   Sending Data

Sending data is easy:

```
int count, len, flags, s;
char *msg;
count = send(s, msg, len, flags);
```

where s is the socket, msg is the address of the first byte of the message, and len is the number of bytes to send.

Fragmentation into packets is handled by the system. Thus, if len is larger than the packet size,[18] then msg will automatically be sent in several packets, all but the last of

---

18. The maximum size of any packet is set by the subscription or negotiated, when flow control negotiation is permitted and used. Regardless, the maximum size will be a power of two in the range 64 through 4096.

which have the "more data bit" set to one, and the last one has this bit set to zero. Reassembly at the receiving side will also be automatic.

X.25/9000 treats each message as one unit, preserving the boundary. Recall that TCP treats data as a byte stream, with no boundaries. Consequently, TCP is free to send as much data as it chooses. It does so on the basis of fairly complicated send-policy algorithms, designed to optimize throughput without choking the network gateways. X.25/9000, however, requires you to specify the maximum message size (if it will be larger than the default size, which is 4K bytes in each direction) via the setsockopt() system call. If you don't, and if you attempt to send a message size larger than that, the attempt will fail with the EMSGSIZE error. On inbound, the system checks the size of the message as it's being reassembled. If the reassembled size is larger than that, it will discard what could potentially be an unlimited-size message and resets the circuit.

For ordinary data, len must be in the range one through the maximum message size defined for the socket. The default is 4096 bytes. Using setsockopt() to increase the outbound size well past the maximum size of any message you will send—even to the maximum allowed by the socket layer—increases the amount of outbound buffering available and so can help improve performance. It costs only a system call in time and only the amount of memory that you've sent. Note, however, that if your application is one that always sends a message and waits for the response (request/reply type), then extra outbound buffering achieves nothing. In this case, you would benefit more from setting the outbound size to only sizeof your_largest_message, or leaving the default of 4096 if that's larger.

To send ordinary data, set the flags parameter to zero. To send INTERRUPT packet data, set flags to MSG_OOB. The returned count indicates the number of bytes transmitted (or minus one for error).

Errors occur if an attempt is made to send over a socket that is no longer connected (ENOTCONN) or is too large (EMSGSIZE).

The send() call is normally nonblocking, except for three cases:

- There isn't sufficient network buffer memory, and the socket is in blocking mode.

- The total number of bytes in the outbound transmission queue, plus len, equals or exceeds the specified outbound socket buffer size (your process will block until the queue drains enough that your data will now "fit" in that maximum size), and the socket is in blocking mode.

- You are using D-bit transmission, and the socket is in blocking mode (your process blocks until the acknowledgment is received).

10.5.1   Using `send()` Over PVCs

The `send()` system call is the same for PVCs as for SVCs, but you will not receive notification if the process at the other end of the circuit aborts, and there is no "circuit opening handshake" as with SVCs. Both exceptions result from the nature of **permanent** Virtual Circuits. If you are sending to an HP/9000/S300 or S800 X.25 on a PVC, and there is no process currently "bound" to that circuit at the remote, each time you send data you will receive a `RESET` Indication (see Section 10.6.2, "Receiving Out-of-Band Data"), and the data will be discarded.

There is more of an advantage to keeping each packet free of unnecessary data in WANs, since they take a significant amount of time to transmit. At 64Kbps, for example, each byte takes an eighth of a millisecond. Furthermore, `DATA` packets are of fixed size (for a given connection). Unnecessary data in the messages may cause extra packets to be sent. For example, if the packet size is 128 bytes, and you have one unnecessary byte in a 129-byte message, the message will be transmitted in two packets. This wastes transmission time and network resources, and it probably wastes money. Many X.25 networks have per-packet usage charges, so this extra byte translates directly into increased costs of operation to the end user.

10.5.2   Sending INTERRUPT Packets

As with "normal data," you can send `INTERRUPT` data only when the socket is bound to a circuit that is in the "ready for data transfer" state. An `INTERRUPT` packet containing only one byte of data may be sent as follows:

```
int s;

char intr = 0; /* Set this variable to contain the interrupt data.
               Here, a value of zero is shown, but any of the 256
               codes is allowed.                                  */

error = send(s, &intr, sizeof (char), MSG_OOB);
```

One byte of INTERRUPT data is all that is allowed by networks that are configured as 1980-style. Those configured as 1984 allow up to 32 bytes. More `INTERRUPT` packet data can be sent, as follows:

```
int s;
unsigned char int_buf[32]; /* set this variable to contain the
                              interrupt data                      */
error = send(s, &int_buf, n, MSG_OOB);
```

This sequence sends n data bytes in one `INTERRUPT` packet (n <= 32). If the interface configuration does not support n bytes of `INTERRUPT` packet data, `EMSGSIZE` is returned. If the socket is in blocking mode, the caller remains blocked until the `INTERRUPT Confirm` is received (this happens automatically when the receiving process reads the event; see Section 10.6.2, "Receiving Out-of-Band Data") or a signal or a `RESET` is received. If the socket is in nonblocking mode, the sending process is (of course) not blocked.

The caller will receive `EINVAL` if an attempt is made to send either ordinary or expedited data before the `INTERRUPT` sequence is completed.

10.6   The `recv()` System Call

To read data from an X.25 socket, call `recv()` or `read()`:

```
int s, len, flags, count;
char *buf;
count = recv (s, buf, len, flags);
```

If the socket is in blocking mode, `recv()` causes the caller to be blocked until there is a complete message available to be read. Partially reassembled messages aren't enough, only complete messages are readable. If the socket is in nonblocking mode and there is not a complete message waiting to be read, EWOULDBLOCK[19] is returned. Otherwise, the message will be copied into `buf` (up to its size or `len`, whichever is less). Unless the `MSG_PEEK` bit is set in the `flags` parameter of the `recv()` system call, the message buffers that held it in the kernel will be released.

Use zero for the `flags` parameter to read in-band data (reading out-of-band data is covered in the next section). Each `recv()` returns at most one complete X.25 message. If `len` is smaller than the amount of data in the message, then only `len` bytes will be transferred to the user buffer and the rest will be discarded (unless `MSG_PEEK` is set). If `len` is equal to or larger than the number of bytes queued in the next complete message, the complete message will be copied to the user buffer. The return value of `recv()` yields the number of bytes that were actually transferred to the user's buffer.

The `recv()` call never crosses message boundaries. For example, if a `recv()` call specifies a length of 200 bytes, and there are two messages, of 50 and 150 bytes, in the inbound queue, the first `recv()` will transfer the first 50 to the user's buffer, and another `recv()` will be necessary to get the other 150 bytes.

---

19. There are three ways to set nonblocking mode for a socket: **ioctl()** with **FIONBIO**, **fcntl()** with **O_NONBLOCK**, and **fcntl()** with **O_NDELAY**. Depending on which of these is used, you will observe slightly different behavior for some of the same circumstances. See the manual pages for further details.

10.6.1   Message Definitions

"Complete message" means that all data specified in the send() system call will be sent in a series of one or more complete X.25 packets; all but the last will have the M-("More data to follow")bit set and will be full. The last packet will have the M-bit clear and need not be full. The Q-bit will have the same value in all packets of the message. The D-bit will be clear in each packet except the last, in which it will be set if so requested by the user (see Section 10.8.4 on X25_SEND_TYPE below). When a packet arrives with the M-bit clear, that packet, and all that preceded it with the M-bit set, comprise a complete message.

10.6.2   Receiving Out-of-Band Data

The same mechanism is provided for telling you about INTERRUPT packets, resets, and VC clears: call recv() with MSG_PEEK set in the flags parameter. It is also used if the socket is in nonblocking mode and a confirmation arrives for a previously issued RESET or INTERRUPT request, or an acknowledgment arrives for a message that was sent with the D-bit set. These are all considered "out-of-band events." Diagnostic packets are **not** delivered to you (but they are logged).

Failure to read out-of-band data in a timely manner can cause the out-of-band data queue to overflow. The queue has a fixed maximum size of just under 300 bytes for each socket, but the actual amount queueable could be slightly less, depending on the particular events in the queue and their ordering. If the queue overflows, it is assumed that the user is not paying attention to the SIGURG signal (no signal handler defined, or the process-ID or process-group-ID wasn't set for the socket). The system will then automatically respond to RESET and INTERRUPT indications (sending their respective Responses), but otherwise discards all such events that arrive after the queue fills. No attempt is made to send SIGURG or to queue another event. This determination is made at the attempt to queue the event. Consequently, if your process is polling the socket often enough, it may not actually need a SIGURG handler, although one is recommended. If the queue overflows, your program may experience "unexplained" loss of data. This can happen because you won't know about state changes in the circuit if you're not "listening" for them. If you let the queue overflow, you wouldn't know if a reset occurred.

The recv() system call, with flags = MSG_OOB, is used to read the first event in the queue. The MSG_PEEK flag is honored, with the following semantics:

1. The first event in the out-of-band queue, if any, is transferred to the user.

2. The queue (normally) retains at least the same size after the read. Other events may of course occur afterwards, and they will be added to the queue in the normal manner.

3. If the OOB queue was nonempty on the first read, a subsequent `MSG_OOB recv()` will (normally) retrieve the same information.

4. Two event types, `INTERRUPT` data and `RESET`, require a response. These responses are **not** issued until the event is read **without** `MSG_OOB`.

5. If a `RESET Indication` occurs, this causes everything in the queue to be discarded, and the new `RESET` event is placed in the queue as its only event. Thus, two separate `recv()`s of the OOB queue, the first with `MSG_PEEK` (and for the second it doesn't matter), may not always return exactly the same data.

The following events may occur:

```
/*
 * Defines for Out-of-Band Events (these are defined in x25.h)
 */
#define    OOB_VC_CLEAR            0x0   /* CLEAR Ind rcvd           */
#define    OOB_INTERRUPT           0x1   /* INTERRUPT Ind rcvd       */
#define    OOB_VC_RESET            0x2   /* RESET Ind rcvd           */
#define    OOB_VC_MSG_TOO_BIG      0x3   /* 2big msg rcvd;ckt reset  */
#define    OOB_VC_RESET_CONF       0x4   /* RESET Conf rcvd          */
#define    OOB_VC_INTERRUPT_CONF   0x5   /* INTERRUPT Conf rcvd      */
#define    OOB_VC_DBIT_CONF        0x6   /* D bit ack rcvd           */
#define    OOB_VC_L2DOWN           0x7   /* Level 2 Down - used for
                                           PVCs only                 */
```

The return value from `recv()` provides the number of bytes transferred to the caller's buffer. Receiving out-of-band data is nonblocking; if zero is returned, there were no OOB events queued. A negative return value means an error occurred, and `errno` must be examined to determine the cause. Otherwise, the first byte of the buffer contains the number of bytes in the event (which should match the return value from the `recv()` call); the second byte contains the event code (matching one of the symbols defined in the foregoing table); and the rest of the buffer contains the event data, if any.

The following code fragment illustrates this usage.

```
#define MAX_EVENT_SIZE 34  /* Defines maximum message size    */

int error, s, n, buflen;
unsigned buf[MAX_EVENT_SIZE];

buflen = MAX_EVENT_SIZE;
if ((n = recv(s, buf, buflen, MSG_OOB)) < 0)
   perror("recv MSG_OOB");
else if (n > 0) {
   switch (buf[1]) {
      case OOB_INTERRUPT:
```

```
            printf("INTERRUPT Packet Received\n");
            for (i = 2; i < n; i++)
                printf("%2x ",buf[i]);
            printf("\n");
            break;
        case OOB_VC_RESET:
            printf("RESET Packet Received\n");
            printf("Cause-code:%2x\n",buf[2]);
            if (n >= 4) printf("Diagnostic code: %2x\n",buf[3]);
            if (n >= 5) printf("Reason code: %2x\n",buf[4]);
            break;
        case OOB_VC_CLEAR:
            printf("CLEAR Packet Received\n");
            printf("Cause-code:%2x\n",buf[2]);
            if (n >= 4) printf("Diagnostic code: %2x\n",buf[3]);
            if (n >= 5) printf("Reason code: %2x\n",buf[4]);
            break;
        case OOB_VC_DBIT_CONF:
            printf("D-bit confirmation arrived\n");
            break;
        case OOB_VC_MSG_TOO_BIG:
            printf("A monstrously large message has arrived;\n");
            printf("the circuit has also been reset.\n");
            break;
        case OOB_VC_RESET_CONF:
            printf("The reset sequence is complete;\n");
            printf("the reset confirm has arrived.\n");
            break;
        case OOB_VC_INTERRUPT_CONF:
            printf("The INTERRUPT sequence is complete;\n");
            printf("the INTERRUPT confirm has arrived.\n");
            break;
        case OOB_VC_L2DOWN:
            printf( "The L2 dropped.\n");
            break;
    }
}
```

Events are queued first-in/first-out. In the HP implementation, OOB_VC_RESET causes the contents of the queue to be discarded and the new reset event inserted as its only event. In the Sun Microsystems implementation, events are also queued first-in/first-out, except that INTERRUPT packets go to the head of the queue.

The buf must be a buffer of unsigned char and at least as large as the buflen parameter specifies. The value supplied in buflen should be two bytes larger than the largest possible `INTERRUPT` packet that can be received.   `INTERRUPT` packets cannot contain more than 32 bytes of data (the maximum allowed under the 1984 version of CCITT's X.25 spec, but the peer application program may never send this much), plus two bytes of out-of-band event header (34 total). Support for more than one byte of `INTERRUPT` data may not be available from the network provider or the switching equipment.   A practical lower bound is five bytes, which is the size of `OOB_VC_CLEAR` and `OOB_VC_RESET`. If `buflen` is smaller than the actual number of data bytes in the `INTERRUPT` packet, only the first `buflen` bytes will be stored in the buffer, and (except for `MSG_PEEK`) the rest of the data for that event will be lost.

10.6.3   What the Individual Event Types Mean

10.6.3.1 OOB_VC_RESET

`OOB_VC_RESET` means that a `RESET` was received on the connection. `RESET`s cause all inbound and outbound data queued anywhere in the path between the DTEs, including the switching equipment, to be discarded. Thus, any data that a user process reads **after** an `OOB_VC_RESET` event has been read was received **after** the `RESET` sequence was completed. Reading this event will automatically cause the `RESET` `Confirm` to be sent. If the `RESET` was sent by a process running in an HP9000 computer, and its socket was in blocking mode, the sending process will be blocked until this `Confirm` arrives. Resets may also be generated by any of the equipment in the "X.25 cloud."   Regardless of where the `RESET` was generated, the `RESET` `Confirmation` is still necessary for all of the nodes in the path to complete their state transitions. The state of the connection is ready-for-data-transfer, with no data queued.

The third byte contains the cause code. The fourth byte will contain the diagnostic code. If this contains zero, the diagnostic code may or may not have been present in the original X.25 packet. The X.25 spec describes this parameter as "optional." The DCE, or the firmware, will substitute a zero if the sending party has not included this field. All HP9000 X.25 implementations include the field.

At most one RESET may appear in the queue at any one time. If the queue contains any `RESET`, it will be the first item in the queue.

10.6.3.2 OOB_VC_L2DOWN

This event can only occur if you are using a Permanent Virtual Circuit (PVC). It means that the PVC is no longer usable because the link layer connection was lost, and the association between socket and circuit was destroyed (associating a socket to a PVC is discussed later). This event can occur only to sockets bound to PVCs. Loss of the link layer connection affects ordinary virtual circuits (called "Switched Virtual Circuits," or

SVCs for short) as well, but in a different way. They are cleared, and OOB_VC_CLEAR events will be generated for them. Any further attempts to send data on the PVC will return an error (EINVAL).

10.6.3.3 OOB_VC_CLEAR

This event can only occur on Switched Virtual Circuits (SVCs). It means that a CLEAR Indication packet was received on the circuit, and therefore the circuit cannot send any more data. The circuit is nonexistent, but you can retrieve any data (out-of-band events or ordinary data) that remain queued. Use recv(), with or without MSG_OOB, to retrieve this data. You can retrieve any "facilities" data with the X25_RD_FACILITIES ioctl(). You can retrieve any CLEAR User Data (like the Call User Data Field, but this data appears in CLEAR packets) with the X25_RD_USER_DATA ioctl(). These ioctl()s are discussed in more detail later in this chapter.

The third byte of the returned buffer contains the cause code. The fourth byte will contain the diagnostic code. The fifth byte will contain two if the circuit has been cleared as a result of loss of the level 2 connection (SVCs only), or zero if the circuit is being cleared for a variety of other reasons.

10.6.3.4 OOB_INTERRUPT

OOB_INTERRUPT means that INTERRUPT packet data is available for reading. If this event is read without MSG_PEEK, this causes the INTERRUPT Confirm packet to be sent automatically. If the sender was a process running in an HP9000 computer and its socket was in blocking mode, the sending process will be blocked until this Confirm arrives.

10.6.3.5 OOB_VC_MSG_TOO_BIG

OOB_VC_MSG_TOO_BIG means that the peer process has attempted to send a message that is larger than the defined size for inbound messages. This protects the system from reassembling huge messages. The size of the upper limit is under your control (see the manual page for setsockopt()). If this event is queued, it implies that one of the following is true:

1. The data in that message has been discarded.

2. The circuit has been reset, as a signal to the sending side that data has been lost, and including all other semantics for RESETs.

3. The other side's program contains a programming error (in sending a message which is too large), or that the receiving side's program contains a programming error (in not specifying a large enough message size).

10.6.3.6 OOB_VC_RESET_CONF

This event is generated only when a `RESET Confirm` packet has arrived and the socket is in nonblocking mode at the time of arrival.

10.6.3.7 OOB_VC_INTERRUPT_CONF

`OOB_VC_INTERRUPT_CONF` is similar to `OOB_VC_RESET_CONF`: It means that an `INTERRUPT Confirmation` packet has arrived and at this time the socket is in nonblocking mode.

10.6.3.8 OOB_VC_DBIT_CONF

This event is only generated if you send an ordinary message `send()` with the `flags` parameter zero and the current setting for the D-bit is set (see the discussion in Section 10.8.4 on `ioctl()` `X25_SEND_TYPE`. `OOB_VC_DBIT_CONF` means that the acknowledgment has arrived for a message sent previously which had the D-bit set, and at this time the socket is in nonblocking mode.

10.6.4 Other Ways **SIGURG** Can Occur

The signal `SIGURG` is not specific to the X.25 subsystem. It can be received for other, non-X.25 reasons. If you have more than one X.25 socket open, you will have to poll each socket to find out which one caused the `SIGURG` signal to be sent (use `recv()`). If you have other kinds of sockets open that can cause `SIGURG` to be sent, you will also have to poll those sockets. It is also useful to remember that calling library routines from a signal handler can be a dangerous practice, because not all of them are, or even can be, written to be reentrant. It is usually better to set a global flag in the handler and return. The mainline code checks this flag at appropriate times. You should remember two things about signals in UNIX:

1. If you are using unreliable signals, signals can be lost. With this type of signal handling, if the same signal arrives while the process is running that signal's signal handler, the signal will be lost.

2. Even if you are using reliable signaling (that is `sigvec()`), the fact that your `SIGURG` signal handler has been called means **only** that **at least one** `SIGURG` signal arrived. There may have been more than one. With "reliable signals," if the process is running the

signal handler for that signal and another signal arrives, the kernel queues the signal. When the signal handler returns, the kernel will reenter the handler. This queue is one deep. If another signal arrives and the process is still in the signal handler, the kernel still remembers that **one** signal arrived, but it doesn't remember if more than one arrived. Thus, it will be necessary to poll each and every socket that is created, using methods appropriate to each type, to make sure that **all** causes of these signals have been discovered.

10.6.5 Setting Process-Group ID in a Socket

Any time you are programming and utilizing X.25 sockets, you should set up a signal handler for SIGURG on each socket. Out-of-band events, such as RESETs, CLEARs, and INTERRUPT DATA packets, affect the status of the circuit, and these events are reported asynchronously. Unless you have a SIGURG signal handler established for each socket, you won't know that they have occurred. Thus, you won't really know the status of the circuit at any point in time.

If you use SIGURG, a process ID or process-group ID must have been assigned to the socket. If you assign the process's processgroup-ID (pid) to the socket, all processes in the same process group will receive the SIGURG. If you only want a single process to receive the signal, then you must set a value equal to the process ID. If you want the entire process group to receive the signal, specify the negative of the process ID. The case where only the process itself is to receive the SIGURG is illustrated in the following code fragment:

```
int pgrp;
pgrp = getpid(); /* Set process group, so this process receives
                                 signal                        */
error = ioctl(s, SIOCSPGRP, &pgrp);
```

The HP implementation switched the significance of the sign at the 8.0 release of HP-UX. Consult the manual pages for specific details.

10.7 System Calls for Sockets

10.7.1 Setting Inbound and Outbound Message Sizes

The setsockopt() system call is used to set options on a socket. Since X.25/9000 only handles messages as a complete unit (in other words, "atomically") if you are going to send or receive messages larger than the default (which is 4096 bytes), you must use the setsockopt() system call to inform the system of the new size. There is one size for inbound (for receiving messages) and one size for outbound (for sending messages).

The parameter SO_RCV is used to specify the receive size; SO_SEND specifies the send size. The inbound side is not required to have the same message size as the outbound side. You may set larger values than these, which may improve performance by increasing the amount of buffer memory used for messages. If too-small values are set, the process may receive OOB_MSG_TOO_BIG out-of-band events (described earlier) or EMSGSIZE errors when attempting to send().

10.7.2   The read() System Call

The read() system call executes exactly the same as recv(), with the flags parameter set to zero (that is, it reads only in-band data).

10.7.3   The select() System Call

The term "select readable" means that a read() or recv() issued on the socket would not block; this can mean that there is data available to be read or, in the case of listen sockets, there is a connection pending; or it can mean that the circuit has been cleared (either a shutdown() executed on the socket or the circuit has been cleared by the peer or by the DCE). Select "writable" means that a write() or a send() issued on the socket would not block. This can mean that a send(), specifying no more data than the "write threshold" (see X25_WR_WTHRESHOLD, Section 10.11.3) bytes, will not block, or it can mean that the circuit has been cleared (this can occur with shutdown(1) or shutdown(2) or if the circuit has been cleared).

There are no "exceptional conditions" defined.

10.7.4   The write() System Call

The **write()** system call executes exactly the same as **send()**, with the flags parameter set to zero (that is, it always sends "normal" data).

10.7.5   The shutdown() System Call

The shutdown() system call has two parameters:

```
shutdown (skt, how)
```

The skt parameter is a socket descriptor. The how parameter may have the values zero, one, two, or three; only the two low bits are significant. If the how parameter equals zero, then the socket is marked incapable of receiving more data, but the circuit retains the same state. If how equals one or two, the socket is marked incapable of more sends and receives. In addition, the circuit is cleared, just as with the close() call, except that shutdown() is effective **only** when the **first** process that is using the socket shuts it down, rather than the last as with close(). All close() and shutdown() calls issued against that socket after the circuit has been cleared do nothing further to the circuit, because it has been cleared; the circuit has ceased to exist in relation to the socket. shutdown with how equal to one or two differs from close() in another way: shutdown() does not release all the resources allocated to the socket, whereas close() does.

If the socket has been marked incapable of receiving (but the circuit remains open), and data is received on that circuit, then the circuit will be cleared if it is a switched virtual circuit, and reset if it is a permanent virtual circuit.

10.7.6   The close() System Call

A close() destroys the mapping between the local process's socket descriptor and the socket. If the caller is not the **last** process to close() the socket, or if it terminates but is not the last process using the socket, this is all that close() does.

Otherwise, the resources associated with the socket, including any and all unread data, facilities, and CUDF field, are released. The specific actions that occur on the circuit for the last close() depend on what has occurred prior to its issue and whether it is a switched or permanent virtual circuit.

If the circuit is a switched virtual circuit (SVC) and has already been cleared, or the socket has been shut down, then nothing happens on the circuit, because it's already been cleared. If the circuit is currently in the connected state, then it is cleared. If there is a circuit bound to this socket, then this binding is destroyed. In the case of "colliding disconnects," the other side's CLEAR Indication is taken the same as a CLEAR Confirm.

In the case of PVCs, the **circuit** cannot be closed (it's permanently open, hence the name), but the user process **must** issue close() against the socket to free resources and remove the binding between socket and circuit. That PVC may then be used by another process. If one process opens its PVC, but there is no process at the other side to receive the data, then all attempts to send data will meet with RESETs (assuming both ends of the PVC are X.25/9000; for other cases, consult that system's documentation to determine what it will do when it receives data on a PVC but there is no process ready to receive data). HP considers that it is the user's responsibility to ensure that proper synchronization between the processes at the two endpoints is achieved. This is fairly simple to do. For example, upon starting up, each process can issue a send() on the socket, after creating it and binding it to a particular PVC. It may then attempt a select(), with a specified time limit and setting the bit in the read-map corresponding to the PVC (others may also be set, if desired). If there is data from the other side, then your process can send an acknowledgment. This simple technique will work no matter what the remote implementation does when data arrives with no listener (for example, discard it, or discard it with a RESET). At this point, you have established contact with the peer process. If the `select()` times out or you receive a reset back, then your peer process is not running, so you'll have to keep trying.

10.8   The `ioctl()` System Call

The Berkeley socket-related system calls don't provide a sufficiently complete mapping to the functionality available in X.25. Rather than create a multitude of additional system calls, the Sun Microsystems and HP implementations provide this additional functionality via a rather large number of `ioctl()` commands. For the most part, these provide optional functionality that is intended for more sophisticated purposes rather than simple usages.

10.8.1   Reading the Host Address

This `ioctl()` command `X25_RD_HOSTADR` obtains the host's X.121 address for you. If there are several X.25 interface cards, you must specify which one you want by name. You can specify the first interface with the null string. `X25_RD_HOSTADR` is useful if you wish to load that portion of the address matching into a bind address. You must first fill in the interface name, identifying which interface you want. For example:

```
struct x25addrstr bind_addr;
bind_addr.x25_family = AF_CCITT;
bind_addr.ifname[0] = '\0';  /* or set name of the interface you
                                                 want           */
error = ioctl(s, X25_RD_HOSTADR, &bind_addr);
```

Don't forget to set the `x25_family` field to `AF_CCITT`.

The French national network, Transpac, and some others, operate on subaddresses only, so you will get a zero-length address when the interface is configured for such a network.

10.8.2   Setting the Cause Code and Diagnostic Code

You can use the `ioctl()` command `X25_WR_CAUSE_DIAG` to set the values of the cause code and diagnostic code that will go out in the next user-generated `RESET` or `CLEAR` packet (it has no effect on subsystem-generated `RESET`s and `CLEAR`s). This `ioctl()`, by itself, neither clears nor resets the circuit; it merely informs the system what cause code and diagnostic code you want contained in the next outgoing `RESET` or `CLEAR` packet you issue. These values remain as you set them until you change them. `X25_WR_CAUSE_DIAG` uses the `x25_cause_diag` data structure:

```
struct x25_cause_diag {
    u_char x25_cd_loc_rem;/* 1 if close was local, 0 if remote */
    u_char x25_cd_cause;   /* holds cause-code                  */
```

```
    u_char x25_cd_diag;    /* holds diagnostic code              */
};
```

This `ioctl()` will have no effect if the circuit is already cleared, or is cleared by the provider or peer before you can `close()` it.

If the X.25 interface is configured as being a DTE and to be compliant with the 1980 CCITT X.25 spec, then it is useless to specify anything other than zero for a cause code if you are going to clear the circuit. The implementation will always send a zero in the cause field of the `CLEAR Request` packet, regardless of what you specified. This is a requirement of the 1980 version of X.25. No error is returned to the user. If, on the other hand, the subsystem is configured as 1984-style, the interface is to behave as a DTE, and the cause code has been set to a value other than zero, and if the `RESET` or `CLEAR` is user-generated, the cause code that appears in the `CLEAR` packet will be the value you specified, but its most significant bit will be set (this too is a requirement of the 1984 spec). If you specified a zero in the cause code, then that field in the `CLEAR` will also contain zero.

The following is an example of an `X25_WR_CAUSE_DIAG ioctl()` call in use:

```
struct x25_cause_diag diag;
int s;                             /* socket                      */
diag.x25_cd_cause = whatever_cause_code_you_want;
diag.x25_cd_diag = whatever_diagnostic_code_you_want;
error = ioctl(s, X25_WR_CAUSE_DIAG, &diag);
```

10.8.3   Resetting a VC

If you wish to reset a circuit, use the `X25_RESET_VC ioctl()` command:

```
    error = ioctl(s, X25_RESET_VC, 0);
```

SVCs (when in the "ready-for-transfer" state) and PVCs may be reset the same way. If the socket does not have a virtual circuit associated with it that is in the ready-for-data-transfer state, `EINVAL` is returned. In the case of SVCs, `EINVAL` will be returned if the circuit is not connected.

Executing this `ioctl()` will normally result in a reset indication being received by the peer user. If the peer is also an HP9000 X.25 implementation, it will receive an out-of-band event (`OOB_VC_RESET`). There is no guarantee that the other side will receive a `RESET Indication` for each `RESET` that is initiated, because if the circuit is already in the process of being reset, the additional `RESET` requests are discarded until the first sequence is completed. Or if the circuit is also being cleared, the `CLEAR` takes priority.

`RESET`s imply the possibility that data was lost. They may also be initiated by the network provider, so you should include logic to respond appropriately, even if your peer process **never** sends a `RESET`.

You may also wish to consider preceding X25_RESET_VC with X25_WR_CAUSE_DIAG in order to set the values supplied in the cause code and diagnostic code fields of the RESET packet. You can use these fields to tell the peer why you are resetting the circuit, subject to the restrictions imposed by X.25 specifications:

- 1980-style networks don't let the DTE set any other code but zero.

- If the network interface is configured as a 1984-style DTE, the most-significant bit of the cause code will be set in the RESET packet before it is transmitted, unless the code value is zero. This is because of the way X.25 is defined: DTEs that issue RESETs are allowed to set the cause code field contain either zero or a value in the range 128 through 255, inclusive. You don't have to set this bit, only to be aware that the subsystem will do so for you.

The user's process will be blocked until the RESET Confirm is received, unless the socket is in nonblocking mode. In the case of nonblocking sockets, the out-of-band event OOB_VC_RESET_CONF will be queued (see Section 10.6.2, "Receiving Out-of-Band Data").

10.8.4   Control of the D- and Q-Bits

Some applications require control over the D- and Q-bits. This control is provided via the X25_SEND_TYPE ioctl() call. Some network providers do not permit the D-bit to be set unless it was set in the CALL Request or incoming call, and both the peer DTE and the underlying network and X.25 implementation support its use. If you use this ioctl(), the D- and Q-bit values specified remain as you set them, until you change them. If you specify D=0, then all DATA packets will be transmitted with the D-bit set to zero. If you specified D=1, then only the last packet will be sent with the D-bit set; all those up to the last one will be sent with D-bit clear. This improves throughput, slightly. The Q-bit is similar, but will be set or clear in each DATA packet, according to the value set in the most recently executed X25_SEND_TYPE ioctl(). The Q-bit is carried transparently through the system (the vendor's implementation as well as the network provider's switching equipment). No special action is taken based upon its value, except that you can determine the value of the Q-bit of the next message available to be read via the X_25_NEXT_MSG_STAT ioctl() described subsequently.

The Q-bit may be used by an application to signify "control"-type information to its peer and thus to distinguish it from "data"-type messages. For example, in a file transfer–type application, synchronization messages (which could be used to recover from resets or premature circuit disconnects without having to back up to the beginning of the transfer) could be sent with the Q-bit set, and file data could be sent as Q == 0 messages. In the X.29 Packet Assembler/Disassembler (PAD), the Q-bit is used to signify messages that change any of the PAD's parameters. Use of the D-bit is also subject to the subscription agreement with the network provider. The Q-bit has no significance to the provider and is not covered by subscription (you can use it whenever you want).

For example,

```
int s, send_type;
send_type = 0;
if (you want the Q bit set) send_type |= 1<<X25_Q_BIT;
if (you want the D-bit set) send_type |= 1<< X25_D_BIT;
error = ioctl(s, X25_SEND_TYPE, &send_type);
```

When the socket is first created, the initial values for the D-bit and Q-bit are both zero. If the D-bit is set, then when you send data, your process will be blocked until the last packet is acknowledged.[20] If you are not sending a message with the D-bit set, then your process will not be blocked on the send unless there is insufficient buffer memory available to hold the message.

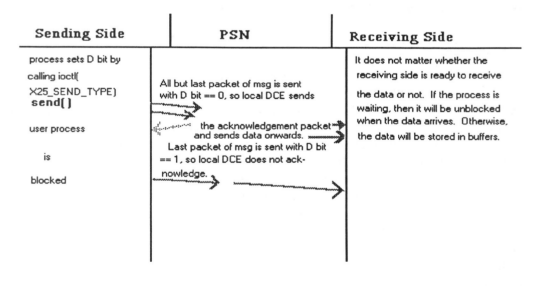

Sending Side	PSN	Receiving Side
process sets D bit by calling ioctl(X25_SEND_TYPE) **send( )**	All but last packet of msg is sent with D bit == 0, so local DCE sends	It does not matter whether the receiving side is ready to receive the data or not. If the process is waiting, then it will be unblocked
user process	the acknowledgement packet and sends data onwards. Last packet of msg is sent with D bit == 1, so local DCE does not ack-	when the data arrives. Otherwise, the data will be stored in buffers.
is		
blocked	nowledge.	

Figure 10.7 DATA Packet Sequence with D-bit set

---

20. Unless the socket is nonblocking. In that case, the process will receive a SIGURG signal and an out-of-band event—OOB_VC_DBIT_CONF—will be queued on the socket when the confirmation arrives; see Section 10.6.2, "Receiving Out-of-Band Data," for more details.

D-bit transmission is illustrated in the diagram shown in Figure 10.7. The diagram depicts the case where a multi-packet message (too large for a single packet) is sent. The user is sending ordinary data with the D-bit set, so the X.25 subsystem will block the process until this sequence is complete. The message requires three DATA packets. The first two are sent with the D-bit clear, so the acknowledgment (ACK in the diagram) comes from the near-side DCE. When the last packet is sent, the D-bit will be set and the M-bit will be clear. This packet is not acknowledged by the near-side DCE, because the D-bit is set. When the packet arrives at the remote DTE, its acknowledgment is carried all the way through the network. When the acknowledgment arrives back to the sender, the sending process resumes execution.

10.8.5   Next Message Status

You can use the X25_NEXT_MSG_STAT ioctl() command to obtain status information on the circuit and the next-available message, its size, and the status of the D- and Q-bits in it. You can also determine if there is call user and or clear user data available to be read. The ioctl() is used by declaring a structure of type x25_msg_stat:

```
struct x25_msg_stat {
    int x25_msg_size;
    int x25_msg_flags;
};
```

Here is an example of how to use this ioctl():

```
struct x25_msg_stat msgstat;
error = ioctl(s, X25_NEXT_MSG_STAT, &msgstat);
```

Upon return, msgstat.x25_msg_size will contain the number of bytes in the next message, or zero if there is no message. The msgstat.x25_msg_flags field returns the D- and Q-bits from the message, but they are valid only at the start of each message. If the x25_msg_size field contains zero, then it is pointless to test the x25_msg_flags field bits X25_D_BIT and X25_Q_BIT bits. The following code fragment illustrates:

```
struct x25_msg_stat msgstat;
error = ioctl(s, X25_NEXT_MSG_STAT, &msgstat);

if (msgstat.x25_msg_flags & (1<<X25_SKT_CONNECTED))
    printf("Circuit is fully connected\n");

if (msgstat.x25_msg_flags & (1 << X25_D_BIT))
    printf("D-bit was set\n");

if (msgstat.x25_msg_flags & (1 << X25_Q_BIT))
    printf("Q bit was set\n");
```

```
if (msgstat.x25_msg_flags & (1 << X25_CA_DATA_AVAIL))
    printf("CALL DATA is available\n");

if (msgstat.x25_msg_flags & (1 << X25_CL_DATA_AVAIL))
    printf("CLEAR DATA is available\n");
```

If X25_D_BIT is set, then the next message available for reading contained at least one packet in its packet sequence with the D-bit set. If X25_Q_BIT is set, then the next message available for reading contained at least one packet in its packet sequence with the Q-bit set. If X25_CA_DATA_AVAIL is set, then there is call user data available to be read, and the next X25_RD_USER_DATA ioctl() issued will begin to read it. If X25_CL_DATA_AVAIL is set, then there is clear data available to be read. Both the X25_CA_DATA_AVAIL and the X25_CL_DATA_AVAIL bits may be set, signifying that there is call user data as well as clear user data available to be read. If X25_SKT_CONNECTED is set, then the socket is fully connected. This is useful in determining, with nonblocking sockets, when the connection handshake has been completed. The socket can go to the connected state before the circuit does, and you can test this bit to resolve this ambiguity. X25_SKT_CONNECTED is set for a PVC when the socket is bound to it and remains set until either the link level connection fails or the user closes or shuts down the socket.

10.8.6   How to Control Which Calls You Accept

If you wish to retain approval control of all incoming calls for your server, you use the X25_CALL_ACPT_APPROVAL ioctl(). You must issue this ioctl() on the listen socket before calling accept(). It is an error (EINVAL) to issue this call against any socket that is not already a listen socket. It cannot be "turned off" once it has been turned on. By default, the option is turned off. Once issued, it also implies that the user has the opportunity to provide facilities in the CLEAR Confirm packet (data is not allowed in CLEAR Confirm) before rejecting the call; this applies to all sockets associated with SVCs. When dealing with public data networks, however, and some private ones, keep in mind that the network may insist that any facilities you place in the CALL Accepted and CALL Cleared packets be those specifically allowed by the X.25 specification (see the Yellow Book, Red Book, or Blue Book, as your network provider's type dictates, for a list).

```
error = ioctl(s, X25_CALL_ACPT_APPROVAL, 0);
```

The parameter s is the listen socket descriptor. This ioctl() will defer the automatic acceptance for incoming calls arriving on that listen socket. Inbound calls are still received the normal way: When a call arrives, it is still bound to a new socket by accept(), and the new socket will be placed in the IS_CONNECTED state, but the state of the circuit is saved internally, preventing data (whether ordinary or

INTERRUPT data) from being sent on that socket until the X25_SEND_CALL_ACPT is issued. Any attempt to send will result in the ENOTCONN error.

The programmer **must** either accept the call with an X25_SEND_CALL_ACPT ioctl() **or** clear the call with close(); shutdown() with argument one or two will clear the call, but it will leave the socket and its resources allocated. Consequently, close() should be the response if you don't want to accept the call.

10.8.7   How to Accept a Call

The ioctl() command X25_SEND_CALL_ACPT is used **only** for new sockets returned by accept(), and **only** when the listen socket has an X25_CALL_ACPT_APPROVAL issued against it. Together, these two ioctl()s give you the power to determine whether to accept or reject the call. This decision may be made on the basis of any or all of the information available, such as the origination or destination addresses, CUDF, or the Facilities field.

Once this ioctl() has been issued, the socket will be in a state supporting data transfers and will remain there until cleared.

error = ioctl(new_s, X25_SEND_CALL_ACPT, 0);

The parameter new_s is the socket returned from the previous accept() system call. It must **not** be a listen socket.

10.8.8   Using Permanent Virtual Circuits (PVCs)

The X25_SETUP_PVC ioctl() request is used to "bind" a socket to a particular permanent virtual circuit (PVC). You have to know the Logical Channel Identifier (LCI) for the PVC you want to use. It must not already be in use by another process. PVCs are analogous to leased lines and are always considered "open." They only terminate at one destination (unlike switched VCs, which can terminate at different destinations on different calls). They may be used by, at most, one socket at a time. Normally, this means at most one process at a time. That is, the X25_SETUP_PVC request will fail and return an error (EBUSY) if the PVC is already in use. However, if a process successfully issues this request and then fork()s a child, both parent and child will have access to this same socket. Similarly, errors occur if you use a newly created socket for connect() while the other tries to use the same socket for X25_SETUP_PVC. If the X.25 interface is shut down, or level 2 drops, the binding between socket and circuit is broken, and you can't use the socket any more. If you still want to use the PVC, you must close() the old socket, create a new one, and bind to the PVC again. This last will be rejected as long as the interface remains shut down or the link level connection opens. To use a PVC, the programer must declare a structure of type x25_setup_pvc_str:

```
struct x25_setup_pvc_str {
   char ifname[X25_MAX_IFNAMELEN+1]; /* Name of X.25 interface to
                                         use                   */
   int lci;                          /* Logical Channel Number */
};
```

Use the `ifname` field to specify which X.25 interface you want to use. Here, as with every other instance where this field is used, specify an empty string if there's only one interface.

The `X25_SETUP_PVC ioctl()` is used as follows:

```
struct x25_setup_pvc_str pvc_str;
int pvc_so;
pvc_so = socket(AF_CCITT, SOCK_STREAM, 0);
/*
 * Although not shown, you must set the interface name in
 * pvc_str.ifname.  The LCI must be stored in pvc_str.lci.
 */
pvc_str.lci = 1; /* Use PVC # 1 in this example.            */
error = ioctl(pvc_so, X25_SETUP_PVC, &pvc_str);
```

As shown in the foregoing example, you must first create a socket, then use the `X25_SETUP_PVC ioctl()` to bind the socket to the PVC. The name of the X.25 interface to use, or the default, and the logical channel number (LCI) of the PVC, must be set prior to making the `ioctl()` call. If the request is successful, then the circuit will automatically be reset. The cause code will be zero and the diagnostic code will be 250 (decimal). If the PVC is currently in a RESET sequence (either from a reset previously generated at the user level, or a network provider- or firmware-initiated one, which has not been completed), the user process will be put to sleep until one of two packets is received: RESET Confirm or RESET Indication. In this case, the second RESET will be skipped. If data is received on any circuit that isn't bound to any socket, the data will be discarded and the circuit reset.

10.8.9 How to Read Call and Clear User Data

The `ioctl()` command **X25_RD_USER_DATA** is available for reading data from the call user data field, if there was any, of the CALL Connected or Incoming CALL packet. The same `ioctl()` can also be used to read the data field from a CLEAR packet. The data from the CALL and the CLEAR are kept separate. Thus, if a CALL has data, and a CLEAR arrives with data before the user process reads either, it is queued after the CALL data. The first X25_RD_USER_DATA `ioctl()` sequence would transfer the call user data field. The second sequence would transfer the clear user data field. The X25_NEXT_MSG_STAT `ioctl()` can be used to tell you which you have. Both are useful for fast select. The mechanism for reading this data is somewhat complicated, owing to the fact that the HP-UX kernel allows no more than 127 bytes of data to be sent through any one ioctl() call. In the following example, X25_NEXT_MSG_STAT is used to determine if there is any call or clear user data. If so, then X25_RD_USER_DATA is used to transfer it to user space.

```
struct x25_userdata userdata;
struct x25_msg_stat msgstat;
unsigned char call_udata[128], clear_udata[128];
int i, call_ndata = 0, clear_ndata = 0, error = 0;
/*
 * Assume that s is a socket which
 * has already been created.
 */
while ( !error ) {
   error = ioctl(s, X25_NEXT_MSG_STAT, &msgstat);
   if (error < 0) {
      perror("ioctl(X25_NEXT_MSG_STAT failed");
      exit(1);
   }
   if (msgstat.x25_msg_flags & (1 << X25_CA_DATA_AVAIL)){
      error = ioctl(s, X25_RD_USER_DATA, &userdata);
      if (error != 0) {
         perror("X25_RD_USER_DATA returned error");
         ++error;
         break;
      }
      if (userdata.x25_cud_len == 0) break;
      memcpy(&call_udata[call_ndata], userdata.x25_cu_data,
            userdata.x25_cud_len);
      call_ndata += userdata.x25_cud_len;
   } else break;
}
/*
 * If error == 0 at this point all of the Call data
   is now in "udata".  "call_ndata" gives the number
   of bytes of data.                                          */
while ( !error ) {
   error = ioctl(s, X25_NEXT_MSG_STAT, &msgstat);
   if (error < 0) {
      perror("ioctl(X25_NEXT_MSG_STAT failed");
      exit(1);
   }

   if (msgstat.x25_msg_flags & (1 << X25_CL_DATA_AVAIL)){
```

```
        error = ioctl(s, X25_RD_USER_DATA, &userdata);
        if (error != 0) {
           perror("X25_RD_USER_DATA returned error");
           ++error;
           break;
        }
        if (userdata.x25_cud_len == 0) break;
        memcpy(&udata[clear_ndata], userdata.x25_cu_data,
              userdata.x25_cud_len);
        clear_ndata += userdata.x25_cud_len;
    } else break;
}
/*
 * If error == 0 at this point all of the clear data is now in
 * "clear_udata". "clear_ndata" gives the number of bytes of data.
 */
```

10.8.10 How To Write Call and Clear User Data

The ioctl() command **X25_WR_USER_DATA** is available for writing the call user data field. This is used in any (or all) of the following situations:

- before connect()
- before accept() when call-accept approval is in effect
- before close() for writing the CLEAR packet data

If there is too much data to transfer in one call, you must make multiple calls, just as we saw for reading. The data will be appended to the data from the previous calls. If you are using more than 16 bytes of data, then you must also set up fast select (see Section 10.10, "Fast Select"). Inbound call and clear user data is kept separate from outbound. You cannot read with X25_RD_USER_DATA what you wrote with X25_WR_USER_DATA. Once a successful connection has been initiated, any outbound call user data that has been defined will be released.

The following example shows the use of user data:

```
struct x25_userdata userdata;
unsigned char udata[128];
int i, j = 0, ndata;

/*
 * Assume at this point that s is a socket, and all data is now
 * in "udata" and that "ndata" counts no. of bytes.
 */
userdata.x25_cud_len = (ndata<=X25_MAX_CU_DATA) ?
                                    ndata:X25_MAX_CU_DATA;
```

```
memcpy(userdata.x25_cu_data, udata, userdata.x25_cud_len);
error = ioctl(s, X25_WR_USER_DATA, &userdata);
if (error) {
   perror("X25_WR_USER_DATA 1");
   exit(1);
}
if (ndata > X25_MAX_CU_DATA) {
   userdata.x25_cud_len = ndata-X25_MAX_CU_DATA;
   memcpy(userdata.x25_cu_data, udata[X25_MAX_CU_DATA],
                                    userdata.x25_cud_len);
   error = ioctl(s, X25_WR_USER_DATA, &userdata);
}
if (error) {
   perror("X25_WR_USER_DATA 2");
   exit(1);
}
```

10.9   Facilities

CCITT defines a header-item-encoding method for facilities and also defines header codes for the facilities that it defines (this information is described in great detail in Section 7 of the CCITT X.25 specification). When the socket is created, the socket will by default not use any facilities. If your application requires that you use X.25 facilities, you must set up an array of type `unsigned char`, containing data formatted according to the CCITT-defined encoding, and pass this array (and its length) to the X.25 subsystem with the `X25_WR_FACILITIES` ioctl(). The X.25 subsystem and/or the packet switches may negotiate the flow-control parameters, if specified, downwards, according to the negotiation rules specified in X.25; in the particular case where a packet size of 64 bytes is specified, the negotiation will be **upward**, because each implementation is **required** to support 128-byte packets. You must not assume that the values for these parameters that are used for a connection are the same as were originally specified. Attempts to negotiate in the wrong direction will cause the call to be cleared.

10.9.1   Setting the Facilities Field

The `X25_WR_FACILITIES` ioctl() is available for setting up the facilities field and can be used in any situation in which `X25_WR_USER_DATA` may be used. There is only one storage area for facilities for each socket. Any new ones that are set (or received) will cause the old storage area to be released, and new storage area allocated to store the new data; old and new facilities data never mix. Inbound and outbound facilities data also never mix. That is, issuing `X25_WR_FACILITIES`, or receiving a

CALL or CLEAR packet with a facilities field, overwrites this area, and the previous contents are lost. If the user has not specified any facilities prior to initiating a call, then the default flow-control facilities will be used in the call. Consequently, when the subscription allows flow-control negotiation, users do not **have** to set this up every time. They may choose to override with their own, but these must be smaller values (silently lowered otherwise). If the user has executed X25_WR_FACILITIES specifying zero-length, then no facilities will be included in the call. The CCITT specification states that if the subscription **allows** flow-control negotiation, then every call request packet must contain the proposed flow-control parameters. However, in certain cases, such as with private networks and certain switching equipment, it may be desirable to allow the user to override and not specify **any** facilities.

The following code shows the use of this ioctl():

```
struct x25_facilities facilities;
/*
 * Assume at this point that s is a socket, and the facilities
 * have been coded properly in facilities.x25_fac[], and that
 * facilities.x25_fac_len contains the number of
 * facilities-field data bytes.
 */
    error = ioctl(s, X25_WR_FACILITIES, &facilities);
```

When writing code for the called side, you should, in general, assume that the facilities data will be delivered in a different order than originally specified by the side that initiated the call.

10.9.2   How to Read Facilities Data

The ioctl() command X25_RD_FACILITIES is available for reading any inbound facilities that have been received (Incoming CALL, CALL Connected, CLEAR Indication, CLEAR Confirm data). If inbound facilities data has not been received, or has been read since it was last received, or if the X25_WR_FACILITIES ioctl() has been issued since they were received, then the returned length will be zero. Facilities data written with X25_WR_FACILITIES cannot be read with X25_RD_FACILITIES. The receipt of any CALL or CLEAR packet overwrites the facilities data area, as does execution of the X25_WR_FACILITIES ioctl().

If **X25_RD_FACILITIES** is executed before the socket goes to the connected state, the default facilities (as specified by x25init) will be returned for the interface associated with the socket. If no such association has yet occurred, then the returned facilities data will be those of the first X.25 interface (the one corresponding to /dev/x25_0).

Thus, the normal sequence would be as follows:

1. Set up the facilities buffer; execute `X25_WR_FACILITIES`
    `ioctl()`; if desired, set up and execute the
    `X25_WR_USER_DATA ioctl()`; then execute the `connect()`
    system call.

2. On the passive side, after the call has been received, read the
    facilities from the `Incoming CALL` packet with
    `X25_RD_FACILITIES ioctl()`. From this and other
    information available with `getpeeraddr()` or
    `X25_RD_USER_DATA`, determine whether to accept or clear the
    call; if the decision is to clear, then close the new socket and exit.
    Otherwise, continue as described in the following steps.

3. If the `CALL Accepted` packet needs to be sent with a facilities
    field, construct that buffer and issue the `X25_WR_FACILITIES`
    `ioctl()` with that data; if desired, `X25_WR_USER_DATA` may
    also be used (fast select). Issue the `X25_SEND_ACPT ioctl()`.

4. Back on the active side, after the connection has been set up, issue
    `X25_RD_FACILITIES` to read the facilities field. This request
    will return to the caller the contents of the facilities field, if present,
    of the `CALL Accepted` packet. It will return zero data length if
    the field was empty.

5. This same `ioctl()` can also be used to read the facilities field
    from the `CLEAR` packet, if there is one. This is useful for fast
    select.

Data may only be read once.

```
struct x25_userdata userdata;
int i, ndata = 0, error = 0;
/*
 * Although not shown, assume that s is a
 * socket which has already been created.
 * The circuit need not already be set up.
 */
error = ioctl(s, X25_RD_FACILITIES, &userdata);
if (error != 0) {
   perror("X25_RD_FACILITIES returned error");
   break;
}
/*
 * If error == 0 at this point all of the
 * data is now in "userdata".
 */
```

10.9.3   Extended-Format **CLEAR** Packets

Calls are cleared in X.25 by means of the CLEAR packet. At the application software level, calls can be cleared at any time with the `close()` system call. Normally, the CLEAR packet contains only a cause code and a diagnostic code field.[21] It is possible to specify a facilities field, a clear user data field, or both. When the CLEAR packet contains either or both of these fields, its format is called "Extended" in X.25. If you wish to send additional information (such as an indication of **why** the circuit is being cleared), you may do so in this manner. As mentioned previously, the X25_WR_CAUSE_DIAG applies only to the next user-initiated CLEAR. In addition to its use prior to setting up a connection, the X25_WR_USER_DATA `ioctl()` can also be used to set the clear user data field (also called CUDF; the context tells you whether CUDF means "call user data field" or "clear user data field"). You can specify up to 16 bytes of data in this field, or, if you specify the "Fast Select" facility in the facilities field, you can specify up to 128 bytes of data in the CUDF.

You may also specify a "facilities" field. Use the X25_WR_FACILITIES `ioctl()` to set the facilities field for the next outgoing packet (applies only for packets whose type permits a facilities field).

Before the connection is set up, X25_WR_FACILITIES and X25_WR_USER_DATA apply to CALL packets; once the connection is established, these same `ioctl()`s apply to CLEAR packets. Neither of them will clear the circuit; they just store information for later use. The X25_WR_FACILITIES and X25_WR_USER_DATA `ioctl()`s may be issued in either order, but they must be issued before `connect()` if you want the corresponding fields to exist in the CALL packet. Similarly, they must be called before `close()` if you want the fields to exist in the CLEAR packet. If the socket is closed without an X25_WR_CAUSE_DIAG `ioctl()` having been executed, the cause code will be defaulted to zero and the diagnostic code will be defaulted to 241 (decimal).

10.10   Fast Select

One of X.25's more interesting protocol features is called "fast select." Applications can use this feature, when available, to handle simple data exchanges quickly. In a nutshell, it's a connection that is never completely set up. All the data exchanged is carried in CALL and CLEAR packets. For example, a credit inquiry might require only two packets, using fast select, rather than six otherwise (two to set up the connection, one DATA packet, one acknowledgment, and two to tear down the circuit). Fast select can only be used if it is programmed correctly, supported by the network provider,

---

21. The diagnostic code field is optional in the X.25 specification. The HP implementation always specifies this field.

subscribed to, and supported by the X.25 interface. You may wish to check the network provider's tariff structure (the price list for its services) to determine whether using fast select is truly as economical as it appears. It is the programmer's responsibility to specify the fast select facility correctly. Incorrect programming will likely result in `DIAGNOSTIC` packets or `CLEAR`s from the network provider.

10.10.1 Fast Select: Calling Side

On the calling side, you encode the facilities you want, including fast select, in an `unsigned char` array and send this data into the kernel using the `X25_WR_FACILITIES ioctl()`. You use the `X25_WR_USER_DATA ioctl()` to send the call user data field into the kernel. If you are using protocol-IDs for call-matching, you must place the protocol-ID ahead of the other call data, and the total length of the CUD field must not exceed 128 bytes. The order in which the `ioctl()`s are issued is unimportant, so long as they are issued prior to `connect()`.

Now you call `connect()`. The X.25 subsystem will construct an X.25 `CALL Request` packet containing the facilities field and the call user data field you told it to use. This combination isn't peculiar to fast select, by the way.

If the calling side elects to make a fast-select call, one of three things can happen:

1. If the called side isn't accepting this type of call, then a `CLEAR` will be returned, with no data.

2. The called side may send a reply and immediate clear. You implement this by issuing a `X25_WR_USER_DATA ioctl()` and then a `close()` on the socket. You must be handling call acceptances (`X25_CALL_ACPT_APPROVAL`). This data will be used in the `CLEAR`'s clear user data field when you close the socket. The same is true for writing the facilities field.

3. When allowed by the caller, the called side can choose to accept the call, turning it into a normal call.

All of this is achieved via `ioctl()` calls. The diagram shown in Figure 10.8 illustrates one simple use of fast select (the second of the three possibilities just listed).

In the situation shown in Figure 10.8, the Caller will receive `ECONNREFUSED`, but there will be call user data available, which can be read with `X25_RD_USER_DATA`. If the other side had rejected the call (`CLEAR`, with no data), the return value from the Caller's `connect()` would also be `ECONNREFUSED`. The two cases are distinguishable because in the latter there would be no user data readable with `X25_RD_USER_DATA`. If `X25_NEXT_MSG_STAT` indicates that the connection is open, then the called side has elected to turn the transaction into an ordinary circuit by accepting the call (see the discussion of `ioctl()` `X25_SEND_CALL_ACPT`. Data may be read via `recv()` (but you should check for call data first). At this time, the call is set up and is treated as a normal call (without fast select). Fast select is no longer considered to be "in effect."

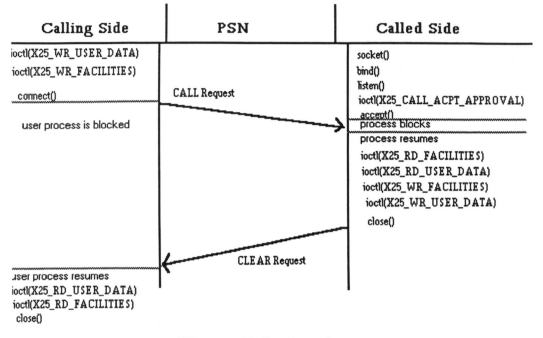

Figure 10.8 Fast Select

10.11   Other `ioctl()` Commands

10.11.1   X25_RD_CTI

This `ioctl()` command allows you to determine the circuit table index (cti) associated with a particular socket.   HP has a tracing and logging facility that is useful for debugging, but it identifies circuits by their CTI rather than their logical circuit identifier (LCI). The `X25_RD_CTI` gives you the CTI, so that you can include it in your own application's logging.   The combination of your application-level logging with the X.25/9000 subsystem's is a very powerful one for debugging.

```
int error, s, cti;
/*  Assume at this point that s is a socket.                    */
error = ioctl (s, X25_RD_CTI, &cti);
if (error < 0) {
   perror("X25_RD_CTI");
   exit(1);
} /*  Use cti as the circuit table index.                      */
```

This request will return EINVAL if issued before the socket is fully connected or after the connection is cleared.

10.11.2 X25_RD_LCI

This ioctl() command allows you to determine the logical channel indicator (LCI) associated with a particular circuit. Using this information, you can can correlate information in the log file with that from a protocol-analyzer trace. With the LCI, the CTI, application-level tracing, and X.25 subsystem-level tracing, it is possible to debug most kinds of problems.

```
int error, s, lci;
/* Assume at this point that s is a socket.                     */

error = ioctl (s, X25_RD_LCI, &lci);
if (error < 0) {
   perror("X25_RD_LCI");
   exit(1);
}
/*
 * Use lci as the logical circuit indicator.
 */
```

This request will return EINVAL if issued before the socket is fully connected or after the connection is cleared.

10.11.3 X25_WR_WTHRESHOLD

This ioctl() command sets the "write threshold" for a socket. It is useful in conjunction with nonblocking I/O and with **select()** calls. Its purpose is to override the usual "Berkeley sockets" semantics of select writeability. As was discussed in Chapter 5, if you select a socket for writability, Berkeley socket semantics dictate that the socket will select writable if there is space for at least one byte of data to be sent. This is fine for byte-stream protocols, such as TCP, because they can transmit the data in whatever-sized chunks the transmission medium can accept. With X.25, however, you want to know when the subsystem has enough buffer space to accept a whole message, not just "at least one byte of data." When the send() system call is executed, how much data can be copied into the kernel's buffers depends on the size of the message and the amount of data still queued for transmission from previous send() requests. If the system didn't limit this, then an application that sends huge amounts of data would monopolize the system's limited amount of buffer memory. Without the X25_WR_WTHRESHOLD ioctl(), select() will return "writable" status if there is space for even one byte. However, if you try to write more than one byte, you could block or, in the case of a nonblocking-mode socket, receive EWOULDBLOCK (or EAGAIN or zero, depending upon which flavor of nonblocking you preferred to use).

To avoid this problem, the HP implementation of X.25 gives you this way to specify a "threshold" value. This may be set once or changed at will. The current value of this threshold is used to determine when select() on the socket will return writable status. That is, select() will return writable status when the space available is at least the size of this threshold value.

The write threshold has no effect on the select() system call's "readable" semantics. The write threshold defaults to one byte, thus preserving the normal "Berkeley sockets semantics" if you want them. Each such call sets the new threshold, overriding the old value. To use this ioctl() most successfully, issue it some time before you wish to write a message of a certain size, specifying that size (or a larger value) as the write threshold. You may choose to set one fixed size for the life of the socket or to vary it from time to time. Later, you issue select(), specifying the read and write masks for the sockets and file descriptors in which you're interested. For each one in the write mask that corresponds to an X.25 socket, if there is sufficient space to queue a message of the socket's write threshold number of bytes, the select() will return a one in the write mask bit position corresponding to that socket; otherwise, it will place a zero in that position.

10.11.4   X25_WR_CALLING_SUBADDR

This ioctl() command is used to specify a subaddress field to be included in the calling address field of the CALL Request packet. It is used by programs that wish to inform the server process of the subaddress to use to return their call. That is, it enables dialog resembling the following:

```
 Client                 Server
 -------------          -----------------
Process-ID 1234
initiates call --->
                        (receive call;  optionally, there may be
                         an exchange of messages, but that doesn't
                         matter to our example)
         <--------      clear call
         (some time later)
         <----          Initiate call
                         back to process-ID 1234
```

As an example, consider a transaction-based application (electronic mail, for instance) in which the originator sends some data that will require a considerable amount of processing time before there is anything more to be sent on the circuit.

Continuing the email example, the mail recipient may return a message to the sender's mail application when the human being reads this "letter." This may not happen for a few hours, or even days, or perhaps never. It is wasteful to keep a circuit open when you don't need it.[22] To save money, it makes sense to clear the circuit, writing the server's code to call the client back when the results are ready. The server "knows" when the results are ready, but how does it call the client back? It can read the client's address; this information is available in the addr field of the accept() system call;[23] but that doesn't identify a particular client process, only the host itself. You can use protocol-ID addressing, but what if the programmer of the client side preferred (for whatever reason) to use subaddressing?

This is where the X25_WR_CALLING_SUBADDR ioctl() comes in. It is used to add a subaddress to the calling address field. Normally, when the X.25 subsystem sends the CALL Request packet, the packet's calling address field contains only the X.121 address of the calling side. When this ioctl() is used, it will cause the subaddress it specifies to be appended to the calling address. The resulting address plus subaddress must not be longer than 15 digits, and the subaddress must be specified before the CALL packet is generated; otherwise the request has no effect.

To utilize this ioctl(), you load the subaddress into an x25addrstr structure. The fields that are meaningful in this request are x25_family, x25hostlen, and x25_host[]. The other fields in this structure are not used for this ioctl(). The x25_family field must be set to AF_CCITT. The x25_host[] field must contain a subaddress consisting **only** of digits, in ASCII. The x25hostlen field must contain the number of subaddress digits.

When the server process is ready to send back the results of its "deliberations," it initiates a new connection just as we have already described. The roles of the two processes reverse: The server calls connect(), the client calls accept().

How can the client "know" a subaddress that isn't already in use, without first creating a socket and binding it to a subaddress? Once this succeeds, then the server must call listen() to specify that the socket is a "listen socket" address.

There may be reasons why you don't want to keep a listen socket around for this length of time; if the server is going to take, say, two weeks to get you an answer, or your own computer may have been rebooted before the answer comes back, you may want to figure out another way to make things work. It isn't necessary that a listen socket be created for the entire time it takes for the "callback" to occur. It **is** necessary

---

22. Different network providers have different charges, but there is usually a charge for the length of time the circuit is open (whether or not data is being transferred), a charge for each packet, and a charge to open the circuit.

23. Any process may obtain the the peer's address (including subaddress, if any) by using the getpeername() system call and the associated socket.

that there be a listen socket, with the matching address, **before** the callback CALL
Indication packet arrives.   Otherwise, this call will be cleared automatically
(because it doesn't match any existing X.25 listen socket).

The code that handles the X25_WR_CALLING_SUBADDR ioctl() does not
check if any other processes have a socket bound to this address.

10.12   X.25 Client/Server Example

To illustrate these points, the "Dinner is ready when the smoke alarm goes off" example
from Chapter 3 is shown in Section 10.12.1 (server) and Section 10.12.2 (client),
converted to use X.25 directly.

10.12.1   Example: Server

```
/* vcserverx25.c -- X.25 server */
#include    <stdio.h>
#include    <fcntl.h>
#include    <sys/types.h>
#include    <netinet/in.h>
#include    <sys/socket.h>
#include    <sys/errno.h>
#include    <netdb.h>
#include    <signal.h>
#include    <time.h>
#include    <x25/x25.h>
#include    <x25/x25addrstr.h>
#include    <x25/x25str.h>
#include    <x25/x25ioctls.h>
#include    <x25/ccittproto.h>
#include    <x25/x25codes.h>
extern int errno;
struct x25addrstr    server_x121_address, peer_addr;
main( argc, argv )   /* argument count, argument vector        */
char *argv[];
{
   int    rc;                   /* system call return code         */
   int    x25_listen_skt;       /* server listen socket descriptor */
   int    x25_accept_skt;       /* server accept socket descriptor */
   int    addrlen, nbytes;      /* sockaddr length; read nbytes req*/
   struct sockaddr addr;        /* client's internet addr & port   */
   char   buf [256];            /* your basic buffer               */
   struct hostent *hp, *gethostbyaddr();/* /etc/hosts lookup       */
   if ((x25_listen_skt = socket ( AF_CCITT, SOCK_STREAM,
                       X25_PROTO_NUM)) < 0) {
```

```
        perror( "X25 Domain Socket" );
        exit(1);
    }

    strcpy(server_x121_address.x25_host, "" );
    strncpy(server_x121_address.x25ifname,'\0',X25_MAX_IFNAMELEN);
    server_x121_address.x25_family = AF_CCITT ;
    server_x121_address.x25hostlen = strlen (
                            server_x121_address.x25_host );
    server_x121_address.x25pidlen = 4;
    server_x121_address.x25pid[0] = 0xFF;
    server_x121_address.x25pid[1] = 0xAA;
    server_x121_address.x25pid[2] = 0xBB;
    server_x121_address.x25pid[3] = 0xCC;
    if ( bind( x25_listen_skt, &server_x121_address,
                sizeof server_x121_address ) < 0 ) {
        close(x25_listen_skt);
        perror( "X25 Domain Bind" );
        exit(2);
    }

    if (listen(x25_listen_skt,5) < 0){ /* wait for a "phone call"  */
                                    /* allowing 5 pending "holds" */
        close(x25_listen_skt);
        perror( "X25 Domain Listen" );
        exit(4);
    }

    while (1) {      /* answer "phone calls"                     */
        addrlen = sizeof server_x121_address;
                    /* need a real mem location                 */
        if ( (x25_accept_skt = accept( x25_listen_skt,
                    &server_x121_address, &addrlen )) < 0 ) {
            close(x25_listen_skt);
            perror( "X25 Domain Accept" );
            exit(5);
        }
        do {
            if ( (nbytes = read( x25_accept_skt, buf, sizeof buf) ) < 0 ) {
                close(x25_accept_skt);
                exit(6);
            }
            else if (nbytes == 0)
                printf( "\nClosing connection...\n\n" );
            else
```

```
        printf( "\nReceived: %s\n", buf );
    } while (nbytes != 0);

    close(x25_accept_skt);  /* close the service descriptor */
    }
}
```

10.12.2 Example: Client

```
/* vcclientx25.c -- Example X.25  client                        */

#include  <stdio.h>
#include  <sys/types.h>
#include  <sys/socket.h>
#include  <netinet/in.h> /* sockaddr_in Internet socket address */
#include  <netdb.h>       /* /etc/hosts entry (hostent)         */
#include  <sys/errno.h>
#include  <signal.h>
#include  <x25/x25.h>
#include  <x25/x25addrstr.h>
#include  <x25/x25str.h>
#include  <x25/x25ioctls.h>
#include  <x25/ccittproto.h>
#include  <x25/x25codes.h>

#define DATA "Dinner is ready when the smoke alarm goes off.\n"

struct x25addrstr destination_x121_address; /* Address of the
                                               remote node       */
struct x25_userdata  userdata ;
usage()
{
    printf("Usage: vcclient <remote's x121 address>\n");
    exit(1);
}

main( argc, argv )        /* argument count, argument vector     */
char *argv[];
{
    int   x25_socket;     /* socket descriptor                   */

    if (argc != 2) usage();
    if((x25_socket = socket(AF_CCITT, SOCK_STREAM, X25_PROTO_NUM)) <
                  0 ) {
        perror( argv[0] );
        exit(1);
    }
```

```
    destination_x121_address.x25_family = AF_CCITT ;
    destination_x121_address.x25hostlen = strlen (argv[1]);
    strncpy(destination_x121_address.x25_host, argv[1],
            X25_MAXHOSTADDR );
    strncpy(destination_x121_address.x25ifname, "",
            X25_MAX_IFNAMELEN );

    /*  Do a connect on the server socket                           */

    userdata.x25_cud_len = 4 ;
    userdata.x25_cu_data[0] = 0xFF;
    userdata.x25_cu_data[1] = 0xAA;
    userdata.x25_cu_data[2] = 0xBB;
    userdata.x25_cu_data[3] = 0xCC;

    if(ioctl ( x25_socket, X25_WR_USER_DATA, &userdata ) < 0) {
       perror("ioctl X25_WR_USER_DATA");
       exit(1);
    }
    if (connect(x25_socket, &destination_x121_address,
                sizeof(struct x25addrstr)) < 0) {
       perror("connect");
       exit(1);
    }
    write( x25_socket, DATA, sizeof DATA );
    close( x25_socket );
}
```

10.13   x25netd: An inetd-like Daemon for X.25

We now turn from the simple examples to a more complex and useful one: An inetd-like daemon that can be just as useful in starting up X.25 server daemons as inetd is for Internet-protocol suite daemons.

x25netd.c is an inetd-like daemon that is used to vector incoming connection requests to the appropriate daemon, based upon a protocol-ID specified in the call. When the listed daemon is started up by x25netd, file descriptor zero is the socket that has the incoming connection (also one and two). The daemon should not attempt to create another socket by socket(), nor use bind(), nor listen(); it must either issue the X25_SEND_CALL_ACEPT ioctl() (to complete the call) or close the socket, if it determines for any reason not to accept it.

x25netd has a configuration file, just as inetd does, but the syntax is different. It reads the file /etc/x25netd.conf to determine X.25 socket bindings. The format of this file is as follows:

- There is one line per entry; lines beginning with a # character are considered comments and are skipped.

- Fields are separated by blanks or tabs.

- The first field is the X.121 address with subaddress field; use − to default to any X.121 address of any available X.25 interface.

- The second field is a string containing protocol-ID, in hex (leading 0x); use − to specify no protocol-ID field.

- The third field is a string containing protocol-ID mask, in hex (leading 0x). Use − to specify the default, which is a string of all-ones for as many bytes as the second field specifies.

- The fourth field (logname) is the user name (must be findable in /etc/passwd, see **getpwent (3C)**) under which the server process will run. The daemon will run with the "group ID" set to the GID of this user name. If getpwent() lookup fails, then /etc/x25netd will log the error (if a log file is in use) and clear the circuit without starting any server daemon.

- The fifth field (chroot) is the directory to which x25netd will **chroot()** (see Section 7 of your UNIX programmer's reference manual) before exec()ing the server process. This is a security protection. The idea is that the system administrator can run the server within some "safe" file system. If the chroot() fails, x25netd will log the error (if a log file is in use), and clear the circuit without starting any server daemon. Note: The user named in the logname field must have permission to chroot() to the directory named in the chroot field.

- The sixth field (cmnd) is the process that will be invoked when an incoming call arrives whose address and protocol-ID fields match the binding in fields one through four.

- The seventh and following fields are parameters, which will be passed to the server when they are exec()ed.

For example, the line

```
# X121adr     Proto-ID      Mask          Log-   Chroot
#                                          name
5551107       0xFFAABBCC    0xffffffff    x25d   /etc/x25/x25daemons
Cmnd                        Parameters
/vcserverX25                p1 p2 p3 p4 p5
```

will cause the daemon `/etc/x25/x25daemons/vcserverX25` to be invoked whenever an incoming X.25 call specifies the X.121 address `5551107` and the protocol-ID field with the first byte equal to `0xFF`, second byte `0xAA`, third byte `0xBB`, and fourth byte `0xCC`. Notice that the `cmnd` field is relative to the `chroot` directory. In this case, the `x25netd.conf` file has the `cmnd` field parameter set to `/vcserverX25`, but the actual command (the executable file) resides in `/etc/x25/x25daemons/vcserverX25`.

The server daemon `vcserverX25` will be invoked under the user-ID for `x25d`, and using the corresponding group-ID. It will have the following runtime parameters: `argv[1]` will contain `"p1"`; `argv[2]` will contain `"p2"`; `argv[3]` will contain `"p3"`; `argv[4]` will contain `"p4"`; and `argv[5]` will contain `"p5"`.

The `x25netd` has some command line options:

- `-i` sets the name of the X.25 interface to use. Default is all interfaces.

- `-v` sets "verbosity" level, for logging. This is a bitmask consisting of the following:

1 = Log errors; if any bits are set, then error logging is forced to be "on."

2 = Log parameter information.

4 = Log info when starting server daemons.

8 = Log miscellaneous information.

16 = Log the file, `/tmp/x25netd.server.out`, for server daemons. If this bit is set, then the `stdout` and `stderr` for the server daemon will be set to output into this file. This file is used, if this bit is set, to log any errors that occur when `x25netd`'s child process attempts the `setuid()`, `setgid()`, and `chroot()` system calls. Use this bit only if you are debugging a server. If this bit is not set, `stdout` and `stderr` are closed when the server is `exec()`ed.

- `-L` sets the name of the log file. If this is not specified, no logging will be performed.

The program first initializes itself and reads the `/etc/x25netd.conf` file. For each noncommented line, it allocates some space (`malloc()` is called), stores the fields from that line, and creates a "listen" socket. It binds this socket to the interface found in the `-i <name>` command-line parameter and the protocol-ID, address, and protocol-ID mask fields. If this request fails, such as when some other program has a listen socket open, then log the error and continue. The mode of this listen socket is set such that incoming X.25 calls are not automatically answered by the X.25 subsystem;

this means that servers must either close the socket or issue the `ioctl()` command X25_SEND_CALL_ACPT on it, which will complete the connection sequence.

The daemon could potentially be asked to establish a very large number of listen sockets. Accordingly, it calls the `setrlimit()` system call (available in Berkeley and Berkeley-derived UNIX systems, but not in HP-UX prior to Release 8.0) to notify the kernel.

Once the configuration file has been completely read and all the listen sockets have been created, the daemon enters its main loop. This consists of building the masks for the `select()` system call and waiting for an incoming call to arrive via `select()`. By using `select()`, it is possible to block the process until an X.25 `Incoming CALL` packet arrives that contains address information matching one of the daemons specified in our `x25netd.conf` file. Other X.25 daemons may establish listen sockets with other addresses without conflict, so long as the address spaces don't conflict. For example, suppose two daemons specified the same X.121 addresses and protocol-IDs 0xAA and 0xAABB. There is an address space conflict here, because an incoming call bearing protocol-ID 0xAABB could match either one. The HP implementation detects conflicts like this and results in an error being returned in the `bind()` system call.

When the `select()` returns, `x25netd` scans the returned bitmap (only the read map is used for this type of situation) until it finds a bit that is set and that matches one of the listen sockets. From this match, `x25netd` has all the information necessary to start that daemon. First, however, it must call `accept()` to create a socket for the call. Since the listen socket has been set to await user-level confirmation of incoming calls (that is, not to accept them automatically) at the X.25 packet and protocol level, the VC has not been established yet, but we do have a socket for referring to it (call this new_s).

Next, `fork()` is called. The parent will close new_s; this is necessary because when the time comes for the daemon to close the socket, we want the daemon to be the last process with the socket still open. Otherwise, the circuit would never close, and eventually the daemon would run out of available socket descriptors, just like any other program that opens files or sockets repeatedly and does not eventually close them.

The child process will eventually **execl(2)** the server, but first it is necessary to do some other work. We must close all the files that `x25netd` had open. This will be its full set of listen sockets, plus the log file, if any, plus `stdin`, `stdout`, and `stderr`. We must be careful, however, not to close new_s, and if we are going to create a log file for the daemon (otherwise, there's no way to print an error message, should any error occur at this stage), we need to create a log file and a descriptor for it, and we don't want to close that descriptor here, either. Once all but these descriptors have been closed, new_s is `dup()`ed (see **dup(2)**) into `stdin` and closed. Next, if there is to be a daemon log file created, the daemon log file descriptor is `dup()`ed into `stdout` and `stderr`.

The server now needs to set the user-ID and group-ID under which we're expected to run; this information comes from using `getpwnam()` to look up the user name for this daemon (from the `x25netd.conf` file). Next, the server calls `chroot()` to set the root directory. Lastly, the server is `execl()`ed. The server will use zero (`stdin`) for the socket descriptor of the connection and must either close it or accept the call with `X25_SEND_CALL_ACPT`.

The parent notes the time at which the test begins and the protocol-ID, command line options of the test, and so forth; and when the child terminates, it also writes into the log file the pid, its `exec()` status, and the time.

Here is the example `x25netd`:

10.13.1 `x25netd.c`

```
#include <stdio.h>
#include <errno.h>
#include <time.h>
#include <fcntl.h>
#include <x25/ccittproto.h>
#include <sys/types.h>
#include <sys/socket.h>
#include <pwd.h>                          /* for getpwnam            */
#include <sys/signal.h>
#include <sys/param.h>
#include <sys/resource.h>
#include <sys/param.h>
#include <sys/ioctl.h>

#include <x25/x25.h>
#include <x25/x25addrstr.h>
#include <x25/x25stat.h>
#include <x25/x25ioctls.h>
#include <x25/x25str.h>
#define MAX_FILE_NAME_LEN 256
#define LBIFNAME ""
#define X25NETDCONF "/etc/x25netd.conf"/*Default for x25inetd.conf
                   file                                           */
#define MAP_INDEX(index) (index / (NBBY*sizeof(int)))
#define MAP_OFFSET(index) (index % (NBBY*sizeof(int)))
char Myname[20] = "x25netd:";
int verbose = 1;
#define MAXARGS 6
struct nsap_s {
   struct nsap_s *next_ent;
```

```
    int           listen_skt;           /* the listen socket      */
    unsigned char x121_addr_len;
    unsigned char proto_id_len;
    unsigned char proto_id_mask_len;
    unsigned char x121_addr[16];   /* X.121 address -- in ASCII */
    unsigned char proto_id[16];        /* protocol-ID            */
    unsigned char proto_id_mask[16]; /* protocol-ID mask         */
    char          logname[8];
    char          pathname[MAXPATHLEN];
    char          chroot_pathname[MAXPATHLEN];
    int           user_id;             /* user ID, for setuid()  */
    int           group_id;
    char          argv[MAXARGS][64];
};
struct nsap_s *nsap_list_head = NULL;

struct rlimit rlimit;
struct x25addrstr addrstr, bind_addr, from;
struct x25_facilities x25_facilities;
struct x25_userdata userdata;
struct x25_msg_stat msgstat;
int atohex();
unsigned char call_udata[128], clear_udata[128];
int call_udlen;
FILE *log_file;
/* Define bit-shifts for verbosity-level masks                  */
#define VPRINTERRORS    0 /* Print out errors                   */
#define VPRINTPARAMS    1 /* Print out parameter/config info    */
#define VMSGS           2 /* Print out more events info         */
#define VMSGS2          3 /* Print out more events info         */
#define VLOGSERVER      4 /* log file for server daemons        */

#define MAXNOBUFRETRY 1000
#define SUCCESS 0
#define FAILURE 1

int   gskt = -1,
      enobufs_cnt = 0,
      mode = -1,
      n_exp_data_len = 32,    /* lnth of expedited data test  */
      n_pkts_rcvd = 0,
      n_pkts_sent = 0,
      n_interrupt_pkts = 0,
      n_reset_pkts = 0;

int sigcldhdl();
```

```
extern long time();
extern char *ctime();
extern int errno;
extern char *getenv();
extern struct x25servent *getx25servbypid();
extern int sys_nerr;
extern char *sys_errlist[];
char  cud_file_name[MAX_FILE_NAME_LEN] = "",
      facilities_file_name[MAX_FILE_NAME_LEN] = "",
      mask_file_name[MAX_FILE_NAME_LEN] = "";
int from_add_len, cti = -1;
int skt = -1, new_s = -1, addr_len, status;
char logfilename[256] = "";
int  logfileopen = 0;
FILE *logfile = NULL;

int from_addr_len, n, protocolidlen = 0, cud_len;
int call_ndata = 0, error = 0;
#define MAP_SIZE (2048/(NBBY*sizeof(int)))
unsigned int read_map[MAP_SIZE];
int sigignore()
{
   return (0);
}
int sigiothdl()
{
   printf("x25netd: SIGIOT received.  Program terminating.\n");
   exit(0);
}
#define MAXENVVARS 256
#define EXECSTRINGSIZE 1024

main(argc,argv, envp)
int argc;
char **argv;
char **envp;
{
   struct x25servent *serv;
   struct sigvec v;
   struct nsap_s *nsap;
   int i, j = 0, k, nn, junk, base, pid, loop_holder, found;
   int n_skts;
   char cc, *cptr, *cptr2, *cptr3, *cpp, *p;

   /*
```

```
 * Initialize & set DEFAULTS.
 */
addrstr.x25_family = AF_CCITT;     /* Set up address-family. */
addrstr.x25hostlen = 0;
/* set default protocol-ID                                  */
addrstr.x25pidlen = 0;
strcpy(addrstr.x25ifname, LBIFNAME);

/*
 * Check parameters.
 */
/*
 * Examine & (if OK) use parameters.
 */
for (i = 1; i < argc; i++){
    if (argv[i][0] == '-') {
        switch(argv[i][1]){
            case 'a':                    /* Set remote's address    */
                if (++i >= argc) {
                    printf("-a option needs a parameter\n");
                    usage(argc, argv);
                }
                if (strcmp(argv[i], "0") == 0) {
                    addrstr.x25hostlen = 0;
                } else {
                    addrstr.x25hostlen = strlen(argv[i]);
                    if (addrstr.x25hostlen > X25_MAXHP1) {
                        printf("Too many address digits.\n");
                        usage(argc, argv);
                    } strcpy(addrstr.x25_host,argv[i]);
                }
                break;

            case 'i' :                   /* Set interface name      */
                if (++i >= argc) {
                    printf("-i option needs a parameter\n");
                    usage(argc, argv);
                }
                strcpy(addrstr.x25ifname, argv[i]);
                break;

            case 'v':                    /* Set "verbosity" level   */
                if (++i >= argc) {
                    printf("-v option needs a parameter\n");
                    usage(argc, argv);
                }
```

```
                   verbose = atoi(argv[i]);
                   if (verbose < 0) verbose = 0;
                   break;
             case 'L':                       /* -L Log file           */
                   if (++i >= argc) {
                      printf("-L option needs a parameter\n");
                      usage(argc, argv);
                   }
                   strcpy(logfilename, argv[i]);
                   break;
          }
       } else {
          printf("Option %s not defined.\n", argv[i]);
          usage (argc,argv);             /*Option not starting w/ - */
       }
   }
   if (*logfilename == '\0')
       logfileopen = 0;
   else {
       if ((logfile = fopen(logfilename,"a")) == NULL) {
          printf("logfile %s couldn't be opened for writing.\n",
                 logfilename);
          perror("");
          logfileopen = 0;
       } else ++logfileopen;
   }
   /*
    * Finished getting parameters.
    */
   verbose |= 1<<VPRINTERRORS;    /* Force to print out errors */
   nn = addrstr.x25hostlen;
   if (nn >= X25_MAXHOSTADDR) nn = X25_MAXHOSTADDR;
   addrstr.x25_host[nn] = '\0';
   memcpy(&bind_addr, &addrstr, sizeof(struct x25addrstr));
   if (logfileopen && (verbose & (1<<VPRINTPARAMS))) {
       fprintf(logfile,"%sinterface name is %s\n",
               Myname, addrstr.x25ifname);
       fprintf(logfile,"%sX.121 address is %s\n",
               Myname,addrstr.x25_host);
       tstamp(logfile);
   }
   /* set up signal handlers                                          */
```

```
/*v.sv_handler = (*int sv_handler()) sigcldhdl;          */
v.sv_handler = sigcldhdl;
v.sv_mask = v.sv_onstack = 0;
sigvector(SIGCLD,&v,0);

/* Ignore SIGHUP                                         */
v.sv_handler = sigignore;
sigvector(SIGHUP,&v,0);

/* SIGIOT handler                                        */
v.sv_handler = sigiothdl;
v.sv_mask = v.sv_onstack = 0;
sigvector(SIGIOT,&v,0);

initialize_listen_skts();
if (fork() != 0) exit(0);
while (1) {

   /* Build the select masks                            */
   n_skts = build_maps();
   if (n_skts == 0) {
      if (logfileopen && (verbose & (1<< VPRINTERRORS)))
         fprintf(log_file,
               "build_maps() returned zero. Terminating.\n");
      exit(1);
   }

   /* We only care about the "read" map.  This is where
   ** the connection indications are shown.  We also don't
   ** care to set a timeout.  We'll just wait until there's
   ** a new connection waiting.
   /
   if (select(n_skts, &read_map, 0, 0, 0) < 0) {
      if (errno == EINTR) continue;
      if (logfileopen && (errno > 0) && (errno <= sys_nerr))
         fprintf(logfile,
               "select()error:%s", sys_errlist[errno]);
      exit(1);
   }
   skt = found;
   for (nsap=nsap_list_head; nsap; nsap=nsap->next_ent){
      if ((skt = nsap->listen_skt) < 0) continue;
      if (read_map[MAP_INDEX(skt)] & 1<<MAP_OFFSET(skt)){
         ++found;
         break;
      }
```

```
   }
   if (!found) continue;

   from_addr_len = sizeof(struct x25addrstr);
   new_s = accept(skt, &from, &from_addr_len);  /* wait     */
   if (new_s < 0) {
      if (errno == EINTR) continue;
      if (logfileopen && (errno > 0) && (errno <= sys_nerr)) {
         fprintf(logfile,
                 "accept()error:%s", sys_errlist[errno]);
      }
      exit(15);
   }
   if (logfileopen && (verbose & (1 << VMSGS2))) {
      fprintf(logfile,"accept() results: from_addr_len = %d\n",
                 from_addr_len);
      fprintf(logfile, "from.x25_family=%d\n",
                 from.x25_family);
      fprintf(logfile, "from.x25hostlen= %d\n",
                 from.x25hostlen);
      fprintf(logfile, "from.x25pidlen= %d\n",from.x25pidlen);
      fprintf(logfile, "from.x25_host= %s\n",from.x25_host);
      for (i = 0; i < from.x25pidlen; i++) {
         fprintf(logfile, "%02x ", from.x25pid[i]);
      }
      fprintf(logfile, "\n");
      fprintf(logfile, "from.x25ifname= %s\n", from.x25ifname);
      tstamp(logfile);
   }
   from_addr_len = sizeof(struct x25addrstr);
   if (getpeername(new_s, &from, &from_addr_len) < 0) {
      if (logfileopen && (verbose & (1<<VPRINTERRORS))){
         if ((errno > 0) && (errno <= sys_nerr)) {
            fprintf(logfile, "getpeername %s",
                sys_errlist[errno]);
         }
      }
      exit(27);
   }
   if (logfileopen && (verbose & (1<<VMSGS2))) {
      fprintf(logfile, "getpeername results: from_addr_len =
                 %d\n",from_addr_len);
      fprintf(logfile, "from.x25_family= %d\n",
                 from.x25_family);
```

```
            fprintf(logfile, "from.x25hostlen= %d\n",
                    from.x25hostlen);
            fprintf(logfile, "from.x25pidlen= %d\n",from.x25pidlen);
            fprintf(logfile, "from.x25_host= %s\n",from.x25_host);
            for (i = 0; i < from.x25pidlen; i++) {
                fprintf(logfile, "%02x ",from.x25pid[i]);
            }
            fprintf(logfile,"\n");
            fprintf(logfile,"from.x25ifname= %s\n",from.x25ifname);
            tstamp(logfile);
        }
        if (logfileopen && (verbose & (1<<VMSGS))) {
            fprintf(log_file, "Starting server %s args %s %s %s %s %s %s\n",
                    nsap->pathname,
                    nsap->pathname,        /* argv[0]                    */
                    nsap->argv[0],         /* argv[1]                    */
                    nsap->argv[1],         /* argv[2]                    */
                    nsap->argv[2],         /* argv[3]                    */
                    nsap->argv[3],         /* argv[4]                    */
                    nsap->argv[4]);        /* argv[5]                    */
            tstamp(logfile);
        }
        pid = fork();
        if (pid < 0) {
            if (logfileopen && (verbose & (1<<VPRINTERRORS))) {
                fprintf(logfile,"x25netd: fork failed");
                if ((errno > 0) && (errno <= sys_nerr))
                    fprintf(logfile, "because %s", sys_errlist[errno]);
                tstamp(logfile);
                continue;
            }
        } else {
            if (pid == 0) {
                char buffer[256];
                int logfilefd = -1, k;

                /* Child process                                        */
                if (logfileopen)
                    fclose(logfile);
                if ((verbose & (1<<VLOGSERVER)) && ((logfilefd =
                    open("/tmp/x25netd.server.out",
                    O_CREAT|O_WRONLY|O_APPEND, 0666)) < 0))
                    logfileopen = 0;
                else
```

```
            logfileopen = 1;
        for (i = 0; i < 2048;i++)
            if ((i != new_s) && (i != logfilefd))
                close(i);

    dup(new_s);                      /* now stdin = new socket */
    close(new_s);
    if (logfileopen) {
        dup(logfilefd);              /* set stdout              */
        dup(logfilefd);              /* set stderr              */
    }
    if (setuid(nsap->user_id) < 0) { /* Set user-id             */
        if (logfileopen) {
            sprintf(buffer, "setuid %d failed %d\n",
                    nsap->user_id, errno);
            write(logfilefd, buffer, strlen(buffer));
            close(logfilefd);
        }
        exit(3);
    }
    if (setgid(nsap->group_id) < 0) { /* Set group-id            */
        if (logfileopen) {
            sprintf(buffer, "setgid %d failed %d\n",
                nsap->group_id, errno);
            write(logfilefd, buffer, strlen(buffer));
            close(logfilefd);
        }
        exit(4);
    }
    if (chroot(nsap->chroot_pathname) < 0) {
        if (logfileopen) {
            sprintf(buffer, "chroot %d failed %d\n",
                nsap->group_id, errno);
            write(logfilefd, buffer, strlen(buffer));
            close(logfilefd);
        }
        exit(5);
    }
    /*
     * Child now execs the server
     * stdin = new connection socket.
     * stdout = closed.
     * stderr = closed.
     */
```

```
            execl(nsap->pathname, nsap->pathname,  /* argv[0]    */
                                  nsap->argv[0],    /* argv[1]    */
                                  nsap->argv[1],    /* argv[2]    */
                                  nsap->argv[2],    /* argv[3]    */
                                  nsap->argv[3],    /* argv[4]    */
                                  nsap->argv[4],    /* argv[5]    */
                                  0);
            /*
             * Uh-oh! If we get here, then the 'exec' failed.
             */
            if (logfileopen) {
               sprintf(buffer, "exec %s failed %d\n",
                       nsap->pathname, errno);
               write(logfilefd, buffer, strlen(buffer));
               close(logfilefd);
            }
            exit(6);
        }             /* Child                                    */
        else {        /* We are the parent.                       */
            if (logfileopen) {
               fprintf(logfile,"Process #%d started ", pid);
               tstamp(logfile);
               }
            close(new_s);
            }
        }
    }
}
/*
** Build readable maps for select() system call.
** Set the appropriate bit for each listen socket we have.
*/

build_maps()
{
    int i, index;
    int skt, max_skt = -1;
    struct nsap_s *nsap;

    memset(read_map, 0, sizeof(read_map));

    for (nsap = nsap_list_head; nsap; nsap=nsap->next_ent){
        if ((skt = nsap->listen_skt) < 0) continue;
        read_map[MAP_INDEX(skt)] |= 1<<MAP_OFFSET(skt);
        if (skt > max_skt) max_skt = skt;
```

```
    }
    return(max_skt + 1);
}

usage(argc,argv)
int argc;
char **argv;
{
    int i;

    printf("x25netd: Allowed flag options:\n");
    printf("-a <address> sets X.121 address for filtering\n");
    printf("-i <interface name>\n");
    printf("-v <verbosity level>\n");
    printf("-L <logfilename>\n");
    /*
     * Print out the parameters we were given.
     */
    printf("Parameters as given:\n");
    for (i = 0; i < argc; i++)
        printf("%s ",argv[i]);
    printf("\n");
    tstamp(logfile);
    exit(1);
}
static int child_pid,waiting,exit_code;
sigcldhdl()
{
    int pid, junk;

    pid = wait(&junk);
    fprintf(logfile,"Process #%d terminated, status %x", pid, junk);
    tstamp(logfile);
    if ((junk & 0xFF) == 0177) {
    /* Process stopped; caught signal                               */
        fprintf(logfile, "process aborted due to signal %d\n",
             ((junk & 0xFF00) >> 8));
    } else if ((junk & 0x00FF) == 0) {
        /* Process stopped, due to exit or _exit call               */
        fprintf(logfile,"Process returned exit status %d\n",
             ((junk & 0xFF00) >> 8));
    } else if (( junk & 0xFF00) == 0) {
        fprintf(logfile,"Process aborted due to signal %d\n",
             (junk & 0xFF));
        if (junk & 0200)
```

```
            fprintf(logfile,"Corefile dumped.\n");
        } else {
            fprintf(logfile,"Process terminated, status is 0x%x\n", junk);
            tstamp(logfile);
        }
}
#include <time.h>
tstamp(log_file)
FILE *log_file;
{
    struct  timeval t;
    struct timezone tz;

    gettimeofday(&t, &tz);
    fprintf(log_file, "%ld:%s", t.tv_usec, ctime(&t.tv_sec));
    fflush(log_file);
}
char *
skipwhite(ptr)
char *ptr;
{
    while((*ptr == ' ') || (*ptr == '\t'))
        ++ptr;
    return(ptr);
}
/*
** Build up the list of listen sockets we're supposed to use to
** wait for calls.  Each one is bound to a different X.121 address,
** protocol-ID and protocol-ID mask triplet, per the contents of
** the /etc/x25netd.conf file.
*/
initialize_listen_skts()
{
    FILE *fp;
    char scan_buf[1024], *cptr_from, *cptr_to;
    struct nsap_s *nsap;
    struct passwd *pw;
    int line_number = 0;
    int field_len;
    int index;
    int k;

    #ifdef BSD4_3
        /* Tell the kernel we want a max. # of socket/file desc */
        /* If kernel won't let us do this, well, that's ok, too...*/
```

```
        rlimit.rlim_cur = rlimit.rlim_max = 2048;
        if (setrlimit(RLIMIT_NOFILE, &rlimit) < 0) {
            if (logfileopen && (verbose & (1<< VPRINTERRORS))){
                if (errno <= sys_nerr)
                    fprintf(log_file,"setrlimit %s",
                            sys_errlist[errno]);
                else
                    fprintf(log_file,"setrlimit %d", errno);
            }
        }
    #endif /* BSD4_3 */

    if ((fp=fopen(X25NETDCONF,"r")) == NULL) {
        if (logfileopen && (verbose & (1<< VPRINTERRORS))){
            if (errno <= sys_nerr)
                fprintf(log_file,"could not open %s: %s\n",
                        X25NETDCONF,sys_errlist[errno]);
            else
                fprintf(log_file,"could not open %s: errno %d\n",
                        X25NETDCONF, errno);
        }
        exit(1);
    }
    while(fgets(scan_buf, sizeof(scan_buf), fp) != NULL) {
next_line:
        ++line_number;
        if (scan_buf[0] == '#') continue;

        nsap = (struct nsap_s *)malloc(sizeof (struct nsap_s));
        if (nsap == NULL) {
            if (logfileopen && (verbose & (1<< VPRINTERRORS)))
                fprintf(log_file, "malloc failure\n");
            exit(1);
        }
        if (nsap_list_head != NULL)
            nsap->next_ent = nsap_list_head;
        else nsap->next_ent = NULL;
        nsap_list_head = nsap;
        nsap->x121_addr_len = 0;
        nsap->proto_id_len = 0;
        nsap->proto_id_mask_len = 0;
        if (stuff_bind_fields(nsap, scan_buf, line_number)){
            exit(1);
        }
        nsap->listen_skt = socket (AF_CCITT, SOCK_STREAM,
```

```
            X25_PROTO_NUM);
    if (nsap->listen_skt < 0) {
        if (errno == EAFNOSUPPORT){
            if (logfileopen && (verbose & (1<< VPRINTERRORS)))
                fprintf(logfile, "Most likely problem: kernel not
                        generated for Level-3 Access\n");
        } else {
            if ((errno <= sys_nerr)  && logfileopen &&
                    (verbose & (1<< VPRINTERRORS)))
                fprintf(log_file, "socket(AF_CCITT,SOCK_STREAM)
                        error, line %d error %s\n", line_number,
                        sys_errlist[errno]);
        }
        exit(8);
    }

    /* Now, we have all the arguments we need.              */

    if ((pw = getpwnam(nsap->logname)) == NULL) {
        if (logfileopen && (verbose & (1<< VPRINTERRORS)))
            fprintf(logfile, "No such logname as %s, line %d\n",
                    nsap->logname, line_number);
        exit(1);
    }
    nsap->user_id = pw->pw_uid;
    nsap->group_id= pw->pw_gid;
    addrstr.x25_family = AF_CCITT; /* Set up address-family. */
    addrstr.x25pidlen =  nsap->proto_id_len;
    addrstr.x25hostlen = nsap->x121_addr_len;
    memcpy(addrstr.x25_host,nsap->x121_addr,
            nsap->x121_addr_len);
    memcpy(addrstr.x25pid,nsap->proto_id, nsap->proto_id_len);
    if(bind(nsap->listen_skt, &addrstr, addr_len =
            sizeof(struct x25addrstr)) < 0){
        if (logfileopen && (verbose & (1<< VPRINTERRORS))) {
            if (errno <= sys_nerr)
                fprintf(log_file, "bind() error, line %d error %s\n",
                        line_number, sys_errlist[errno]);
            else
                fprintf(log_file,"bind() error, line %d, errno %d\n",
                        line_number, errno);
        }
        goto next_line;
    }
    if (listen(nsap->listen_skt, 20) < 0) {
```

```
        if (logfileopen && (verbose & (1<< VPRINTERRORS))) {
            if (errno <= sys_nerr)
                fprintf(log_file, "listen() error, line %d error
                        %s\n", line_number, sys_errlist[errno]);
            else
                fprintf(log_file,"listen() error, line %d, errno
                        %d\n", line_number, errno);
        }
        goto next_line;
    }
    if (ioctl(nsap->listen_skt, X25_CALL_ACPT_APPROVAL,0) < 0){
        if (logfileopen && (verbose & (1<< VPRINTERRORS))) {
            if (errno <= sys_nerr)
                fprintf(log_file, "ioctl(X25_CALL_ACPT_AAPPROVAL)
                        error, line %d error %s\n", line_number,
                        sys_errlist[errno]);
            else
                fprintf(log_file, "ioctl(X25_CALL_ACPT_AAPPROVAL)
                        error, line %d, errno %d\n", line_number,
                        errno);
        }
        goto next_line;
    }
    if (logfileopen && (verbose & (1<< VPRINTPARAMS))) {
        fprintf(logfile,"X121 address %s #digits %d\n",
                nsap->x121_addr, nsap->x121_addr_len);
        fprintf(logfile,"listen socket descriptor %d\n",
                nsap->listen_skt);
        fprintf(logfile,"proto-ID len %d bytes, mask len %d
                bytes\n", nsap->proto_id_len,
                nsap->proto_id_mask_len);
        fprintf(logfile,"proto-ID: ");
        for (k= 0; k< nsap->proto_id_len; k++)
            fprintf(logfile,"%-2x",nsap->proto_id[k]);
        fprintf(logfile,"\nproto-ID mask: ");
        for (k= 0; k< nsap->proto_id_mask_len;k++)
            fprintf(logfile,"%2x",nsap->proto_id_mask[k]);
        fprintf(logfile,"\n");
        fprintf(logfile,"user-name: %s\n",nsap->logname);
        fprintf(logfile,"pathname: %s,",nsap->pathname);
        fprintf(logfile," chroot name: %s\n",
                nsap->chroot_pathname);
        fprintf(logfile,"user ID: %d,",nsap->user_id);
        fprintf(logfile," group ID: %d, ",nsap->group_id);
```

```
            for (k=0;  k <MAXARGS;  k++)
                fprintf(logfile,"%s ",nsap->argv[k]);
            fprintf(logfile,"\n");
            fprintf(logfile,"\n");
            fflush(logfile);
        }
    }
    if (logfileopen && (verbose & (1<< VPRINTPARAMS))) {
        fprintf(logfile,"==================== BEGIN =========== \n");
        fflush(logfile);
    }
    fclose(fp);
    return;
}

stuff_bind_fields(nsap, scan_buf, line_number)
struct nsap_s *nsap;
char *scan_buf;
int  line_number;
{
    char *cptr_from, *cptr_to, *cptr_to2;
    int field_len;
    int index, even_odd_flag, k;

    cptr_to = nsap->x121_addr;
    cptr_from = scan_buf;
    /* Skip whitespace before the X.121 address field, if any. */
    cptr_from = skipwhite(cptr_from);

    /* Copy the X.121 address.                                   */
    while ((*cptr_from != ' ') && *cptr_from != '\t') {
        if ((*cptr_from == '\n') || (*cptr_from == '\0'))
            return(FAILURE);
        *cptr_to++ = *cptr_from++;
        ++nsap->x121_addr_len;
    }
    *cptr_to++ = '\0';
    /* Skip whitespace before the proto-ID field.                */
    cptr_from = skipwhite(cptr_from);

    /* Copy the protocol-ID (if any).                            */
    cptr_to = nsap->proto_id;
    cptr_to2 = nsap-> proto_id_mask;  /* protocol-ID mask         */
    if (*cptr_from != '-') {
        /* Make sure field begins with "0x"                      */
        if ((*cptr_from == '\n') || (*cptr_from == '\0'))
```

```
            return(FAILURE);
        if (*cptr_from++ != '0') goto conv_error;
        if (*cptr_from != 'x' && *cptr_from != 'X') goto conv_error;
        ++cptr_from;
        /* Copy the protocol-ID.                                 */
        even_odd_flag = 0;
        while ((*cptr_from != ' ') && (*cptr_from != '\t')) {
            if ((*cptr_from == '\n') || (*cptr_from == '\0'))
                return(FAILURE);
            k = atohex(*cptr_from++);
            if (k == 'Z') {
conv_error:
                fprintf("proto-ID hex field conversion error, line
                        %d\n", line_number);
                return(FAILURE);
            } else {
                if ((even_odd_flag++ %2) == 0) {
                    *cptr_to = k << 4;
                    *cptr_to2 = 0xf0;
                } else {
                    *cptr_to = *cptr_to | (k & 0xf);
                    ++cptr_to;
                    ++nsap->proto_id_len;
                    ++nsap->proto_id_mask_len;
                    *cptr_to2++ = 0xff;
                }
            }
        }
    } else ++cptr_from;
    *cptr_to++ = '\0';

    /* Skip whitespace before the proto-ID mask field.          */
    cptr_from = skipwhite(cptr_from);

    /* Copy the protocol-ID mask (if any).                      */
    cptr_to = nsap-> proto_id_mask;  /* protocol-ID mask         */
    if (*cptr_from != '-') {
        /* Make sure field begins with "0x"                     */
        if ((*cptr_from == '\n') || (*cptr_from == '\0'))
            return(FAILURE);
        if (*cptr_from++ != '0') goto conv_error2;
        if ((*cptr_from == '\n') || (*cptr_from == '\0'))
            return(FAILURE);
        if (*cptr_from!= 'x' && *cptr_from != 'X') goto conv_error2;
        ++cptr_from;
```

```
        even_odd_flag = 0;
        nsap->proto_id_mask_len = 0;
        /* Copy the protocol-ID.                                          */
        while ((*cptr_from != ' ') && (*cptr_from != '\t')) {
            if ((*cptr_from == '\n') || (*cptr_from == '\0'))
                return(FAILURE);

            k = atohex(*cptr_from++);
            if (k == 'Z') {
    conv_error2:
                fprintf( "proto-ID mask hex field conversion error,
                    line %d\n", line_number);
                return(FAILURE);
            } else {
                if ((even_odd_flag++ %2) == 0)
                    *cptr_to = k << 4;
                else {
                    *cptr_to = *cptr_to | (k & 0xf);
                    ++cptr_to;
                    ++nsap->proto_id_mask_len;
                }
            }
        }
    } else {
        ++cptr_from;
    }
    *cptr_to++ = '\0';

    /* We now have the X.121 address, the protocol-ID and
    ** protocol-ID mask address bindings, and their lengths.
    ** The next field is the user-ID (aka logname).
    */
    cptr_to=nsap->logname;
    /* Skip whitespace before the user logname field.               */
    cptr_from = skipwhite(cptr_from);

    /* Copy the name.                                                */
    field_len = 0;
    while ((*cptr_from != ' ') && (*cptr_from != '\t')) {
        if ((*cptr_from == '\n') || (*cptr_from == '\0'))
            return(FAILURE);
        if (++field_len >= 8) {
            if (logfileopen && (verbose & (1<< VPRINTERRORS)))
                fprintf(log_file,"user name field too big, line %d\n",
                    line_number);
```

```
            return(FAILURE);
        }
        *cptr_to++ = *cptr_from++;
    }
    *cptr_to++ = '\0';

    /* Now get the chroot path-name for the server              */
    cptr_to = nsap->chroot_pathname;
    /* Skip whitespace before the chroot pathname field.        */
    cptr_from = skipwhite(cptr_from);

    /* Copy the chroot pathname.                                */
    field_len = 0;
    while ((*cptr_from != ' ') && (*cptr_from != '\t')) {
        if ((*cptr_from == '\n') || (*cptr_from == '\0'))
            return(FAILURE);
        if (++field_len >= MAXPATHLEN-1) {
            if (logfileopen && (verbose & (1<< VPRINTERRORS)))
                fprintf(log_file,"pathname len too big, line %d\n",
                        line_number);
            return(FAILURE);
        }
        *cptr_to++ = *cptr_from++;
    }
    *cptr_to++ = '\0';

    /* Now get the pathname for the server                      */
    cptr_to = nsap->pathname;
    /* Skip whitespace before the pathname field.               */
    cptr_from = skipwhite(cptr_from);

    /* Copy the pathname.                                       */
    field_len = 0;
    while ((*cptr_from != ' ') && (*cptr_from != '\t')) {
        if ((*cptr_from == '\n') || (*cptr_from == '\0'))
            return(FAILURE);
        if (++field_len >= MAXPATHLEN-1) {
            if (logfileopen && (verbose & (1<< VPRINTERRORS)))
                fprintf(log_file,"pathname len too big, line %d\n",
                        line_number);
            return(FAILURE);
        }
        *cptr_to++ = *cptr_from++;
    }
    *cptr_to++ = '\0';
```

```
    /* Now, if there are any other fields, these will be
    ** passed as run-time parameters to the server.
    */
    for (index = 0; index < MAXARGS; index++)
        nsap->argv[index][0] = '\0';
    for (index = 0; index < MAXARGS; index++) {
        /* Skip whitespace before the argument field.          */
        cptr_from = skipwhite(cptr_from);
        if ((*cptr_from == '\n') || (*cptr_from == '\0'))
            break;

        /* Copy the run time argument.                          */
        field_len = 0;
        cptr_to = nsap->argv[index];
        while ((*cptr_from != '\n') && (*cptr_from != '\0') &&
                (*cptr_from != ' ')  && (*cptr_from != '\t')) {
            if (++field_len >= 63) {
                if (logfileopen && (verbose & (1<< VPRINTERRORS)))
                    fprintf(log_file,"argument len too big, line %d\n",
                        line_number);
                return(FAILURE);
            }
            *cptr_to++ = *cptr_from++;
        }
        *cptr_to++ = '\0';
    }
    return(SUCCESS);
}
atohex(cc)
char cc;
{
    if (cc >= '0' && cc <= '9')
        return(cc - '0');
    if (cc >= 'a' && cc <= 'f')
        return(cc - 'a' + 10);
    if (cc >= 'A' && cc <= 'F')
        return(cc - 'A' + 10);
    return('Z');                       /* not legal hex digit       */
}
```

10.13.2   X.25 Server Used with **x25netd**

Here is a modified vcserverx25 (called vcserverX25, to distinguish it) for use
with x25netd. It is the same as the earlier example, except that the listen socket setup
is removed.

```
/* vcserverX25.c -- X25netd-spawned X.25 server daemon          */
#include     <stdio.h>
#include     <fcntl.h>
#include     <sys/types.h>
#include     <netinet/in.h>
#include     <sys/socket.h>
#include     <sys/errno.h>
#include     <netdb.h>
#include     <signal.h>
#include     <time.h>
#include     <x25/x25.h>
#include     <x25/x25addrstr.h>
#include     <x25/x25str.h>
#include     <x25/x25ioctls.h>
#include     <x25/ccittproto.h>
#include     <x25/x25codes.h>
#include     <x25/x25ioctls.h>

extern int errno;
struct x25addrstr        server_x121_address, peer_addr;

main( argc, argv )              /* argument count, argument vector */
char *argv[];
{
   int    rc;                 /* system call return code         */
   int    x25_listen_skt;     /* server listen socket descriptor */
   int    x25_accept_skt;     /* server accept socket descriptor */
   int    addrlen, nbytes;    /* sockaddr length; read nbytes req*/
   struct sockaddr addr;      /* client's internet addr & port   */
   char   buf [256];          /* your basic buffer               */
   char   *if_name, *x121_addr;
   struct hostent *hp, *gethostbyaddr();  /* /etc/hosts lookup */

   x25_accept_skt = 0;  /* x25netd gave us our skt on stdin.   */
   ioctl(x25_accept_skt, X25_SEND_CALL_ACEPT, 0);

   do  {
     if ( (nbytes = read( x25_accept_skt, buf, sizeof (buf) ) ) < 0 ) {
        close(x25_accept_skt);
        exit(6);
     }
```

```
      else if (nbytes == 0)
         printf( "\nClosing connection...\n\n" );
      else
         printf( "\nReceived: %s\n", buf );
   } while (nbytes != 0);
   close(x25_accept_skt);   /* close the service descriptor    */
   exit(0);
}
```

The earlier client example, **vcclientx25.c**, works with this version of the server, given that **x25netd** is set up and running first.

10.14   Glossary of X.25 Terms

calling side — Refers to the code that initiates the connection

called side — Refers to the code that is called.

CTI — Circuit Table Index. The host-side identifies circuits by a combination of an interface card identifier and a circuit table index. This is an internal matter, unless you are troubleshooting a problem with a protocol analyzer. Then you need to know which Logical Group/Channel the circuit is using, so you can correlate what you see on the analyzer traces with the internal logging at the host.

CUDF — call (or called or clear) user data field. Refers to a field in any of the CALL or CLEAR packets. This field may be up to 16 bytes long (128, if fast select is used), and is a way in which the caller may specify additional information to the called process, such as setup options or some form of identification code.

D-bit — A bit in the X.25 DATA packet which is under the control of the programmer. This bit controls where the flow control acknowledgment is generated. If set to zero, the acknowledgment is generated by the DCE that is connected to the sender. If set to one, the acknowledgment comes from the DCE that is connected to the receiver. Thus, when the acknowledgment arrives for a DATA packet whose D-bit was set to one, the sender can assume that the data was received by the remote DTE. This is **not** the same as confirmation of delivery to the remote user process, however. There are many things which could prevent the peer process from receiving this data, such as if the process is aborted, the link is reset, or the data link level connection is lost.

DCE — Data Circuit Equipment (such as the modem and the packet-switching equipment immediately on the other side of the link to the DCE).

DTE — Data-Terminating Equipment (such as the computer and X.25 interface)

fast select — Term meaning that the caller is going to make a quick call (the data is contained in the CALL packets) and clear the circuit right away. The packets exchanged are CALL Request/CALL Indication, CLEAR Request/CLEAR Indication. Fast select is commonly used for such things as a simple database lookup or update, in which the data length in each direction is less than or equal to 128 bytes. Fast select can be economical in terms of packets sent and time, but it is not necessarily economical in monetary terms (some networks charge as much to use fast select as if a full circuit were set up and more than a dozen packets exchanged).

LCI — Logical Channel Identifier. This term combines the four-bit field of the X.25 header called Logical Group Identifier with the eight-bit circuit identifier.

M-bit — A bit in the X.25 DATA packet which tells the receiver whether this packet is the final packet in this message (M == 0). If the M-bit is set, there are more packets to follow in this message. The M-bit is what gives X.25 its message-oriented nature (as opposed to TCP, for example, which has no message boundaries in the protocol itself).

Protocol-ID — Refers to a convention, started with X.25/PAD, in which the intended recipient (that is, which server) of an inbound connection is distinguished by using a certain number of bytes (or bits) in the call user data field (CUDF). The determination of which bits in this field is left to the applications programmer.

PVC — Permanent Virtual Circuit. These are particular circuit numbers that, by agreement with the network provider, are considered "permanent" in the sense that they don't have to be established by the DTE. It is a mistake to assume that the word "permanent" in their name means that they are always available for use, however.

Q-bit — A bit in the DATA packet that is controlled by the applications programmer. The X.25 protocol simply carries this bit without modification. The receiving process can determine whether the Q-bit was set or clear. The significance of its state is entirely up to the designer of the application program; X.25 places no significance on it whatsoever. It is common to use the Q-bit to identify "control" type messages or "high-priority" messages. In a simple application having only two message types, you could use the Q-bit to identify the message type, thereby economizing on message size and network bandwidth.

virtual circuit (VC) — Same as a connection.

Bibliography

Bach, Maurice J., [1986], *The Design of the UNIX Operating System*, Prentice Hall, Englewood Cliffs, NJ, ISBN 0–13–201799–7 025.

Comer, Douglas E., [1991], *Internetworking With TCP/IP, Volume I: Principles, Protocols, and Architectures*, Prentice Hall, Englewood Cliffs, NJ, ISBN 0–13–468505–9.

Comer, Douglas E. and Stevens, David L., [1991], *Internetworking With TCP/IP, Volume II: Design, Implementation, and Internals*, Prentice Hall, Englewood Cliffs, NJ, ISBN 0–13–472242–6.

Davies, D.W., et al., *Computer Networks and Their Protocols*, John Wiley & Sons, New York, ISBN 0–471–99750–1.

Deasington, R. J., *X.25 Explained —Protocols forPacket Switching Networks*, Halsted Press (a division of John Wiley & Sons), New York, ISBN 0–470–20731–0.

Kong, Mike, et al., [1990], *Network Computing System Reference Manual*, Prentice Hall, Englewood Cliffs, NJ, ISBN 0-13-617085-4.

Leffler, S., McKusick, M., Karels, M., and Quarterman, J., [1989], *The Design and Implementation of the 4.3BSD UNIX Operating System*, Addison-Wesley, Reading, MA, ISBN 0–201–06196–1.

Malamud, Carl, [1992], *Stacks*, Prentice Hall, Englewood Cliffs, NJ, ISBN 0–13–484080–1.

Miller, Mark A., [1989], *LAN Troubleshooting Handbook*, M&T Books, 501 Galveston Dr., Redwood City, CA, ISBN 1–55851–056–7.

Miller, Mark A., [1990], *LAN Protocol Handbook*, M&T Books, 501 Galveston Dr., Redwood City, CA, ISBN 1–55851–099–0.

Partridge, Craig, [1988], *Innovations in Internetworking*, Artech House, Norwood, MA, ISBN 0–89006–337–0.

Rochkind, Marc J., [1985], *Advanced UNIX Programming*, Prentice Hall, Englewood Cliffs, NJ, ISBN 0–13–011818–4.

Rose, Marshall T., [1991], *The Simple Book: An Introduction to Management of TCP/IP-based Internets*, Prentice Hall, Englewood Cliffs, NJ, ISBN 0–13–812611–9.

Stevens, Richard W.,[1990], *UNIX Network Programming*, Prentice Hall, Englewood Cliffs, NJ, ISBN 0–13–949876–1.

X.25: The PSN Connection, An Explanation of Recommendation X.25, published by Hewlett-Packard, Part Number 5958–3402.

Tanenbaum, Andrew S., *Computer Networks*, Prentice Hall, IEnglewood Cliffs, NJ, ISBN 0–13–165183–8.

Young, Douglas A., [1989], *X Window Systems: Programming and Applications With Xt*, Prentice Hall, Englewood Cliffs, NJ, ISBN 0–13–972167–3.

RFC Information

Copies of Requests For Comments (RFCs) may be obtained, either in printed or electronic form. For most of the protocols in the so-called "Internet suite of protocols," you will find the technical details in one (or sometimes more) RFCs. If you have access to a computer that can access the Internet, you can obtain RFCs quickly using `ftp`. The host name is `nic.ddn.mil` (IP address 192.67.67.20, user name `anonymous`, password `guest`; `cd rfc`; and `get rfc-index.txt` in ascii mode. This index contains a brief description of the RFCs, by number. Alternatively, if you have a copy handy, you can consult *Internetworking With TCP/IP: Volume I*, Appendix 1, "A Guide to RFCs," which tells you a little more about the RFCs, and which ones are important in which areas. When you know the RFCs you want, you just repeat the above `"get"` sequence, for example, `get rfc1157.txt`.

If you don't have Internet access, you may have electronic mail access (many of the electronic mail networks have gateways to interconnect them; this isn't the same as Internet gatewaying, but it does allow users who otherwise have no access to send email), send email to `Service@nic.ddn.mil`, subject field specifying the RFC you want, for example, *Subject: RFC 1060*. If you want more information, send a message with the subject field `help` and you will receive more information on how to use the service.

NFSNET Network Service Center (NNSC): If you have access to a computer that can send electronic mail to `info-server@sh.cs.net`, send a message in which the first line specifies the keywords `REQUEST:rfc` and the second line specifies the keyword `TOPIC:` followed by the RFC number you want, for example, `1060`.

RFCs are available in printed form, for a modest fee, from the DDN Network Information Center:

```
Postal:     DDN Network Information Center
            SRI International
            333 Ravenswood Ave.
            Menlo Park, CA 94025
            US

Phone:      +1 800-235-3155
            +1 415-859-3695

E-Mail:     NIC@NIC.DDN.MIL
```

OMNICOM, Inc., 115 Park Street, SE, Vienna, VA 22180–4607, is one source for copies of most of the standards of interest in data communications, such as OSI and X.25.

Index

UNIX Training and Consulting

"**Rules of Teaching.** *The first rule of teaching is to know what you are supposed to teach. The second rule of teaching is to know a little more than what you are supposed to teach.*"
George Polya, HOW TO SOLVE IT

Our instructors are personable, subject-matter experts who spend 75% of their professional time helping clients with their projects, and 25% developing course notes and teaching. Please call us when you need practical training or results-oriented project assistance. We'll be glad to help you.

C Programming	System Administration
Korn Shell Programming	Device Drivers
UNIX for Software Developers	SVR4/OSF Internals
C++ Programming	X11/Motif Programming
Network Programming	Network Administration

.sh consulting
3355 Brookdale Drive
Santa Clara, CA 95051

(408) 241-8319   uunet!ames!dotsh!wdr
                  dotsh!wdr@ames.arc.nasa.gov

Clients

AT&T Bell Laboratories (SVR4)	IBM (AIX/OSF)
Advanced Micro Devices	ICL Datachecker
Amdahl (UTS)	Mentor Graphics
Apple Computer (A/UX)	NASA Ames/Huntsville
Bank of America	NCR
Bellcore	NEC America
CDC (ETA)	Oracle
DEC (ULTRIX)	Pacific Bell
Dell Computer (SVR3)	Santa Cruz Operations (SCO)
Harris (HC/UX)	Sun Microsystems (Solaris)
Hewlett-Packard (HP-UX/OSF)	Sybase
Hitachi Data Systems (OSF)	U.C. Berkeley

The source code presented in this book is available on diskette for a $30.00 distribution fee. A QIC-24 tape is also available for a $60.00 distribution fee. Please photocopy this page and mail a check or money order for the proper amount (U.S. funds, drawn on a U.S. bank, please) to the address given below. You may use a credit card:

VISA ☐ or MASTERCARD ☐ Expiration Date: _____

Credit Card Number: _____

Signature: _____

Your order will be processed promptly and professionally.

John Wiley & Sons, Inc. is not responsible for orders placed with *.sh consulting*.

Mail to: **Phone:** 408 - 241 - 8319

Attn: Network Source Code
.sh consulting
3355 Brookdale Drive
Santa Clara, CA 95051

Name: _____

Address: _____

_____

_____

Diskette: 5.25" HD (1.2 MB) ☐   3.5" HD (1.44 MB) ☐

Tape: QIC-24 cartridge tape ☐

Diskettes and tape are in UNIX tar format.